HISTORY AND THE ENLIGHTENMENT

HISTORY
AND THE
Enlightenment

HUGH TREVOR-ROPER

Carlyle

predigurned

(Hitler

235

YALE UNIVERSITY PRESS
NEW HAVEN AND LONDON

Published with assistance from the Annie Burr Lewis Fund

For information about this and other Yale University Press publications, please contact:
U.S. Office: sales.press@yale.edu   www.yalebooks.com
Europe Office: sales @yaleup.co.uk   www.yaleup.co.uk

Set in Arno Pro by IDSUK (DataConnection) Ltd.
Printed in Great Britain by TJ International Ltd, Padstow, Cornwall

Library of Congress Cataloging-in-Publication Data

Trevor-Roper, H. R. (Hugh Redwald), 1914–2003.
   History and the Enlightenment/Hugh Trevor-Roper; [edited by John Robertson].
      p. cm.
   Includes bibliographical references and index.
   ISBN 978-0-300-13934-1 (ci: alk. paper)
   1.   Historiography. 2.   Enlightenment—Influence. 3.   History—Philosophy.
4.   Historians.   I. Robertson, John, 1951- II. Title.
   D13.2.T74 2010
   907.2—dc22
                                                                           2009026500

A catalogue record for this book is available from the British Library.

10 9 8 7 6 5 4 3 2 1

Contents

Editor's Introduction
John Robertson

To Hugh Trevor-Roper, reading the great historians of the past was a source of pleasure, inspiration and scholarly interest. His discovery of that pleasure may be traced to the years of the Second World War. Before the war he had tended to divide his work as a historian from his pleasures; now that he himself was a participant in events, as an officer in the intelligence services, reading good history became a pleasure. After the war and his return to Oxford that pleasure became a source of inspiration (and occasional frustration) as he struggled to identify, and then to write, the major work of history of which he knew himself to be capable. It was not until the 1960s, however, that historiography – the study of the history of historical writing – became a focus of his own scholarship. The first of the essays collected here was written and published in 1963, and a further five were published before the end of the decade; the remainder derive more or less directly from the interests he established, and the style of intellectual history he began to cultivate, during that period. In this Introduction, I shall elucidate the circumstances in which his interests took this new direction, and say something of his conception of historiography.

With one exception, that on Conyers Middleton, all the essays in this volume have already been published. They are collected here, however, for the first time: hitherto they have lain scattered in a wide variety of learned journals and edited volumes, some of them, such as the *Revue romaine d'histoire*, not the most accessible. (Trevor-Roper was free of the insistent, ungenerous pressure to publish only in the 'top' journals for the benefit of Research Assessment Exercises, and could honour commitments to those who had invited him to give the essays as lectures or conference papers in the first place.) It is clear that collected publication was Trevor-Roper's intention:

there survive among his papers various manuscript plans for series of volumes. If this collection does not correspond exactly to any of the volumes he projected, neither did the volumes published in his lifetime: *Catholics, Anglicans and Puritans* (1987) and *From Counter-Reformation to Glorious Revolution* (1992). As he told Noël Annan in 1994, he also hoped to publish the essay on Middleton, which was first given as the Leslie Stephen Lecture in Cambridge in 1982, and for which he had since done considerable further research, rewriting it several times.[1] The present volume is designed to augment the series of collected essays, although with the qualifications that it has required the editor to select from among essays on the same or very similar subjects, and that a few important essays have fallen between the several volumes.

Appropriately, since he is the subject of three of these essays, and a major presence in several more, Edward Gibbon seems to have been the first of the great historians to whom Trevor-Roper turned during the war. The stimulus was Logan Pearsall Smith, who had befriended Trevor-Roper and drawn him into his Chelsea circle out of admiration for his first book, *Archbishop Laud*, published in 1940. Pearsall Smith persuaded Trevor-Roper of the importance of style, a quality which Trevor-Roper acknowledged he had discounted in writing the book on Laud, despite Pearsall Smith's enthusiasm for it.[2] So in 1940 he read Gibbon anew, and recognised in the *Decline and Fall* just those qualities missing in his own book. By 1951 he would write to the art historian and connoisseur Bernard Berenson, who had succeeded Pearsall Smith as an older friend and intellectual foil:

> I am now re-reading, for the nth time, that greatest of historians, as I continually find myself declaring, – Gibbon. What a splendid writer he is! If only historians could write like him now! How has the art of footnotes altogether perished and the gift of irony disappeared! I took a volume of Gibbon to Greece and read it on Mount Hymettus and the island of Crete; I read it furtively even at I Tatti, where 40,000 other volumes clamoured insistently around me to be read; and I cannot stop reading him even now.[3]

Berenson's own contribution to Trevor-Roper's discovery of the great historians was Jacob Burckhardt. Burckhardt is first mentioned in their correspondence in 1949; in 1955 Trevor-Roper was reading him again in order to write a review of an English selection of his letters; for this purpose he had also reread the works on the Renaissance and Constantine the Great, and the *Weltgeschichtliche Betrachtungen*. 'They really are a wonderful rediscovery to make. What 19th century historian saw historical forces so clearly?' By 1958 the recurring enthusiasm was tempered by a note of criticism: Burckhardt, he now wrote to Berenson, suffered from a timidity which occasionally 'freezes up his thought': there was something 'ungenerous' about his fear of ideas.[4] Earlier that year Trevor-Roper had also enthused about the Scottish historians of the eighteenth century, Hume, Millar and Adam Smith. But now he identified a historical problem as well as another set of inspiring historians: how could one account for that 'extraordinary phenomenon of the Scottish intellectual ferment of the 18th century', and the 'revolution in historical study' which it began?[5] By the end of the 1950s, it is clear, Trevor-Roper had come to recognise that the great historians whom he had been reading for pleasure and stimulus also required historical study in their own right, like any other dimension of the past.

For the moment, however, this interest in historians was still a diversion, for then his energies were directed, indeed concentrated as never before, on two major projects. One was a full-scale study of the Civil War of the mid-seventeenth century, and of the collapse of the monarchy which precipitated it. Trevor-Roper envisaged this as both a structural study of the failure of a state and as a narrative of the choices made by those who took the Stuart kingdoms into the conflict. Both were essential to an explanation of the Civil War: Trevor-Roper wanted to apply the social analysis which he had derived from his earlier intervention in the Gentry Controversy, but to avoid any hint of determinism, which he detested. The other, complementary project was a re-examination, and a historical refutation, of the major theses of Max Weber's historical sociology. Trevor-Roper had read Weber, and in particular *The Protestant Ethic*, in the 1930s, and he acknowledged Weber's influence on his early work on Laud. In other words, he had read Weber as historians still now read Habermas or Foucault, as contemporary sources of inspiration, or, as it would now be said, as 'theorists'. By the late 1950s, however, Trevor-Roper had rethought his own understanding of the issues addressed by Weber, and was ready to settle accounts with his theories. He now rejected both the idea that Protestantism, or more particularly the Calvinist, puritan doctrine of the calling, was the ideological begetter of capitalism, and the thesis that the modern state was born in early modern Europe. On the contrary, as he intended his study of the English Civil War to show, the mid-seventeenth century saw the failure of the Renaissance state, brought down by the enthusiasm of monarchs and their courts for levels of expenditure which the societies they ruled over were unable or unwilling to sustain.

In the event, neither of these projects resulted in a book. The failure to complete the study of the Civil War, of which he wrote some 200,000 words, and which he at one time projected in three volumes, was the greater; the reasons why it never reached publication, and the scale of the loss, have been tellingly but sympathetically assessed by Blair Worden in his biographical memoir of Hugh Trevor-Roper for the British Academy.[6] All that did make it into print were essays on the Long Parliament and Cromwell's parliaments, and on Scotland and the Puritan Revolution. The historical critique of Weber fared better, since it was articulated in two of Trevor-Roper's finest essays, the title essay of the collection *Religion, the Reformation and Social Change* (1967), and its immediate successor in the volume, 'The General Crisis of the Seventeenth Century'. The first argued that the great capitalists who dominated trade and financed the war efforts of Protestant and Catholic powers alike in the early seventeenth century were 'Calvinists' only of convenience; under their outwardly Calvinist allegiance they were really Arminians, who rejected the dogma of predestination in favour of free will, and were therefore heirs to the eirenic, undoctrinaire religion of Erasmus. The second essay explained the concurrent collapse of the great European monarchies in the middle decades of the century as a crisis, not of feudalism challenged by capitalism, but of the institutional structures and cultural excesses of the Renaissance state. Incomparable in its style, this essay contains one of the finest, most beautifully balanced sentences ever written by a historian.[7] In the same volume were the essays on Parliament and on Scotland already mentioned. Additionally, there were new essays on 'The Religious Origins of the Enlightenment' and on 'The European Witch-craze'. These, however, are better read as expressions of the reorientation of Trevor-Roper's interests in the early 1960s which also led him to the serious study of historiography.

The critical year, it seems, was 1962. He had attempted to revise the book on the Civil War in 1961, but had given up. Instead, he started turning parts of it into essays. Then, at the end of 1962, he took stock. Over the Christmas vacation of 1962–63 he began, once again, to keep a journal, something he seems not to have done since the mid-1940s. He first recorded his response to Chester W. New's *Life of Henry Brougham to 1830*, a book which excited him 'more than any other historical work read this year (1962)'. 'And then', he writes, 'I made a resolution. In fact I made several. I resolved to be better-tempered, more tolerant, etc.; to resume this notebook; and to re-read the Greek tragedians.' He enjoined himself 'to go quietly through the whole canon, even if I fall behind in the latest historical periodicals'. How well he kept the first and third resolutions he did not record. The first may have been intended primarily for his family, a recognition that his frustration over the uncompleted work on the Civil War had taken a toll. But he did resume the notebook, taking it with him to Paris, where he spent the Hilary term of 1963.[8]

He went at the invitation of Fernand Braudel, and lectured, in French, on the English Civil War. But he found himself neglected by his hosts at the Ecole Pratique des Hautes Etudes, and was by now unconvinced that the methods of the *Annales* school were all that was needed to revivify the study of history.[9] Instead, he undertook a course of reading that was quickly to result in a significant reorientation, or rebalancing, of his interests, which would henceforth include historiography and, more generally, intellectual history. It would be a mistake, I think, to look for a specific intellectual inspiration for the new turn in his studies. The resolution to read the Greek tragedians at the expense of the most recent historical periodicals underlines Trevor-Roper's resolute intellectual individualism; he was not looking for a new fashion to follow. Instead, the immediate incentive was a promise. He had been invited by Theodore Besterman to address his inaugural International Conference on the Enlightenment in Geneva in the summer, and offered to read a paper on 'The Historical Philosophy of the Enlightenment'. So he read in preparation: John Wesley's Diary, Voltaire's *Essai sur les moeurs* and some of Pietro Giannone's *Storia civile del regno di Napoli* and *Il Triregno*, along with a life of Giannone and his autobiography. Trevor-Roper did not confine his reading to the promised paper; subsequently he turned 'to that other topic which interests me, international calvinism'. But historiography had at last captured and concentrated his attention. The notebook contains three sustained exercises in comment and assessment, which give content to the new direction in his interests.

One is devoted to Wesley. Wesley embodied anti-Enlightenment. He was 'an abject conservative', whose preaching evoked the evangelism of the Puritan Revolution without its reforming edge. Hating the reformers of the past, 'he was even more violent about their successors in his own day, the men of the Enlightenment'. Voltaire was judged by Wesley a coxcomb, Rousseau a shallow, supercilious infidel. Montesquieu lacked clearness of thought: he was no more to be compared to a Lord Forbes or a Dr Beattie than a mouse to an elephant. This was the Beattie, Trevor-Roper added, whom Hume had called 'that bigoted silly fellow'. But Hume, to Wesley, was 'the most insolent despiser of truth and virtue that ever appeared in the world'. As for William Robertson, his 'philosophical history' was not merely 'profoundly dull', but excluded God from the government of the world. Gibbon is never mentioned by Wesley, but his denial of the miracle of the darkness covering the world at the time of the crucifixion is briskly refuted. By contrast, Wesley dismissed Captain Cook's anthropological discoveries as 'fiction': Hume or Voltaire might believe them, but not Wesley.[10] All this repelled Trevor-Roper. And yet he was clearly also fascinated. To understand the Enlightenment and its historians, he needed first to understand their antithesis. He had recognised that the Enlightenment did not own or epitomise the eighteenth-century mind; its proponents had to clear their own intellectual space, and fight to defend it.

Exemplary of the Enlightenment, by contrast, was Pietro Giannone, subject of a second free-standing commentary. 'Of all the books which I have read recently', Trevor-Roper began, 'none has so seized my mind as Giannone's Autobiography.'

> I was drawn to Giannone by my interest in the historiography of the Enlightenment. I read his *Storia Civile* – not all of it, I must admit – and some of his *Triregno*, as also Panzini's life of him, in Paris. Then I got his autobiography. It is fascinating, a terrible story. How truly might Gibbon, at the beginning of his autobiography, congratulate himself on the accidents of his birth and nation when the greatest of his predecessors, only a generation before, had suffered, merely for his historical views, this incredible persecution!

Paolo Sarpi had at least been supported by the republic of Venice when he defended its independence from the papacy. Yet Giannone had been betrayed by the princes of Italy for doing the same on their behalf. After enduring exile in Vienna, he had been kidnapped by agents of the duke of Savoy, and cast into a succession of Savoyard prisons as a token of the duke's good intentions towards Rome. Why? Giannone believed it was because the princes were corrupted by hopes of preferment in the Church for members of their families. To this, Trevor-Roper added that there must also have been fear: fear that if they turned against Rome, the monks and the friars would turn their peoples against them. But Giannone had also been undone by a personal trait which made him particularly attractive to Trevor-Roper: 'his love of rural solitude'. Like Horace, Giannone came from Monte Gargano, in Apulia; again and again in his autobiography he alluded to the charms of rural peace. And it was this love for the country that had induced him to leave the safety of Geneva, cross the lake and visit Savoy, where he was kidnapped. Only after his death did the several princes of Italy discover their mistake and resist the Church; by then Giannone had become a hero and an example to the Enlightenment historians, Gibbon above all.[11]

It is not surprising, then, that the paper Trevor-Roper wrote and published that summer on 'The Historical Philosophy of the Enlightenment' (the first of the essays in this volume) should have started from Giannone, or that Wesley should have featured more than once as a foil, his crass judgments on Robertson and Montesquieu setting off Trevor-Roper's assessment of their true importance. But it is also significant that Trevor-Roper concluded the essay by looking forward into the nineteenth century, to the historians who divided and contested the legacy of the Enlightenment's historical philosophy. Even as he focused on the Enlightenment and historiography, Trevor-Roper sought to illuminate the wider importance of the subject, identifying its philosophy and assessing its legacy.

One other, related interest comes into focus in the 1963 notebook, and is the subject of a third set of comments. This is the phenomenon of the Scottish Enlightenment. Trevor-Roper had been puzzled by the phenomenon earlier, in 1958. But now Giannone helped put him back on its trail. In an addendum to his commentary on Giannone's autobiography, Trevor-Roper noticed that there had been a Scottish dimension to the English translation of Giannone's *Storia civile* by Captain James Ogilvie. Among the subscribers who made the publication possible were large numbers of Scots. 'Surely, I said to myself, This is relevant to that great problem, the Scottish Enlightenment.' For here, before the conclusive defeat of Jacobitism in 1745, was evidence of tories, even Jacobites, interesting themselves in an Enlightenment history. Pursuing 'this slender trail', Trevor-Roper had written to the Keeper of the Public Records of Scotland, Sir James Fergusson of Kilkerran. But his reply had been disappointing: Kilkerran had dismissed 'your phrase, the Scottish Enlightenment', as 'unfamiliar to me'. Elsewhere in the notebook Trevor-Roper commented on the reasons for the Scots' lack of interest in their own Enlightenment. Up until the very end of the nineteenth century, Scottish scholars such as Henry Grey Graham had written good books about eighteenth-century Scottish history. But in the twentieth century the Scottish universities had become ever more insular, taking refuge in their tribal boast that Scottish education was the best in the world. As a result, their professors thought that Scottish history should be written only by Scotsmen, born in Scotland, and graduates of Scottish universities. Trevor-Roper determined to break that monopoly. Could they not see what an extraordinary problem the Scottish Enlightenment presented? The contrast between England in the eighteenth century, 'sunk in torpor' after 1688, and the Scotland of Hume, Robertson, Millar and Adam Smith could not be more striking. 'How did it happen? What was the social, what the intellectual basis of this extraordinary efflorescence? What a problem to answer, or even to face!'[12]

Here, evidently, was the origin, and much of the argument, of the second of the essays in this volume, 'The Scottish Enlightenment'. This too was a lecture to the Enlightenment Congress, meeting for the second time in Edinburgh and St Andrews in August 1967. Although Trevor-Roper did not repeat his accusations against the Scottish historical professoriate, they did not miss the opportunity to take offence. The essay's comments on the backwardness of pre-Union Scottish society, and on the bigotry of its Presbyterian clergy, were ample provocation. Nevertheless, Trevor-Roper won: the specifics of his argument might be (and continue to be) disputed; but that the Scottish Enlightenment had occurred and constituted a fascinating historical problem was accepted by increasing numbers of historians across the world, from North America to Japan, and even, eventually, in Scotland. The essay concentrates on the social explanation of the phenomenon, as a response to the experience of 'catching up' on England and the other advanced nations of Europe. Less often noticed is that Trevor-Roper also insisted on the intellectual content of the Scottish Enlightenment, its 'philosophy': this was to be found in its preoccupation with understanding 'the social mechanism of progress', through the study of political economy, sociology and history.

Another invitation prompted a further step in Trevor-Roper's engagement with historiography. In 1965 he gave the Trevelyan Lectures in Cambridge on whig and tory historians. The six lectures set off the first whigs (John Foxe and John Milton) against the first tories (William Camden and the earl of Clarendon), then traced the fluctuating fortunes of the two sides through the whig Rapin, the 'tory' Hume and the radical whig 'Mrs Macaulay' (Catherine Macaulay), before concluding with 'the whig triumph' of Lord Macaulay. Shortened versions of the lectures on Clarendon, Hume and Lord Macaulay were subsequently broadcast and published in *The Listener* later in the year; but the Trevelyan Lectures themselves were not made into a book.[13] Instead, Trevor-Roper broadcast and published further lectures in 1966, on Camden and, alongside him, a new interest, the Scottish humanist and Calvinist George Buchanan.[14]

While in Cambridge to give the lectures, Trevor-Roper encountered Duncan Forbes, a Scotsman of a very different temperament and intellectual style, but whose teaching and, eventually, publications would do at least as much as Trevor-Roper's to establish the Scottish Enlightenment as a major historical problem. Predictably, if regrettably, the encounter was not a meeting of minds.[15] But Forbes and Trevor-Roper were at least agreed on the importance of Hume, as a historian and as the intellectual catalyst of Enlightenment in Scotland. An early, common expression of this was their reviews of the Italian historian Giuseppe Giarrizzo's *David Hume politico e storico* (1962). Trevor-Roper's review is the essay on Hume reprinted in this volume. It is matter for regret that he did not write at greater length on Hume, whose style he admired even above Gibbon's. But Giarrizzo, already the author of what at the time was the only serious historiographical study of Gibbon, successfully provoked Trevor-Roper (as he did, very differently, Forbes) into sketching why Hume had been of such significance.[16]

Gibbon too had been the subject of a broadcast lecture, reprinted in *The Listener* in 1964.[17] During the 1960s Trevor-Roper began lecturing regularly to undergraduates in Oxford on 'Gibbon and Macaulay', a paper which he introduced into the syllabus for the Preliminary Examination in Modern History taken at the end of the first term. (Undergraduates, who in those days sat an Oxford Entrance Examination after A Levels, had nine months before going up to university in which to travel the world with copies of Gibbon and Macaulay in their rucksacks.)[18] Of the two, there is no doubt which most engaged his scholarly interest. Gibbon had been his first inspiration when he learned the importance of style; now he asked the key historical question – how had Gibbon identified the decline and fall of the Roman Empire as the most pressing, the most challenging question facing a modern historian of the mid-eighteenth century? The first of the essays on Gibbon reprinted here was his answer. By contrast, Trevor-Roper's interest in Macaulay was commensurate with his assessment of the limitations of Macaulay's achievement. There was much to admire, not least in the confident effrontery of Macaulay's style; but his very strength was the narrowness of his vision of English history. The introduction to a volume of selections from the *History of England* which is reprinted here was Trevor-Roper's most extended treatment of Macaulay; but it contributed less to scholarship on its subject than the essays on Gibbon.

One insight, however, stands out: Macaulay's debt to Sir Walter Scott. Trevor-Roper was a firm admirer of his fellow-Borderer, and celebrated Scott's contribution to the development – and enlargement – of historical vision in the immediate aftermath of the Enlightenment.[19] This conviction lies at the heart of 'The Romantic Movement and the Study of History', first given as the John Coffin Memorial Lecture in London in 1969, and reprinted here. The key to Trevor-Roper's argument was the linking of Scott with Niebuhr; together they were the inspiration, first, of Macaulay's *Lays of Ancient Rome*, then of his conception of history as 'romance'. But, as he pointed out, their inspiration was equally important to the young Ranke. The lecture thus reconstructed and reinforced the bridge by which Trevor-Roper sought to join the historical philosophy of the Enlightenment to that of the nineteenth century, and the subjects of his later essays, Carlyle and Burckhardt.

In 1973 Trevor-Roper delivered a further set of lectures in Chicago, on 'Historical Change and Historical Philosophy 1750–1850'; the final lecture was devoted to Ranke.[20] Three years later the bicentenary of the publication of Volume I of the *Decline and Fall* prompted further invitations to lecture and write on Gibbon. One of these, again from Chicago, yielded the second of the essays on Gibbon reprinted here, 'Gibbon and the Publication of *The Decline and Fall of the Roman Empire, 1776–1976*'; it is included as a clear statement of Trevor-Roper's understanding of the argument of Gibbon's book.[21] In the following year, the prospect of Devolution for Scotland (a prospect Trevor-Roper abhorred) prompted a second, shorter essay with the title 'The Scottish Enlightenment'. This gave more emphasis to the Union of 1707 as an agent of social and intellectual change in eighteenth-century Scotland, and displaced the religious origins of Enlightenment in Scotland from Jacobite Episcopalians on to Presbyterian Arminians.[22] There are grounds for preferring the second essay to the first;[23] but the earlier essay is reprinted here, on grounds both of priority and of greater impact, since it served far more frequently as a reference point for debate.

The falling-off in Trevor-Roper's engagement with historiography in the 1970s reflected the attention he was giving to other interests. These had coexisted with writing on historians in the 1960s: in the crucial year of 1963 he had also given the lectures which became *The Rise of Christian Europe* (1965). But in the 1970s he was working on four books: the first, *Princes and Artists* (1976), a response to a question concerning the artistic patronage of the Habsburgs which he had first asked Berenson in 1952; the second, *The Hermit of Peking* (1976), a study of the Sinologist and fantasist Sir Edmund Backhouse; the third, the study of Scottish historical myths which became *The Invention of Scotland* (2008); and the fourth, a major work on the life and political and intellectual worlds of Sir Theodore de Mayerne, Huguenot and physician to Henri IV of France and James I of England. Although this last was only published posthumously, as *Europe's Physician* (2006), it represented the fulfilment of the other new interest identified in the journal of 1963, the intellectual world of international Calvinism – an interest which had been enhanced later in the 1960s by Trevor-Roper's contact with Frances Yates.

Once he had set aside the books on Scotland and on Mayerne, he returned in the 1980s to a related line of enquiry from the 1960s, into the 'religious origins' of the Enlightenment, and also to historiography. The Arminian or Socinian ancestors of Enlightenment were the subject of the major essays on 'The Great Tew Circle' and on 'Hugo Grotius and England', published in other volumes of his essays in 1987 and 1992.[24] In historiography, there were new essays on Cantemir, Middleton, Carlyle and Burckhardt, all published here. The essay on Middleton I shall come to in a moment. That on Cantemir was prepared for a gathering in Bucharest at the Académie des Sciences Sociales et Politiques de la République Socialiste de Roumanie in 1985; he had been drawn to Cantemir, he explained, by Gibbon's interest in him and his writings. By contrast, the interest of Thomas Carlyle's historical philosophy to Trevor-Roper lay in the way it had been forged in direct opposition to that of the Enlightenment. This essay, too, was first a lecture in Cambridge, before being printed in the *Times Literary Supplement* in 1981. Among the several letters of praise it elicited, that of Alan Taylor was notably generous: 'your piece on Carlyle is among your finest performances, beyond all praise. I read it with unstinted enjoyment – and agreement. Humble congratulations.'[25] The subject of the final essay in this collection, Jacob Burckhardt, was of course an old enthusiasm of Trevor-Roper's. A lecture to the British Academy in December 1984, it distilled the series of lectures on Burckhardt which he had for many years given in Oxford, to undergraduates in their first term who had chosen to study the *Weltgeschichtliche Betrachtungen* as a text in the German language.[26]

Two more essays were written in the 1990s. One, on 'Gibbon's Last Project', was occasioned by a conference to mark the bicentenary of Gibbon's death. The other, on the English translation and publication of Pietro Giannone's *Civil History of Naples*, was Trevor-Roper's attempt to resolve the puzzle surrounding the translation – the same puzzle on which he had alighted with such enthusiasm in the journal in 1963, and had subsequently written in the 1967 essay on 'The Scottish Enlightenment'. If a full resolution of the puzzle still eluded him, it was nonetheless fitting that Giannone, who had inspired the turn to historiography in 1963, should have been the subject of the last essay he published on a historian.

Though written at the beginning of the 1980s, the essay on Conyers Middleton, Cambridge controversialist, deist and critic of miracles, merits separate introduction, since it is published here for the first time. It was first given as the Leslie Stephen Lecture at the University of Cambridge in 1982. Trevor-Roper seems to have chosen its subject out of a long-standing puzzlement over Leslie Stephen's hostility to the English deists. 'Why did Leslie Stephen so <u>hate</u> the Deists?' he later asked Stephen's biographer, Noël Annan.[27] But his interest in Middleton transcended the occasion of the lecture. He continued to work on the essay for several years afterwards, reading Middleton's correspondence with Lord Hervey in the Suffolk County Record Office and the British Museum and extending the analysis of his works, until it attained the form in which it is now published.

In part its inspiration was local, the result of his own translation in 1980 from Oxford to Cambridge, to be Master of Peterhouse. Not only had Middleton caused repeated ructions in the university of which Trevor-Roper was now a part; he had specifically picked a fight with the Master of Magdalene College, Daniel Waterland, the most determined and persistent defender of the doctrine of the Trinity in the Church of England of his day. Trevor-Roper was intrigued by the doctrine of the Trinity, which he regarded as 'palpable nonsense'.[28] His own long war against the Anglo-Catholic clique in Peterhouse, which had helped secure his election as

Master in the mistaken belief that he would leave them to run the college, only piqued Trevor-Roper's curiosity. While there he asked Alasdair Palmer, a younger friend who admitted once to having been 'a committed Christian', to explain how anyone could believe 'those quaint, superannuated doctrines of the Incarnation, Resurrection, Ascension, etc., which, in the Creed, we solemnly say that we believe'. How was it that, in the twentieth century, there were people 'who apparently take this stuff not (as is surely permissible) as an agreeable allegory, or harmless poetic myth . . . but literally'? . . . . 'All this is extremely worrying to me as I sit, now and then, in the chapel of Peterhouse, placing myself, by versatile imaginative effort, as the various parts of the service follow one another, among the fanatical Bedouin of ancient Judaea, the hooligan clergy of Byzantium or the Roman Maghreb, the scholarly Anglican bishops of the 17th and the snivelling Methodist hymnologists of the 19th century.'[29]

If local circumstances lent colour to the investigation of Middleton, however, the serious, underlying purpose of the essay emerges towards its end. Middleton was a vital missing link in Trevor-Roper's explanation of Gibbon's attitude to religion, which he took to be that of a sceptical deist. It was reading Middleton's *Free Enquiry* which precipitated Gibbon's youthful conversion to Catholicism; but once he had been retrieved from that, Gibbon adopted and maintained 'a position, which, in respect of religion, was identical with that of Middleton'. To the deist Middleton, therefore, was to be attributed the thinking which informed Gibbon's history of the Christian Church and the Roman Empire. In its scholarly depth as well as in the elegance of its argument, the essay on Middleton stands comparison with the long essays on Great Tew, Laud and Laudianism, and Grotius and England, which were also written in the 1980s (although interestingly Trevor-Roper did not attempt to associate Middleton with the Erasmian, Arminian tradition of Grotius and Great Tew which he celebrated in those essays). Together, these four essays are the major scholarly achievement of his years in Cambridge.

To some readers of this volume, the essays collected here will evoke the period in which they were written. Those who read them when they were first published, or who heard Trevor-Roper lecturing on Gibbon and Macaulay and on Burckhardt, in the 1960s and 1970s, will find themselves on familiar ground. (Even so, the lectures did not always follow the script. One who attended a lecture on Gibbon as an undergraduate remembers

Trevor-Roper beginning to quote from one of the more scabrous footnotes, starting to giggle, and finally leaving the lecture in hysterics. The undergraduate has enjoyed the *Decline and Fall* ever since.)[30] The essays were undeniably the product of circumstances, personal, institutional and intellectual, from which we are now at a distance, and it has been the purpose of this Introduction to illuminate the circumstances in which they were originally written.

But distance should not obscure the essays' contribution to the history of historical writing, or historiography. When Trevor-Roper began to write on the subject, it was still, almost exclusively, the preserve of literary scholars. Anglo-Saxon scholarship on Gibbon in particular was still wide open to Giarrizzo's derisive comment of 1954 that it amounted to no more than 'banal methodological observations and idle chatter'.[31] In the historical study of Gibbon, Trevor-Roper was preceded only by Giarrizzo and Arnaldo Momigliano. Momigliano was more interested in Gibbon's historical method, and in his relation to ancient Roman and ecclesiastical historians, than in Gibbon as an Enlightenment historian;[32] Trevor-Roper's contribution was to set Gibbon in a wider context, as the heir of Giannone and Montesquieu, and the contemporary of the historians of the Scottish Enlightenment, Hume and Robertson. Trevor-Roper also pioneered the study of the afterlife of the Enlightenment's historical philosophy, showing how much of it carried over into the work even of those who noisily professed to reject it.

In an appendix, I have indicated the main lines of scholarship on the subjects of Trevor-Roper's essays since they were written. The intention is to offer guidance on further reading to those interested; but in many cases the later work is also testimony to the impact of Trevor-Roper's essays on the field. Among the scholars prominent in that survey are John Burrow and John Pocock. Younger by ten or more years, neither was a pupil of Trevor-Roper; indeed, both were Cambridge-educated, and John Pocock was supervised by Herbert Butterfield, a historian for whom Trevor-Roper had limited respect (mainly on account of his professed identity as a Christian historian). If there was intellectual distance between them, however, there was also cross-fertilisation, and both Pocock and Burrow have made major contributions to the study of Enlightenment history and its legacy. In turn, the work of all three has been the point of departure for a younger generation, led by Colin Kidd and David Womersley, Karen O'Brien and Mark Phillips, whose contributions are likewise indicated in the appendix. The teaching of historiography also continues to thrive within History at Oxford, where William Thomas, a Macaulay scholar, took over the lectures on Gibbon and Macaulay, to be succeeded in turn by Peter Ghosh and Brian Young.

The essays which follow, then, are historiography in a double sense. They have made important, in several cases ground-breaking, contributions to a now-flourishing field of historical enquiry. At the same time, they can and should themselves be read historiographically, as among the finest examples of English historical writing of the last four decades of the twentieth century. This is a world now moving away from us, but still far from lost; and Trevor-Roper's essays will be among its most enduring products.

Trevor-Roper valued the great historians of the Enlightenment and their nineteenth-century heirs for three things. First of all, for their style. That style was not uniform – the polemical clarity of Middleton was quite distinct from the limpid, deceptively easy prose of Hume, as that was in turn from the great, arching periods of Gibbon; in the nineteenth century, the relentless momentum of Macaulay's short sentences vied with the inflated, metaphysical exuberance of Carlyle. But they had all shared a commitment to style, to good writing as indispensable to the persuasive expression of argument. Ever since his first reading of Gibbon, at Pearsall Smith's prompting, in the 1940s, Trevor-Roper had endorsed that view of the importance of style: history is a rhetorical art.

Second, Trevor-Roper valued the historical vision generated by the Enlightenment. He belonged to the post-war generation of historians who had no difficulty in writing of 'the Enlightenment', and he was unaffected by the later debate, instigated by John Pocock, over whether it is helpful to think of one Enlightenment, unified by the definite article. For Pocock and many others (though not the editor of the present volume), it makes better sense to think in terms of plural Enlightenments, even within historiography.[33] Trevor-Roper did not think of the Enlightenment philosophy of history as monolithic – indeed, the argument of the original essay with this title was that it generated two rival philosophies, one deriving from Voltaire, the other from Montesquieu. But he nevertheless continued to think of the Enlightenment historians as a group, who had, by their several contributions, transformed the intellectual ambitions of historical writing. In place of the 'civil' history of Machiavelli and his heirs, the Enlightenment historians had taken political and constitutional history out of itself, and placed it in wider frameworks of social development. The theorists of this ambition had been Montesquieu and his heirs among the Scots, Adam Smith and John Millar; the narrative practitioners had been Hume, Robertson and Gibbon. The same practitioners, joined by the erratic genius of Voltaire, had also absorbed the lesson of Giannone and of Middleton: that the history of the Church must be written in the same, secular, social perspective. The new intellectual ambition of the Enlightenment historians, however, was also valuable for what most of them avoided: an excessive, utopian confidence in the inevitability of progress. Such confidence was mistakenly attributed to the Enlightenment by Hegel, Marx and their followers in the nineteenth century and beyond; but it was not characteristic of Montesquieu, Gibbon or the Scots. Nor was it characteristic of the nineteenth-century historians whom Trevor-Roper most admired, Carlyle and Burckhardt. Their philosophies of history might in other respects have been hostile to that of the Enlightenment, and, in the case of Carlyle, in some respects positively dangerous. But they shared the conviction that progress and its benefits were never to be taken for granted.

Whatever their differences, moreover, the Enlightenment historians and their heirs approached history with a philosophy. For this Trevor-Roper valued them just as much as he did for their style. History, even well-written history, was of no value to Trevor-Roper without a philosophy to inspire it and shape its methods. He would put this point with particular clarity in a letter to Gideon Cohen in Jerusalem in 1983. Cohen had sent Trevor-Roper a copy of the letter he had submitted to the editor of the *Times Literary Supplement* in which he sought to correct Trevor-Roper's claim that Burckhardt had a philosophy of history. Burckhardt, he reminded Trevor-Roper, states explicitly in the *Weltgeschichtliche Betrachtungen* that he repudiates all philosophy of history, because history and philosophy are antithetical. To this Trevor-Roper replied:

> I don't think that we really differ much, if at all. If we do, it is only in the use of language. When I say that Burckhardt, though he disclaimed a particular philosophy of history, nevertheless had a general philosophy of history which sprang from the same roots as those particular philosophies which he rejected, I am using the word 'philosophy' in an 18th century sense: the sense in which Gibbon, for instance, used it. My point is that Burckhardt's whole attitude to history, though unsystematic, and opposed to the

intellectual and indeed metaphysical systems erected by Hegel and even by Ranke, nevertheless constituted (in 18th century terms) a 'philosophy'; and that that philosophy sprang from the same root (i.e. Herder and Goethe) as those systems – which, however, had been distorted by intervening forces (the forces of German political history) from which Burckhardt (not being German) was exempt. The 'philosophy' of Winckelmann, Herder and Goethe is a very different kind of thing from the philosophy of Hegel, or indeed of any professional philosopher; but I hope that I am in a reputable tradition when I call it too a philosophy: I don't see why that amiable Greek word, and indeed Greek concept, should be annexed exclusively to rigorous systems! This is perhaps a prejudice of mine, since I want to save the word, and need such a word to apply to the thing which I respect, and do not like to see it monopolised by systems which I do not respect.[34]

History written without a philosophy, Trevor-Roper believed, is liable to lose its sense of purpose, and to lapse into antiquarianism. The philosophies of the historians who are the subjects of these essays were not identical. The philosophies of Carlyle or, to a lesser extent, Burckhardt were consciously opposed to the Enlightenment philosophy of Giannone, the Scots and Gibbon. But in every case it was the presence of a philosophy which made their works worth studying, for without a philosophy, these essays argue, no great, or even interesting, history can be written.

Editorial Note

THE ESSAYS PUBLISHED in Trevor-Roper's lifetime are reprinted as they were published, with minor corrections where these were indicated by Trevor-Roper in offprints, or where the original typescript made it clear that an error had occurred in the process of publication. A very few corrections have been made by the editor, all of them of minor slips. Consistency has been applied to the use of capitals and italics, and to punctuation and spelling, which were previously subject to the vagaries of different journal and volume editors.

The notes have required more intervention. Wherever possible, Trevor-Roper referred to what he believed to be the most accessible editions of texts at the time of writing. Everyman, World's Classics and Penguin editions were favoured, particularly in the case of Gibbon. He did not believe it necessary to give a full reference to a work whose title he gave in the text of the essay. He also did not trouble the reader with references for quotations which he assumed the reader would know already. Without wanting to give a false impression of Trevor-Roper's annotation, I have silently corrected some slips (as of page numbers), and amplified references to ensure that the essentials of full title, place and date of publication are given on first citation. A greater level of intervention has been necessary to provide references for quotations where I have been able to track them down: these new references are placed within square brackets. In the case of Gibbon, I have also added references to the editions of the *Decline and Fall* and the *Autobiography* which scholars now use, namely David Womersley's Penguin edition of the former, and the older edition of all the drafts of the *Autobiography* by John Murray. Finally, I have added a few references to later scholarship where it has a bearing on a particular point of fact or interpretation.

Two of the essays, those on Carlyle and Burckhardt, were published without notes. The first, which was published in the *Times Literary Supplement,* I have left without annotation, but have listed the sources on which, his preparatory notes reveal, it was based. In the case of Burckhardt it has been possible to supply references for the quotations, since these are given in the typescripts of the lectures from which the essay derived. I have followed Trevor-Roper in using available English translations of Burckhardt's letters and books.

The previously unpublished essay, on Conyers Middleton, has been printed from the last and fullest of the several typescripts left by Trevor-Roper. It is also exceptional in being much more intensively annotated. Building on this foundation, I have sought to complete the annotation by amplifying still-abbreviated references and by adding new ones where a quotation was unattributed or a work referred to in the text was not clearly distinguished. Since this essay is published here for the first time, I have also included references to recent work by other scholars on specific points discussed by Trevor-Roper, where I am aware of it; these references are within square brackets.

Acknowledgments

I owe a great debt of gratitude to Judith Curthoys, archivist of Christ Church, who has received the Dacre Papers and made them available to scholars in awkward circumstances, and who has willingly searched out items still uncatalogued. I am likewise grateful to the staff of the Bodleian Library for their kindness and ingenuity in tracking down incomplete titles. Rosemary-May Services of Honiton retyped the previously published essays. For the publishers, Robert Baldock has been supportive and patient, Candida Brazil a helpful and authoritative editor, and Robert Shore a vigilant, constructive copy-editor.

Individuals who have helped by tracking down references and making suggestions include Alan Bell, Peter Ghosh, Colin Kidd, John Pocock, Angus Ross, Adam Sisman and Brian Young; in particular, Colin Kidd and Brian Young read and made valuable editorial suggestions for the essay on Middleton. To all of them I am very grateful. A still greater debt is to Stephen Taylor, whose help in preparing the Middleton essay for publication has been invaluable; his knowledge of the Hervey Papers and loan of Xerox and electronic copies of that correspondence made the editor's task much easier than it would otherwise have been. Most of all, however, I have to thank Blair Worden, Trevor-Roper's literary executor, for encouraging me to undertake the volume, for making available a great deal of relevant material, for reading and commenting helpfully on my introduction – and for his patience.

The publishers and the editor are most grateful to the following for permission to reproduce essays included in this volume: The Voltaire Foundation, University of Oxford (for 'The Historical Philosophy of the Enlightenment', 'The Scottish Enlightenment', 'The Idea of *The Decline and Fall of the Roman*

Empire', and 'Gibbon's Last Project'); *The Historical Journal,* Cambridge University Press ('Pietro Giannone and Great Britain'); The *Revue Roumaine d'histoire* ('Dimitrie Cantemir's *Ottoman History* and its Reception in England'); *History and Theory* ('David Hume, Historian'); *The Journal of Law and Economics,* Chicago ('Gibbon and the Publication of *The Decline and Fall of the Roman Empire,* 1776–1976'); The University of London ('The Romantic Movement and the Study of History'); Penguin ('Lord Macaulay: *The History of England*'); the *Times Literary Supplement* ('Thomas Carlyle's Historical Philosophy'); and the British Academy ('Jacob Burckhardt').

CHAPTER 1

The Historical Philosophy of the Enlightenment

IT IS APPROPRIATE, from Lake Leman, to look back not merely, in general, at the Enlightenment, but, more particularly, at the historiography of the Enlightenment. In Geneva the greatest of its Italian historians, Pietro Giannone, found his only safe retreat. Here lived Giannone's friend and protector Jacob Vernet, the link between him and his French successors Montesquieu and Voltaire. Here Montesquieu published his *De l'Esprit des lois*; here Voltaire completed and published his *Essai sur les moeurs*. Here, at Lausanne, Gibbon laid both the first foundations and the final stone of his *Decline and Fall of the Roman Empire*. The eighteenth-century revolution in historical writing, we may say, began on this lake; or at least this lake provided the geographical link between the separate makers of that revolution. If Montesquieu and Voltaire had been confined to France, could they have inspired Hume and Robertson? If Giannone had been confined to Italy, how much of his work would we possess? If Gibbon had been stuck in Oxford, he himself assures us, he would have been a barnyard fowl quietly moulting on his own dunghill and we should never have had the *Decline and Fall*. And without them, what would modern historiography be?

For it is with these men that historiography, as a continuous science, begins. I say 'as a continuous science' because it has, of course, earlier beginnings in Renaissance Florence. But from those earlier beginnings its progress was not continuous. When the 'philosophical historians' of the Enlightenment looked back at the two predecessors whom they all explicitly acknowledged, Machiavelli and Guicciardini, they saw them across an intervening gulf in which they might recognise one or two isolated allies – a Thuanus, a Davila, a Paolo Sarpi – but no continuous tradition. The seventeenth century, they would admit, had seen a great growth of erudition; but there had been a decline of criticism. Reformation and Counter-Reformation, the serried, rival tomes of the Protestant Centuriators of Magdeburg and the Catholic annalist cardinal Baronius, had alike opened an era of intellectual regression. Since then there had been a great deal of learned accumulation, but criticism, 'philosophy', had – with rare exceptions – been in suspense. In that field, as Gibbon once observed, there had been 'a century of slumber'; and it was the task of the eighteenth century to begin again. To Voltaire, the period of the Renaissance appeared as the beginning of the modern world; it was then, he wrote, that the human spirit had experienced, 'comme dans notre monde, une révolution qui a tout changé'; and he recognised Machiavelli and Guicciardini as the only historians worthy to be named since Antiquity. Gibbon agreed with him. Machiavelli and Guicciardini, he wrote, 'were justly esteemed the first historians of modern languages till, in the present age, Scotland' – that is, Hume, Robertson and Adam Smith – 'arose to dispute the prize with Italy herself'.[1]

But if the past had been uneven, the future, it now seemed, would be smooth. Looking ahead, neither Voltaire nor Gibbon feared that the intellectual revolution which they had witnessed or helped to make might be reversed. The break-through had occurred. The arts, wrote Voltaire, once established and protected by national independence, cannot be extinguished: they will always spring again. The gains of science, wrote Gibbon, are permanent: no temporary eclipse can stay the progress which they ensue. And among the arts and sciences thus permanently established, they saw their own achievement: 'philosophical history', 'critical history', 'universal history' had come to stay.

What was the 'philosophic history' of the Enlightenment, and how is it to be distinguished from the historiography of the seventeenth century, the century of Bossuet and Maimbourg and Fleury and Tillemont, of the Bollandists and the Maurists, and indeed from the historiography of the nineteenth century, the century of Ranke and Macaulay and Michelet, of the *Monumenta Germaniae historica* and the Rolls series? The broad lines are clear enough. The 'philosophical' historians rejected the mere accumulation of detail and fact. They also rejected splendid examples, the Plutarchian heroes so popular since the Renaissance. Instead they looked for explanation. In this they had predecessors, of course; but unlike those predecessors they altogether rejected theological explanations. Theological explanation had already been undermined by the seventeenth-century sceptics: the eighteenth-century historians threw it silently overboard and loud was the cry from those who saw it going. 'This philosophical history (so called)', thundered that great enemy of the Enlightenment, John Wesley, is not merely 'profoundly dull' (he was referring to the most novel and most interesting parts of Robertson's *History of America*); it not merely ignores the central, heroic figures (but where in all this, he asked, on reading the *History of Charles V*, is Charles V?); it also – and this, of course, is its greatest crime – excludes God from the government of the world, postulating other, secular causes; and so he discharged his successive salvos against all its exponents in turn: against Gibbon's Hanoverian precursor Mosheim, who, he said, (though a professor of theology) had 'no sense of inward religion'; against the 'infidel' *abbé* Raynal, whose *Histoire des deux Indes* had provoked the outburst; against that 'most insolent despiser of truth and virtue that ever appeared in the world', David Hume; and against that disgrace to his cloth, Principal Robertson of Edinburgh University, who, though a minister of religion, contrived to explain the discovery and conquest of America without ever mentioning the Providence of God![2] The outcry against Gibbon, when his first volume appeared, was even more hysterical. But Gibbon knew how to deal with it, and there is no need now to revive the victims of his famous *Vindication*.

But this was only the beginning. Because they rejected all such theological explanations, the philosophical historians also, by a necessary consequence, rejected any theoretical predilection for Europe or Christendom, and refused to confine the course of history within the time-honoured channels so deeply dug and so faithfully watered by so many Christian writers. In particular, they took a malicious pleasure in devaluing a certain intolerant, insanitary and superstitious tribe which had arrogantly claimed a disproportionate place in the unfolding of the divine plan of human history, the Jews. How absurd it would seem to a civilised Chinaman, exclaimed Voltaire, if he were told that a certain bishop at the other end of the Eurasian landmass – he was referring, of course, to Bossuet – had written a 'universal history' which made no reference to China at all, but deduced the whole course of humanity from the parochial bickerings of those fanatical barbarians! Once God, and his whimsical preferences, had been removed from historical causation, all humanity came naturally and equally in, and most of the great eighteenth-century historians – Mosheim, Voltaire, Robertson, Gibbon – extended their range to other continents and other civilisations, from whose material they impartially drew their conclusions. They believed mankind to be everywhere essentially the same, subject to the same laws, and capable of comparative treatment, even in religion. Finally, having thus rejected the old philosophy of history and widened their field of study, the 'philosophical historians' looked for a new philosophical content. To reanimate the mass of historical data into which the old ideological structures had decomposed, they put forward two new concepts whose acceptance may be said to have created the positive historiographical revolution of the Enlightenment. These new concepts were the concept of the organic nature of society and the idea of progress.

Of course these ideas did not explode suddenly upon the intellectual world of Europe. The more we study the roots of any intellectual revolution, the longer and more complex they always turn out to be. The eighteenth-century Enlightenment grew slowly out of seventeenth-century heresy – out of the Arminianism, the Socinianism, the Libertinism, the Quakerism, the Platonism, the Pietism which, in the gradual disintegration of dogma, had merged in undenominational deism. The way for it had been cleared by the scepticism of Bayle and Le Clerc; the new motivation was supplied by the ideas of Locke and Newton. Out of this great intellectual change of the seventeenth century, the idea of progress gradually and naturally disengaged itself. Long before it was made explicit, it was implicit in the attack of the 'moderns' upon the 'ancients'. If, by 1700, the 'moderns' could, in Mr Willey's phrase, look back on the sages of Antiquity from an eminence as lofty as their own, it was clear that the old idea of a golden age, perhaps even of the fall of man, was out of date.[3] Already there had been progress. What had begun could be continued; and the function of history must be, at least in part, to trace the stages by which it had come.

Similarly the idea that human societies have an internal dynamism, dependent on their social structure and articulation, was not new. It had been held by Machiavelli, varied and documented by many of his successors. The great legal and institutional writers of the seventeenth century, Grotius and Pufendorf, had given it substance; and Grotius and Pufendorf were among the cherished masters of the 'philosophical historians' of the next century. In fact it was because the ground had been so well prepared that the intellectual revolution of the eighteenth century, when it came, was so complete. Within two years the two new concepts which lay at it base, and had already pene-trated men's minds, were made explicit. In 1748 Montesquieu published his great work *De l'Esprit des lois*. In 1750 Turgot, in his *Discours* to the Sorbonne, traced the concept of progress in history. Thereafter the great works of philosophical history appeared, precipitated if not originally inspired by these two ideas: Hume's *History of England*, Voltaire's *Essai sur les moeurs*, Robertson's *Charles V* and the *History of America*, and, greatest of all, Gibbon's *Decline and Fall of the Roman Empire*.

Of course, these writers had their immediate predecessors, men who had foreshadowed Montesquieu rather than been inspired by him. In particular there had been two. There had been Mosheim, the judicious, impartial Mosheim who, for all his Lutheran orthodoxy, had been influenced by the English deists and the German Pietists against whom he wrote, and who treated the Church no longer as the repository of the divine plan but as a purely secular institution, a *coetus hominum* like any other human society. And there had been Giannone, the great, unfortunate historian of Naples, who from his days as a law student had seen that history and law were inseparable and had studied the legal codes of Theodosius and Justinian, as he wrote in his autobiography, 'not as ends in themselves but as effective means to understand the origins and changes of the Roman Empire and how, from its ruins, there arose so many new rulers, laws, customs, kingdoms and republics in Europe'.[4] In those words how many of the great histories of the Enlightenment are foreshadowed! It is the very doctrine of Montesquieu, Voltaire, Gibbon, all of whom read and admired Giannone – most of all, perhaps, Gibbon. Gibbon described Giannone's *Storia civile del regno di Napoli* as one of the three works which most directly inspired him; his passion for Godefroy's commentary on the Theodosian code echoes Giannone's panegyric of that 'immortal', 'stupendous' work; and his own great work was the realisation of Giannone's dream. But still, between Giannone and Gibbon, as between Giannone and Voltaire, stands Montesquieu; and it was Montesquieu whose genius, generalising the ideas not only of Giannone but of so many other writers, gave a new formative spirit to that laborious accumulation of scholarship which the scepticism of their predecessors had reduced to formless disorder.

A glance at the dates tells the tale. In 1748 Montesquieu's great work was published at Geneva. Next year David Hume, having read it in Turin, wrote to the author sending him some Scottish evidence and a copy of his own *Philosophical Essays*. Montesquieu at once recognised a kindred spirit and wrote back sending a presentation copy of his work, two chapters of which Hume promptly had translated and published in Edinburgh. Thereafter

Hume resolved to be a historian: the utter vacuity of English historiography (as he told a friend) was suddenly brought home to him; and he set to work to fill it. When his first volumes were out, and Montesquieu was dead, a French correspondent assured him that 'you are the only one who can replace the Président de Montesquieu'.[5] Meanwhile Hume's friend William Robertson was writing his *History of Scotland* which already, in its account of Scottish feudalism, shows the influence of Montesquieu: an influence which would be even more marked in the great introductory chapters, or rather books, of his histories of Charles V and America. John Wesley, as usual, sniffed the dangerous scent: he poured scorn on those 'dry verbose dissertations on feudal government', and roundly declared that Montesquieu himself had 'neither strength nor clearness nor justness of thought' and 'is no more to be compared to Lord Forbes and Dr. Beattie than a mouse to an elephant'.[6] But Wesley, here as everywhere, was the voice of the past, vainly lamenting the loss of belief in the doctrine of the Trinity, eternal punishment, the reality of witches, etc. A few years later another Scotsman, a pupil of Adam Smith, looking back on the foundation of the new science of sociology and political economy, would write: 'the great Montesquieu pointed out the road. He was the Lord Bacon in this branch of study. Dr. Smith is the Newton'.[7]

While Hume and Robertson were writing in Scotland, Edward Gibbon was studying in Lausanne, and was finding his chief delight, as he afterwards wrote, 'in the frequent perusal of Montesquieu, whose energy of style and boldness of hypothesis were powerful to awaken and stimulate the genius of the age'. After his return to England in 1758, Gibbon published his historical *credo*, his *Essai sur l'étude de la littérature*, which is at once a definition of 'philosophical history' – history related to and explained by the social institutions in which it is contained – and a paean in praise of Montesquieu. Even the style of it, he afterwards wrote, had been fatally influenced by that of Montesquieu. Thereafter he would apply Montesquieu's method to the vast subject he had undertaken; and in the last volume of that work he would stop to pay a final tribute to the master whose *Esprit des lois*, he said, had been the greatest influence not only on him but on historical enquiry for forty years.

Meanwhile there had been Voltaire. In the years before the publication of *De l'Esprit des lois*, Voltaire was already a historian. He had published his history of Charles XII in 1731 and had been engaged on his *Siècle de Louis*

XIV from 1735. But although Voltaire, like Giannone and others, independently held many of the views of Montesquieu, neither of these books reveals the fully developed historical philosophy of the Enlightenment. When Gibbon read *Le Siècle de Louis XIV*, which had been published in 1751, he complained of Voltaire's 'vicious' method of separating the various aspects of history into distinct chapters when in fact they are causally connected. It is the judgment of a man who had learned from Montesquieu on a man who had not. But meanwhile Voltaire too was learning. Since 1744, with the advice and encouragement of Vernet, the friend of Giannone and Montesquieu, he had been at work on his *Essai sur les moeurs*. Its first version was published, after what Mr Furio Diaz calls two 'tormentosi anni' of revision, in 1754. Two years later the second version showed 'the first signs of interest in Montesquieu'. In 1769, in the third version, the first to contain the new essay on 'La philosophie de l'histoire', 'the influence of Montesquieu', says Mr Brumfitt, 'has become clearly visible'.[8]

Moreover, through Voltaire, the influence of Montesquieu also received wider diffusion. Perhaps the most signal tribute to Voltaire as a historian, and the clearest evidence of the real interdependence of the historians of the Enlightenment, is that paid to the *Essai sur les moeurs* of the 'infidel' Voltaire by the Presbyterian clergyman and Moderator of the General Assembly of the established Kirk of Scotland, William Robertson. At the end of his famous dissertation on the progress of society from the end of the Roman Empire to the reign of Charles V, Robertson gave a note upon his sources. He admitted that, among them, he had not explicitly cited Voltaire's work; but that, he said, was only because Voltaire had not followed the modern practice of quoting chapter and verse. If only 'that extraordinary man, whose genius, no less enterprising than universal, has attempted almost every different species of literary composition', had complied with this recently adopted practice, then, said Robertson, 'a great part of my labours would have been unnecessary, and many of his readers, who now consider him only as an entertaining and lively philosopher, would find that he is a learned and well-informed historian'.[9]

Thus, in the third quarter of the eighteenth century, the revolution in historical studies was completed. Montesquieu had declared the principles on which historians should work, Turgot had suggested the thread they should pursue. History was no longer to be 'a dull chronicle of speeches and battles'; it was to be, as Giannone had urged, *storia civile*, a history of society. Montesquieu himself (we know from his notebooks) had contemplated writing an *Histoire civile de France* comparable with Giannone's *Storia civile di Napoli*.[10] 'Civil history' meant the explanation of social change, illuminated, as Gibbon wrote, by 'criticism and philosophy'; and it was to show, as Voltaire and Robertson showed, the progress of mankind: 'si vous n'avez autre chose à nous dire', wrote Voltaire, 'sinon qu'un barbare a succédé à un autre barbare sur les bords de l'Oxus et de l'Iaxarte, en quoi êtes-vous utile au public'?[11] How completely these views were accepted can be seen by comparing the greatest works of 'philosophical history' written after the death of Montesquieu: Voltaire's *Essai*, Robertson's two dissertations, Gibbon's *Decline and Fall*. In all we find the same basic assumptions: that history is universal; that its course, though it may be affected in detail by human decisions, is fundamentally determined by the structure of society, that is (in Robertson's words), by 'the division of property, together with the maxims and manners to which it gave rise'; that such axioms enable a science of history to be developed and the mechanics of progress to be identified; and, moreover, that this science itself supplies new evidence to the historian. Mere literary evidence, though contemporary, is devalued if it lacks what Voltaire called *vraisemblance*, that is, as Hume and Gibbon applied the concept, if it is incompatible not only with *bon sens*, but with the necessary consequences of economic or social facts. And to all these writers the significant substance of history is the same. The improvement of wealth, the discovery of useful arts, the elaboration of industrial technique, and the creation and preservation of appropriate social institutions are of more interest to them than dynasties, wars, or what even the clergyman Robertson described as 'those uninviting studies' of theology which had consumed so much of the intellectual activity of unenlightened ages.

Such was 'philosophic history' in the great generation of its practitioners. And yet how brief was their unanimity! Even as they practised it, a rift was opening out which would split them apart into mutually suspicious parties, soon to be ranged in fierce opposition. Voltaire would disown Montesquieu, who would become – posthumously – the patron saint of English whiggery, and Gibbon would disown Voltaire, who would become – posthumously – a hero of the French Jacobins. In his last years Gibbon would look back with disillusioned eyes on the Voltaire to whom, in Lausanne, he had once paid personal homage and whom, as he dryly remarked in his autobiography, 'I then rated above his true value'; and about the same time Mirabeau would be surprised to hear, on the lips of the king of Sweden, the almost forgotten name of Montesquieu whose 'rêveries surannées ne sont plus estimées que dans quelques cours du nord'.[12]

If we look for the agreement between the philosophic historians it is easy to find it. Montesquieu and Voltaire were brought together by many shared views and by a common struggle against the *dévots* who attacked their works. The admiration of Robertson embraced them both. Voltaire and Gibbon also had much in common: the more one reads both, the more one is surprised by the identity of their views. The *Essai sur les moeurs* forestalls many judgments of the *Decline and Fall* – on 'the supine indifference of the pagan philosophers' to the astounding miracles of the Jews and Christians, for instance; on the 'secondary causes' of the establishment of the Christian Church; on the worthlessness of Eusebius of Caesarea as a historical source; on the triumph of 'barbarism and religion' over the Roman Empire; on the register of crime, folly and misfortune which constitutes the bulk of human history; and on the thin, firm line of progress which nevertheless runs through and animates that bulk, giving it its only significance. Gibbon's conclusion that the profit of the crusades lay only in the financial ruin of the nobility which led indirectly to the enfranchisement of their industrious subjects is also identical with that of Voltaire. Like Voltaire, he sees in manufactures, rather even than in commerce, the machinery of social change. Like Voltaire, he contrasts the useful arts with useless metaphysics and explains heroes by the times and societies which produce them. Voltaire and Gibbon are alike in their scale of values, in their humanity, in their combination of a quest for purpose with a refusal to systematise. But the differences between Montesquieu and Voltaire, and between Voltaire and Gibbon, are no less obvious than their resemblances. Montesquieu did not conceal his distaste for Voltaire, and Voltaire loudly criticised *L'Esprit des lois* by which he was quietly influenced. In the *Decline and Fall* Gibbon never gave credit to Voltaire for his acute observations, only censure (sometimes exaggerated censure) for his faults. While Robertson, whom Gibbon venerated as 'the Livy of Scotland', praised the universal genius of Voltaire and rebuked those who dismissed him as no more than 'a lively and entertaining philosopher', Gibbon himself scoffed at the pretensions of this 'lively philosopher' to 'universal monarchy' in the arts and sciences. He allowed that Voltaire, in the *Siècle de Louis XIV*, by confining himself to recent times, had chosen a subject suitable to his labour-saving habits. Of the *Essai sur les moeurs* his general verdict is that Voltaire had 'varnished over' his hasty reading of modern compilations with 'the magic of his style' and had produced 'a most agreeable, inaccurate, superficial performance'. These seem ungenerous comments on two works into which Voltaire has put so much labour and thought. 'Je jetterais mon ouvrage sur le feu', Voltaire had written of *Le Siècle de Louis XIV*, 'si je croyais qu'il fût regardé comme l'ouvrage d'un homme d'esprit'. And his *Essai* required of him, ideally, he said, 'la patience d'un bénédictin' – that is, of a Mabillon or a Montfaucon – 'et la plume d'un Bossuet'.[13]

The rift between Voltaire and Gibbon, to which every reference to Voltaire in Gibbon's work bears witness, was not merely personal. It was not merely the reflexion of a scholar's distaste for what he supposed (however unfairly) to be mere journalism. It was part of a wider rift between Montesquieu and his disciples on one hand, the French Encyclopaedists on the other. The rift opened, I suggest, very soon after the publication of *L'Esprit des lois* and was cased largely by events in France. The key to it, so far as Gibbon is concerned, is to be found in his first published work, his *Essai sur l'étude de la littérature*, begun before leaving Lausanne in 1758 and published in England in 1761. In this work Gibbon openly declared war on the French *philosophes* whom hitherto he had admired. He accused them, in effect, of abandoning the principles of Montesquieu, deserting true 'philosophic history', jettisoning respect for facts and subordinating truth not merely to literary presentation but to particular polemical purposes. Had not d'Alembert proposed that at the end of each century a selection be made of such knowledge as was worthy of preservation and the rest burnt – that the *Encyclopaedia*, in effect, should replace the evidence which it interpreted and whose survival might disturb its conclusions? Would not Chastellux declare that there was 'far greater need of forgetting than of remembering' the past? Against such arrogant modernity Gibbon, himself essentially a modern, disdaining 'the trash of the last age', was nevertheless, by his historical conscience, his fundamental respect for the identity and independence of the past, moved to defend the erudition of his predecessors, which he also respected, and to formulate his own conception of 'philosophical history'. Facts, he insisted, are sacred: 'a Montesquieu, from the meanest of them, will deduce consequences undreamed by ordinary men'; they must never be subordinated to the tactical purposes of today. For the rest of his life this was his philosophy, and all his attacks on Voltaire are on these grounds. Voltaire is careless of accuracy, contemptuous of the labours of those scholars who had supplied even the philosophers with their facts, more concerned to damage his enemies than to discover the truth; in his dogmatic modernity he presumes to despise even the greatest masters of Antiquity; in his neurotic opposition to the Church he is 'the dupe of his own cunning'; his prejudices, since he claims to be a philosopher, are less excusable than those of his Jesuit enemies; at times, and in his way, Voltaire – the champion of tolerance, the author of a *Traité sur la tolérance* – is, says Gibbon, 'a bigot, an intolerant bigot'.[14]

But why did Voltaire and his friends deviate, if they did deviate, from the principles of Montesquieu, and why did Gibbon and his friends cling to those principles? Essentially, I suspect, because the society around them was different. Intellectually, all the 'philosophical historians' were reformers. They all believed in progress, in the republican virtues, in the useful arts of peace and the social forms which fostered those arts. But how was such reform to be achieved in practice? That, according to the views which they all accepted, depended on the state of society at the time. But in the 1750s the society of France and Italy was not only very different from the society of England and Scotland: it was also becoming daily more different. In Protestant countries reformers could be content to understand the world: reform could be achieved, piecemeal, through an intelligent appreciation of the existing forces of society and an intelligent co-operation with their natural tendency. England was already, said Montesquieu, 'une république qui se cache sous les formes d'une monarchie'. If only English kings and statesmen had shown a little more tact here, a little more imagination there – this was the burden of Hume's *History* – there would have been no need of civil war in 1642 or revolution in 1688. But in Catholic countries the position was very different. There the philosophers felt obliged not merely to understand but to change the world. They would have to fight against the existing forces of society. And that meant – necessarily according to their views – not merely a change in political direction, a change of persons. If politics (as all agreed) were conditioned and limited by the organic structure of society, then piecemeal political change might indeed be best attained by complying with that structure, as in England, but a radical change of political direction could only be achieved by radical change of the organic social structure too: that is, by revolution.

Montesquieu himself was an essentially unrevolutionary man. Perhaps before 1748 there was no need for him to be revolutionary. At all events he took the structure of French society for granted, distrusted apostles of abstract liberty, and relied, for progress towards real liberty, on the checks and balances supplied by the various organs of society. If he sought reform in the state, history taught him to rely on those 'intermediate powers' – the Church, the *parlements*, the nobility – whose feudal institutions had prevented the growth of royal tyranny in the Middle Ages. If he sought reform in the Church, he had no desire to see a frontal, anticlerical revolution: he preferred, as he once said, to see learned theologians and grave bishops not rudely cast down from their seats but sliding gently, gently into the abyss . . .[15]

Whether they were appropriate in France or not, such views were perfectly adapted to Protestant countries where the social power of the old regime had already been broken. Gibbon had no love for the Anglican Church, but it could not impede progress or persecute heresy and he conformed with it himself, just as he praised Socrates, Epicurus, Cicero and Plutarch who inculcated 'decent reverence' for the religion of Greece and Rome and reproved Voltaire for insulting 'the religion of nations'. The Kirk of Scotland had certainly been fanatical enough in the last century, and the memory of that fanaticism was still vivid to Hume, who had enjoyed many a running fight with enraged dominies in the sinuous, malodorous wynds of Edinburgh. By comparison he found Anglicanism tolerant and even popery had distant charms. So Hume's *History* infuriated the whig zealots by its indulgence to the pre-Reformation Church of Rome, the Italian politeness of whose superstition distinguished it from 'the gross rusticity' of 'enraged and fanatical' reformers, and by its open preference for the Anglican court of Charles I to the 'barbarous Zeal' and 'ridiculous cant' of his Scottish and puritan enemies. But in fact, in Hume's time, even the Scottish Kirk was in retreat. What real harm could it do when the Great Secession had relieved it of its fanatics and it was governed, year after year, by his own urbane friend and fellow-historian, that lukewarm clergyman, William Robertson? Clerical power in England and Scotland might be capable of loud squeaks against 'infidelity', but it was no longer a real force in society, capable of thwarting social and intellectual progress.

So the views of Montesquieu found an easy reception in Protestant England. But what of Catholic France? In the two years following the publication of *De l'Esprit des lois* the great struggle over the *vingtième* ended with the victory of the Church. It was the beginning of the *réaction seigneuriale*. From now on it seemed absurd to hope that the existing framework of

French society could be made to forward progress: that 'feudal' institutions would provide the balance against absolutism. On the contrary, Church, nobility, *parlement* were all socially reactionary bodies whose power was growing, not dwindling. The more one accepted Montesquieu's general theory, that it was the social power of institutions, and the mental attitudes derived from them, rather than political authority, which determined the history of nations, the more one was forced to the conclusion that, in Catholic countries in general, and in France in particular, political authority must be used to break down the existing organs of society and to create new. These inescapable social facts might not be so obvious in liberal, metropolitan society, but once one moved into the provinces, they were only too clear. Voltaire was horrified to find rural slavery still in force in the Jura. Gibbon was disgusted by the *corvées* imposed on the peasants of Savoy: in every gilded moulding in the royal palace of Turin, he wrote in his diary, he saw a Savoyard village dying of hunger, cold and poverty.[16] In Italy, the fate of Giannone himself was an eloquent warning. The political power of the viceregal court of Naples or of the emperor at Vienna might protect him for a time, but only for a time; in the end the social power of the Church – the power of the monks and the religious orders and the rich clerical offices dangled before lay families – had driven him from city to city till he had found a refuge in Protestant Geneva – only to be kidnapped, abducted, and imprisoned to death in Catholic Savoy. In Spain the liberal minister Campomanes might assist Robertson's researches and even sponsor a Spanish translation of his work. But it could not last: political liberalism had to yield to social reaction, and before long the translation was stopped and the work banned throughout the Spanish Empire. And in provincial Toulouse there was the terrible Calas case which resolved Voltaire to dedicate his life to a revolutionary programme: *écrasez l'infâme*.

Thus while Montesquieu became the historical prophet of the Protestant, and particularly of the English and Scottish, world, the historians of Catholic Europe turned away from his too tepid philosophy. If history had a function in politics, if the 'chain of events' of which it gave evidence in the past – that purposive thread which Voltaire himself saw so clearly, and which he accused Montesquieu of failing to observe – were to be applied usefully to the present, then the writing of history must bear some relation to the needs of politics. In free, Protestant countries it might be different. In Scotland, as Voltaire wrote, Hume might compose histories worthy of the name, but it was different in

France where serious writers were 'gênés et garrottés par trois sortes de chaînes: celles de la cour, celles de l'Eglise, et celles des tribunaux appelés parlements'. Protestant countries had had their social revolutions, in the sixteenth century. There the forces of progress, which had slowly revealed themselves in the Middle Ages, had triumphed. The traditions of those countries, the spirit of their laws, had adapted themselves to a new social structure. The pressure of those traditions, thus modified, could therefore remain beneficient pressures, 'checks and balances' to be respected. One could expect, in Montesquieu's phrase, 'que le pouvoir arrête le pouvoir'. But in France, in the Catholic countries generally, it was different. Their tradition, the spirit of their laws, reflected an unreformed society, and necessary change could not be contained within its existing channels. New channels must be dug, the inveterate organs of society – the court, the Church, the *parlements* – must be purged; in particular the Church, since it dominated the others and created the intellectual system of resistance, must be not merely purged but destroyed. Voltaire himself had always seen the Church as the enemy. From 1750, thanks to political events in France, hatred of the Church would dominate his historical thinking. And so, while the infidel Hume received the congratulations and encouragement of the primates of England and Ireland on his *History*, and was invited to stay in Lambeth Palace;[17] while Robertson quietly managed the deliberations of the established Church of Scotland; and while Gibbon happily conformed with the established Church of England, confident that the forces of society made progress merely a matter of enlightened policy, the French *philosophes* behaved very differently. In Professor Carl Becker's phrase, they could not, even as historians, 'afford to leave the battlefield of the present, where they were so fully engaged', for the realities of the past.[18] Montesquieu, they held, had been too busy 'finding the reasons for that which is' instead of 'seeking that which should be'. So Voltaire sought to redress the balance. He took sides in history, became not an observer but a partisan, indeed a furious partisan, and, in his zeal to discredit the institutions which he wished to see destroyed, appeared to Gibbon 'a bigot, an intolerant bigot'.

Soon after Voltaire's death, while Gibbon was still alive, political events further widened the gulf between them. The great French Revolution broke out. It was not what Voltaire had preached. He had preached reform of the structure of society by the political power of enlightened kings. In England the Parliament might have asserted the claims and founded the institutions of liberty against despotic, or would-be despotic, kings, but in France it was the monarchy which must establish it against the fossilised *parlements* and the social power of the Church. To the French monarchy, 'aimé et respecté par nous' – if it would only imitate the hero of his *Henriade*, or even of his *Charles XII* – i.e. Peter the Great – Voltaire would wish 'un pouvoir immense'. But essentially it was the reform, the progress, which mattered, and the monarchy was valued not for itself but as the instrument of reform. If it failed, if, instead of changing them, it should yield to the social forces around it, then he, or his disciples, would wish the same 'pouvoir immense' to another instrument. Instead of reforming the monarchical state, they would support a revolutionary republican state. The historical philosophy of the French *philosophes* looks forward, through the French Revolution, to the radical tradition of the nineteenth century, to the politicians and the historians who saw the state as the reformer of society.

On the other hand Gibbon, as he looked from Lausanne at the unrolling of events in revolutionary France, expressed himself, more than ever, a disciple of Montesquieu, and drew together with the man who was to become, for nineteenth-century Europe, the most influential of all Montesquieu's disciples. In the same 1750s in which Gibbon had disengaged himself from the French *philosophes*, another English whig, Edmund Burke, had discovered that Montesquieu was the greatest genius of the age and had sought to rewrite the history of England on his principles.[19] Now, in the 1790s, Burke's *Reflexions on the French Revolution* were hailed by Gibbon with enthusiasm: 'I admire his eloquence, I approve his politics, I adore his chivalry, and I can even forgive his superstition.'[20] Thereafter the rift widened still further. As the revolution in France was transformed into the subjugation of Europe, the disciples of Montesquieu became more conservative while those of Voltaire became more radical, and German conservatives and English whigs, finding that the social structure and traditions of their countries repudiated the revolution that was thrust upon them by a foreign conqueror, turned increasingly to Burke for their new historical philosophy. Where the radicals had seen the state as the necessary reformer of society, the new conservatives now saw society as the necessary corrector of the state. The organic conception of society which triumphed among German conservatives like Savigny and Niebuhr, and among English whigs like Acton, can be seen as the nineteenth-century continuation of Montesquieu and Gibbon. Did not Acton declare that, to him, Burke's speeches of the 1790s were 'the Law and the Prophets'? And are not

Acton's most famous dogmas, that power corrupts and that liberty sprang not from political victory but from structural deadlock, translated almost verbatim from *De l'Esprit des lois*, book XI, ch. iv?

Thus the two schools into which philosophical history had divided in the watershed of the 1750s became irreconcilably opposed, and in that hardening division the old concept of philosophical history foundered. In the nineteenth century, after the War of Nations against France, history, from being universal, became, once again, national. If history, after all, is subject to social structure, then surely – since social structure varies from nation to nation – history must vary from nation to nation too. There *can* be no 'universal history'. Besides, in the nineteenth century, there were so many more facts to study: on one hand, the European archives had been opened, revealing the political secrets of centuries; on the other hand, the convulsions of the revolutionary period had put a premium on sober, sobering facts as against intoxicating theories. So the pious accumulation of facts, which had characterised the seventeenth century, returned to fashion. So also, with Carlyle, did the Plutarchian heroes, and, with Chateaubriand, the Christian god. In many ways it seemed a return to the century before the Enlightenment. If universal, philosophical, impersonal history survived the shock of revolution at all, it survived in a very different atmosphere: as the pious, conservative universal history of Ranke, so respectful of the past that he left all judgment to God, suddenly restored to his heaven, and the bold, radical universal history, or at least theory of history, of Marx, who, like Voltaire, regarded the past as an armoury of weapons by which the continuity of history, so respected by conservative historians, must be broken and its course changed.

CHAPTER 2

The Scottish Enlightenment

THE FIRST INTERNATIONAL Congress on the Enlightenment took place in Geneva. It is appropriate that the second should be in Scotland. For if French-speaking Switzerland was the crucible of the Enlightenment, the meeting-place of those intellectual *émigrés* of Europe who inspired it, Scotland, another Calvinist country, was its outpost in the Anglo-Saxon world. By the later eighteenth century, the universities of Geneva and Edinburgh could be described by Thomas Jefferson as the two eyes of Europe.

The phenomenon of the sudden Scottish revival, after its dark age in the seventeenth century, is very perplexing. Foreigners, perhaps, were not fully aware of it. They saw it as part of the progress of liberal, whig, Hanoverian England. How were they to detect the subtle difference between London and Edinburgh, between two societies which spoke the same public language, which had long been ruled by one monarch, and were now fully united? The Scots themselves, by their terror of provincialism, aided the confusion. They tried hard to bury their identity. This was the time when they invented for their country the new name of 'North Britain', and when the great Scotch writers took such pains to 'purify' – i.e. to anglicise – their vocabulary: when they went through each other's works to purge them (in Hume's phrase) of all native impurities *alias* 'Scotticisms',[1] and when a docile class of 300 ambitious young Scotsmen would attend, here in Edinburgh, the fashionable elocution lectures in which Thomas Sheridan, the father of the dramatist, expounded, in a rich Irish brogue, the pure English pronunciation. But the English, being closer, observed the truth. While they made merry at Scotch manners, Scotch frugality, Scotch complacency, and did not take too seriously the tribal boasts of Edinburgh shopkeepers, they recognised that a great change had occurred north of the border. As Gibbon wrote to Adam Ferguson, he particularly appreciated tributes from 'the northern part of this island', to which taste and learning seemed to have fled from the smoke and hurry of London; and later he would declare that in the study of 'philosophic history' modern Scotland could dispute the prize with Renaissance Italy, 'and it is with private as well as public regard that I repeat the names of Hume, Robertson and Adam Smith'.[2]

How did this extraordinary change occur? By what social, political or intellectual alchemy did a country which had recently seemed so barbarous suddenly – in the fashionable jargon of the sociologists – 'take off'? At the end of the seventeenth century Scotland was a byword for irredeemable poverty, social backwardness, political faction. Its universities were the unreformed seminaries of a fanatical clergy. A century later, in one field at least, it was the teacher of Europe; and some of the most enterprising Englishmen sent their sons, some of whom would become British cabinet ministers, not to Oxford or Cambridge, but to Edinburgh or Glasgow: the Edinburgh of William Robertson, the Glasgow of John Millar.[3]

Surely there is something mysterious about this transformation. Surely it is a historical problem worthy of our study. And yet, I find, it is a problem from which modern Scottish historians turn impatiently away. Not for them, in this century, the sociological curiosity, the 'philosophic history', which their predecessors may claim to have founded. They prefer to reiterate their atavistic war cries: to remember Bannockburn, or to debate, for the thousandth time, the admittedly very debatable virtues of Mary Queen of Scots. These are no doubt inexhaustible subjects. Let us not seek to exhaust them. Let us turn rather to this worthier problem, which has hardly been broached.

What did cause the Scottish Enlightenment, that efflorescence of intellectual vitality which suddenly became obvious after the defeat of the last Jacobite rebellion in 1745, but whose causes must lie deeper in the past? Was it the Union with England of 1707, that great act of statesmanship which, at so small a price, opened England and the English empire to the hitherto cramped and introverted commerce and talent of Scotland? Was it the Kirk of Scotland – not its doctrine, of course (no one would suggest that), but the moral and mental discipline which it imposed on its subjects? Both these answers have been given, but neither of them, I think, can entirely satisfy the critical mind.

The liberating effects of the Union are of course unquestionable. It enriched Scotland materially; it enlarged its intellectual horizons; it transformed its society. But the Enlightenment did not come from England only, nor can any intellectual movement be explained merely by economic causes. Besides, the spirit precedes the fact. The spirit which made the Union possible – that liberal spirit which could see beyond the narrow glories of a tribal past to a new prosperity and a higher culture in a wider unity – was necessarily older than the union which it made. It was also, by 1707, well developed: strong enough to prevail over the vested interests of local burghs and the nationalist rhetoric of impassioned 'patriots'. Therefore, without denying the debt of the Scottish Enlightenment to the English union, we must also look for deeper, earlier springs. They must be sought in the reigns not of the first Hanoverians but of the last Stuarts.

What then of the Kirk, that essential organ of national identity in those Stuart days? In the nineteenth century it was fashionable to claim great things for the Calvinist spirit. Look at the country round Rome, cried Macaulay, in an unusual burst of national exultation, and then look at the country round Edinburgh, and admire the fertilising effect of the religion of the north![4] Marxist and Weberian sociologists have since taken up, and modulated, the cry. But today we cannot accept such simple solutions to complex problems. Calvinism may have been a liberating force in its first days. It may have been the religion of political and social resistance in the seventeenth century. But only a false analogy, or a blind loyalty, can see it as progressive in 1700. By that time the Church of Scotland was as obscurantist as the Church of Rome had ever been. Politically it opposed the Union. Intellectually it stamped on every new idea. Economically (in the words of Henry Grey Graham) 'it seemed to dignify dirt and to consecrate laziness'.[5]

Where then shall we look for the source of light? If we are to face this question, perhaps it is best to begin by asking: what was the peculiar character of the Scottish Enlightenment? For what distinguished Scotland in the eighteenth century was not merely the emergence of a number of literary men who attracted attention in their time and are now, with few exceptions, very properly forgotten. Many of those Scotch writers, who so complacently admired each other's 'genius', were thoroughly second-rate. Some of them were not 'enlightened' at all – merely busy or quaint. Even those who were innovators, even the greatest of them, with the solitary exception of Hume, were dull dogs. Their writing is flat and their conversation was dry: no *bon mot* is recorded from them.[6] With the same conspicuous exception, they were also all university professors; which may explain something. How different was Hume! What trouble he took over his own style! How he remonstrated with his friends about theirs! But it was no use. Being good Scotsmen, they were not to be changed; and by now they have paid the price. They are unread. By the next century, the Scotch philosopher, like Peacock's Mr McQuedy, was by definition a bore. He was a bore because, by then, the once-exciting substance of his thought had been absorbed. Only the style was left; and the style, alas, does not tempt us. Robertson, the Moderator of the General Assembly of the Kirk, might be an admirer of Voltaire. But he did not write like Voltaire. He wrote like a Moderator.

What then was the once-exciting content of that work? What was it that distinguished the Scotch philosophers of the eighteenth century from their Scotch predecessors and their foreign contemporaries? To answer this question we need not trouble ourselves with the camp-followers – with Stewart and Beattie and Reid and Hamilton. We may not, alas, digress to those more attractive but irrelevant artists and writers, Allan Ramsay, Cameron, the Adam dynasty, Boswell, or even that most influential Scotsman of them all, James Macpherson, the creator of Ossian. We must concentrate on the real intellectual pioneers: Francis Hutcheson, David Hume, Adam Ferguson, William Robertson, Adam Smith, John Millar. What was the general interest uniting these men whose lives, together, spanned the eighteenth century? For together, these are the Scottish Enlightenment.

It can be expressed very briefly. All these men were interested, above all, in the social behaviour of mankind.[7] Francis Hutcheson, the teacher of them all, the founder of the new 'Scottish philosophy', argued that the mind of man was governed neither by theological determinism nor by its own reasoning faculty but by a common or moral sense that was innate, instinctive and fundamentally virtuous and benevolent. There was nothing very Scottish about this philosophy, which would certainly have outraged any Scottish philosopher of the past. Hutcheson himself was born an Irishman, and he drew his philosophy from English teachers: Bacon, Newton and Locke, as filtered through Shaftesbury. But it was in Scotland that this English philosophy acquired its new social character. This instinctive moral sense, which Hutcheson postulated, though possessed by all men, was (he believed) directed differently at different times under different social pressures. It follows therefore that, in order to know man and the development of his ideas, we must know about society and the different forms of society within which man operates and by which his thinking is determined. So, insensibly, the study of man merges in the study of his social context, and the pupils of Hutcheson, from being moral philosophers, concerned with the problem of virtue, became social historians, concerned with the problem of progress. Hume, after his *Treatise on Human Nature*, became the historian of England. Ferguson stepped aside from moral philosophy to write his *Essay on Civil Society*; Adam Smith moved on from his *Theory of Moral Sentiments* to his *Wealth of Nations*. All these were concerned, essentially, with the social mechanism of progress. As Bagehot would say of *The Wealth of Nations*, it showed 'how, from being a savage, man rose to be a Scotchman'.

Thus, in the course of the century, the Scottish philosophy defined itself. It moved from psychology to sociology. It redefined the terms of political economy and founded the new political philosophy of 'utilitarianism'. It was the benevolent Hutcheson who first used the famous phrase 'the greatest happiness of the greatest number'. It was the sceptical Hume who first advanced the criterion of 'utility'. It was the radical Millar who annexed Hume's philosophy to whig politics and so showed the way to the great Scottish whig historians and utilitarian philosophers of the nineteenth century, Macaulay and Mill.

This, then, is the original contribution of the Scottish philosophers, and it is this, above all, which has to be explained. Why was it Scotsmen, rather than other men, who were so preoccupied with the problem of social change? All new ideas, I believe, are generated by social circumstances. Machiavelli and Guicciardini could not have founded 'philosophic history' had it not been for the remarkable changes which they had witnessed in their own city of Florence, and equally the eighteenth-century Scots could not have disputed the prize with them had they too not observed remarkable changes in their society. What were those changes? In the rest of this lecture I shall suggest an answer to this question. I shall suggest that in the years after 1680 – the years in which the new spirit was incubated, although it took some time to hatch – the internal condition of Scotland forced men to think in a new way. It was not only that those years were years of economic decline – of failing trade, financial disaster and catastrophic famine, all of which helped to precipitate the Union. They were also years in which the Scots, by resuming their broken contact with the rest of Europe, discovered themselves. That discovery, I shall suggest, was almost as disconcerting to them as the European discovery of America had been to Renaissance Europe.

First, the resumption of contact with Europe. Here I foresee an objection. Was such contact, it will be asked, ever broken? Were not the Scots, at all times, a cosmopolitan people? Did they not travel abroad, to France, to Holland, to Germany, to Poland and beyond? Indeed they did; but not equally at all times; and particularly not in the seventeenth century. For the events of the sixteenth century, I believe, had dug a great gulf between Scotland and the rest of the world, and the events of the seventeenth century had so widened that gulf that, when the bridge was at last rebuilt, those Scotsmen who had once crossed it hardly recognised themselves.

Consider the cosmopolitanism of the Scots. Before the Reformation they had gone, especially, to France. Paris was then the intellectual capital of Scotland, and almost every literary Scotsman had completed his education there. But after the Scottish Reformation that had changed. Paris was then a papist city, and the Scots who sought education abroad (unless they were cast-off Catholic émigrés) sought it only in safely Calvinist institutions: in the Huguenot academies of France, in Calvin's own academy of Geneva, or in the universities of Heidelberg, Leiden, Groningen, Utrecht. Unfortunately, in the later seventeenth century, few of these Calvinists seminaries gave a liberal education. The Huguenot academies in France, with the exception of the heretical Saumur, were timorous, narrow, defensive. Geneva was dominated by the bigots. Heidelberg had been ruined by the wars. And if the Dutch universities were different, that did not necessarily help the Scotch students there; for the majority of them went to study theology or law: pure Calvinist theology, good Roman law. Neither the theological nor the legal faculties of the Dutch universities were open to new ideas.[8] Only if a Scotsman went to study natural science in Holland was he likely to discover the modern world. It may be remarked that the new philosophy which entered Scotland in the later seventeenth century was brought largely by scientists – mathematicians and medical men – who had studied abroad: either at Leiden or (since few or none of them were Presbyterians) in Oxford, Padua or Paris.[9]

If Scotland, in the seventeenth century, was intellectually severed from France, at least it was dynastically united with England. But this dynastic union, we all know, was not a success. It transferred the court and its patronage to London and left Scotland, justly afraid for its independence, increasingly subject to an intolerant, defensive Kirk. In the 1650s, indeed, a brief flicker of Enlightenment was reflected from the pikes and muskets of Cromwell's army. But the reflexion did not outlast the conquest and with the return of the Stuarts, and the restoration of the old tensions, the energies of Scotland were once again distracted and consumed by faction. To the Scottish national historians, to those home-bred antiquaries who showed such zeal in recording the annals of national resistance – men like Robert Wodrow in his manse of Eastwood near Glasgow – those years from 1660 to 1690 were a heroic period: the period of the 'killing times', of the guerrilla war against episcopacy, of the holy murder of Archbishop Sharp, of the Cameronians, of the battle of Bothwell Brig, of the disaster of Killiecrankie and the final victory of the cause in the settlement of King William. But periods of heroism, of national resistance, can be periods of wastage, even of barbarisation. To those who look in history for more than the defence of ancient, anarchic liberty (which is often local tyranny),[10] the last half-century of Scottish history before the Union is a dark age of introversion and social war.

Thus Scotland, in the seventeenth century, suffered from a double isolation. Cut off from France by religion, from England by politics, refreshed mainly by the stale waters of Calvinist bigotry fed to it through the narrow conduits of Utrecht and Sedan and Geneva, it was also further insulated behind the barricades of a defensive nationalism. The first conditions of the Enlightenment were the breaking down of these barriers, the reopening of old contacts with Europe, the discovery of fresh streams of thought. These conditions were ultimately achieved at the end of the seventeenth century. They were achieved not by the national Kirk, the chief organ of isolation, but by its enemies and rivals: by its open enemies, the Episcopalians and Jacobites; by its secret enemies, the 'Arminian' heretics within the fold; and – perhaps most important of all – by that body of men without whom no intellectual movement can bear fruit: the new class of educated laity. Let us look, in turn, at each of these groups of men whom the patriotic historians of Scotland have so often ignored.

First, the open enemies of the Kirk, the Episcopalians and the Jacobites. The Episcopalians, of course, were the English party: they provided the link with England. Their service to Scotland, in those years, was invaluable: almost all the foreign culture which reached Scotland in its dark age came through them. There were men like the statesman Sir Robert Moray, royalist, freemason, mathematician and natural scientist, who had served Richelieu in France, become a friend of Huygens in Holland, and would be one of the founders, and the first president, of the Royal Society in London: Charles II's chief adviser on Scottish affairs, an 'erastian' who supported the laity against the clergy, 'the greatest man that his country produced in this age', as his *protégé* Bishop Burnet would write.[11] There were scientists like

David Gregory, who, having succeeded to the post and the papers of his uncle James Gregory, student of Padua and friend of Newton, would deliver in Edinburgh the first lectures on the Newtonian system ever to be given in Britain, only to be driven out by clerical inquisition and become Savilian Professor of Astronomy at Oxford. Or there were clergy like the Garden brothers of Aberdeen: James, who would correspond with John Aubrey on natural phenomena; George, who, when driven out of his living by the Kirk, would become the centre of that curious group of 'mystics of the north east' which G.D. Henderson has described,[12] and which created a new religious and intellectual link with the Continent. After the revolution of 1690, many of these anglophil Episcopalians retired from the public stage; but privately they continued to operate as a leaven in the Presbyterian lump; and meanwhile the revolution itself, unexpectedly, created new links between Scotland and the outer world. It did so, immediately, by sending many of the Jacobites, as exiles, abroad, and thus resuming a partial contact with France.

The Jacobites . . . how can one do justice, in a paragraph, to the influence on the Enlightenment of these alienated subjects of Scotland? It is a wonderful subject, and yet largely neglected. The conventional Scotch writers seem determined to ignore it: for how could a 'progressive' movement owe anything to such blind reaction? And yet 'progress' and 'reaction' are never easy to separate: the words themselves are but artificial labels, retrospectively imposed. In fact, almost every Scotsman of intellectual distinction from the beginning of the movement until 1715, and even beyond, was at least half a Jacobite. The College of Physicians in Edinburgh was the creation of the earliest Jacobite party: of King James himself, as duke of York and governor of Scotland; of James Drummond, earl of Perth, afterwards his hated minister; and of Perth's *protégé* Sir Robert Sibbald, who had learned the subject in Leiden and in France. All these were or would become Roman Catholic. They were supported by the duke's English physician and the Scotch bishops.[13] Among later Jacobites we find John Arbuthnot, scientist and wit, Queen Anne's physician, Fellow of the Royal Society and friend of Pope in London, and his brother Robert, the banker in Paris; Archibald Pitcairne, physician, poet and professor at Leiden, perpetually in trouble with the Kirk; Thomas Ruddiman, the most accurate of antiquaries and the most scholarly (when he wanted to be) of editors; Fr Innes, of the Scots College in Paris, the founder of critical history in Scotland, who would publish his work in London but then slip back to France to dedicate it to 'the

King' – i.e. the Old Pretender; his brother Lewis Innes, the Pretender's secretary, also a scholar and antiquary; the Chevalier Ramsay, another Roman Catholic, who set out from the mystical circle of Dr Garden in Aberdeen to join the mystical circle of Mme Guyon at Blois and become tutor to the Young Pretender and first projector of the *Encyclopaedia*.[14] In Edinburgh the only two reputable printers were both Jacobites;[15] even the others were not Presbyterians but Episcopalians. Lord Kames was a Jacobite. David Hume himself was a Jacobite till 1745. George Keith, Lord Marischal, the friend of Frederick the Great, of Voltaire, of Rousseau, of Boswell, and everyone else, was an exiled Jacobite. These Jacobites were not merely adherents of a fallen dynasty. Many of them thought little enough of the Stuarts: 'to think', Lord Marischal would exclaim in 1764, 'that I have sacrificed myself for that beastly family!'[16] Their Stuart loyalty was often accidental. Basically, at their best, they were an independent-minded élite who refused to conform with the narrow ideological nationalism of their time. The flight of some of them abroad, and their intercommunication with the Jacobites at home, created a new link between Scotland and the Continent whereby disruptive foreign ideas, so jealously excluded by the Kirk, gained admittance to what might seem at first unlikely homes.

Meanwhile the revolution was creating another, more direct foreign contact. The Kirk itself was being transformed. It was being liberated from the narrow nationalist Calvinism of the past and refreshed by new, heretical ideas brought largely from the country of its new king: Holland.

Through most of the seventeenth century, the Calvinist Churches of Europe, in Holland as in Scotland, in Switzerland as in France, had been on the defensive. Threatened by aggressive 'popery' from without, they were determined to tolerate no treachery within, and heresy was persecuted by the ruling clergy as fiercely as the society around them would allow. In Scotland that allowance was great. If ever the Hydra of heresy raised any of its heads – 'Arminianism', 'Socinianism', 'Independency' – there was a rustle of black gowns as the clergy competed to tread on it. In 1625 the 'Arminian' John Cameron was driven out of Scotland to Saumur. In the 1640s the Kirk seemed triumphant over all its enemies: it crushed the Arminian 'Aberdeen doctors', 'in whom fell more learning than was left behind in all Scotland besides',[17] and it stamped on the first sparks of 'Independency' in England. In the 1650s, under the protection of Cromwell, the enemies of the Kirk raised their heads again: that was the golden age for Scottish heretics, even for Scottish Catholics.[18] But it did not last long. Even in its eclipse, the Kirk clung to its doctrine of intolerance: the very idea of toleration was to it 'the mystery of iniquity'. Had I known, wrote the Rev. Samuel Rutherford, from St Andrews, to his reverend and dear brother Mr John Scot at Oxnam, near Jedburgh, had I known that you had summoned me to Edinburgh 'for so honourable and warrantable a truth of Christ as a testimony against tolera- tion', neither failing health nor 'my daily menacing gravel' would have held me back.[19] In the 'killing times' of the restored Stuarts, that honourable and warrantable truth of Christ was asserted from the catacombs. With the fall of the Stuarts and the accession of a Dutch Calvinist king, it looked as if it would be asserted, at last, from the throne.

In fact it was not. For the victory of William of Orange did not merely restore the Presbyterian party to power in Scotland: it also liberalised it by restoring its contact with the continental Churches, particularly in Holland, precisely at the time when those Churches were being undermined by the heresy which they had so long kept at bay. The exiled Huguenots of France, no longer controlled by their clergy, were becoming a solvent force. 'Arminianism', 'Socinianism' were triumphing in Holland and Switzerland. They might even reach Scotland. The two Scotch clergymen who accompa- nied William of Orange from Holland to England, and were to be his advisers on Church affairs in England and Scotland – Gilbert Burnet and William Carstares – were very different from the home-bred Baillies and Rutherfords and Wodrows who had never crossed the sea.

Carstares's influence in Scotland was to be enormous. For our purpose his most important work was to be the reform of the Scottish universities. In the middle of the seventeenth century the Scottish universities had been at their lowest ebb. Scottish learning had then, in the words of one Scotch historian, 'relapsed into a dark age of its own' which the General Assembly had tried to make permanent by fixing the philosophical syllabus on a firm Aristotelian basis throughout the land.[20] But Carstares, who had seen the revival of medical studies in Edinburgh through the accidental appearance of foreign-trained professors, now sought to subject the whole university system of Scotland to the same treatment. Himself trained in Utrecht, he returned to Holland to look for such professors, and having installed his own brother-in-law, William Dunlop, as principal of Glasgow University, he urged him to do the same. He obtained royal orders increasing the endowments of the universities and adding new professors, who were 'to be fetched from abroad', on the nomination of the king. Professors from Holland, he told Dunlop, 'are very good, and I suppose will please the King most'. Then he secured his own appointment as principal of Edinburgh University and set out to reform the whole structure on the pattern of 'the most famous universities abroad'.

The years after 1688 are indeed the great reforming period of the Scottish universities, and especially of Edinburgh and Glasgow, which were to lead the way in Enlightenment. There the arts faculties were reorganised on Dutch models; new chairs were founded in those new subjects which had become fashionable in Holland and Switzerland: universal history, the laws of nature and nations, the physical sciences; Bacon and Newton replaced Aristotle and Sacrobosco; and Edinburgh set the example, which the other universities would follow, of abandoning the old system of 'regenting', whereby the same teacher taught his pupils all the subjects in his course, and replacing it by that specialisation of labour in which Adam Smith was to discover the essential condition of progress.[21]

Thus from 1688 onwards, not because of whig or Presbyterian victory, but because of the defeat of narrow nationalism, the end of isolation, the resumption of foreign contact, the dark age of Scotland came to an end. The heretics within the Church, the Episcopalians and Jacobites without, sustained by their émigré friends in Holland, England, France, regenerated the structure and content of university teaching and enabled liberal ideas to spread even inside the Kirk. The strict believers observed with horror the growth of heresy and ultimately seceded in protest against it. They were particularly incensed by the teaching of the 'Arminian' John Simson, who had been trained in Leiden and was, incidentally, the teacher of Francis Hutcheson. Well might Dugald Stewart afterwards ascribe the 'sudden burst of genius' in eighteenth-century Scotland to a 'constant influx of information and liberality from abroad'.[22]

But if the ideas came from abroad, how was it that they found such a ready reception in so primitive a country? Where was the interested laity which is so essential an element in any intellectual renaissance? Once again, we face a neglected problem. What would we not give for a social history of seventeenth-century Scotland: for a book which could compare – if any book can compare – with H. Grey Graham's Social Life of Scotland in the 18th Century: for a detailed picture of that closed society on the eve of its opening?[23] For it takes an effort to see past the public face of seventeenth-century Scotch history, to hear the quiet voices which are drowned by the din of nationalist heroes, rhapsodical clergy,

Cameronian bigots – even to imagine a society so completely different from the world around it. At first sight – to the sight of those horrified Englishmen who visited it – Scotland was a mere desert, inhabited (if at all) by barbarous people whose whole way of life was at worst nasty, at best unintelligible. Returning travellers wrote of it as they might write of a visit to Arabia: those long treeless wastes; the squalid towns in the plains; the savage, unvisited tribes in the hills; the turbulent tribal chieftains; the rabble-rousing *mullahs* with their mysterious religious organisation. Only for a brief moment, in the 1650s, had Cromwell opened up the country and discovered some of its profounder qualities. Then the darkness had descended as the country had gone native again.

The major trouble was the total lack of communications. No roads, no coaches, hardly a cart. Wheeled vehicles were altogether unknown in Ayrshire till 1723; in Banff till 1728. When a cart appeared in East Kilbride, twelve miles from Glasgow, in 1723, the crowds collected round so wonderful a machine: it might have been a satellite from the moon. Heavy goods sent the twenty miles from Stirling to Glasgow had to be carried round Cape Wrath, over 700 miles of rough and boisterous sea.[24] This total lack of internal communication dissolved the country into a kind of archipelago of isolated coastal areas connected with each other by sea. It led to a concentration of life in little local pockets, almost like monasteries in the Middle Ages.

And yet, in some of those pockets, there could be a surprising development of culture. In the manse of the minister there might be only orthodox works of theology. The burgh merchants, concerned only with local trade, might have very limited horizons. A few Edinburgh lawyers perhaps remembered their days in Leiden or Groningen or Utrecht and bought some of the books occasionally imported by sea from London or Amsterdam. But all these were deeply conservative classes, fundamentally opposed to novelty. The great men, who had been courtiers in London and built up splendid cosmopolitan libraries, were exotic exceptions. But here and there, and perhaps more often than we suspect, in grim rural castles and peel-towers and obscure town houses, eccentric lairds and merchants trading by sea kept in touch, through the heretical Calvinist or the Jacobite freemasonry, with foreign ideas.

Nowhere, perhaps, was this independent-minded lay society stronger than in the largest island of the archipelago, the North-East. Cut off from the rest of Scotland by mountains and firths, it communicated direct, by sea, with England and Europe. Its nobility, its lairds, were often themselves exporters:

at Findhorn they had their own 'unfree' (that is, free) port.[25] It had its own universities of King's College and Marischal College at Aberdeen: early centres of religious and scientific liberalism. It had its own religious and political loyalty: for it was royalist, Episcopalian and Jacobite. In the seventeenth century it was less severed from the intellectual life of France than other, more orthodox parts of Scotland, and Aberdonian émigrés breathed the fresh air of Richelieu's Paris;[26] indeed, the greatest of the 'Aberdeen doctors', John Forbes of Corse, wished to remodel King's College on the pattern of the University of Paris. In the eighteenth century, the same area was the solid basis of Jacobitism: in 1715, and again in 1745, the two counties of Aberdeen and Banff would supply the main strength of the Jacobite armies: they did more harm to the Hanoverian cause, it was said, 'than all the Highlanders put together'.[27] But this Jacobite, Episcopalian society, which gave such trouble to the Kirk – which resisted the Reformation, rejected the Covenants, accepted Cromwellian rule, welcomed all kinds of heresy, and rebelled against the re-establishment of Presbyterianism – was, in many ways, the cultural bastion of Scotland. This impression is inescapable when we look closely at its record. Here I will content myself with two illustrations.

In the 1720s that great Aberdonian scholar, the Jacobite hedge-priest Fr Innes, was creeping through Scotland gathering material for his explosive *Critical Essay*. One of his ports of refuge was with the Maule family of Panmure. Lord Panmure had been attainted as a Jacobite after 1715 and had fled abroad; but his brother, though also in arms with him, contrived to live on in the confiscated castle. We happen to possess a list of his library at that time. There we find, among the religious books, along with the Fathers and the Reformers, the worst of the great Arminians, Hooker, Grotius, Limborch; of the Socinians and Latitudinarians, even of the deists; among the secular books, Machiavelli, Erasmus, Montaigne, Comenius, Hobbes and the *Dictionary* of Pierre Bayle. It is the library, already, of a gentleman of the Enlightenment.[28]

The same year, 1729, which saw the publication of Innes's *Essay* saw also the publication of an English translation of one of the first and greatest works of the new 'civil history' which was to be perfected by Hume, Robertson and Gibbon. This was Pietro Giannone's *Storia civile del regno di Napoli*, the work which was the inspiration alike of Montesquieu and Gibbon. The translator was a Scotsman, James Ogilvie, of whom nothing is known save what can be deduced from his work: *viz*, that he had travelled abroad, that he knew

French and Italian, and that his friends, patrons and sympathies were all Jacobite.[29] But what interests us is not so much the translator as the readers of this famous work of social history. The list of subscribers fills five folio pages. When Giannone himself saw that list, he was amazed: so many lords and gentlemen, archbishops and bishops, all buying the book for which he himself had been hounded out of Italy and for which he would die in a Savoyard prison.[30] What Giannone could not discern was the great preponderance, among these names, of Scotsmen; and, among them, of Scots lairds from that Jacobite island in the North-East. Three copies were ordered by Marischal College, and orders poured in from Arbuthnots, Brodies, Duffs, Forbes, Gardens, Gordons, Grahams, Grants, Keiths, etc. – and of course Ogilvies galore. The inhabitants of Aberdeenshire are respected for their prudence in economic matters, and it seems unlikely that this massive investment in two folio volumes of Italian history was solely due to skilful salesmanship by an obscure and impoverished fellow-Scot. It is more rational to assume that this great work of 'philosophic history' was of genuine interest to an enlightened laity in the far North-East.

But if the Episcopalian Jacobite North-East was the largest island of the seventeenth-century archipelago, the most open, in many ways, to foreign influence (for Edinburgh, 'that most unmercantile of cities' as Lord Cockburn called it, has always been somewhat self-enclosed and Glasgow had not yet risen to importance), there were plenty of smaller islets in that sea, little active cells in that scattering of dissevered monasteries of culture. There always had been, of course, even in the earlier seventeenth century. Most of them had been local or at most national in their interest, like Sir John Scot of Scotstarvet or Robert Gordon of Straloch; but there were Europeans too. There was John Napier of Merchistoun, the only Scotsman of genius in his century, as Hume called him, inventing logarithms and calculating the days of Antichrist in his draughty peel-tower, or Sir Thomas Urquhart of Cromarty, the Scottish Rabelais, devising his universal language and his singular pedigree in his ancestral fortalice. But these were heroic eccentrics, who could take for granted the bizarre contradictions around, as within, them. What distinguished their successors at the beginning of the new century, as new ideas came in from abroad and new prosperity from the Union, was they did not. They realised that the society around them – that self-sufficient, self-enclosed, arrested society which their predecessors had accepted – was, by the standards of the outer world, in 'the full light and freedom of the eighteenth century', an archaism; and this realisation made them think. It is in this sense that I make the comparison with the transatlantic discoveries of the sixteenth century.

But between the European discovery of America in the sixteenth century and the Scottish self-discovery of the eighteenth there was, in the intellectual field, a great difference. A revolution had occurred in the general outlook of men. The old biblical fundamentalism had gone. In the sixteenth century men had asked religious questions: how were the Red Indians descended from Adam, how had they survived the Deluge, how was it that they were naked and yet unashamed?[31] In the eighteenth they saw them as their own prototypes and asked secular questions: how did man progress from that stage to this? How insistently they asked this question we see, again and again, in the great French writers. We see it also in their Scottish disciples. We can see it already in the first half of the eighteenth century. We see it particularly after the problem had been squarely posed in that most provocative work of the century, Montesquieu's *De l'Esprit des lois*.

If the Scotch read Giannone's *Civil History of Naples* in 1729, how much more did they read, twenty years later, the great work of Giannone's French disciple Montesquieu! We know how they discovered him. It was David Hume himself who read *De l'Esprit des lois* within a year of its publication, in Turin. Reading it, he was as excited by it as Gibbon would be, a few years later, in Lausanne. Hume brought the book back to Scotland and published two chapters of it, in French, at Edinburgh. Soon the whole text was published, in both French and English, in Edinburgh and Aberdeen.[32] The effect was instantaneous. It was Montesquieu who inspired Hume's *History,* Ferguson's *Essay on Civil Society*, Robertson's histories, Smith's *Wealth of Nations.* Of the new science of sociology, that peculiar contribution of the Scottish Enlightenment, John Millar would afterwards write that Montesquieu was the Bacon, Adam Smith the Newton.[33]

Thus to the question, why was it in Scotland that this new science took such root and throve so well, I suggest my answer. It was not merely the new contact with the outer world, or the prosperity brought by the Union – although both these were essential too. It was also because Scotland itself presented the problem in a domestic, and a peculiarly vivid, form. Scotland in 1700 was an archaic, closed society. It had not always been so. The closure was artificial: the result of defensive nationalism. But that closure, that fixation, had taken place in a period of general European expansion. In the

two centuries since 1600, Western Europe had expanded economically and
intellectually. It had been transformed socially and politically. But Scotland
had no share in these great changes. Its horizons, physical and intellectual,
were still those of 1500. 'A Leith skipper of the later 15th century', says
Mr Smout, 'would certainly have known most of the routes his successors
sailed in 1700.'[34] Trade since then had been static. Shipbuilding had
declined. Education, in spite of the efforts of Andrew Melville and Alexander
Henderson, had been fossilised. Society had contracted on itself. Politics had
shrunk to faction. The contrast between Scotland and Europe, in 1500, had
been natural, the consequence of obvious physical differences. In 1700 it was
not natural. It was artificial and bizarre.

But now that closed society was beginning to open. We have seen that it
was opening already before the Union, under the influence of those new
contacts generated by the events of the 1680s. The Union opened it wider.
But as yet the opening was very partial. There were pockets of enlightenment;
but equally there were pockets of antique, immobile custom consecrated by
timeless conservatism and a sclerotic Church. Frances Hutcheson was
lecturing on Locke and Shaftesbury in Glasgow while carts were unknown
twelve miles away. Hume was to witness 'the most perfect and accurate
system of liberty' nearly overturned and 8 million men nearly reduced to
slavery by 5,000 Highlanders, 'the bravest, but still the most worthless
amongst them'. Ferguson, who was hailed by Gibbon as the creator of a new
science,[35] began his career preaching in Gaelic to Highland soldiers. Adam
Smith, as a child, was kidnapped by gypsies in Fife. Travelled Scots might be
artists, philosophers, architects; those at home might live in vertical towers,
eating their way through one salt-beef after another, without a tree or a
vegetable on the estate, treating their ailments with powdered toads, bottled
woodlice and cataplasms of snails. The anglicised 'Union Dukes' of Argyll and
Queensberry might live in princely splendour at Inverary and Drumlanrig;
the unreformed Lord Lovat at Castle Dounie lived and slept in one room
surrounded by 400 retainers gnawing mutton bones and sleeping on straw.[36]
Such archaisms had been taken for granted in the seventeenth century, for
there had been no obvious standard of comparison. In the eighteenth century
it could not be, for there was. Cosmopolitan Scotsmen, like Lord Kames,
might deplore the archaic structure of Scotland; romantic Scotsmen, like
Sir Walter Scott, might delight in it; but the essential thing is that they were
conscious of it. They saw, as Dr Johnson saw when he visited the Hebrides,

a society whose existence polite Europeans could not conceive; and that, as he admitted, was a profound, stimulating intellectual experience: it forced men furiously to think.

The idea of progress does not occur to a uniformly primitive society which seeks only to conserve ancient traditions. It could never have occurred to Covenanting Scotland. The problem of progress does not impose itself on a mature society, which too easily assumes its own virtue. How little direct impact it made on whig England![37] It is when a society finds itself faced, whether from outside or within itself, at the same time, by two distinct and strongly contrasting worlds, a world of antique custom inherited from the past and world of rapid movement inspired by new ideas from abroad, that thinking men are forced to speculate on the social ambience of man and the mechanism of its change. This happened to the highly developed nations of Western Europe at the time of the Renaissance, when they discovered the natives of America and asked about their own relationship with them. It happened to the Scots of the eighteenth century when they resumed their contact with Europe and thereby discovered the dualism in themselves. All through the eighteenth century they were stimulated by that discovery. Only at the end of that century was the process of assimilation complete. By then, as Lord Cockburn wrote, 'the feelings and habits which had prevailed at the union, and had left so many picturesque peculiarities on the Scotch character, could not survive the enlarged intercourse with England and the world'.[38] But they had served a useful purpose. Before sinking into the past as the raw material of the new romanticism, they had helped to stimulate that analysis of human progress which is the peculiar contribution of the Scottish Enlightenment.

CHAPTER 3

Pietro Giannone and Great Britain

I

In one of those footnotes to *The Decline and Fall of the Roman Empire* which cast such shafts of light on European intellectual history, Gibbon sets out the pedigree of what he and his contemporaries called 'philosophic', and his predecessors 'civil history': that is, history seen in its totality, the product of its own internal laws, deducible from its own course by secular human reason. In such total history, the history of the Church is not privileged: it is subject to the same laws, an integral part of the whole. The pioneers of this history in the modern world, says Gibbon, had been the great Florentines, Machiavelli and Guicciardini; 'their worthy successors', the Venetians Paolo Sarpi and Enrico Davila, had continued their work; and now, after 'a century of slumber', Scotland had arisen 'to dispute the prize with Italy herself'.[1] By 'Scotland' he meant, of course, Hume, Robertson and Adam Smith, the disciples, like himself, of Montesquieu. But behind Montesquieu stood an earlier pioneer who, in some ways, being also a historian, was closer to him than Montesquieu himself: the great Neapolitan philosophic historian, the real founder, and indeed protomartyr, of the 'civil history' of the Enlightenment: Pietro Giannone.

In this essay I wish to examine a curious episode in this chapter of intellectual history: an episode which has not, I think, been noticed before; which provokes some interesting general questions; and which is particularly appropriate to this conference, because it lights up a moment, and unexpected circumstances, in which Scotland took over the torch from Italy.

But first, a few general words about Giannone. Giannone was a Neapolitan lawyer and scholar who sought, by his writings, first, to free the institutions of

his country from the inveterate, legally entrenched feudal power of the
Catholic Church; then, when that attempt had failed, to free Christianity itself
from the stifling and corrupting embrace of a political church. Each of these
two phases of his career resulted in the writing of a great book and consequent
personal persecution. The first book was his *Istoria civile del regno di Napoli*
whose publication in 1723 forced him to flee from Naples; the second would
be known to posterity as *Il Triregno*, the mere apprehension of whose publication brought upon him an even greater persecution. Both books were
historical in method: in the first, ecclesiastical history, in the second, theology,
was taken from its privileged position and subjected to the discipline of
historical explanation. In the writing of both, Giannone was influenced by
English writers: the first was inspired by Francis Bacon's *Advancement of
Learning* and 'the golden book' of the Caroline civil lawyer Arthur Duck;[2] the
second owed much to the English Church historians Bingham and Dodwell
and the English deists Toland, Collins and Tindal. However, in this essay I am
concerned not with what Giannone derived from Britain but with what he
contributed to it; and since his *Triregno* was suppressed by the Church
authorities for two centuries,[3] that contribution was confined to his first work,
the beginning of all his troubles, *The Civil History of Naples*.

That great work, though essentially a work of scholarship, was both historically and politically revolutionary: historically, because it ignored the traditional
and privileged separation of ecclesiastical from political history; politically,
because it justified the programme of those reformers who sought, throughout
Catholic Europe, to remove ancient 'feudal' obstructions to modern progress
and 'enlightenment'. Such reformers were particularly vocal in the kingdom of
Naples, where, in the last two centuries, under the rule of the Spanish
Habsburgs, feudal power had been positively strengthened. After the outbreak
of the War of the Spanish Succession in 1700, they saw their chance. In 1707 the
kingdom was transferred from the new Bourbon rulers of Spain to the
Habsburgs of Austria. The reformers would have preferred complete independence; but the Austrian Habsburgs were at least more enlightened than the
Spanish had been. So, when Giannone began his work, he could hope for a
favourable reception; and when he had finished it, nearly twenty years later, he
dedicated it to the reigning emperor, Charles VI.[4]

Alas, he was disappointed. Whatever his own views (and Charles VI was
less 'enlightened' than his brother Joseph I, whom he had succeeded) the
emperor was far away in Vienna while in Naples the clergy were close at hand,

numerous and powerful. They saw the danger and knew how to meet it. Immediately on the publication of the book, they organised popular demonstrations in the city. They questioned whether the blood of St Januarius would deign to liquefy after such an insult to the Church. Their indignation was transmitted to Rome, where the Holy Office would denounce the book as scandalous and seditious, on no account to be read or translated by the faithful, and a copy of it would be ceremonially burnt. In Naples the cardinal-archbishop excommunicated the author; the newly appointed viceroy, himself a cardinal, advised Giannone to flee for his life; and Giannone, his theory of clerical power now visibly confirmed, acted on the advice. Secretly, under a false name, he crossed the Apennines to the Adriatic coast, took the first boat that he could find to Trieste, and finally found safety in Vienna.

It was in Vienna that the second period in Giannone's intellectual history began. There he was free, once more, to read and write; he had access to good libraries and to the German book market; the British ambassador also supplied him with the works of English writers; and although the imperial court was less sympathetic than he had hoped, he was sustained by an annual pension, charged to the revenues of Sicily, and enjoyed the protection of the great patron of avant-garde intellectuals, the old military hero Prince Eugene of Savoy. It was in these happy years, the lull in his angry and tormented life, that Giannone composed, and almost completed, his second great work, *Il Triregno*. There for the moment we shall leave him, enjoying something like peace in the delightful gardens of his noble patrons and the rural solitude of their country estates, and turn our eyes back to Italy.

It happened that in 1723, while Giannone was fleeing from the storm he had raised, an erudite Englishman, Richard Rawlinson, was in Italy. A man of adequate means, son of a former lord mayor of London, Rawlinson was a zealous and eccentric antiquary: in politics a high tory, in religion a non-juror, indeed a priest among the non-jurors, in loyalty a Jacobite, who recognised James Stuart, 'the chevalier de St. Georges', *alias* 'the Old Pretender', as James III, legitimate king of Britain. He had already made scholarly tours of England, the Low Countries and northern France; now he was making a more ambitious and more protracted tour of Europe. Leaving England in the summer of 1720, he had moved at a leisurely pace through France, South Germany and Tyrol. Then he had crossed into Italy and quickened his pace as he headed for Rome, for he was eager to pay his respects to the exiled Stuart court, which had been at Rome since 1718, and to rejoice at the expected birth of a royal infant. His loyalty was rewarded. On the last day of that year, 1720, he was able to celebrate in Rome the birth of an heir to the dynasty, the future 'Young Pretender', *alias* Bonny Prince Charlie. For the next four years Rome would be Rawlinson's base. There he would show his loyalty to the Pretender on suitable occasions, attend papal ceremonies, and act as a guide to English tourists. Thence he would also make long, leisurely excursions to other parts of Italy.[5]

In his travels, as in all his life, Rawlinson was very inconspicuous. It was said of him that he had seen France, Germany and Italy but had never himself been seen by anyone anywhere. If he was a priest, he was a hedge-priest, seldom if ever known to officiate. The main purpose of his travels was to acquire, assiduously but indiscriminately, antiquarian evidence: books, manuscripts, coins, medallions, copies of inscriptions; which he did so effectively that his vast and miscellaneous collections would ultimately exclude all else, and almost himself, from his London house. In Italy he would make a great haul, which he would send, in stages, to the port of Leghorn in the grand duchy of Tuscany, to be shipped to England.

In January 1723 Rawlinson was back in Rome after an extended tour of Tuscany, Venice and North Italy, and would remain there till the autumn. He was therefore in Rome when the work of Giannone was condemned, and he followed the controversy with interest. Then, in the autumn, he set out on another journey of exploration: this time to the south, first to Naples, then to Sicily. From Sicily he determined to visit Malta, then ruled by the Knights Hospitaler under their Grand Master. His first attempt was frustrated: his ship was driven back by storms; but he was not deterred, and finally he landed at Valletta. There, on 8 January 1724, his eye was caught by an interesting document, pinned to the door of the great church of St John the Baptist, the cathedral of the Knights. It was a copy of the 'damnatory Bull', as he called it, against the *Civil History* of Giannone.

To Rawlinson, already interested in the affair by his experience in Rome, the temptation was irresistible. His practised hand quickly detached the document to join his collection. Next day he revisited the church and noted with interest that another document had replaced it: an announcement in the joint names of the Grand Master of the Order and the papal nuncio offering a reward for the apprehension of the sacrilegious thief. Shortly afterwards, as a distinguished visitor to the island, Rawlinson was ceremoniously received by the Grand Master who treated him with great respect. I like to think of that solemn exchange of courtesies: I wonder if Rawlinson savoured the irony of the situation. I suspect not: he does not seem to have been that kind of a man. Anyway, he clung to his trophy, which was duly despatched to Leghorn and now nestles, with the rest of his collection, in the Bodleian Library at Oxford.[6]

Rawlinson was clearly pleased with his *trouvaille*, to which afterwards, in marginal notes and occasional publications, he would often refer. One such occasion occurred while he was in Italy. There, in Venice, he picked up a copy of the recent Italian translation of the popular French work, *Méthode pour étudier l'histoire* by the enterprising and versatile *abbé* Nicolas Lenglet de Fresnoy. In order to occupy himself during what he called a 'summer's recess in Italy', and to perfect his knowledge of the language, Rawlinson translated it into English. The *abbé*'s text contained a brief account of Giannone's work and the rumpus it had caused. In his translation, which he would publish in 1728, after his return to England,[7] Rawlinson would comment that 'a proposal has recently been published for a translation by Captain Ogilvie'. Who had published this proposal, and where, he did not say; nor did he offer any particulars about Captain Ogilvie.

It happened that in this same year, 1728, the controversy over Giannone's book, which was still rumbling on in Italy, was quickened by a new development: the violent public attack made on Giannone by the Italian Jesuit Giuseppe Sanfelice. To this attack Giannone, now safe in Vienna, replied with a masterpiece of withering irony, his *Professione di fede*. Although it was not printed, this work, which delighted all critics of the Jesuits and their extreme ultramontane claims, was widely circulated in manuscript. Once again Rawlinson, now back in England and a bishop – an invisible hedge-bishop, of the non-jurors only – was quick off the mark. He obtained, presumably from a friend in Italy, an elegant copy of Giannone's manuscript, and this too is now among his papers in the Bodleian Library.[8]

Meanwhile another actor steps on to this ill-lit stage. He was, or at least afterwards appeared to be, a somewhat dubious character. His name was Archibald Bower.

Bower was a Scotchman, born in Dundee. Brought up as a Roman Catholic, educated at the Scots College at Douay, he had been admitted as a Jesuit in Rome and for twenty years had taught Latin and Greek at various Jesuit colleges in Italy; but in 1726, the same year in which Rawlinson returned to England, Bower had declared himself disgusted by the cruelties of the Inquisition, which he had witnessed, and left for England. There he was received into the established Church and started a new career as a private tutor and a journalist in London. In 1730 he began to edit a literary periodical, *Historia literaria, or an exact and early account of the most valuable books published in the several parts of Europe.*

Whatever his personal character, Bower was a learned man, of modern 'enlightened' ideas. His periodical, which would run for four years, aimed high. It offered reviews of 'none but the most valuable books and such as are last published and have not been mentioned by any other of our journalists'. In fact, the books reviewed in it would include works by John Toland, Richard Simon, Isaac Newton, Samuel Clark, Muratori, Montfaucon, Boerhaave, de Crousaz – the intellectual high-flyers of the time. But by far the fullest treatment was given to a long and enthusiastic review of Giannone's *Civil History*. Indeed, it looks as if the whole venture was inspired by that work, for the first four issues of the periodical were devoted to it, and the fifth contained a critique – a very contemptuous critique – of Sanfelice's attack on it. In sum, Bower praised Giannone's work as 'the most perfect history of Naples that is extant in any language': it had reached 'a degree of perfection above censure or criticism'.

All this publicity was very timely, for meanwhile the first volume of the English translation of Giannone's work – a stout folio volume of 750 pages – had been published in London. It was the first translation of the book into any foreign language. It was also an entirely independent venture: neither Giannone nor any of his friends had any part in it or foreknowledge of it. The publisher was Andrew Millar, an enterprising young Scotch printer in London, and the translator, as previously announced by Rawlinson, was Captain Ogilvie – Captain James Ogilvie.

Thus we see, in the years 1728–30, what looks like a concerted operation to publicise Giannone's work in England. At the centre of it is Rawlinson. He had been there at the beginning, first in Rome, then in Malta. Now he had used his translation of Lenglet de Fresnoy's book to advertise Ogilvie's translation. In his translation Ogilvie included a copy of the 'damnatory bull' which had been supplied to him by 'his learned and worthy friend Mr Rawlinson'; and at the same time, as an additional advertisement, on 29 August 1729, Rawlinson himself published a facsimile of that 'bull', explaining, in an unpublished note, that Ogilvie's transcript was not quite accurate. Finally, just when Ogilvie's translation was on sale from five booksellers in London, it was further boosted by Bower's elaborate and sustained review. To have produced so large a work, Ogilvie must have been at work on it for some time, and it looks as if Rawlinson was his promoter.

Who then was Captain James Ogilvie? Here we come to a real problem on which I have spent many a fruitless hour. No English writer, as far as I know, has tried to identify him. The only explicit account of him comes from Giannone's eighteenth-century biographer, the *abbé* Leonardo Panzini.[9] Panzini was a conscientious scholar who had access to Giannone's correspondence, knew his son Giovanni, and is generally reliable. According to him, Ogilvie himself wrote a civil letter to Giannone explaining that he had heard so much about his book, and its fame, both in Britain and abroad, that he had set out to translate it 'nell'ozio di un viaggio che in qualità di capitano di vascello aveva fatto alla Nuova Zembla', and enclosing ten copies of the work (it must have made a huge parcel) for himself and his friends, together with a gift of 500–600 German florins as a token of his admiration. Panzini admits that he cannot find this letter, or any trace of this story, in Giannone's papers, but says that he believes it to be true, having heard it from a trustworthy person who was in Vienna and friendly with Giannone at the time.

Can we believe it? Can we believe that a British naval officer, in command of one of His Majesty's ships, sailing (but why?) through the Polar Sea to (of all places) Nova Zemlya, had the leisure to read and translate this huge work? And if Giannone had received such a letter, why has it disappeared from his correspondence, and why does he himself say nothing about it in his own autobiography in which he refers, at some length and with great satisfaction, to this English translation – and also, incidentally, to Bower's helpful publicity? According to his own account, Giannone received not ten copies but one copy of the translation, and it had been sent to him not by Ogilvie but by his own German friend Johann Burckhard Mencke, the editor of the *Acta eruditorum* at Leipzig, who, we happen to know, had subscribed for a copy, having evidently been informed in advance about the publication – perhaps by Rawlinson. This account, which is first-hand and documented, is much more plausible than the story published by Panzini, which is undocumented and rests only on hearsay from an unnamed 'friend' of Giannone in Vienna. The terms used clearly exclude Giannone's son, who only joined Giannone after he had left Vienna and who would surely have been cited if he had been able to confirm the story. So in the end, although it has been repeated by all modern commentators, I think it best to reject Panzini's story altogether, regarding it as either a misunderstanding or a fantasy or a hoax, and to start again from firmer ground, if such can be found.

Can we find it? Perhaps we can, for in the preface and the dedication of his work Ogilvie himself gives some vague but tantalising hints. He tells us that he had suffered a disastrous 'change of circumstances' in the 'fatal year that involved so many in irretrievable ruin', but that his 'distressed condition' had then been relieved by the generosity of Lord Grandison, to whom he now dedicated the first of his two volumes; that he had then travelled in Italy with Grandison's brother-in-law, Lord Falkland, 'from whom he received many favours', and to whom he had intended to dedicate the second volume, but that, Falkland having died, he will now dedicate it to his son and successor in title; and he adds that it was through his travels with Lord Falkland in Italy that he was able to undertake the translation of the work.

This is not very precise. Indeed, it seems deliberately imprecise. But if we look more closely into the patronage behind Ogilvie's venture, we may discover the reason for his imprecision – and also something about himself.

Ogilvie's two named patrons were both, as he emphasises, of impeccable royalist background, their families conspicuous in the Cavalier pantheon. The famous Lord Falkland, Lucius, the 2nd viscount, had been killed fighting for Charles I; Lord Grandison's family, the Villiers, had risen through their sex appeal in the courts of James I and Charles II.[10] Both families, by the end of the seventeenth century, were impoverished. Lord Grandison's mother, we are told, had swooned with horror when she learned that her son had married the sister of the even more impoverished Lord Falkland: she had hoped for a rich marriage to repair his broken estate. However, he had afterwards inherited an 'ample fortune'[11] and Ogilvie refers to the 'magnificence and splendour', as well as the 'exact Oeconomy and order', of his household. As an Anglo-Irish landlord, he was bound to support the Protestant establishment, but his sympathies seem to have been Jacobite, and he was evidently very close to his brother-in-law, who had no such inhibitions.[12]

For Falkland – Lucius Cary, 6th viscount – was a committed Jacobite. He had served Queen Anne – a legitimate Stuart sovereign – in the army in Spain, but his attempts to secure patronage at court had failed, and after the Hanoverian succession he burnt his bridges: he emigrated to France, to the Pretender's court at St Germain-en-Laye, and became a trusted agent of the Pretender, acting under the orders of the Pretender's chief adviser there, the émigré Irish aristocrat Arthur Dillon, commander of the 'Dillon regiment' in the service of Louis XIV, ennobled as Count Dillon in the peerage of France and created Earl Dillon by the Pretender. In July 1722, when the Jacobite plan for a foreign invasion to coincide with a Jacobite rising in England had failed, Falkland was sent secretly to England by the express orders of the Pretender, to visit the Jacobite leaders and assess the situation. From England he reported, first, under a false name, to Dillon in France, and then, on his own arrival in France, direct to the Pretender in Rome.[13] On 13 December 1722 the Pretender rewarded him with a Jacobite earldom. It thus seems likely that Falkland's visit to Italy, on which he was accompanied by Ogilvie, occurred at the end of 1722, in which case he would have been there when his fellow-Jacobite Rawlinson returned to Rome for a stay of several months. So Falkland, Ogilvie and Rawlinson were probably together in Rome in February 1723 when the storm over Giannone's *Civil History* broke out. Afterwards Falkland returned to St Germain where, his first (Protestant) wife having died in England, he married the daughter of Count Dillon and became a Roman Catholic. As far as we know, he lived for the remainder of his life at St Germain. He died there in 1730 and was buried in the Catholic church of St Sulpice.

This Jacobite tinge to the whole affair is deepened when we look further. For later, in 1735, after he had published the second volume of his translation of Giannone's *Civil History*, Ogilvie would translate another solid work, this time from the French. This was a 'History of the Troubles of Great Britain' – in fact mainly of Scotland – from the coronation of Charles I as king of Scotland in Edinburgh in 1633 till the restoration of Charles II in 1660, written by an *émigré* Scotch Roman Catholic priest, Robert Menteith, who called himself Menteith de Salmonet. Menteith had written the first part of this work in 1649, after the execution of Charles I, and had dedicated it to his revered patron the archbishop of Corinth *in partibus*, better known as that notorious turbulent priest, Cardinal de Retz.[14] Three years later, he had shown his hand even more clearly by writing a 'Remonstrance' to the exiled Charles II, urging him to turn papist as the best means of recovering his throne.[15] This was not a very happy suggestion, even at the time; it would have been particularly inopportune after 1688, and Ogilvie, wisely, did not take notice of it.

Fluent in French and Italian, financially ruined in a year fatal to many of his friends, travelling companion of an impoverished Jacobite peer, friend and collaborator of a migratory Jacobite hedge-bishop, translator of Catholic political propaganda in the Stuart interest – such is the character of the mysterious

Captain Ogilvie which emerges from his own arcane admissions. But let us press the evidence a little harder; perhaps we can then extract a little more.

When Giannone, in Vienna, received from his German friend Mencke Ogilvie's translation of his work, he was, he tells us, both delighted and astonished: delighted to find that his work was read and appreciated in England, a country 'in which the sciences and literature are so flourishing today', astonished at the quality of the support which it had evidently received there. For Ogilvie's translation was prefaced by a long list of subscribers – and such subscribers too! 'milordi, arcivescovi, vescovi ed altre persone illustri', page after page of them, subscribing some for four, some even for six copies. How different from the reception of the original work in his own country, where it had been banned and burnt and himself hounded into exile, and where the great and the good (as he could ruefully remark when he came to write his autobiography) had signally failed to protect him.[16]

We too may look, and perhaps look a little more closely and critically, at that list of subscribers. It is indeed a remarkable list: seven dukes, two marquises, sixteen earls, seven viscounts, thirteen barons, twenty baronets – that is good enough for a start. But the further breakdown is even more revealing. More than half the subscribers are Scots, and those Scots come, especially, from the North-East of Scotland, the heartland of the Scotch Jacobites and non-jurors: Ogilvies, Grants, Gordons, Grahams, Brodies, Forbes, Arbuthnots. There are also no less than fifty army officers, all Scotch and predominantly from the 7th Hussars (*alias* 7th Dragoons *alias* Brigadier-General Ker's Dragoons).[17] Among the identifiable individuals, both Scotch and English, though there are some grand names of the whig establishment – Sir Robert Walpole, the earl of Macclesfield, the two archbishops – there is a disproportionate number of well-known tories and Jacobites: Colonel Cecil, the Jacobite agent in England; two Jacobite bankers in Paris; John Gordon of Glenbucket – Old Glenbucket, 'out' in '15, and destined to be 'out' again in '45; Lord Lansdowne, a committed Jacobite *émigré*, created a duke by the Pretender; Sir John Hynde Cotton, the open Jacobite M.P. for Cambridgeshire; Dr Arbuthnot, Queen Anne's Jacobite physician, and his two Jacobite brothers; Sir John St Aubyn, M.P. for Cornwall, the incorruptible enemy of the whig establishment. The Ogilvies themselves, of whom there are eleven on the list, were a Jacobite tribe: one of them, another Captain James Ogilvie, had been the most trusted of all Jacobite secret agents, the chief link between the Jacobites in Britain and the Pretender and Louis XIV – but he was dead now; and I note incidentally that the head of the tribe, as a subscriber, is boldly named as earl of Airlie although his earldom had been forfeit for high treason after 'the Fifteen' and would not be restored till 1826.

From all this I think it is clear that this precocious translation into English of the most radical and original work of 'philosophic history' was a Jacobite venture. What an agreeable thought with which to disconcert those who see Jacobites merely as mental fossils buried permanently beneath the detritus of the Glorious Revolution! Perhaps the whole operation was planned in Rome in 1723 – we may recall that Bower too was in Italy at that time – and so Rawlinson's theft of the document in Malta early in 1724 may have been a deliberate act in a planned programme of research and publication. Rawlinson's note in his version of Lenglet de Fresnoy's *Méthode*, which he explicitly states was translated in Italy, suggests that the operation had been planned, and the translator engaged, while he was there.

As for the translator, he was clearly a man of some account in Scotland. Probably, like Lord Falkland, he had served in the British Army under Queen Anne, perhaps in the 7th Hussars, but then, like so many of his friends and kinsmen, had been involved, and ruined, in the rebellion of 1715 – for that, I now feel sure, was 'the fatal year' to which he so obscurely refers. Jacobites were accustomed to being obscure in their movements, ambiguous in their professions of loyalty, arcane in their language: hence the unobtrusive life of Rawlinson, the imprecise language of Ogilvie: for there is nothing in his dedication to indicate the true politics of his patron or the true nature of his Italian journey. After 1715, I suspect, Ogilvie, like Falkland, lived mainly abroad, but no doubt he came to London to deal with his publishers. Perhaps he is the Captain James Ogilvie who, in 1735, the date of publication of his second translation, was in the Fleet prison for debt and whose daughter married Lord Banff (another Ogilvie) in the prison chapel. Perhaps, perhaps not.[18]

This little episode raises some larger and more general questions. Why did the *Civil History of Naples*, the book or the subject, seem significant to Scottish Jacobites? Why did British non-jurors and Roman Catholics welcome a work which the rulers of the Catholic Church had so emphatically condemned? And what part, if any, did this episode play in the process to which I referred at the beginning of this paper: the transfer of the tradition of 'civil history', 'philosophic history', from Italy to Scotland? To these questions I can only give somewhat speculative answers; but having set out what seem to me the objective facts, I shall not shrink from speculation.

II

In an essay published many years ago,[19] I suggested that the intellectual revival of Scotland in the eighteenth century – what we now call the Scottish Enlightenment – drew some at least of its inspiration from Jacobite, Catholic or Episcopalian circles; and I referred to writers like Robert Sibbald, Thomas Ruddiman, and the brothers Lewis and Thomas Innes. These men, and their seventeenth-century precursors – Bellenden, Dempster, Mackenzie of Rosehaugh – were scholars and antiquaries rather than philosophers, and they preferred to write on secular subjects. Since they were dissenters from the Presbyterian Church of Scotland, which had fastened its control over the Scottish universities, they worked in isolation, outside the academic world. Intellectually, if not always physically, they were *émigrés* like the Roman Catholics Dempster, Bellenden, Sibbald, the Innes brothers, or internal *émigrés* like the Episcopalians of the North-East. If they wrote on religion at all they avoided questions of dogmatic theology and ecclesiastical organisation; they tended, like the doctors of Aberdeen, Archbishop Leighton, Forbes of Corse, the Garden brothers, towards mysticism. Such men enjoyed a brief period of favour while the Catholic duke of York was regent of Scotland; but when the duke, as King James II, was overthrown, that period was over and they were marginalised again. Only when the settlement of 1688 had been securely established, and the intolerance of the Kirk modified – that is, only after 1745 – did their ostracism cease. Then at last the two cultures of Scotland – the suppressed or *émigré* lay culture of the dissenters and the now liberalised Calvinist culture of the Kirk – were united, and former Jacobites, no longer politically suspect, could contribute openly to Scottish intellectual life. It is within this context, I suggest, that the Scottish interest in Giannone may perhaps be understood.

But why, in particular, should Jacobites be interested? Some of them, after all, were themselves, like their king, Roman Catholic. Even if they were not, they could not be unsympathetic to his religion. To this I would answer that their religious attitude was in fact a bond of sympathy with Giannone. For Giannone always professed to be a good Catholic, opposed only to the political and social power which the Church had acquired and which, in Naples, threatened freedom of thought, civil society and the authority of the state. This was not very different from the attitude of Scottish Jacobites – or indeed of English Catholic laymen. Dissenters from the established Church in their own country, they too were critical of clerical power, the alliance of Church and state, censorship, inquisition; and although they might profess loyalty to a foreign Church, they were unwilling to allow to it the repressive authority which they denied to that of their own country. As Catholics they were suspect in Rome as 'Gallicans', 'Febronians', 'Jansenists'. Giannone in Italy was regarded as a 'Jansenist'. The Innes brothers were notorious as Jansenists: they made the Scots college in Paris a Jansenist seminary – and the Scots college, in their time, was 'an adjunct of the Pretender's court and the repository of his archives'.[20] Menteith, like his patron cardinal de Retz, was regarded as a thorough-going Gallican: his book, which Ogilvie would translate, was condemned by Cardinal Mazarin as a handbook of sedition.[21] If any consistency is to be found in the career of Giannone's admirer Archibald Bower, it is similar. In Italy, he rebelled against the Jesuit Order, was revolted by the Inquisition, and declared himself a Protestant; but once back in England, he would slide back into a Catholicism which, being disestablished, was unobjectionable. Thus the support which Giannone was surprised to find in Britain, and particularly in Scotland, is perhaps not so surprising after all. English and Scottish Jacobites shared with him a distrust of 'ultramontane' Catholic claims.

However, let us not press coincidence too hard or seek to extract too much from it. For although Giannone's work was offered to, and indeed pressed upon, British readers by a Jacobite group, its impact seems to have been very limited, nor was its central message perceived, even by its promoters. I have already suggested that the Jacobite scholars were distinguished rather as antiquaries than as philosophers. Their merit was their independence of the ruling orthodoxy of their societies. Therefore they were attracted to Giannone by his learning, his independence, his documented anticlericalism. Perhaps also there was a particular sympathy between Naples and Scotland: two ancient kingdoms whose independence had been surrendered to more powerful states, here to England, there to Spain and then Austria.[22] But the true originality of Giannone's work – his conception of civil history, his reinterpretation of ecclesiastical history as an inseparable part of secular history, subject to the same rules and the same methods – escaped them, as it escaped most of his contemporaries, admirers as well as detractors: all, perhaps, except Montesquieu, who wished to see a civil history of France comparable with Giannone's civil history of Naples.

Giannone himself was very conscious of his originality. In the preface to his work he made this clear. The reader, he there wrote, must not expect from him descriptions of battles, scenery, climate, antiquities, arts: other writers had provided enough – indeed more than enough – of that: 'this', he insisted, 'is entirely a civil history, and therefore, if I am not mistaken, entirely new'. If this novelty was not appreciated, if the book was seen merely as a polemic against the Church, he could be very indignant. One of those who excited such indignation was no other than the *abbé* Lenglet de Fresnoy. In the book which Rawlinson was to translate and annotate, he described Giannone as a 'learned, bold, even rash' author whose book, having provoked the Inquisition, and forced him into exile, had become very rare. Giannone, as his biographer admits, was somewhat sharp-tempered and quick to take offence; and on reading this no doubt well-intentioned comment, he reacted violently. In a remarkably aggressive letter he accused the unfortunate *abbé* of prodigious ignorance, brazen effrontery, mendacity and spite. And why? Precisely because he had represented the book as an audacious attack on the Church. Had he not cited its title as *The History of the Kingdom of Naples*, thus confusing it with those other histories of which there were more than enough? The correct title, Giannone pointed out, was *The Civil History* and that showed that it was 'per la nuova forma e per la materia che tratta tutto differente dalle altre storie di quel Regno'.[23] This terrible attack on the poor *abbé* occurred in 1730: the very year in which Giannone purred with pleasure on receiving the English translation of his work.

Thus the first attempt to bring the work of Giannone to Britain – the Jacobite/Jansenist attempt – was limited in scope and success. Neither the promoter nor the readers, if any, appreciated its originality. Britain, in the 1730s and 1740s, was intellectually in a trough; historical philosophy, if it had emerged from party politics, had merely lapsed into Pyrrhonism. But a generation later the work of Giannone entered by another route, and this time it brought its message with it. To follow its course, we must now turn back to the personal history of Giannone, whom we left enjoying a period of relative tranquillity under aristocratic protection in Vienna.

III

Giannone's stay in Vienna came suddenly to an end in 1734. In that year the political balance of Europe was once again convulsed by war. A Spanish army invaded the kingdom of Naples; the Austrians abandoned it; and it became, once again, as before 1536, an independent kingdom under its own king, this

time a Spanish Bourbon prince. Since Giannone's imperial pension had been
charged to the Sicilian – i.e. the Neapolitan – revenues, it could no longer be
paid to him in Vienna. However, the position in Naples now seemed much
more favourable. He still had powerful friends there; his excommunication
had been lifted; and so he might hope to resume his legal career in his native
country. He decided to return.

The mere thought of such a return alarmed the authorities in Rome, and
they resolved to prevent it, if necessary by force. The Holy Office mobilised
its agents and prepared to kidnap its enemy once he had set foot in Italy.
Forewarned, Giannone took refuge in Venice, a free republic, where he had
a powerful protector. But even in Venice he soon found that he was not safe.
So, once again, as in 1723, secretly and by night, under a false name, he
slipped out and headed westward, across the breadth of Italy, to Modena, to
Milan, to Turin, always just one step ahead of his pursuers from the Holy
Office. Finally, as he felt the enemy closing in on him, he took the last leap to
freedom: he was carried across the Alps to the safety of Geneva. Thence,
from the security of a fortified Calvinist city, he proposed to launch his
counter-attack against political Catholicism: he would finish and publish his
Triregno – 'the terrible *Triregno*, as it had been called' – and supervise a long-
planned French translation of *The Civil History of Naples*.

The sequel is well known. In Geneva, though safe, Giannone found
himself cramped, both physically and spiritually. He missed the consolations
of Vienna: those delightful rural walks which had calmed his troubled spirit
in Mödling and Laxenberg. He also, as a good Catholic, eager to show his
orthodoxy, missed – or claimed that he missed – the spiritual consolations of
his Church. Fortunately, an officious new friend, one Giuseppe Gastaldi,
offered to solve both problems at once. He had, he explained, an agreeable
rural villa at Vesenaz in Catholic Savoy, just across the lake from Geneva . . .
why should not Giannone spend Holy Week with him there? Every need
would be met: there was even a priest who spoke Italian. Giannone went,
with his son, who had joined him in Venice, by boat to Vesenaz. How
delightful to be in the open country again, 'in the spring, when it was so
smiling and green'! Alas, it was his last day of freedom. In the middle of their
first night there, they heard a sudden commotion. Armed men had
surrounded the villa. The unfortunate guests were seized, handcuffed, thrust
into a carriage, and transported to the royal capital of Chambéry. All the way
they were escorted by a guard of fifty armed outriders, and their false friend,

'that Judas', Gastaldi, rode ahead in triumph, crying out, as the cortège rattled through astonished villages, 'A great man! A great man! Make way for a great man!' Few historians have travelled in such triumph; but the triumph was not Giannone's: it was over him.

When Gastaldi's coup was reported to his masters, there were compliments from all sides. The governor of Savoy crowed at the success of his long-prepared stratagem. Ministers and cardinals exchanged congratulations. King and pope sang *jubilate* together.[24] By another neat stratagem, Giannone's papers, left in Geneva, were also secured. The dreaded *Triregno* was suppressed. Rome had won.

Giannone never emerged from his Savoyard prisons – a series of prisons: the fortress of Molans and then Ceva, and finally the citadel of Turin. Under pressure he recanted his alleged heresies, but his pleas for freedom were still ignored. He was allowed to read and write, but not to publish. Whatever he wrote was confiscated and disappeared, for over a century, into the archives of the house of Savoy. So he was soon forgotten, and his death, twelve years later, was hardly noticed. He spent his life, he ruefully observed, defending the rights of secular rulers against clerical power and they had betrayed him to that power, by which they too were imprisoned. The Church, as an engine of social control, and as a source of sinecures for younger sons, was more important to them than the defence of their own authority. The thesis of *The Civil History of Naples* was confirmed by the fate of its author.

However, there was one place in which his memory and his published work continued to flourish. His stay in Geneva had been brief, but the drama of his kidnap would not be forgotten there. Nor would the tricks by which the court of Savoy and the Holy Office had secured and suppressed his papers. Already, while he was still in Vienna, extracts from his *Civil History* had been published in Geneva,[25] and a group of French *émigrés* in Lausanne, inspired by the example of Ogilvie, had been planning a French translation of the whole work. It was on account of this interest that Giannone had decided to seek refuge in Geneva.[26] In the twenty years after his abduction the interest increased. Geneva and Lausanne became the main – almost the sole – centres of publication of his works. Even the *Triregno* would have been published there if the Holy Office had not got in first. At the centre of all these operations was the man to whom Giannone himself had entrusted his papers, Jacob Vernet.

Jacob Vernet was an important person in Geneva. A Calvinist pastor and professor of theology, he was nevertheless a man of liberal views and acted as intermediary between the printers of Geneva and Lausanne and the French philosophers who relied on them to evade the Paris censorship. His first notable contact was with Montesquieu, whom he met in Rome in 1728–29 and whose *De l'Esprit des lois* he would see through the press in Geneva twenty years later.[27] During the same Italian journey he must have become acquainted, in Rome or in Naples, which he also visited, with the case of Giannone. It was, after all, the time of Giannone's controversy with the Jesuit Sanfelice. After his return to Geneva, he joined the editorial board of the *Bibliothèque italique*, the journal in which extracts from Giannone's *Civil History* would be published in 1730–31. When Giannone arrived in Geneva, Vernet at once became his trusted friend and agent.

After Giannone's abduction, his friends in Geneva and Lausanne continued to work for a French translation of the *Civil History*. It was held up by publishing delays in Lausanne, but was finally published in Geneva (with the false imprint of The Hague) in 1742. It included supplementary notes, corrections and additions by Giannone himself, supplied by Vernet. By 1753 these notes had also been incorporated in a new edition of the original Italian text, also published in Geneva, again with the false imprint of The Hague. It was followed two years later by Giannone's 'posthumous works' in defence of the *Civil History*, also published in Geneva, this time with the imprint 'Palmyra'. Further editions of both these works would be published a few years later at Lausanne.[28] Meanwhile, in 1755, Voltaire had established himself at Geneva (where he published his *Essai sur les moeurs*), and also at Lausanne: he had houses in both places. There he too interested himself in the case of Giannone and, as so often, used it to sharpen a private quarrel – this time against Vernet. He accused Vernet of having treacherously sold the manuscript of the *Triregno* to the Roman authorities, who of course had suppressed it. The charge provoked Vernet to write a full and documented account, proving, to everyone except Voltaire, that he was entirely innocent.[29] This led to further publicity for Giannone's work, especially in Geneva and Lausanne.

Thus all through the 1740s and 1750s, while his works were banned in Italy, the name of Giannone was well known and his *Civil History* readily available in Geneva and Lausanne. Among those who could not fail to be drawn to it was the young Edward Gibbon, whom his father had deposited with a pastor of Lausanne, M. Pavillard, in 1753, in order to reconvert him to Protestantism and complete his interrupted education. As a boy, Gibbon had read a vast amount of history, but his reading had been indiscriminate, without a guiding thread or directing philosophy. That missing element he discovered in Lausanne where he was captivated by the works of Montesquieu. Montesquieu provided him with his philosophy of history; but for history itself his model, the first strictly historical work which he records as read by him at Lausanne, was Giannone's *Civil History*, in which, as he would afterwards write, 'I observed with a critical eye the progress and abuse of sacerdotal power and the revolutions of Italy in the darker ages'. Gibbon first read Giannone's work in the French translation of 1742. Afterwards he would acquire and use the Italian text of 1753, also published in Geneva. It was, he would write, one of the three seminal works which 'may have remotely contributed to form the historian of the Roman Empire'.[30]

In his commonplace book, compiled at Lausanne, the young Gibbon made copious notes on Giannone's *History*; but it was not only the content that excited his interest. From it, and from another work which he cites as equally important to him – Pascal's *Lettres provinciales*, which he would read 'almost every year with new pleasure' – he learned, as he tells us, 'the use of irony and criticism on subjects of ecclesiastical gravity'.[31] That was certainly a lesson which he learned well.

Six years later, when he was looking for a historical subject, Gibbon showed that he was still under the spell of Giannone. The first subject which he proposed to himself was the expedition of Charles VIII, king of France, into Italy in 1494 to claim the crown of Naples. It was an event which lit a long, explosive train: the revolution in Florence, the Spanish intervention, the Spanish conquest of Milan and Naples, the subjection of the papacy, and, effectively, the extinction, for three centuries, of Italian liberty. So dramatic a turning-point could not fail to appeal to a historian. But after some research,[32] Gibbon turned against it: that French invasion, he observed, was 'too remote from us' – he was then thinking of more modern subjects – 'and rather an introduction to great events than great in itself'.[33] So he abandoned it, and left it to be taken up, in the next century, by the young Ranke.[34]

Nevertheless, the subject of Neapolitan history lingered in Gibbon's mind, and two years later, when he was back in Lausanne, preparing for his famous 'Grand Tour' of Italy, we find him rereading Giannone's work with undiminished enthusiasm: 'la candeur, la pénétration et la liberté de cet excellent jurisconsulte', he wrote, 'feroit toujours estimer son ouvrage par tous les sages'.[35] While in Italy, he took time off from Rome to visit Naples – the customary southernmost station of the Grand Tour – and he can hardly have failed to think of Giannone when he witnessed, and (like most English visitors) was shocked by, the condition into which the kingdom had sunk under the new Spanish Bourbon dynasty. The reformers of the previous generation had indeed secured one victory: the independence of the kingdom had been restored; but in their main purpose they had totally failed: clerical and political reaction was more deeply entrenched than ever.[36]

When he came to write *The Decline and Fall of the Roman Empire*, Gibbon again turned to Giannone's work. His interest in the legal system of any society, and its intimate connexion with its structure and ideas – the lesson he had learned from Montesquieu – led him naturally to it. Fleury's *Institutes of Canon Law* and Giannone's *Civil History of Naples*, he wrote, were 'two of the fairest books which have fallen into my hands';[37] and when he came to the Dark and Middle Ages, Giannone was again one of the principal guides whom, as he said, he 'always consulted and never copied'.[38] As well he might be, for their philosophy and method were very similar. In his autobiography, which Gibbon could never read, for it was buried in the archives of the house of Savoy in Turin, Giannone had stated that the purpose of all his studies had been to discover and understand 'the origins and changes of the Roman Empire, and how, after its ruin, there had arisen so many new rulers, new laws, new customs, new kingdoms and republics in Europe'.[39] This was precisely what Gibbon had set out to do in his later volumes. What he then wrote of the Byzantine Empire, that it was '*passively* connected with the most splendid and important revolutions which have changed the state of the world',[40] could equally be applied to medieval Naples, exposed to the invasions, ambitions and high politics of Goths and Lombards, Arabs and Normans, Angevins and Aragonese, emperors and popes.

At numerous points in his narrative – on the Theodosian code, on Gothic Italy, the contest over images and investiture, Charlemagne and Frederick II, the converging Mediterranean ambitions of Byzantines and Normans, 'Saracens', 'Franks' and Turks – Gibbon enters into dialogue, sometimes into dispute, with 'the exact Giannone', whose 'Gallican' moderation – the effect of his situation as 'a lawyer who dreaded the power of the Church' – he found so congenial. Of course, by this time he had discovered other sources for Italian history, especially Giannone's friend Muratori, another congenial 'Gallican' guide; but afterwards, when he was composing his memoirs, it was Giannone whose name he chose to emphasise, in the words which I have quoted, as his first historical model.[41]

Thus, through Gibbon, absorbed into his work, mediated by it, Giannone's *Civil History* was brought, for the second time, to Britain. Its first arrival, a direct and massive invasion, launched so paradoxically, as it seems, by a group of Jacobites in Rome, had aroused little interest. In spite of all the orchestrated publicity, it seems to have elicited no response from historians. Gibbon himself seems to have been unaware of its existence, although his crypto-Jacobite father may have been one of the original subscribers to it, as his deist mentor, Conyers Middleton, certainly was.[42] In any case, that first reception had brought only a limited message: the 'Gallican', 'Jansenist' message which had been emphasised by Lenglet de Fresnoy and which Giannone himself had disclaimed as inadequate. The second reception, which was mounted in the Calvinist Pays de Vaud and was mediated through Gibbon, carried into Britain the original philosophy of which Giannone himself was so conscious. We may regret that Gibbon had never been able to read the *Triregno*; but perhaps, if he had, that formidable work, which so terrified the Holy Office in Rome, would not have had a comparable influence on him: he had, after all, himself read and digested the English deist authors who had inspired Giannone. In that respect, the influence ran the other way.

CHAPTER 4

Dimitrie Cantemir's *Ottoman History* and its Reception in England

I DISCOVERED THE writings of Dimitrie Cantemir, prince of Moldavia, long ago, when I first read Edward Gibbon's *Decline and Fall of the Roman Empire*. There, in his description of the fall of Constantinople in 1453, Gibbon tells us how the victorious sultan, Mahomet II, after performing 'the *namaz* of prayer and thanksgiving on the great altar, where the Christian mysteries had so lately been celebrated before the last of the Caesars', went from the cathedral of Santa Sophia to 'the august but desolate mansion' of the Christian emperors. As he viewed those abandoned halls, 'a melancholy reflexion on the vicissitudes of human greatness forced itself on his mind, and he repeated an elegant distich of Persian poetry: "The spider has wove his web in the imperial palace and the owl hath sung her watch-song on the towers of Afrasiab".' In his footnote Gibbon gives his source. 'This distich', he says, 'which Cantemir gives in the original, derives new beauties from the application. It was thus that Scipio repeated, in the sack of Carthage, the famous prophecy of Homer. The same generous feeling carried the mind of the conqueror to the past or the future.'[1]

This romantic detail, which so appealed to Gibbon, delighted me; and I was delighted also, through it, to discover that there was at least one writer who has preserved the Turkish version of that dramatic story: for obviously no Greek would have known, or recognised, or been able to quote, a distich of Firdausi. I was therefore drawn to Cantemir; and many years later was lucky enough to purchase a copy of his work, as published in English in 1735.[2] I derived a further if incidental pleasure from finding that my copy had once belonged to a member of my own family, who has proudly added his own name to the printed list of original subscribers. The publication, in 1973, by the Romanian Academy of Sciences, of the Latin text of Cantemir's *Descriptio*

Moldaviae introduced me to this other work of Cantemir, which I found no less fascinating; and it is as a result of reading these two works, and such other writing of Cantemir as I could discover, that I decided to write this paper for this conference. In it, I propose to ask some questions and make some suggestions about the purpose and the impact of the publication, in England and France, of Cantemir's *Growth and Decay of the Ottoman Empire* – 'the *Ottoman History*' as I shall conveniently abbreviate it – the work which was used by Gibbon.

I believe that this subject deserves some attention, first, because of the inherent interest of anything by Dimitrie Cantemir; secondly, because it is one of the very few moments of cultural contact between Britain and the Principalities before 1800; thirdly, because it contains some genuine problems. I will come to these problems in due course. Meanwhile, though such details are well known to my Romanian colleagues, let me, for the sake of completeness, briefly summarise the story of the publication.

It begins in 1732, with the arrival in London of Dimitrie Cantemir's son Antioh. Antioh had been two years old when his father had escaped to Russia, in the coach of Peter the Great, after the disastrous battle of the Pruth; he had been brought up as a Russian prince, but with the high sophistication of his father; and at twenty-three, being already known as 'the most cultivated man in Russia', he was sent by the Empress Anna as ambassador to England to restore the diplomatic relations between the two countries which had been severed since the Northern War. He remained in London for six years; then he was transferred as ambassador to Paris. He died in Paris in 1744, aged thirty-five. It was while he was ambassador in England that an English translation of his father's *Ottoman History* was published in London, and it was at the end of his life in France that a French translation of the same work was published in Paris. The original text has never been published.

Of the background to this double publication in the West we know something from published documents: from the correspondence of the German *savants* in Moscow and St Petersburg who handled the manuscripts; from Antioh Cantemir's own correspondence;[3] and from the writing of his private circle in England and France, and especially of the Piedmontese *abbé* Ottaviano Guasco, an ambiguous character who however managed to obtain the friendship, and to become the intimate companion, both of Cantemir and of Montesquieu.[4] From these sources we know, or can deduce, that Antioh Cantemir first planned to publish his father's works when he was a student at the Academy of St Petersburg in 1726–27. For this purpose his immediate assistants were his father's last two secretaries, who had also been his own tutors, the German Johann Gotthilf Vockenrodt and the Russian I.V. Ilinsky. He could also rely on the German scholars whom Peter the Great had drawn to his new Baltic capital, and particularly on the orientalist Gottlieb Siegfried Bayer, who had come to St Petersburg in 1726.

The two works which Antioh Cantemir was most anxious to publish were the *Ottoman History* and the *Description of Moldavia*. It is generally assumed that Dimitrie Cantemir had written both these works in Latin, but there is some evidence that this was not so: that the former had originally been written in Greek and the latter in Romanian, and that Ilinsky had translated them into Latin, presumably for publication in the West.[5] We know that the *Ottoman History* had also been translated into Russian by a certain Demetrius Grozin, 'translator in the School of Mathematics of the Russian Navy'; but this Russian translation may not have been intended for publication: it may have been designed as a memorial for the Russian government, like Dimitrie Cantemir's *System of the Mohammedan Religion*, which was also translated into Russian as a state paper. At all events, it seems clear that Antioh Cantemir's intention was to publish the two works in Latin. Bayer, whom he put in charge of the project, and who received the Latin text in April 1729, did not know the Russian language. He did not need to know it, since the academic establishment of St Petersburg was almost entirely German.

Antioh Cantemir's plan, as revealed by his correspondence, was to publish the *Ottoman History*, and to dedicate it to the czar, Peter II. For this purpose he approached Dr Blumentrost, the German president of the Academy of St Petersburg, who agreed to sponsor the project. In the following months, Bayer in St Petersburg, assisted by Vockenrodt and Ilinsky in Moscow, prepared and annotated the text and compiled the Latin *Life of Dimitrie Cantemir* to accompany it. Illustrations were prepared: a portrait of the author was copied, to serve as frontispiece, and copper-plate engravings were made of the series of portraits of the Ottoman sultans which Dimitrie Cantemir, during his long residence in Constantinople, had caused to be copied by the Ottoman court painter Leuni Celebi. Publication would probably have been by the Academy's press in St Petersburg or by a learned press in Germany.[6]

For two years, from 1729 to 1731, the material for this Russian or German publication was assembled. The learned Germans in Moscow and

St Petersburg exchanged their details and their doubts. The avant-garde archbishop of Novgorod was brought in. Antioh Cantemir, now in Moscow, directed the operations. Then, suddenly, that whole machine was stopped. In 1732 Antioh was appointed ambassador to London; and the enterprise migrated with him to the West. The Latin text of the *Ottoman History*, together with Bayer's biographical essay and annotations, the portraits of the author and of the sultans, all went with him in his baggage. So did the Latin text of the *Description of Moldavia* and the map which Dimitrie Cantemir had drawn, during his brief reign as hospodar, to illustrate it.[7] Antioh Cantemir apparently intended to publish the *Description* in Holland, for he left that text with a bookseller named Changuion in Amsterdam, and he had the map of Moldavia printed there. The *Ottoman History* and the portraits accompanied, or followed, him to London.

Once in London, Antioh Cantemir wasted no time. An active and efficient diplomatist,[8] he nevertheless busied himself in literary matters. In spite of weak eyes which obliged him to visit an eye-specialist in Paris,[9] he wrote satires, learned languages, translated ancient and modern literature, compiled a Russian-French dictionary, dined out, haunted the opera. He also took steps to ensure the publication of the *Ottoman History* – not now in Latin but translated into a modern language. He himself began to translate it into Italian, with the aid of Paolo Rolli, the Italian tutor to the English royal family, whom he had engaged to teach him the language; but his other activities prevented him from finishing this translation.[10] Meanwhile the work was being translated into English. For this English translation, Cantemir was indebted to a powerful ally: Caroline of Ansbach, the German wife of the German king of England, George II.

We are told by the *abbé* Guasco, who must have had it from Antioh Cantemir, that while in London Cantemir had been a favourite of Queen Caroline, and that it was she who sponsored the translation and publication of the *Ottoman History*. This is likely enough. Queen Caroline piqued herself as a patron of letters – the only such patron at the court of George II. Her name heads the list of subscribers to the published text; it is followed by that of her son, the Prince of Wales; and the subscribers include the queen's confidante Lady Sundon, together with Lady Sundon's brother Captain Dyves, as well as a number of Hanoverian and other German officials: Mr Hattorf, Mr Hotzendorf, Mr Müller, Mr de Reich, Colonel Schütz. That Antioh Cantemir was personally acquainted with Queen Caroline is clear from a letter to him from his sister Maria, dated 23 June 1733. In this letter Maria promises to send Antioh a portrait of herself 'so that the English Queen should see that she was not mistaken in comparing me with Venus'.[11] Unfortunately Queen Caroline's letters for the period do not seem to have survived.

The English translator employed by Cantemir was a man of some note. He was Nicholas Tindal, nephew of the well-known deist writer Matthew Tindal. Like his uncle, Nicholas Tindal was an Oxford man and a clergyman. For the last ten years he had been beneficed as vicar of Great Waltham, Essex, a college living; but he does not seem to have been tied to his parish, for in 1726–28 he had left his curate in charge of it and gone off to sea, as chaplain to Admiral Sir Charles Wager, whose powerful fleet had blockaded, first the Russian fleet in Reval, then the Spanish fleet in Cadiz. While at sea, or while killing time as chaplain to the English factory in Lisbon, Tindal had translated the successive volumes of Paul de Rapin-Thoyras' recent, and highly successful, whig work, *L'Histoire d'Angleterre*. After returning to his parish duties (to which he soon added the mastership of the Free School at Chelmsford), he embarked – with the aid of his curate Philip Morant – on a new venture. This was to be a massive *History of Essex* based on a huge collection of original manuscript sources recently put at his disposal. By 1733 he had published two slim portions of this work, which he undertook to complete in three quarto volumes, in two years' time. Then his plans were convulsed by an unfortunate event: the death, in London, of his uncle Matthew, the deist.

The death of Matthew Tindal brought in its train a scandal which caused a considerable shock to his nephew and some agreeable diversion to the literary world. Nicholas Tindal had confidently expected to inherit his uncle's property; he was therefore chagrined when a parasite of his uncle's last years, one Eustace Budgell, produced a last will, whereby all Matthew Tindal's property was bequeathed to himself. Nicholas Tindal declared this document a forgery, but was unable to invalidate it at law. Fortunately, by this time, he had discovered new patrons. Presumably through Wager, he had become known at court and had been allowed to dedicate a new folio edition of his translation of Rapin to the Prince of Wales. Perhaps he had also met Antioh Cantemir, who had recently arrived in London. Cantemir must have known Wager, the former admiral of the Baltic, and Tindal must have been familiar to him, at least by name, for Cantemir had briefed himself for his London embassy by reading Rapin's *History* and Tindal's commentary on it.[12] At all events, at precisely this time, Tindal decided to change his literary interests.

Abandoning his ambitious *History of Essex*, he applied himself instead to the unfamiliar subject of Ottoman history.

It is easy to see what may have happened. In 1733 Antioh Cantemir, encouraged by Queen Caroline, was looking for a translator. Tindal had made his name as a translator and was known at court. What was more natural than that he should be approached? It is true, Tindal was already committed to a large work of antiquarian scholarship: the *History of Essex*. However, there was not much profit in private scholarship, and Tindal, defrauded (as he believed) of his inheritance, was easily seduced by an offer from the court. Incidentally, Queen Caroline was not only a patron of letters: it was well known that she also disposed of the patronage of the English Church. It was she who made bishops and deans ... The temptation, to a clergyman, was obvious. So Tindal readily dropped the *History of Essex*. That was left to a curate, who would ultimately produce it thirty-three years later. Meanwhile the *Ottoman History* was rapidly translated – the obedient curate being called in to work on the notes.[13] The publishers, James Knapton and Sons, were the publishers of Tindal's translation of Rapin. They had also been his allies in the battle against Budgell. The portraits of the sultans were re-engraved by a well-known Huguenot artist settled in London, Claude du Bosc.

So much for the translation and publication of the work. We now turn to its impact. How was it received by English historians and critics?

Here we seem on firm ground. English and Romanian scholars alike assure us that the *Ottoman History* was greeted with the general enthusiasm accorded to a work of recognised importance. Thanks to it, we are told, 'Dimitrie Cantemir s'est fait connaître et s'est imposé comme un historien européen de premier ordre pour son époque'. As evidence, these scholars point to the eminence of the translator, the royal patronage, the long list of distinguished subscribers. The book, they tell us, was an immediate success and 'having received its consecration in England ... continued its European destiny'. It 'strongly appealed to the reader of the time' and 'had a far-reaching impact on the learned people of Europe'. In particular, we are told, it struck the imagination of Voltaire, who warmly commended its impartiality as a corrective to the 'absurd fabrications' and 'miserable fantasies' of the received historians.[14] Hence the French translation of 1743, which secured for the author 'a great renown'.[15] Finally, there is the unanswerable evidence of the second English edition, twenty-one years after the first. 'The reprinting of

Cantemir's work in 1756', we are told, 'was full proof both of its value and of the interest it had aroused among the British public.'[16]

All this is very impressive; but who, we may ask, were the readers who tumbled over each other to buy and praise the book? One enthusiast did indeed declare himself. This was Jean Bernard le Blanc, a French *abbé* who was in England at the time and who set up as a professional anglophile: he translated Hume's *Political Essays* and published *Letters from England* to the *philosophes* of France. In one of these letters, he assured a friend in Paris that Cantemir's book had been a great success: 'monsieur le Prince de Cantemir a dû être content de l'accueil que les Anglois ont fait à l'ouvrage de son père, traduit en leur langue'.[17] However, the good *abbé* was not entirely disinterested, for he was in fact Antioh Cantemir's literary agent. Brought to England by the duke of Kingston, he had there become intimate with Cantemir. He was now seeking to pave the way for Cantemir's arrival in Paris, to ensure that he was well received by its literary circles, and to further his plan of sponsoring a history of Russia. We cannot regard him as a true or objective judge of English literary opinion.

Who then did represent that opinion? Who, in the England of 1735, was most likely to read, and appreciate, a historical work on the Ottoman Empire? If we glance at the literary world, and the literary patrons of the time, a few obvious names come to mind.

I have mentioned the duke of Kingston, the patron of the enthusiastic *abbé* le Blanc. As such, we might expect him to show an interest. In fact, he did not even subscribe to the work. However, he had a sister, the famous bluestocking and prolific letter-writer Lady Mary Wortley Montagu, who had herself lived in Constantinople and had studied and described the manners of the Turks. And Mary knew Antioh Cantemir's circle – she was indeed in love with Francesco Algarotti, an intimate friend of Cantemir. We therefore naturally expect her to show an interest in this important new work. Surprisingly, she totally ignored it. Then there is Sir Robert Sutton. He had been ambassador in Constantinople for fifteen years, including the period when Dimitrie Cantemir was living there.[18] He must have known Cantemir personally, and he subscribed to the book. His own reactions are unknown; but he too had a literary *protégé* who was devoted to his interests. This was the tyrant of contemporary scholarship Dr Warburton, afterwards bishop of Gloucester. Warburton expressed himself emphatically, not to say dogmatically, on a remarkably wide range of subjects, but in his numerous writings he never refers to Cantemir's book. As ambassador in London, Antioh Cantemir had regular and friendly relations with the English ministers: in particular with the prime minister, Sir Robert Walpole; the duke of Newcastle; the lord chancellor, Lord Hardwicke; and Lord Harrington, the secretary of state. All of these obediently subscribed to the publication. They expressed – as far as we know – no views on it; nor indeed should we expect that they should: busy ministers have little time in which to comment on scholarly works. But they too had literary friends and kinsmen. Walpole's son, Horace Walpole, was the most communicative of men of letters and had, moreover, a special *penchant* for royal and noble authors. Antioh Cantemir knew him well and refers to his agreeable, if too voluble, conversation. Harrington's cousin, Lord Chesterfield, was acknowledged by all as the undisputed arbiter of literature. But although Chesterfield subscribed to it, neither he nor Walpole seems ever to have commented on this striking new work. The lord chancellor was the patron of an active and learned scholar, Dr Thomas Birch. Birch's wide interests included Turkish affairs: he would afterwards publish the copious documents of the most famous English ambassador in Constantinople, Sir Thomas Roe.[19] But Birch too, though he subscribed personally to Cantemir's work, is silent about it. In short, as far as we can see, none of the statesmen who dealt officially with the Russian ambassador, or their literary friends and relations, showed any interest in his book.

The same is true of the statesmen of Opposition. The best known of these was Henry St John, Viscount Bolingbroke. Bolingbroke piqued himself as a philosopher and a student of history. He was in touch with European ideas, and was the patron, while they were in England, of Montesquieu and Voltaire. He expressed a particular interest in the rise and decline of empires, and in 'corruption' as the agent of such decline. Walpole, he believed, was corrupting, and thereby destroying, the British Empire. Surprisingly, the growth and decay of the Ottoman Empire, through the same agency, seems not to have engaged his interest. Bolingbroke's literary friends – Lord Marchmont, Alexander Pope – were equally unconcerned. Indeed, wherever I have looked, I find the same remarkable indifference. English statesmen, scholars, historians, men of letters – not one, as far as I can discover, ever mentions Dimitrie Cantemir's *Ottoman History*. As far as the evidence goes, it seems to have been totally unread.

What, then, of the 'second edition' published by Andrew Millar in 1756, which has been so regularly cited as proof of wide public interest? Alas, on closer examination, even this evidence evaporates. For if we scrutinise that edition, we soon see that it is not a second edition at all. It is simply the first edition with a new title-page and without the list of subscribers. In fact, it is clear that Millar, who had bought up the bankrupt business of Knapton and Sons in 1755, found a number of unsold copies of this book, published over twenty years ago, and sought thus to dispose of them. So far from being 'full proof . . . of the interest it had aroused among the British public', the so-called 'second edition' proves the reverse. It was not a second edition at all: it was a publisher's remainder.

If the book was not read, was it, at least, reviewed? I have examined all the principal literary reviews of the time – *The Gentleman's Magazine, The London Magazine, The Literary Magazine, The Universal Spectator, News from the Republic of Letters*, etc. All pass over it in silence. The only review which I have discovered is an anonymous notice printed in the *Grub-street Journal*, a successful literary periodical which was said to have been controlled by the poet Alexander Pope. The reviewer pretends that, on first hearing of the proposed publication, he had been excited by the promise of 'a true and genuine account of the Turkish affairs, freed from the fictions and mistakes of European writers', but that on seeing the specimen pages published with the prospectus, his expectations were 'not a little damped'. He had therefore caused private suggestions to be made to the publisher that, 'on better consideration, the translation, or at least the revisal, of the work' should be entrusted to some better-qualified person – that is, better qualified than Mr Tindal. Since that had not been done, he now proceeded to slaughter the book as 'full of mistakes and inaccuracies', and 'egregiously deficient' in both oriental learning and history.[20] His criticism was largely irrelevant: it was directed at the vocabulary rather than the substance of the work, the translator rather than the author; and herein perhaps lies its explanation. The *Grub-street Journal*, at this time, was waging a continuous vendetta against deism in general, against Matthew Tindal in particular, and against his nephew Nicholas Tindal by association. The review of Cantemir's *History* seems to be an extension of this personal vendetta against its translator.[21]

We know, indirectly, of one other contemporary criticism of Cantemir's *History*. In a letter to an unidentified correspondent in Constantinople – probably the Russian ambassador – on 6 July 1736, Antioh Cantemir refers to doubts spread in England about the authenticity of the portraits of the sultans in his father's book. He thanks his correspondent for providing him with evidence to dispel these doubts; and he asks him to help him further by obtaining portraits of the last two sultans, *viz* Ahmed III (1703–30) and Mahmoud I (1730–54), in order to bring the collection up to date.[22] I have not discovered who had expressed these ungenerous and undocumented criticisms, but at least it is clear that they had been made. I wish that I had been able to find a single contemporary expression of appreciation to balance them.

If we are to summarise the English part of the story, we can describe it as the triumph of Antioh Cantemir's filial piety over English indifference. Young though he was, Antioh Cantemir evidently made his mark as a diplomatist in London. He had good relations with English politicians. But although he was himself a scholar and a man of letters, he seems to have made no impact at all on the English literary world. His literary circle in London is clear from his correspondence. It consisted exclusively of foreigners, members of a little bohemian club founded and presided over by himself. Most of them were Italians – literary *abbés*, raffish diplomatic agents of petty German or Italian courts, *bon vivants, dilettanti*, not to say rakes.[23] It was the German Queen Caroline who helped him to an English translator of his father's book. Thanks to that royal patronage, English politicians and others – Hanoverian courtiers, friends of the author, of the bookseller, of the translator – subscribed for copies. But very few Englishmen seem actually to have read it; much of the stock remained unsold for twenty years; and not a word of appreciation has been recorded. As far as England is concerned, the book fell completely flat.

What, then, of its history in France? Here too, I believe, the accepted story needs revision. Too much has been deduced from the selected comments of Voltaire, detached from their context. But Voltaire's historical judgment was not sound: it was generally at the mercy of his non-historical prejudices; and his judgment of Cantemir's *Ottoman History* is no exception. Let us look at his comments in their proper context.

In his *History of Charles XII of Sweden*, which he had written in England in 1727–31, Voltaire had referred, naturally enough, to Dimitrie Cantemir, whose rule as prince of Moldavia was rudely terminated by the unexpected victory of Charles XII and the Turks over Peter the Great. He had described him, summarily, as 'a Greek' who, counting on the support of the Greek people, as of the Greek Church, had treacherously turned against his Turkish benefactors, only to discover that his Moldavian subjects, who 'love the Turkish domination' – i.e. share Voltaire's hatred of the Christian Church – refused to follow him.[24] Antioh Cantemir, in England, read the *History of*

Charles XII, together with other works of Voltaire, and formed a very low opinion of their author. Voltaire, he wrote to his French friend the Marquise de Monconseil, was a man 'qui se pique d'écrire sur les matières, q'il n'entend pas'. His work on Charles XII was a novel, not a work of history, and his *Lettres sur les Anglois* was merely the gossip which he had picked up in London cafés: 'I would advise him to write satires and epigrams, but to keep off philosophy'.[25] Later, when he was in Paris as ambassador, Cantemir wrote to Voltaire pointing out that his family was not Greek but of Tartar origin: he was, he said, descended from the great conqueror Timur or Tamerlane. To document his statements he lent to Voltaire a copy of the *Ottoman History* – presumably the printed English text.[26] Voltaire replied in a letter of unctuous flattery, suggesting that although there were technical difficulties at present, he would put the matter right at the earliest opportunity. Cantemir's reply was remarkably, even exquisitely, dry.[27] In fact, in the next edition, so far from meeting the objection, Voltaire merely aggravated his insults. Cantemir, he now wrote, was of Greek origin, but absurdly pretended to be descended from Timur. Later, in his *History of Russia* (Antioh Cantemir being now safely dead), Voltaire rubbed it in again. 'All the Hospodars are Greeks', he wrote, as if that concluded the question of Cantemir's nationality; and he sneered even more contemptuously at his alleged Tartar pedigree.[28] In fact Voltaire was wrong, and his attempt to save his own face only showed that he was egregiously wrong: he could not distinguish between the Phanariot hospodars of his own time, and their native predecessors. But Voltaire's error supported his anti-Christian prejudices and he was not prepared to correct it.[29]

However, having received Cantemir's work, Voltaire did cast an eye over it and although he spurned Cantemir when Cantemir was inconveniently right, he eagerly embraced him when he was conveniently wrong. When describing the capture of Constantinople, Cantemir had accepted a story that, although half the city had been taken by storm, the other half had been surrendered on advantageous terms, scrupulously kept.[30] Voltaire seized uncritically on this story because it enabled him to extol Moslem justice and tolerance against Christian bigotry. It is on this point that Voltaire cries up 'the veracious Turkish annals recorded by Prince Cantemir' against the superficial and inaccurate Christian documents.[31] But in fact, once again, it was prejudice, not criticism, that had determined his choice. On this point, Cantemir is unquestionably wrong. As Gibbon would remark, after setting out the evidence, 'Voltaire, as usual, prefers the Turks to the Christians'.[32] It is as simple as that.

Thus Voltaire's intellectual admiration of Dimitrie Cantemir's *History*, on examination, goes the same way as its 'great renown' in England. All that we can say is that Antioh Cantemir tried to persuade Voltaire by lending him the book; that Voltaire cast a superficial glance through it, seized upon an erroneous statement which conveniently supported his own prejudices, and on that account, and in that particular, loudly declared it to be impartial and veracious. Where the book was accurate and valuable, or conflicted with his prejudices, he ignored it, or dogmatically declared it to be false.

Meanwhile Antioh Cantemir, who had at least penetrated the literary world of Paris as he had never penetrated that of London, pressed on with his attempts to give further publicity to his father's work. He had already translated half of it into Italian. Now he called on his new friend, the *abbé* Guasco, to complete the work. At the same time he was seeking to have it translated into French. In 1736 he employed Jean Rousset de Missy, the French historian and russophil, to translate it for publication in Holland. It was for this proposed Dutch edition that he sought, and secured, the portraits of the last two sultans. Six months later, having heard nothing from Rousset, he sent a copy of the English translation to Mme. de Monconseil in Paris and asked her to find another translator. He offered to transfer the new portraits to this new translator, and thus give his work an advantage over that of the dilatory Rousset.[33] In 1740 he engaged the support of the *abbé* Prévost – another anglophile, like his fellow *abbé*, le Blanc, and also, like him, a translator of David Hume. Prévost puffed the work vigorously in two articles in his periodical *Le Pour et le contre* and urged that it be translated into French. Finally, in 1743, the work was at last translated and published. Once again, it was the indispensable *abbé* Guasco who had organised the operation. The translation was dedicated to the duc de Noailles, a close friend of Antioh Cantemir.[34]

Meanwhile, Antioh Cantemir had evidently recovered his father's map of Moldavia from the Dutch printer, and was able to lend it, in Paris, to the greatest of French geographers, Jean-Baptiste Bourguignon d'Anville, who copied it, and caused it to be printed.[35]

The reactions to Dimitrie Cantemir's work in France are not part of my subject, and I have not studied them in detail, but my impression is that, here too, they were negative. Perhaps they were even more negative than in England.[36] For by now the essential motor of publicity – Antioh Cantemir himself – was no longer there to ensure that notice was taken. On 11 April 1744 Antioh Cantemir died in Paris. The *abbé* Guasco and the duchesse d'Aiguillon were constant in their attendance in his last illness; but after his death both transferred their attentions to Montesquieu. Montesquieu consoled Guasco for his loss: he would easily find other friends, he wrote, although Russia would have difficulty in finding another ambassador like Cantemir.[37] After that, we hear no more of Cantemir in France: the name, thanks to Antioh, was to belong to Russian literature.

For as it was Antioh Cantemir who had brought the works of his father to the West, so it was his energy, and no doubt his resources, which alone had driven that machine. It was he who, in Russia, had first projected the publication. It was he who, in London and Paris, with his group of busy *abbés* – Guasco, le Blanc, Prévost – had discovered the translators, tuned the press, provided the copy. Those efforts achieved some results even after his death; the German version, which appeared in Hamburg in 1745, was based (like the French) on the English translation of 1735 and was almost certainly a by-product of Antioh Cantemir's activities in England; for the Latin manuscript which he had brought with him was by now lost or mislaid.[38] But in general, with the removal of his driving spirit, the interest, always faint, seems to have died away.

The English translation of the *Ottoman History* lay unread in the libraries of subscribers or unsold in the warehouse of the publishers. Guasco's Italian version was never published. The *Description of Moldavia*, after lying neglected in the printing house in Amsterdam, found its way back to St Petersburg, but not yet into print.[39] The ablest English writer on Turkish affairs, Sir James Porter, who, like Dimitrie Cantemir, spent sixteen years at Constantinople, and whose *Observations on the Religion, Laws, Government and Manners of the Turks* would be so highly praised by Sir William Jones, never mentioned his distinguished predecessor.

It would be pleasant to record that Nicholas Tindal, at least, obtained some reward for his services as a translator: that, after losing his inheritance and abandoning his antiquarian researches, he gained a bishopric, or at least a deanery. Alas, even here we are disappointed. Queen Caroline died in 1737, too early to be of any use to him, and the vicar had to fall back on his old patron, Admiral Wager, who appointed him, next year, chaplain of Greenwich Hospital. This, and the rectory of Alverstock, Hants, would keep him for the rest of his long life.

So much for the history of the publication and reception of Dimitrie Cantemir's work. The story, as I have reconstructed it, does not bear out the standard version of a wide interest and busy sales. But this does not, of course, devalue the work. It merely poses another, more general question: why did historical works whose importance has been recognised by posterity excite so little interest in the 1730s? For although modern scholarship has of course overtaken Cantemir's *Ottoman History* as a historical source,[40] it retains its importance in the development of historical philosophy, and its apparent neglect in the West, where Antioh Cantemir took such pains to publish it, invites explanation.

To answer this question we must look at the historical attitudes of the 1730s unprejudiced by later evidence. The mid-eighteenth century was not an era of profound or sensitive scholarship, especially in England. When we look at the London literary scene at that time and see it dominated by the thin philosophy of Bolingbroke and Pope, the acrimonious feuds of Warburton and Hurd, we may agree with David Hume that all polite letters had sunk beneath a welter of 'barbarism and faction'. Paris, until the appearance of Montesquieu's *De l'Esprit des lois* in 1748, was not much better. The fashionable philosophers of the time lived on their predecessors. It was an age of scepticism, of elegant vulgarisation, of complacent cosmopolitanism, not of intellectual receptivity or vigorous thought.

This was particularly true in historical scholarship. The poverty of English historical scholarship in the mid-eighteenth century was a frequent complaint at the time: indeed, the whole idea of history had, by then, been devalued, drained of its philosophic content. History was seen simply as a second-class form of literature – second-class because it was easy and required no originality of mind. As the great arbiter of literature, Dr Johnson, put it, there was in it 'but a shallow stream of thought': the historian simply took his material from his predecessors and adapted it to suite the taste of his contemporaries. The only guiding principle, as Voltaire said, was *le bon sens*.

Perhaps the best statement on the subject is Dr Johnson's essay in *The Rambler* on 18 May 1751. After dwelling on the ease of the historian's task, who has no other labour than to arrange and display the material already 'put into his hands', he enquires why, even in so unexacting a profession, so few have excelled, and, in particular, why 'our nation, which has produced so many authors eminent for almost every other species of literature, has been hitherto remarkably barren of historical genius'. The explanation must be, he presumes, that we have never really tried. Only lack of effort, he supposes, could explain the failure of a literate people to excel in so easy a branch of literature.

However, we have, Johnson thinks, produced one good historian, whom he proceeds to name. The name which he gives is surprising. Like his contemporary David Hume, who also lamented the failure of England to produce great historians, Johnson looks back to the age of Elizabeth and James I. But whereas Hume, with his 'philosophic' views, chooses as the best historical work by an Englishman William Camden's *Annals of Queen Elizabeth*,[41] Johnson selects Richard Knolles' *General History of the Turks*, published in 1603. Knolles, he says, 'has displayed all the excellencies that narration can admit'; and he adds that 'Nothing could have sunk this author in obscurity but the remoteness and barbarity of the people whose story he relates. . . . The nation which produced this great historian has the grief of seeing his genius employed upon a foreign and uninteresting subject; and that writer who might have secured perpetuity to his name by a history of his own country, has exposed himself to the danger of oblivion by recounting enterprises and revolutions of which none desires to be informed'.[42]

So much for English interest in the history of the Ottoman Empire in 1751. If none desired to be informed of that 'foreign and uninteresting subject', even by the greatest of native historians, how could anyone be tempted by the compilation of a Moldavian prince whose mind had been formed not in enlightened whig England but under the guidance of a Cretan monk, and imbued, among the tortuous politics of Iasi and Constantinople, with the imported, and now outdated, mysticism of Jean-Baptiste van Helmont? And if no one could be expected to read about the imperial history of the Turks, how could anyone show an interest in the obscurer works of the author: in the arcane annals of tributary principalities, the customs of an enslaved and illiterate people, the elevation and deposition of successive 'hospodars', the treachery and intrigues of those last native princes, Dimitrie Cantemir himself and his hated rival, Constantine Brancovan? In such an atmosphere it is not surprising that, the *Ottoman History* having fallen flat, the *Description of Moldavia* was never printed in England or France.

However, in the later eighteenth century, the climate changed. If any one man changed it, it was Montesquieu. It is a pleasant coincidence – though perhaps no more than a coincidence – that Montesquieu and Antioh Cantemir were known to each other in Paris, indirectly bound together by their friendship with the duchesse d'Aiguillon, with the oculist Gendron, and, above all, with the strange figure of the *abbé* Guasco, whom most other men disliked, but who was the intimate friend of both the President and the Prince. Antioh

Cantemir would project a translation of Montesquieu's *Lettres persanes* into Russian; it would be agreeable to think that the title of Montesquieu's work *Considérations sur les causes de la grandeur des Romains et de leur décadence* was supplied to him by Cantemir's *Incrementa atqe Decrementa Aulae Othmanicae*, mediated to him by his son. However that may be, it was Montesquieu who transformed the study of history, giving it – especially in England, where his influence was to prove greatest – a new sociological content, and making the merely literary comments of Dr Johnson seem hopelessly and finally dated. The same transformation gave a new significance to Dimitrie Cantemir's work, which had fallen so flat in 1734.

The change was signalised by two great English scholars of the later eighteenth century, both enthusiastic disciples of Montesquieu. The first of these was Gibbon. Gibbon was born in 1737, two years after the English publication of Cantemir's work. At a very early age, he plunged into the study of oriental history – so deeply that Dr Johnson, who disliked him, afterwards professed to believe that he had been converted to Islam. 'Before the age of sixteen', Gibbon would afterwards write, 'I was master of all the English materials which I have since employed in the chapters on the Persians and Arabians, the Tartars and the Turks'.[43] That included Cantemir. By the time when he came to reread and use these materials, Gibbon's historical philosophy had been formed by Montesquieu, the 'chief delight' of his studious years, the dominating influence on his first published work, the acknowledged master behind *The Decline and Fall of the Roman Empire*. So in the chapter of that work in which he introduces the subject, and discusses the sources of Ottoman history, he not only pays a notable tribute to Cantemir – the first public tribute by an English writer – but also takes the opportunity to repudiate the philosophy of those who had ignored him. He does so by referring to precisely that essay of Johnson which I have cited as representing the stale and feeble historical philosophy of the mid-century. 'In one of the *Ramblers*', he writes, 'Johnson raises Knolles (*A General History of the Turks . . .*) as the first of historians, unhappy only in the choice of his subject. Yet I much doubt whether a partial and verbose compilation from Latin writers, thirteen hundred folio pages of speeches and battles, can either instruct or amuse an enlightened age, which requires from the historian some tincture of philosophy and criticism.' This is a complete reversal of Johnson's idea of history. It is the measure of the revolution caused in historical studies by Montesquieu; a revolution which, incidentally, restored to historical significance the structure and fortunes of societies hitherto thought eccentric or obscure, and caused Gibbon to regret that Cantemir's work on 'the ancient and modern state of his principality, which has long been promised' – for Cantemir himself had mentioned it, in the notes to his *Ottoman History* – 'is still unpublished'.[44] Gibbon did not know that the *Description of Moldavia* had in fact, by that time, been obscurely published, in a German translation.[45] Like Porson, and most of his contemporaries, he believed that life was too short to learn German.

The second of the English disciples of Montesquieu who, in the changed climate caused by his work, recognised the value of Cantemir's work was Gibbon's friend Sir William Jones, the great orientalist who first among Europeans mastered Sanskrit and demonstrated the kinship of the Indo-European tongues. In his 'prefatory discourse' to his projected *Essay on the History of the Turks*, Jones examined critically the previous historians of the Ottoman Empire and, after refuting Voltaire's superficial and erroneous statements about Cantemir, paid his well-known tribute to the *Ottoman History*, which, as he wrote, 'far surpasses in authority and method every work on the same subject in any European dialect'. Then Jones, in his turn, acknowledged his debt to the philosopher who had transformed the study of history. That part of his essay, he wrote, 'which relates to the *Causes of the Rise and Decline of the Turkish Empire* was written after the model of M. de Montesquieu's *Considerations on the Greatness of the Romans*; nor am I under any apprehension of being censured for imitating so excellent a pattern, to which I may justly apply the words of Cicero, "Demosthenem imitemur. O dii boni! quid ergo nos aliud agimus, aut quid aliud optamus? At non assequimur" '.[46]

Thus the historical work of Dimitrie Cantemir, if it fell flat in the 1730s, found its welcome half a century later. It owed that welcome to an intervening revolution in the study of history. It is pleasant to think that Antioh Cantemir, who tried so hard to plant his father's works in the West, and whose efforts were frustrated by the temporary shallowness of that soil, should have succeeded in the end thanks to a revolution in thought launched by the profoundest of his Western friends, Montesquieu.[47]

CHAPTER 5

From Deism to History: Conyers Middleton

IN THE 1690s there began in England a concerted attack both on the central doctrines and on the external proofs of orthodox Christianity. From one quarter, the divine inspiration of the Bible was questioned. Thereby the historic context and cosmological significance of Christ's mission were made to tremble. From another, the doctrine of the Trinity, which had become the badge of orthodoxy in the fourth century, and had been defended by fire and faggot ever since, was openly challenged. With it, not only the authority of the Fathers who had invented and imposed it, but the divinity of Christ himself, was put in doubt. These challenges were not indeed new, but they were now delivered far more forcefully than before, from inside as well as outside the established Church; and they aroused a forceful response. In that last decade of the seventeenth century, 'Arian' – that is, anti-Trinitarian – works were ritually condemned in both universities; new Blasphemy Acts were passed by Parliament in a vain attempt to stay the infection; and the alarm of the establishment was increased by the appearance of an alternative religion only loosely connected with traditional Christianity and quite incompatible with Trinitarian doctrines: 'the religion of Nature', or 'deism'.

The 'deist controversy' was launched in 1696 by John Toland's *Christianity Not Mysterious*; it was continued and extended by the successive works of the 'free-thinker' *par excellence*, Anthony Collins; and it is generally held to have reached its peak in 1730 with Matthew Tindal's *Christianity as Old as Creation*. Certainly it was in the 1730s that the reaction began in earnest – although it was a reaction which illustrated the despair rather than the confidence of the orthodox. It was in that decade that Bishop Butler attempted to refute deism by raiding its philosophic armoury and exhibiting his own gladiatorial skill in his *Analogy of Religion*. It was then that William Law urged more timid souls to avoid the battle and follow him into the protective cloud of mysticism. It was then that John Wesley pumped into the enfeebled body of orthodoxy the warm breath of Methodism. It was then that William Warburton first took up, in its defence, his disconcerting weapons, bludgeoning with abuse those whom he had temporarily dazed by paradox. It was then too that the antiquary William Stukeley sought, as he put it, 'to combat the Deists from an unexpected quarter' by showing that the religion of Abraham and the doctrine of the Trinity had been known and perpetuated in Britain, from the earliest times, by the supposed Druids of Stonehenge. However, none of these champions was able, in the end, to do more than prop up the fainting body of the old orthodoxy. For in the same decade the deist cause was reinforced, and effectively transformed, by the emergence of a new champion, more formidable than all his predecessors: the Cambridge clergyman Conyers Middleton.

Conyers Middleton was famous in his own time, both as a thinker and as a stylist. As a thinker, his 'covert assault on the orthodox dogmas', according to Leslie Stephen, was 'incomparably the most effective of the whole deist controversy'.[1] After his death, he had a great influence both on Voltaire and on Gibbon. Voltaire read and marked all his works with close attention: as Norman Torrey has shown, Middleton, not Bolingbroke, was his real tutor in deism.[2] Of Gibbon we shall speak later. As a stylist, Middleton displaced Addison as the model of limpid English; which was painful for the orthodox, since Addison had been entirely sound in religion. Middleton's style, a nineteenth-century bishop was forced to admit, was one which, 'for elegance, purity and ease, yields to none in the whole compass of English literature'.[3] Nevertheless there is, in the English language, no biography of him, no adequate study. His friend Horace Walpole wrote a very brief account of him; so did another friend, the Cambridge antiquary William Cole.[4] Both these accounts are valuable for their personal impressions, but both are factually inaccurate, especially when dealing with Middleton's early years. Leslie Stephen wrote an unsympathetic notice of him in the *DNB*. But the only modern study of his published writings is in Italian,[5] and his unpublished writings and correspondence have been almost totally ignored.[6] Let me therefore begin with some account of his career before going on to his ideas and their influence.

It began, effectively, in 1710 when, as a young Fellow of Trinity College, he joined the opposition to the tyranny of the Master, the famous Dr Bentley.

He was at that time an active tory, the *protégé* and agent of those who managed the tory interest in the university. His first patrons were the tory grandees, the earls of Anglesey and Oxford,[7] and he spent much of his time at Lord Oxford's great house at Wimpole, near Cambridge. He seems also to have been a high churchman.[8] One day in 1710 an officious proctor surprised him at a noisy dinner party of tories and Jacobites in an upper room of the Rose Tavern. According to the proctor's report, loud and derisive laughter rent the air; 'a chamber-pot, or something of that nature', flew through the open window, and toasts were drunk to the high-tory, high-church hero Dr Sacheverell.[9] Those, of course, were the high-flying days of tory triumph in the reign of Queen Anne; and perhaps we should do no injustice to Middleton if we were to see him, at that time, as a young clerical buccaneer seeking, like Swift or Atterbury, to slash his way upwards with the weapons of scholarship and wit, sharpened by party zeal.

However, that phase did not last; for soon afterwards we find him respectably married to an elderly widow: the first of three evidently happy marriages.[10] His wife, we are told, had 'an ample fortune', which was useful, since marriage obliged him to give up his fellowship at Trinity. But he did not give up his hostility to the Master. Indeed, he pursued it more vigorously than ever. It was his challenge to Bentley's right, as regius professor, to charge him four guineas for bestowing on him his doctorate of divinity which extended the academic civil war from the college to the university, and it was on his suit that Bentley, in 1718, was cited before the vice-chancellor's court and, on default, formally deprived of his degrees. This was a moment of glory for Middleton: the hitherto invincible Master of Trinity had at last, it seemed, been overthrown and Middleton, who never spared his opponents, was determined to savour and perpetuate his victory. In the words of his obituarist, 'it cannot be denied that the conqueror indulged his genius in the triumph', fearlessly trampling upon his adversary in the three pamphlets which he published on the occasion. The first of these three pamphlets, which all appeared in 1719–20, was entitled 'An Impartial Account' of the quarrel, and it made Middleton famous; for although anonymous, he afterwards avowed it in order to save his ally Dr Colbatch from the charge of having written it. This was followed by a further attack designed to secure a royal visitation of the college and the deprivation of the Master.[11] These attacks were so formidable that the vice-chancellor prepared to demand that Bentley be deprived of his regius professorship of divinity. Not content with having humiliated Bentley in the university, Middleton now went on to ruin him, as he hoped, in the world of scholarship. Bentley had loudly and rashly announced his intention of producing a new text of the Greek New Testament, with 6,000 emendations, and had confidently published proposals and collected subscriptions for it. In 1721–22 Middleton published two further pamphlets designed to halt the subscriptions and wreck the project.[12] Bentley contemptuously declared that he 'scorned to read the rascal's book', but as he never published his much-trumpeted edition, Middleton was able to claim that it was his criticism that had stopped it. The claim was not in fact true, but it was plausible and, at the time, universally believed.[13]

Thus, in 1721, Middleton had established his position as 'the most determined and dangerous' of Bentley's enemies,[14] and his triumph seemed complete. However, Bentley was never a man to admit defeat, and in fact, in the course of the struggle, Middleton had exposed a vulnerable flank. In one of his pamphlets he had included a passage which might be construed as an accusation of partiality against the government and the law courts. Bentley at once saw his opportunity and seized it. He prosecuted Middleton in the King's Bench for libel upon himself, his college and the king's justice. Middleton was found guilty, kept long in suspense, and in the end fined £50 and forced to make a public apology. After this success, Bentley turned upon Middleton's ally Dr Colbatch, the leader of the Fellows of Trinity. The result was no less gratifying. Then Bentley prepared to deal with his last enemy, the vice-chancellor and Senate of the university. His campaign ended in total victory. On 26 March 1724 the university, complying at last with a peremptory court order, restored the Master of Trinity to all his degrees. The wheel had come full circle, and the invincible Master could resume and extend his tyrannical reign.

The dramatic struggle had of course a political content. Bentley was a whig, imposed upon Trinity College by a whig government. His enemies were, or included, the Cambridge tories. Middleton himself was a tory, and his activity in the struggle made him a tory hero. In 1721 he was held to have deserved well of his party, and indeed to have suffered some bruises on its behalf. His patrons therefore decided to reward and compensate him, and it happened that an opportunity lay conveniently (and, in all the circumstances, somewhat ironically) to hand. This opportunity was provided by the late bishop of Ely, Dr John Moore. Dr Moore, by virtue of his office, had been the Visitor of Trinity College, and as such, in 1714, he had had to pronounce judgment in the action brought in his court by the Fellows of Trinity against their Master, Dr Bentley. Unfortunately, before he could deliver his sentence (which was of deprivation), he had suddenly died. His death had thus robbed the college of otherwise certain victory. However, in another way, it had served the university, for the bishop's famous library – he was a great bibliophile – was bought by George I and by him presented to Cambridge as a loyal whig university. The size of this gift, being twice the size of its existing library, was something of an embarrassment to the university, which had nowhere to put it. In 1721 the problem had not yet been faced; and so the university tories proposed that a new office of *Protobibliothecarius* or librarian-in-chief be created to cope with it, and bestowed on a sound tory, *viz* Dr Middleton. The vote of the Senate was on strict party lines and Middleton was elected by a handsome majority.[15]

There was not much that Middleton could do as librarian until there was somewhere to put the books, and for the next two years he was fully occupied in defending himself against Bentley's counter-attack; but in 1723, the building of the new Senate House, which was to liberate space for the library, had begun, and Middleton published a sensible and rational scheme for the classification and shelving of the books.[16] Unfortunately, even in this professional document, he could not resist the temptation to strike a blow – indeed, more than one blow – at Bentley. Moreover, by a double imprudence, he once again cast reflexions on the judiciary. Bentley saw his opportunity and reacted at once. As his biographer puts it, 'although he had already been engaged, within the last three years, in no less than five distinct suits before the King's Bench, he did not hesitate to add a sixth by prosecuting Dr Middleton for libel upon that high tribunal'. This brought further vexation to Middleton and, in the end, another fine of £50.

By the end of 1723 Middleton's days of triumph were over. The long battle with Bentley had ended in defeat, and defeat had depressed him in body and mind. Once jovial and corpulent, he had become sad and thin, and his doctor advised him 'for the recovery of his health and spirits' to travel abroad. The library being still unbuilt, leave of absence was easily granted, and an opportunity offered itself which could not be rejected. Lord Coleraine, a scholarly peer – he was vice-president of the Society of Antiquaries – was travelling to Italy and invited Middleton to accompany him. The invitation was accepted. In Italy, Middleton parted from Coleraine and remained there, mainly in Rome, for over a year.

Middleton always liked to live in style, and in Rome he was able to do so. His enemies afterwards said that he hired a *palazzo* and impoverished himself by living like an English *milord*. Certainly he moved in good society. He became friendly with literary men and scholars, with *monsignori* and archbishops, and met the future Pope Benedict XIV.[17] He also made a fine collection of antiquities, which he would afterwards sell to Horace Walpole, and he had a medallion of himself struck by an Italian artist. He then returned to England via Paris, where, like Gibbon after him, he visited 'the Benedictine workshop' of the Maurist monks at St-Germain-des-Prés, and he conversed with their greatest scholar, Montfaucon.[18] When he was back in Cambridge, he corresponded with his learned foreign friends on scholarly matters, procured English books for them, and used them as agents to supply the Cambridge library.

To Middleton, as to so many Englishmen at all times, the visit to Italy was the revelation of a new world. As a classical scholar, his great passion was for the works of Cicero; and it was with a kind of spiritual exaltation that he found himself 'taking a turn in those very walks where Cicero and his friends had their philosophical disputations, or standing on that very spot where he had delivered some of his famous orations'.[19] But Rome had more to reveal than classical associations. The visible superimposition of the Catholic religion upon pagan Antiquity aroused in Middleton, as afterwards in Gibbon, a vivid sense of historical continuity across a great ideological chasm. There he saw, for the first time, the public rites and ceremonies of the Roman Church, performed in all their metropolitan splendour, and recognised in them the direct continuation of the pagan practices with which his classical studies had made him familiar. He was not, of course, the first person to make this observation. But whereas earlier Protestants had observed only to condemn, Middleton sought to understand. How was it, he asked, that these beliefs and practices, so eloquently denounced by the early Fathers, had been quietly incorporated into Christianity in what had always been regarded as the purest age of the Church? Once he had posed this question to himself, disconcerting answers presented themselves to his mind, and he began to see the early history of Christianity in a new light.

It may be that this was not the only effect of his Italian visit on Middleton's mind. It is impossible to be positive on this because we know so little about his intellectual position before 1724. We only know that he was a churchman and a high tory, politically involved with tories and Jacobites, learned in the classics, and a doctor of divinity. His interests may of course have been wider than this, but we have no evidence that they were. After his return from Italy, he appears in a different light. His mind is now of a more liberal, even whiggish cast. He is a strong anti-papist, avows 'Revolution principles', repudiates his 'former credulity', and declares himself, in intellectual matters, a convinced Newtonian. In Italy he had of course seen the effects of papal government. This, no doubt, accounted for his changed attitude towards Jacobitism. But he may also have met Italian 'libertines' who, at that time, were enthusiasts for English ideas, especially the ideas of Bacon and Newton. In any case, the Italian visit, which left many traces in Middleton's library,[20] must have enlarged an active mind hitherto cramped within the walls of a contentious college and university.[21]

On his return to Cambridge, Middleton resumed his duties as librarian: a post which he would hold for the rest of his life. It has been said that he treated it as a sinecure, as his successors certainly did,[22] but we must remember that, throughout his time, the new library remained unbuilt, owing to controversies over its architecture, and Moore's books could never be organised according to Middleton's plan. Certainly his own correspondence does not suggest that he was indolent. According to it, he spent several hours in the library every day; he made reports on it to the vice-chancellor and heads of houses; he worked out and put into execution schemes for placing the books and drawing up catalogues; and he was active in procuring books from abroad. However, he did not enjoy this work. He preferred reading books to administering them. 'This drudgery of dealing with the outsides only', he wrote on one occasion, 'has almost surfeited me. It gives me some taste of Adam's temptation in Paradise, with the Tree of Knowledge forbidden me; and the old Serpent has not been wanting, by offer of some fair fruit, to invite me to eat and be wise.' But he submitted for the sake of the salary, the beggarly £50 a year which, he would complain, is 'the only preferment I have in the world'.[23]

It seems that the visit to Italy had achieved its original object and restored Middleton to health, for on his return to Cambridge we find him once again ready, even eager, for controversy. He even resumed his personal battle against Bentley and obtained a small but satisfying victory: Bentley was obliged to return the four guineas which had been the original cause of dispute, plus twelve shillings' costs. Then Middleton, whose energy and ammunition were still unspent, looked around for further big game. The first victim judged worthy of his attention was Bentley's closest and most faithful friend, Dr Richard Mead.

Dr Mead, physician to the royal family and to all the great world in London, was not only the most successful medical practitioner in England: he was also a universal man. Classical scholar, bibliophile, collector, generous patron of art and letters, benevolent and influential, he lived, according to Dr Johnson, 'more in the broad sunshine of life than almost any man'. In 1723, when he was fifty years old and at the height of his success, he had delivered, in Latin, the annual Harveian Lecture at the Royal College of Physicians, and had chosen as his subject the social position of physicians in the ancient world. His audience had been gratified to learn that their profession had been held in high esteem in Greece and Rome, and that its practitioners had been rich and honoured. Dr Mead dwelt particularly upon Antonius Musa, the personal physician of the emperor Augustus, who was celebrated by the poets of the time: the Mead of the original Augustan Age. Having been well received by the assembled physicians, the lecture was printed for a wider audience.

It was at this point that Middleton, as a classical scholar, was tempted to intervene. In a pamphlet of perfect scholarship, expressed in no less perfect Latinity, he showed that the great doctor was quite wrong. Physicians had indeed been highly regarded in Greece, but in Rome they had not even been admitted to citizenship: they were invariably foreigners, or slaves, or freedmen – that is, slaves who, being enriched by this lucrative but menial art, had been able to buy their liberty. The profession, in fact, was not honourable at all, but 'servile and ignoble'. As for Antonius Musa, though he had risen to fame and wealth at the imperial court, he was originally a slave, presented to Augustus by the client king of Numidia. Such a conclusion was unlikely to please the College of Physicians, or the patrician Dr Mead.[24]

Dr Mead did not deign to answer Middleton's attack, but his less eminent colleagues hastened to expunge this social slur on their profession. Middleton thereupon published a second essay, annihilating their feeble arguments, and when that too failed to draw the great man out of his silence, wrote an 'Appendix' to it, summarising the case. He ended by advising medical men to concentrate on their useful vocation and leave antiquarian studies to scholars who lived obscurely in libraries and had nothing better to do.[25]

However, Middleton never published his 'Appendix'. While it was still in manuscript, he happened to visit his patron, the earl of Oxford, at Wimpole. There he met Dr Mead himself, who had come in his professional capacity. The two antagonists found each other's company agreeable; a treaty of peace was negotiated by the earl; and to seal it, Middleton surrendered to him the manuscript of his essay, to be preserved as a curiosity in the famous Harleian Library. It would be published after Middleton's death, by his executor, when the earldom of Oxford was extinct, Wimpole had passed to another family, and the Harleian manuscripts were public documents in the British Museum.[26]

Up to this time, Middleton's published works had all been of a secular character. They had been either explorations of classical Antiquity, or attacks on the scholarship and academic politics of Bentley. But now he changed course and, while never abandoning his secular studies, began to apply his critical mind to a new set of problems. They were the problems which had first exercised him during his year in Rome. Ever since his return to England, he had reflected on these problems, and now he began to examine them with an originality of mind, and a freedom of expression, which were to make his name and ruin his career. The first product of these studies – the beginning, as he would afterwards declare, of all his troubles – was a slender volume entitled *A Letter from Rome*.

The thesis of this little work was simple and not, in itself, novel. It was that those ceremonies and forms of Catholic devotion which Protestants regarded as idolatrous were identical with, and copied from, and continuous with, those of pagan Rome. One by one, Middleton takes the distinguishing marks of popery which strike the visitor to the Holy City – the incense, the holy water, the altar lamps, the votive pictures, the images, the processions, and the miracles allegedly wrought by them – and shows, first, that they had all been denounced as 'profane, damnable and impious', 'superstitious, abominable and irreconcilable with Christianity', by the early Christian Church, so long as it was in opposition, and, secondly, that they were all embraced by the same Church, once it was established. Pagan temples then became Christian churches, pagan heroes were quietly turned into Christian saints. The process, moreover, was continuous, without interruption. It was not (as good Anglicans maintained) only in the Middle Ages that the Catholic Church deviated into idolatry: the deviation began at the moment of its establishment. Indeed, the idolatry was then carried further; for whereas among the pagans 'men of sense' laughed at such follies, the Catholics, even if they were educated, now took them seriously, and made them worse. 'Was there any man ever so mad', asked Cicero, 'as to take that which he feeds upon for a God?' But what a Roman pagan thought 'too gross even for Egyptian idolatry to swallow' became, for his Catholic successors, 'the principal part' and 'distinguishing article of faith'. The fanatical priests of Bellona, Ashtaroth and Isis, who mutilated themselves, were despised by the old Romans. 'If there be any Gods who desire to be worshipped after this manner', said Seneca, 'they do not deserve to be worshipped at all.' But in Rome Middleton had seen 'that ridiculous penance of the *flagellantes* or self-whippers, who march with whips in their hands and lash themselves as they go along, on the bare back, till it is all covered with blood'. When Caligula extended his left toe to a suppliant to kiss – or perhaps only to admire the elegance of his shoe – the 'Persian servitude which he thus exacted was thought unworthy of a man' but now it is 'the standing ceremonial of Christian Rome and a necessary condition of access to the reigning Pope'. To Catholic writers who defend these concessions as necessary in order to convert the heathen from paganism, Middleton replies that this argument – the argument of the Jesuits in China – 'however useful at first for reconciling heathens to Christianity, seems now to be the readiest way to drive Christians back again to heathenism'.[27]

Middleton's *Letter from Rome* was first published in 1729. It was an immediate success, and ran quickly through three editions. Like all of his early works, it was published anonymously, but its authorship was no secret; for who else could have written it? Middleton had been forced to avow an earlier pamphlet against Bentley, and his inimitable style was known. Inevitably the book aroused indignation among the English Catholics; and the bigots of Anglicanism, exasperated by the rise of deism, were quick to detect in it the first whiff of that dangerous heresy.[28] But Middleton had friends in Cambridge. He was protected by the favour of the earl of Oxford, thanks to which he was made a doctor of divinity in Oxford in 1730;[29] and next year he received a small tribute from his own university when he was appointed to a new post: the professorship in natural science recently endowed by the will of John Woodward.

John Woodward was a London physician who combined religious orthodoxy with an interest in geology. He had made a great collection of fossils – he appears as Mummius in Pope's *Dunciad* – and was eager to exhibit it, and his own foibles, to suitably deferential visitors. Not all visitors were sufficiently deferential. A learned German, who was finally admitted at the sixth application, found him 'an affected learned charlatan' and insufferable egotistical bore: 'you must listen to his opinion', he wrote, on the Flood and the antediluvian creatures and postdiluvian fossils, 'till you are sick of it. He repeats whole pages of his works, accompanying them with running panegyrics'; and the

German added that the house was full of mirrors in which Woodward constantly contemplated himself: 'in all he does he behaves like a conceited fool and a woman. He is unmarried but *criminis non facile nominandi suspectus*'. This was in 1710.[30] On his death in 1728 he was eager to perpetuate both his collection and his geological ideas, and to continue, through a deputy, to bore later hearers. So he bequeathed his collection to the University of Cambridge and endowed a chair whose incumbent was directed to exhibit the fossils regularly to 'curious and intelligent persons' and to demonstrate, from them, the literal truth of the Book of Genesis and the correctness of Woodward's geological theories. This was the chair to which Middleton was now appointed.

Middleton accepted the chair for the sake of the salary – about £100 a year – but he did not relish the detailed conditions attached to it. He did his best. He gave the stipulated four lectures a year,[31] and presented Woodward as the Newton of the subterranean world, discovering God in the entrails of the earth as Newton had done in the infinite sky. But it was a tedious and distasteful task from which he gladly sought relief in 'the best old authors, Greek and Latin', and, above all, in Cicero, 'whose works are a treasure-house of the knowledge and learning of those who lived before him'. These works, he explained, were his chosen companions, and made him impatient of theological sophistry. ' 'Tis my misfortune', he wrote, in words which would afterwards be quoted against his memory, 'to have had so early a taste of Pagan sense as to make me squeamish in my Christian studies.'[32]

His squeamishness was soon shown. In 1731 – the same year in which he took up his post as Woodward Lecturer – Middleton yielded once again to his besetting temptation. The same passion for truth, and for attacking error in its most eminent exponents, which had led him to challenge Bentley and Mead, now prompted him to aim a beautifully rounded pebble at the forehead of another giant of the academic establishment, Daniel Waterland.

Daniel Waterland, Master of Magdalene College, Cambridge, was described by Leslie Stephen as 'the greatest living champion of orthodoxy'.[33] Macaulay, in his own copy of Middleton's works, commented more summarily, 'Waterland an ass'.[34] The two judgments are not incompatible. The orthodoxy which Waterland represented, and of which he made Cambridge the citadel, was the divine inspiration of Moses, the Prophets and the Evangelists, the literal truth of the Book of Genesis – he would have no truck with allegory – and the absolute necessity of the doctrine of the Trinity as the solid bulwark against the solvent tide of Reason in religious matters. In other words, he was an uncompromising

defender of precisely those positions which the deists, in the last forty years, had
attacked. He had established his reputation in 1719 with his *Vindication of
Christ's Divinity*, in defence of the Trinity, a work which gained him the title of
'our modern Athanasius'. Now, in 1731, he turned to the Old Testament and,
in a work entitled *Scripture Vindicated* – vindicated, that is, against Tindal's
Christianity as Old as Creation – insisted not only on the literal truth of the whole
Bible, from the Creation and the Garden of Eden onwards, but also on its
perfect morality: the frauds of Jacob, the wholesale extermination of the
Canaanites and the Amalekites, the treacherous murders of Ehud, Sisera and
Agag, the fate of the forty-two children who, for mocking the baldness of the
prophet Elisha, were eaten by bears – every sanguinary act of the chosen people,
or of the God who had chosen them, was solemnly defended by Waterland,
who would rather justify nonsense and barbarism than yield an inch of ground
to the hated deists.[35] As Leslie Stephen wrote, Waterland's grave vindication of
the morality of the Old Testament is so outrageous that it might be mistaken for
an ironical attack on it by Voltaire.[36]

For Middleton, who could not swallow the universal Deluge, even when
given body by Woodward's fossils, this was too much. He took up his pen
and in a *Letter to Dr Waterland* elegantly and mercilessly cut the Master of
Magdalene College to pieces. He destroyed Waterland's fundamentalism at
its very base by pointing out that already, by introducing Satan into the story
of the Fall, Waterland has himself deviated into allegory – for Genesis says
nothing of Satan in the Garden of Eden, only of a talking snake; he demonstrated that the practice of circumcision, which Waterland had accepted as
the mark of election dictated by God to Moses, was merely one of the
customs which the barbarous Hebrews had adopted from the more civilised
Egyptians; he disposed of Waterland's 'silly notion' about the Tower of
Babel; and he told Waterland that his whole method of 'rescuing the Word
of God from reproach and blasphemy' by literal interpretation can only 'lead
you into error and absurdity and expose you to the contempt and ridicule of
all rational men'.

Having thus disposed of the 'crude and senseless cant' of Waterland,
Middleton offered what he regarded as a more effective defence of
Christianity against Tindal and his allies. Christians, he declared, should
abandon obsolete and untenable positions and fight, on more defensible
ground, and with more sophisticated weapons, for the essentials of the faith.
For Middleton did not wish, like the more radical deists, to abolish

Christianity and replace it by the religion of Nature. Such a policy, he believed, was both irrational and immoral: irrational because reason is proved by history to be inadequate, and indeed, by its inadequacy, is the cause of religion; immoral because the abolition of the established religion would destroy social discipline, the only practical guarantee of morality. This, he observed, was a truth well understood by the ancients. 'The moralists of the heathen world' – Socrates, Cicero and others – 'though they clearly saw the cheat and forgery of the established religion, yet always persuade and recommend a submission to it', well knowing its necessity both as a means of social control and as a preservative of freedom. For ''tis not the believers of religion but infidels and atheists who in every country have always been the severest persecutors and cruellest oppressors of all civil as well as religious liberty'. Thus Tindal wished to ban, as clerical imposture, all beliefs that went beyond the reach of human reason. This, says Middleton, is mere bigotry: 'governments must be disturbed, churches dissolved, priests proscribed, because they will not in every point submit to his infallible rules' – which is 'worse than Roman Popery'. So, beyond the reach of reason, Middleton would leave room for religion; for 'though God perfectly understands every purpose of man, yet there are . . . many things effected by his power and ordained by his will which man is not capable of comprehending'.[37]

Like Bentley and Mead before him, Waterland did not deign to notice Middleton's attack; but other clergymen hastened to the defence of orthodoxy. First in the field was Zachary Pearce, a former Fellow of Trinity College. Pearce was, if possible, even more fundamentalist than Waterland, and he was particularly incensed against Middleton for having sought to weaken the authority of Moses. As the confidant of God, the author of the Pentateuch, and the founding father of the Jewish state and religion, Moses was an essential figure, upon whom the whole system of Christian theology ultimately depended. So Pearce stood firm for the literal truth of the Book of Genesis. He was even prepared to meet Middleton's objection by jettisoning Satan: if Moses said that a serpent talked, then a serpent talked: Moses, after all, had it direct from God in that celebrated *tête-à-tête* on Sinai; and we know that because Moses said so. Pearce was particularly indignant with Middleton for treating Moses as a mere politician, and he accused him of infidelity.[38] Middleton indignantly rebutted the charge. The true way of defending religion, he wrote, was not 'to enlarge the compass of its fortifications' and so invite an attack which could not be repelled, but 'to demolish its weak outworks, that serve only for shelter and lodgement of the enemy', and to concentrate on the defence of what was defensible and worth defending; and he dismissed Waterland and his allies as 'a set of rash dogmatical divines' who, instead of tempering their medicine to the patient, 'expect to treat rational creatures as farriers do their horses: tie them up by the nose, and so make them swallow whatever they think to throw down'.[39]

The battle would continue, with changing adversaries, for three years; and in the course of it Middleton would further define both his position and his method.[40] The central problem concerned the character of Moses. To Middleton, Moses was an astute tribal leader who, having been brought up among the civilised Egyptians, had known how to make himself the leader of a 'rude and illiterate' tribe and had imposed upon it rites and ceremonies drawn from Egyptian experience. In order to increase his authority, he had pretended that the peculiar institutions and customs which he founded, such as circumcision, and the useful fictions which he declared, such as the story of Genesis, had been communicated to him in a personal colloquy with God. This was of course quite untrue, and therefore any serious argument about the 'divine inspiration' of those agreeable fables was irrelevant; but this was no discredit to Moses: he had merely done what other wise legislators and founders of states would do, especially if they had to deal with 'perverse and obstinate people'. Numa Pompilius, for instance, the second king of Rome, had ascribed the religion which he had invented for his subjects to similar colloquies with the nymph Egeria: a story which the Roman writers, while commending his policy, 'were not so silly as to believe'. These were 'politic fables' such as Plato had recommended for the better government of the people. Men of sense were not expected to take them seriously.

Thus, in the course of his controversy with Waterland, Middleton not only destroyed the foundations of orthodox theology, he also applied to the Old Testament the historical method which he had already used in his *Letter from Rome*. That is, he took the history of religion out of its insulation and applied to it the criteria of secular history. The true interpretation of the Old Testament was found to lie not in a particular revelation to the Jews, asserted by themselves, but in historical continuity with Egypt, just as the history of the early Church was to be explained, in part at least, as a continuation of Roman paganism. But Middleton also did more than this. He secularised not only the history but the function of religion. Implicitly denying its divine origin, he justified it as a psychological necessity and an engine of social control. As such, he sought to place it firmly in lay hands, for in clerical hands it would lead, as he had seen in Rome, to absurdity, intolerance and persecution. If the clergy 'labour to impose their own fictions as divine truths', he wrote, the laity should resist them, lest the authority of the priest grow too strong for that of the magistrate. For this reason the doctrines of the Church must never be exempt from criticism. Fair criticism, he insisted, never harmed true religion, and was very good for the health of the clergy: it 'keeps them in breath and exercise'.

Such views might be acceptable to whig politicians: they would hardly recommend their author to the high-church clergy who dominated the university, or even to their lay patrons. Once again, anonymity was no protection, and there was an outcry. The Public Orator demanded that Middleton be expelled from the university and his books burnt. There was an attempt to deprive him of his librarianship. His tory friends fell away. The most spectacular desertion was that of the earl of Oxford.

Oxford had been Middleton's patron for many years. He had backed him against Bentley, called personally on him in Cambridge, used him to build up his great library, corresponded with him on the most friendly terms. Recently he had promised to appoint Middleton as 'governor' to accompany the young duke of Leeds on his foreign travels. Middleton had actually written the *Letter to Dr Waterland* at Wimpole, and the earl had read it and expressed his delight in it. But when it was published, and the hue and cry raised, the great man promptly changed his tune. As a friend of Middleton put it, 'he could not long withstand the noisy clamours of his party', and he promptly disowned the author.[41] A dry letter put Middleton in his place, and another governor, 'a man wholly unknown to the polite and learned world', was found for the duke of Leeds. Oxford was, after all, high steward of Cambridge University. He might hope to be elected as its next chancellor.[42] He could not afford to be compromised by a public attack on one of its dignitaries who was also an oracle of the tory clergy. Middleton was much hurt by this defection. 'Your Lordship knows', he protested, 'with what zeal and attachment to yourself and your family I have followed you, as a kind of domestic for many years past.' But the earl was inexorable, and after some vain expostulation, Middleton realised that he 'must despair of all further favour or civility from that quarter'. So he detached himself from the tory embrace and became a professed whig. This change of loyalty was, he declared, a great relief to him: now he could express his views more freely.

It was made easier for him since alternative patrons were at hand, eager to support so able a convert to their cause.[43]

One of these new whig patrons was Arthur Onslow, Speaker of the House of Commons, whom Middleton described as 'the protector of those clergy who are animated by sentiments of reason and liberty'. Onslow assured Middleton that he believed in complete freedom of discussion, 'without which a university would contradict its nature and (shall I say?) its name'.[44] A little later, Onslow was joined by Sir Robert Walpole himself, who was brought in by his son Horace, an undergraduate of King's College, and Lord Townshend, whose son was M.P. for the university. But the earliest and most devoted of Middleton's new friends was the most intimate of courtiers, the vice-chamberlain, John, Lord Hervey.

Lord Hervey, the heir of the earl of Bristol, whom George II had raised to the peerage in his own right, has been immortalised, as 'Lord Fanny' and 'Sporus', in the most vicious of Pope's satires.[45] Eccentric in manners, effeminate in appearance – the cause of Horace Walpole's remark that the human race was divided into men, women and Herveys – his memoirs show him as an acute political observer and his private correspondence as an accomplished classical scholar and man of taste. He also fascinated Queen Caroline, the most intelligent of Hanoverian queens. Since Queen Caroline was the ultimate arbiter of all Church patronage, and had complete authority over the king, Hervey was recognised as a man of influence, and was cultivated by Walpole himself; and since it is clear that Hervey genuinely admired Middleton – Middleton's writings, he said, were the only modern works which could lure him away from classical authors – Middleton's future seemed assured. With such a patron, how could he fail to prosper?

For Middleton was not one of your crusted old college codgers. He too was a man of the world, and a man of taste. The Cambridge antiquary William Cole, with whom he enjoyed 'a most intimate and familiar acquaintance', described him as 'one of the most sober, well-bred, easy and companionable men I have ever conversed with'. He carried his learning lightly. He had cultivated tastes. He was interested in art and architecture, loved music, frequented the opera, held regular concerts in his house, played the violin, the cello and the harpsichord. He moved easily in the *beau monde* and was welcome in the houses of the great. Horace Walpole, from an undergraduate, became his lifelong friend: three days before Middleton's death, Walpole would forbid his house to a clergyman who had published an attack on 'my friend Dr Middleton'.[46] So did

Philip Yorke, 2nd Earl Hardwicke, the son of the lord chancellor.[47] The poet Gray, who was hard to please, declared that Middleton's house was 'the only place one could find to converse in at Cambridge'.[48] This was 'a noble house' which Middleton had built for himself – 'he always had a great turn for building' – 'in the most cheerful part of town', next to Caius College, overlooking the newly built Senate House, and conveniently close to the library.[49] It was well appointed too, furnished 'in the most elegant manner and in the highest taste, with pictures of some of the best masters, statues, busts and other antiquities'. There the most intelligent undergraduates of the time gathered for conversation. They referred to it as 'our club', and Middleton's friendship, as one of them wrote, 'was one of the most valuable acquisitions I made at Cambridge'.[50]

With such social gifts, and such political patrons, Middleton, it seemed, had only to choose his preferment. His demands were not extravagant. As he himself put it, he had no pretensions 'to riot in the feast with the Elect', but only 'with the sinners to gather up the crumbs that fall from the table'.[51] That meant, not a bishopric or a deanery but a dignified prebend or the headship of a college: the natural and proper endowment for a scholar in the days when an academic profession independent of the Church did not exist. Such a position was perfectly compatible with a dash of learned heresy. Bentley, after all, was Master of Trinity while disbelieving the doctrine of the Trinity. Benjamin Hoadly was a bishop although his theological views were even more offensive to the high-church party. These men had been promoted by the whig party, now firmly in power. Middleton was now a good whig – as active in whig politics in Cambridge as he had previously been in tory politics. Why then should he not be promoted?

The difficulty was that the deist controversy had, by now, thoroughly alarmed the high churchmen, and they had mobilised their forces – not only in the tory party. Waterland was their intellectual leader. Edmund Gibson, the learned bishop of London, had established himself as their most effective patron, for he had the ear of ministers and the queen. They also had a popular organ in the *Weekly Miscellany*, a periodical recently founded by two clerical tribunes, William Webster and Richard Venn, and discreetly supported by both Waterland and Gibson.[52] Thus the latitudinarian whig grandees who might have patronised Middleton found themselves opposed by a determined clerical pressure group, which had a base in the country and leverage at court, and which was determined to prevent, if it could, any further patronage of 'deism' in the Church.

The story of Middleton's quest for preferment begins immediately after his alliance with Lord Hervey in the summer of 1733. Middleton explained his position frankly. Whig patronage, he said, enabled him to act in his true character as a believer in Reason. His present fortunes – some £700 a year from the estate of his first wife – were 'sufficient to make a single man easy', but his librarianship was precarious and his lectureship, which obliged him 'to demonstrate the reality of an universal Deluge from the proofs of Woodward's cockleshells', was a tedious distraction from classical studies.[53] Moreover, it had a further disadvantage: 'that sour old Batchelour Woodward, so unlike his antediluvian worthies', had insisted that his lecturer be unmarried.[54] Middleton had been a widower when he was appointed, but now he was planning a second marriage, and so would have to resign the post. For these reasons he was eager for security – not merely financial security, but the security of an established position: 'rank and dignity'. Only from such a position, he felt, could he afford to speak freely. Till then, he would accept the advice of his friends and seek 'to mitigate still the resentment of our divines' by a show of orthodoxy.[55]

When Middleton wrote these last words, he was on his way to Dorset to stay with a clerical kinsman, the Rev. Conyers Place, whose daughter he was proposing to marry. Mr Place had 'a great zeal for the honour of Revelation and as great a contempt for Reason' and was even then busy 'writing down Natural Religion by denying its very existence'.[56] However, the urbane Middleton was able to coexist happily with him, and found relief in private heresy. On his way, he stopped in Salisbury, hoping 'to spend a day philosophically' with the notorious deist Thomas Chubb, who kept a shop there, and whom he 'had a great inclination to be acquainted with, for the sake of his writings'. Unfortunately Chubb was not at home, so Middleton was 'disappointed of that pleasure'. While Middleton was in the country he heard that the lord chancellor was dying, and begged Hervey to recommend him to his successor. Another friend, he said, was doing the same, and perhaps their joint efforts would procure him 'some little preferment . . . independent of our ruling prelates'. Hervey promised to work on the new lord chancellor. He also commended Middleton to the queen and made her read the *Letter from Rome*, which she praised highly.[57]

Thus, in the autumn of 1733, all the signs were good and in correspondence with his patron Middleton could afford to express himself freely. He was indeed being harried by Waterland and his friends, who sought, as he said, 'to tame me, as people do wild beasts, by suffering me to take no rest; but I shall have the grace still to follow my Reason in spite of all this Nonsense, and am more thankful to God for what I do not believe than for what I do. In the one, I may possibly be biased by custom, authority, interest; but the other is the triumph of my reason over prejudices that enslave the greatest part of mankind.' He was particularly pleased with the approval of Queen Caroline. Those who attacked him so strongly – the high churchmen, the high tories, the papists – were 'the known enemies to Her Majesty and her family, an inviolable attachment to whose interest is the only merit and virtue that I pretend to'.[58]

The opportunity for action occurred in December 1733, through the death of Samuel Harris, the first occupant of the recently founded regius chair of history at Cambridge. This seemed an ideal solution of Middleton's problems: ' 'tis a post', he wrote, 'that greatly suits my circumstances and situation in life, will not be invidious to the clergy, nor unpopular in this place'. Only the die-hard Jacobites, he thought, would object to such an election, which would show that he stood fair 'in the opinion of the heads and body of the whig party'. Hervey promised his support, lobbied the queen and Sir Robert Walpole, concerted tactics with other supporters. But it was no good. Academic waters run deep, and have their own tides. The late Dr Harris had been a Fellow of Peterhouse, and Peterhouse was determined to keep history, or at least the chair of history, as its monopoly. So another Fellow of Peterhouse, one Shallet Turner – 'a genteel man' but otherwise, Middleton thought, not a serious rival – was fetched back from Paris, where he had been living for several years, and placed in the chair; after which he returned to Paris where he would live for most of the next twenty-seven years.[59] He would make occasional visits to Cambridge, but only to stay with his friend the Master of Trinity. He never gave a lecture or contributed anything to the study of history. Middleton's historical teaching (if any) would have been unorthodox, but he would have given greater distinction to the chair.

It was perhaps unfortunate for Middleton that this first trial of strength occurred when it did. At the very time when the regius chair fell vacant, the clerical pressure group had made its power felt at court. The new lord chancellor, Lord Talbot, had nominated Thomas Rundle as bishop of Gloucester. Rundle was a liberal clergyman, suspected of deism. At once the clerical tribunes moved into action. They delved into Rundle's past. They discovered that he had been a friend of the infamous Chubb. They alleged that long ago, in a private conversation, he had expressed doubts about God's command to Abraham to sacrifice his son: doubts which could be traced to Chubb.[60] They mobilised Bishop Gibson; and Bishop Gibson so bullied the lord chancellor that the appointment, already announced, was reversed. In these circumstances the prime minister might well hesitate before putting another alleged deist and admirer of Chubb into a professorial chair in Cambridge.

Middleton was much put out by this failure and gave free vent to his depression. He felt that he had ideas to express, but that, through his own insecurity, and the newly revealed power of the bigots, he was 'debarred from the liberal satisfaction of declaring' them. So there seemed 'nothing left but to reserve them for a legacy to my country and to an age when the progress of reason and good sense may have opened people's minds to receive them; for at this place where I am doomed to live, we are so cramped by the terrors of orthodoxy that to whisper our scruples is like imparting treason to a friend, and puts him under a necessity of betraying us for his own safety'.[61]

Meanwhile the orthodox were in full cry. Dr Waterland had gone into print again, on one of his favourite themes: *The Importance of the Doctrine of the Trinity*, or at least of persecuting those who doubted it. The *Miscellany* supported the action of Bishop Gibson against Dr Rundle and urged all good Christians to keep up the pressure by denouncing to their bishops any ordinands known to have associated, in their youth, with deists or infidels; and Bishop Gibson himself, in a public letter, justified his action against Rundle, claiming a right and duty to advise the king's ministers, 'who expect it of him', on the fitness or unfitness of persons recommended for promotion. In the face of such provocation, Middleton soon forgot his resolve to publish only orthodox sentiments. He could never resist the temptations of controversy; and he decided to put both the bishop and the Master in their place.

In his answer to Gibson, Middleton pretended to believe that the published letter had not been written by the bishop but had been ascribed to him by some 'grovelling writer' who had sought, by such means, to curry his favour. He then accused this supposed author of claiming, for his patron, at the expense of other bishops, an inquisitorial power, such as could only be exercised through espionage into the opinions of the clergy and the right to 'direct the ecclesiastical polity of the kingdom and keep this whole body of the clergy in order': in fact, to return to the days of popery when bishops were lord chancellors and a bishop of London's officer 'could imprison and murder any citizen in the Tower of St Paul's without being hanged for it' – a reference to the notorious case of Richard Hunne in 1514. Middleton showed this document to Hervey, who was delighted with it, but doubted the prudence of publishing it. Middleton, this time, was prudent.[62]

To Waterland's work on *The Importance of the Doctrine of the Trinity*[63] – this 'surprising piece of nonsense and irreligion' as he called it – Middleton wrote a longer answer, in the form of a second letter to the author. Wisely declining to discuss the truth or falsity of the doctrine, which he regarded as purely speculative, he attacked Waterland for 'the consequences you draw and the discipline you build upon it, which I take to be subversive of the very foundations of Protestantism'. For Waterland would make this speculative doctrine a necessary article of belief, a condition not only of preferment but also of toleration. He had preached sermons on the duty of shunning and affronting heretics; he had openly declared that 'heresy was a worse crime than felony or treason'; and on these grounds he had urged the faithful to hate the heretics no less than the heresy, 'as if', said Middleton, 'the end of Christian preaching was not to inspire charity and meekness but to inflame our passions, and send men from the pulpit, like drunkards from taverns, furious with zeal and resolved to knock down the first sober Christian they met'.

Then, to show on what rotten grounds Waterland sought 'to restrain the most valued and envied part of English liberty, that of judging for ourselves in matters of religion' and 'to build up again the old bulwarks of Popery', Middleton turned to the historical basis of the doctrine to which Waterland was so addicted: that is, the tradition of the Fathers and the corroborative evidence of miracles. Having examined both, Middleton showed that the former was tenuous, inconsistent and futile, the latter spurious or irrelevant: for even genuine miracles could only prove the truth of Christianity in general, not of particular doctrines included in it, or added to it. After exposing the evidence, he cited with approval the letter in which the Christian Emperor Constantine told the contending bishops at the Council of Nicaea that their whole dispute on this subject was 'a most trifling, contemptible, impertinent contest concerning things of no use or importance, a squabble about empty words . . . the fruit of idleness and leisure misemployed', and he invoked the best and most orthodox scholars in order to assure Waterland that the age of the Fathers 'whose interpretations you magnify as the touchstone of truth' was in reality 'the proper era of nonsense and absurdity'.[64]

Having written this second letter, Middleton consulted his whig patrons. Would its publication be of service, he asked Speaker Onslow, 'to the cause of liberty, and at the same time of no disservice to myself; for I have already suffered enough to have some regard also to that consideration?'[65] The Speaker expressed his delight with the piece. So did Lord Hervey. Hervey then passed it on to the famous, or infamous, Dr Hoadly, who had recently been advanced (to the fury of the high-church pressure group) to the rich bishopric of Winchester. All three men urged publication, though with some prudent changes. Middleton made the changes, but then, 'on a nearer view of the danger', had cold feet. It was all very well for Hoadly to express such views: he was already safe in his bishopric, and 'had secured the good castle of Farnham for his retreat'.[66] But Middleton's only office was his Cambridge librarianship, of which he could easily be deprived. Indeed, in 1736 there would be another serious attempt to deprive him.[67] So he buried the letter – or rather, put it into store for later use[68] – and instead published a scholarly treatise on a more inoffensive subject: the origin of printing in England.

This treatise was a by-product of his work as university librarian, and, like everything that he wrote, was provocative, scholarly – and right. At that time it was the received opinion that the art of printing had been brought to England by a German, one Frederick Corsellis, one of Gutenberg's workmen, who had set up the first English printing press at Oxford, with smuggled German equipment, in the reign of Henry VI. This opinion had been established in the reign of Charles II by one Richard Atkyns, a Gloucestershire gentleman, who saw some profit in it,[69] and it had been eagerly embraced by the patriots of Oxford. It had just been reasserted in a three-volume *General History of Printing*.[70] It was, however, a complete myth. Its only basis was a book which bore an Oxford imprint and the date 1468. Middleton exposed the fabrication of the myth, argued that the date must be a misprint for 1478 – an argument which has since been proved correct by more refined biblio-graphical techniques[71] – and restored the honour of introducing the art into England to Caxton at Westminster.[72]

Middleton did not overvalue this small but significant contribution to knowledge. 'Your Lordship will think me sadly employed in turning over such rubbish', he wrote to Hervey, 'but it is just the reverse in the learned world of what it is in the active world: the more obscure and trifling our pursuits are, the greater fame of learning is acquired by attempting them; and a few more performances of this kind may raise me to a rank of glory with the great Hearne of Oxford.'[73] The great Hearne of Oxford did not agree. As a sound academical patriot, he altogether repudiated Middleton's work.

Middleton, he pointed out, was a Cambridge man and a notorious infidel, who had denied the inspiration of Moses and who now sought, by a poor mean envious twelve-penny pamphlet, to rob Oxford of its just claim to be the first seat of English printing.[74]

Meanwhile, encouraged by Hervey, Middleton had taken up a more ambitious project. This was a documented life of Cicero. For Cicero was his hero, as a philosopher, as an orator, even, less plausibly, as a statesman. Again and again, in his letters, Middleton would dwell on his love and respect for Cicero, 'one of the greatest masters of Reason that Antiquity ever produced'. Indeed, he identified himself with Cicero: for was not Cicero, the philosopher of 'probability', the disciple of the Greek Academy, equally opposed to the rigid stoics and the uncompromising sceptics, the forerunner of Middleton, similarly poised between the rigid churchmen and the uncompromising deists? Was not Cicero too a whig, a champion of liberty, and a priest of the traditional religion of which he outwardly observed the forms but quietly ridiculed the doctrines? In writing Cicero's life, Middleton wished, as he said, only to prolong his own name 'by engrafting it on his. For whatever our divines dispute of the salvability of the Heathens, I desire no better company in this, or better lot in the next life, than with him.'[75] In other words, better Hell with Cicero than Heaven with Waterland. The sentiment, for a Christian clergyman, was not entirely orthodox, but it was in a sound tradition. Erasmus, with his *sancta Socrates, ora pro nobis,* would have agreed.

Middleton began his *Life of Cicero* in the autumn of 1734, immediately after completing his work on the history of printing. It would occupy him for seven years: seven years of hard and often frustrating study, in which his spirits often flagged but were regularly sustained by his patron. Hervey indeed took a personal interest in every stage of the work, corresponded with Middleton on matters of detail, and kept him to the task when he seemed to deviate from it. He also never lost sight of opportunities of preferment.

By the autumn of 1736 Middleton believed that he had recovered his credit in the Church – or at least among the more liberal churchmen. By keeping a low profile and a public silence on religion, and by dutifully attending church services morning and evening every Sunday in order 'to wipe off the stain of infidelity',[76] he had made 'daily progress' towards respectability. In February 1736 his enemies in the university had tried, once again, to deprive him of his post as university librarian – some valuable books had been stolen and others mutilated – but the Caput, the all-powerful committee which controlled university legislation, had unanimously quashed the motion.[77] That showed that he had the support of the university establishment. And of the Church establishment too: for recently he had enjoyed an agreeable dinner with the bishop of Salisbury, which was surely 'a testimonial of some merit in me, though not perhaps of a kind that will procure me a stall in his cathedral'.[78] Another encouraging sign was the flattering attentions of an erudite and interesting country clergyman, William Warburton, who spontaneously approached him at this time, and to whom we shall return. Altogether, Middleton now began to feel more confident, and pleased himself with the thought of some sustaining sinecure. What he most coveted, he explained, was a canonry of Westminster, Windsor or Canterbury, or the Mastership of Trinity College, in that order, 'though any one of them would fully satisfy me' – even, he added, in reversion; for although Bentley had now at last been formally deprived of the Mastership of Trinity, the Fellows had so far been quite unable to turn him out.[79] Middleton's confidence was increased in January 1737, when he learned, from the son of Lord Townshend, that Sir Robert Walpole was 'truly inclined to do me service, and that I shall probably find the good effects of it in a short time'.[80] Scarcely had Middleton received this good news when the prime minister himself confirmed it by summoning him to London and suggesting that he might wish to succeed the late Dr King as Master of the Charterhouse in London.

The Mastership of the Charterhouse was an ideal sinecure for a scholar. It was dignified and well endowed. From 1685 to 1715 it had been held by Thomas Burnet, a clergyman who combined scientific interests with very unconventional theology. Middleton was enchanted by the idea. This, he wrote, was 'a preferment which of all others would be the most agreeable to me'.[81] The post was in the gift of the governors, who were all grandees of the establishment: Sir Robert Walpole himself, Lord Townshend, the duke of Newcastle, the archbishop of Canterbury, the bishop of London and others. The new archbishop was John Potter, whom Middleton described as an excellent man and his friend[82] (he did not know that Waterland had hailed his appointment as a victory for orthodoxy).[83] Of the bishop of London, the formidable Bishop Gibson, he could not say so much. But in Church matters there was always, in the background, the influence of Queen Caroline. How fortunate that both she and her confidante Lady Sundon had been secured for Middleton! Lord Hervey had seen to that. Altogether, Middleton felt sure of election, and he pleased himself with the thought that he would now escape to a comfortable haven in London from the provincial animosities of Cambridge and the persecuting zeal of Dr Waterland.

Alas, once again he was to be disappointed. After long debate, the prize was ultimately awarded not to him but to 'one Mr Mann, an old friend and companion of Lord Godolphin'. Mann was the candidate pressed by the duke of Newcastle. Like Middleton, he was a scholar and a heretic, but he was more prudent than Middleton: it was not till he had been safely instituted as Master that he shocked the archbishop by confessing that he did not believe in the Trinity. Middleton was much mortified by this failure. So were his patrons. Lord Townshend told him that it was the first time that the duke of Newcastle's recommendation had prevailed over that of Sir Robert Walpole. But one evening at Houghton Walpole himself explained to Middleton the true reason for his defeat. 'Bishop Sherlock', he said, 'was the person that wholly obstructed it'; and Archbishop Potter and Bishop Gibson had, no doubt happily, responded to his pressure. Against the absolute veto of the episcopal governors, even the prime minister, even Queen Caroline, could do nothing.[84]

So Bishop Sherlock was the enemy. But who was he, and what had he to do with the case? He was bishop of Salisbury, and should have been out of the way, in his diocese, where Queen Caroline had told him to reside. He was not even a governor of the Charterhouse. But – unlike Archbishop Potter and Bishop Gibson, both Oxonians – he was a Cambridge man. As such he was well known to Middleton, and Middleton had some reason to regard him as a friend. They had been allies in the past. As Master of St Catherine's College, Sherlock had supported Middleton against Bentley – indeed, it was he who, as vice-chancellor, had formally deprived Bentley of his degrees. And this personal friendship had continued. In 1733, after his attack on Waterland, Middleton had received 'some particular compliments and significations of favour from Dr Sherlock'; at the time of the vacancy of the regius chair he had confidently named Sherlock as one of his referees in case there should be 'any cry against me on the part of the bishops'; he had expressed delight when Sherlock had been raised to the episcopal bench; and only recently he had enjoyed that most agreeable dinner with him. Now, it appeared, this false friend had come up to London, intervened in the election, put pressure on the clerical electors, and blocked Middleton's otherwise certain promotion. Middleton was naturally very angry at this treachery. He had it out with Sherlock in a personal interview. Of course, he obtained no satisfaction. But he did not forget: he stored up his revenge.

Though shaken by his defeat, Middleton did not despair of promotion, and next year another opportunity presented itself. Bentley had a stroke, and it seemed that death might at last rid the Fellows of Trinity of their otherwise irremovable tyrant. Middleton at once let it be known that he was a candidate for 'that desirable preferment'.[85] Sir Robert Walpole told him bluntly that his application was vain: the post had been promised to Dr Smith, the Plumian professor of anatomy, and Middleton was anathema to the clergy.[86] But Middleton was not discouraged: he wrote direct to the duke of Newcastle, who had so recently shown his superior influence, pressing his case. 'Sir Robert indeed', he admitted, 'when I had the honour of waiting upon him last, seemed to intimate an apprehension of giving offence to the clergy by showing any favour to me': but all that, he assured the duke, was now over: he believed himself to be well liked in the university now and only opposed by a few bigots in the Church – that is, Newcastle must have reflected, by the archbishop of Canterbury, the bishops of London, Salisbury, etc.[87]

As Bentley recovered, the vacancy did not occur, and Middleton then lowered his sights: a prebend at Ely or Canterbury would satisfy him, he said, or the Mastership of Jesus College – did not the bishop of Ely, who at that time nominated the Master of Jesus, owe his see to Lord Hervey?[88] Finally, he decided to take the bull by the horns: to tackle the archbishop of Canterbury himself and find out why he had turned against him, and whether fair words could not turn him back.

In the summer of 1739 Middleton waited on the archbishop at Westminster. He protested that he was a good Christian, only concerned to defend the essentials of the faith against the attacks of modern sceptics. To do so effectively, he explained, it was necessary to allow some of their premises, and adopt their style. If his language was somewhat tart and lacking in clerical gravity, that was in the tradition of anonymous pamphleteering. The archbishop was not convinced. Middleton's books, he said bluntly, contained nothing from which he could deduce that the author was a Christian. Middleton declared that he should not be judged by those early works and pointed to his recent silence as evidence that he had retracted them. The archbishop was still unconvinced. The conference was long and became disagreeable. It ended without reconciliation: indeed, the gulf separating the two clergymen was widened by it.[89]

Even so, Middleton did not give up. Nor did his patron. 'I am determined', Hervey wrote, after an encouraging dinner with Sir Robert Walpole, 'to obtain something for you both agreeable and beneficial, if my power can bring it about.'[90] But how could anything be brought about if the bishops were inexorable? Next year, Middleton decided to make one last effort. He would write to the archbishop and try to persuade him, if he would not give positive support, at least to be neutral and not block any recommendation by his lay patrons, 'for that is all that I can expect or would desire from him'.[91] As usual, he consulted Hervey before taking this step. Hervey was not sanguine: he did not know how the archbishop would react, he said, but 'in general I do not take his opinions or prejudices to be of a very waxen make'.[92] However, a plan of action was agreed. Middleton was to write the letter, and Hervey and the bishop of Ely would 'take the opportunity of softening the Archbishop' in the House of Lords, and try to 'make him at least a neutral power, if we can get him no further'.[93]

So once again Middleton took up his pen and sought to reconcile his deist views with orthodoxy. He recapitulated his previous conversation with the archbishop, and repeated his previous arguments. He stood firm on his essential beliefs: that the Book of Genesis could not be accepted as literal truth and that (consequently) not all parts of Scripture were divinely inspired. But he insisted that the Christian religion could survive these admissions. 'I look upon our religion', he wrote, 'as a wonderful scheme of the divine wisdom and goodness, proposed and revealed in a miraculous manner, and at different times, as the exigencies of man required, from the beginning of the world to the coming of Christ, in order to secure to us that happiness for which we were originally created.' He ended by asking for a charitable construction of his views and an end to the ban on his preferment; for, 'although in my advanced life and easy circumstances, no accession of fortune can bring any great accession of comfort to me, yet it cannot be indifferent to any man to be marked out by a person of Your Grace's high station and character as a pestilent member of the society in which he lives'.[94] As Hervey had foreseen, the archbishop did not melt. He did not trouble to answer Middleton's letter, but simply retailed its content to his friends, who soon carried it to Cambridge and circulated it with their own commentary round the whole university.[95]

Lord Hervey was desolated by his failure to secure any preferment for Middleton. In his last surviving letter, written from his sickbed, he would protest that, 'sick or well, your interest is never forgot or neglected by your very faithful humble servant'.[96] However, if his efforts in that direction were in vain, at least he could help in another. Thanks to his encouragement, the

Life of Cicero was at last completed, and Hervey took over the whole task
of publication. He reviewed the text, offered advice, organised advance
publicity. He sang its praises to his friends, and read passages to Princess
Caroline, who said that it was 'the prettiest and most entertaining thing that
she had ever read in her life', and could not wait for the next instalment.[97]
When it was ready for the press, he arranged every detail of the printing. He
was indefatigable in collecting subscriptions. The success of his efforts was
spectacular. Over 2,000 persons subscribed, including royalty, half the
nobility and fourteen bishops. Hervey even hoped that 'the stern inflexibility
of the Archbishop will look on this performance as a propitiation for your
former sins'.[98] This, however, was too much to hope. The archbishop made it
plain that he smelt heresy in anything written by Middleton. Even a life of
Cicero, he believed, would be a 'covert attack on revelation', by implicitly
recommending 'a heathen character' and heathen morality. Since the archbishop smelt infidelity even in Thomas Blackwell's recent life of Homer, he
evidently had a particularly fine nose.[99]

Middleton's *Life of Cicero* was published in 1741,[100] simultaneously with a
new, augmented edition of his popular *Letter from Rome*. It filled two stout
quarto volumes, and was dedicated, in florid style, to Hervey. The dedication
excited much ridicule, and Middleton afterwards regretted it; but the book
was a great literary (and commercial) success – and justly so. A modern
scholar has described it as the only important work of Roman history written
in the first half of the eighteenth century.[101] It also created a new literary
form – the biography with documents – which would be imitated by Mason
in his *Life of Gray* and Boswell in his *Life of Johnson*. It remained a classic for
over a century and, although criticised by both Gibbon and Macaulay,[102] can
still be read with pleasure and instruction. The weakest part of it is its
treatment – its uncritical admiration – of Cicero the politician. But then
Middleton himself, as his whole career shows, was *naïf* in politics. For our
purposes the most interesting part of the work is the conclusion, in which
Middleton seeks to extract from Cicero's writing 'the key into his real
thoughts', and, in particular, his attitude to religion. For Cicero, whom every
English gentleman of the eighteenth century was taught to admire, was, like
Middleton himself, both philosopher and priest: a philosopher of the New
Academy and a priest of the old Roman religion. As a priest, he conformed to
the old Roman religion which, 'like all men of liberal education', he privately
ridiculed but publicly respected as 'an engine of state, or political system,

contrived for the uses of government and to keep the people in order'. As a philosopher, he believed 'that there was one God, or supreme being, incorporeal, external, self-existent, who created the world by his power and sustained it by his Providence'. So much was deducible from the evidence of nature. Beyond that he would neither dogmatise nor dispute but would settle for probability. The probability was that the soul was immortal, and survived the death of the body in 'a state of happiness or misery' according to its deserts: that is, according to its observance or non-observance of the moral law. Whether these were really the views of Cicero has sometimes been questioned. They were certainly the views of Middleton.

The *Life of Cicero* established Middleton's fame as a scholar. However, it must be admitted that a certain cloud lingers over it. It is not merely that Middleton's idealised portrait of Cicero the statesman is not always supported by the documents cited, and indeed is sometimes punctured by them. There is also a graver charge. Although Middleton told Hervey, and repeated in his book, that his task was 'new and unattempted by any man', that 'no man had ever attempted the same work before me, or at least in this large and comprehensive form',[103] it has been stated that he was in fact a plagiary: that he made surreptitious use of the little-known work of an unavowed precursor, William Bellenden.

William Bellenden was a Scottish scholar who lived in Paris in the early seventeenth century. There he taught Latin and served King James I in some diplomatic capacity. He was an admirer of Cicero, and he conceived the idea of writing a history of Rome, documented from the works of three great Roman writers: Cicero, Seneca and Pliny. At the time of his death only the first part had been completed: a volume of over 800 closely printed folio pages describing events, year by year, from the foundation of the city to the end of the republic, almost exclusively in the words of Cicero. The book, *De tribus luminibus Romanorum*, was printed in Paris in 1634, after the author's death; but as the greater part of the impression was lost at sea, copies are very rare. The poet and critic Thomas Warton was the first to suggest that Middleton had stolen his matter from this almost unknown work.[104] Warton's challenge was taken up by Samuel Parr, who rediscovered Bellenden and edited another of his works. Parr admired Middleton and was at first unwilling to believe the charge; but after a careful collation of the two texts he declared himself convinced. Middleton, he concluded, was a man of great intelligence and an inimitable style, but he lacked candour and

sincerity: 'this I must admit, unwillingly, sadly, perforce'.[105] Like Parr, I too
was at first reluctant to believe this; but my defences were destroyed when I
lit on the catalogue of Middleton's books, as sold by auction after his
death.[106] The list includes one work described as '*lib. Rar.*', a rare work: it is
De tribus luminibus Romanorum by William Bellenden.[107]

In extenuation it can be said that Middleton did not merely plagiarise
Bellenden. He describes his own method of work, in convincing terms. The
structure of his book, which is different from that of Bellenden, argues its
independence; and the whole work bears the distinctive imprint of his mind.
But the fact remains that Middleton possessed and used Bellenden, and
although he cited other, slighter books which he had found useful, he kept
silent about this more solid work. It would have been more generous to have
commemorated a scholar whose memory had been accidentally obliterated
and whose labours, at the least, had lightened his own.

However that may be, Middleton's *Life of Cicero* made him suddenly
prosperous and enabled him to realise an old ambition. He liked to escape from
Cambridge; he had rural tastes (in earlier years he had kept a country house in
Kent);[108] and he had long wished to find 'some retreat for old age in this agreeable country'.[109] Now, with the profits of *Cicero*, he was able to buy an estate at
Hildersham, eight miles from Cambridge, 'the pleasantest spot in the whole
country, always dry and clear, with a trout stream running through it and a good
road to it over the hills'. Here he converted 'a rude farm into a neat and genteel
villa', in which he planned to enjoy 'a quiet and philosophical old age, neither
meditating hurt nor fearing any to myself'. He was now resolved, he said, 'to
keep clear of all offence, being disposed to spend the remainder of my days in
quiet, and to avoid controversy'.[110] He now spent his time between Cambridge
and Hildersham. To improve his income, he took a few private pupils. The
established college Fellows greatly resented this invasion of their monopoly and
represented his pupils as rich booby squires such as they themselves would
disdain to teach; but the young men had their uses: the father of one of them,
Sir John Frederick, presented Middleton with a living in Surrey. Middleton
went there for his induction, expressing his satisfaction that he was to be instituted by the only bishop whom he respected – the heretical Bishop Hoadly of
Winchester. After that he never visited the place; which also was held against
him.[111] He treated it as a sinecure, although, as such, it was a sad comedown
from his previous hopes: the Mastership of the Charterhouse, the headship of a
Cambridge college or a comfortable cathedral stall.

For another six years Middleton maintained his resolve to avoid contro-versy. He was now over sixty, and with the fall of Walpole in 1742 and the death of Hervey in 1743 his hopes of preferment finally vanished. Had he been willing, he wrote in 1744, to renounce his books and speculations, 'I might, perhaps, in my old age, have been cushioned up to the chin and slum-bering in the stall of some cathedral; but the old sin of thirsting after forbidden knowledge has driven me from that Paradise'.[112] So he continued to lie low, publishing only dry classical studies, mainly by-products of his *Cicero*,[113] and planning a companion life of Demosthenes.[114] Then suddenly, in 1747, when he had nothing left to hope or fear from the clergy, he decided to cast caution aside. He would publish and be damned. In that year he took out of store his suppressed second Letter to Waterland and saw that it could be an ingredient in a new bombshell which would finally blow up all his intel-lectual enemies, even if he too should be atomised by the explosion. At this point, therefore, we return, with him, to the battlefield from which he had so long absented himself: the deist controversy.

The stolid defenders of orthodoxy, when first assailed by the nimble cavalry of the deists, had drawn up their wagons around three essential bastions of their system: the Mosaic revelation, which had announced the grand strategy of God and his chosen instruments; the prophecies, which were the blueprints for its execution; and the miracles, which proved that the Christian Church was its fulfilment. Between them, these three positions formed the external defensive system of Christian theology: if they should fall, nothing was left of it except what any man might loot for himself out of the sacked citadel. In his *Letter to Waterland*, Middleton had dealt with Moses and his revelation. There remained the prophecies and the miracles. These had already been heavily battered – the prophecies by Collins and the miracles (since the manuscript of Collins' work on that subject had been first bagged and then burnt by the bishop of London) by Woolston. Middleton now decided to attack them both, from a new direction; and to begin with the miracles.

How exhilarating to be free at last: to be able to enjoy the liberal satisfac-tion of declaring one's sentiments, and not to be constrained to leave them as a secret legacy to posterity! Loftily declaring that, unlike his adversaries, who, as 'true soldiers of the militant Church', had been ready to fight for any establishment that offered them pay and rewards, he had never been 'trained to pace in the trammels of the Church, nor tempted with the sweets of its preferments', Middleton declared his basic philosophy. It was empirical and historical. Biblical history was not a reserved area, subject to special rules of interpretation. 'The case is the same in theology as in natural enquiries: it is experience alone, and the observation of facts, which can illustrate the truth of principles', and we must proceed empirically, from the concrete evidence, properly tested, not deductively, 'from the supposed integrity and piety of the Fathers'.[115] In this spirit, and on these principles, Middleton set out to examine the miracles, not indeed of Christ and the Apostles (those were prudently excluded from the survey) but of the early Church. To prepare the public for the shock (and perhaps to whet its appetite) he began by publishing a *Preliminary Discourse* in 1748. The book itself followed in the first months of 1749. It was entitled *A Free Inquiry into the Miraculous Powers Which Are Supposed to Have Subsisted in the Christian Church.*[116]

Middleton's *Free Inquiry* was aimed, with almost indecent precision, at a peculiarly delicate part of the official doctrinal structure. All good Christians agreed that Christ and his Apostles had worked miracles. All good Protestants agreed that modern miracles were fraudulent. But when had the genuine miracles ceased? The official Protestant view was that they had ceased when they were no longer necessary: when the Church was sufficiently well established not to need these extraordinary aids. But when, precisely, was that? How did one distinguish the last true miracle from the first false miracle? Once this question was posed, all kinds of difficulty arose. Therefore, for two centuries, by tacit agreement, it had not been posed. Middleton now posed it. It had to be posed, he said, in order to resist insidious Catholic propaganda. For Roman Catholics were in a far happier position. For them, miracles had never ceased: were not Spain and Italy full of curative relics, liquefying blood, winking Madonnas, all proving that theirs was the true Church? This propaganda, said Middleton, was very effective: it was making converts among the bewildered young;[117] so it was necessary to pose the question, and answer it: necessary in the interest of the established Protestant Church of England, of which he offered himself as the defender.

In his suppressed second Letter to Waterland, Middleton had already prepared the way for this enquiry. He had there applied to the early Fathers, the inventors of the doctrine of the Trinity, the same methods which he had previously applied to Moses – with far more damaging results. For whereas Moses, under Middleton's treatment, had at least retained something of his stature, changing from the chosen mouthpiece of God to a consummate tribal politician, the early Fathers, when similarly placed in their historical context, had fared far worse: from inspired interpreters of truth they had sunk to weak and silly men, 'more absurd, if possible', even than Dr Waterland.[118] The traditions passed on by these men, said Middleton, quite apart from their inherent improbability, could have no value; nor, of course, could the miracles for which they were the only authority. No doubt it was because of this conclusion that he had decided, in the end, to suppress his work.

The problem, however, had continued to exercise him, and in the intervening years he had written a number of papers on various aspects of it. The method, in all of them, was the same; so was the conclusion: they limited still further the authority of the Bible, the inspiration of the Apostles and the credibility of the miracles. Now, by concentrating his attention on the last subject, he had made, he believed, an important discovery. In the first half-century after the death of the last of the Apostles, when the infant Church, lacking their authority, particularly needed evidence of divine support, no miracles were reported; when they were first reported, it was on evidence that no man of sense could accept; and thereafter the reports had multiplied *pari passu* with the abuses of popery – 'I mean, the institution of monkery, the worship of reliques, invocation of saints, prayers for the dead, use of images, of the sacraments, of the sign of the cross, and of consecrated oil' – all of which, indeed, had been the chief means of such pretended miracles. In other words, the miracles even of the primitive Church, if they validated anything, only validated the abuses of popery – or they were invalidated by them. Between these two conclusions the reader was free to choose; but choose he must, for the middle position – the comfortable compromise of Protestant orthodoxy – had collapsed; and he must choose (Middleton insisted) on rational grounds, by examining, in its historical context, 'the joint credibility of the facts . . . and of the witnesses'.

It need hardly now be said that Middleton's examination of the facts and the witnesses left little of either. The Fathers who believed miracles were shown to be 'weak and silly men', 'void of common sense'; those who endorsed them, like St Jerome, were unscrupulous operators; the most reputable of them, like Chrysostom, admitted that they had ceased. All the evidence of these men anyway was hearsay, for not one of them claimed to have been an eyewitness of the miracles which he recorded. On such authority, nothing could be believed; nor indeed could such miracles be believed on any authority, for 'no force of testimony can alter the nature of

things'. Nature is regular; so is human nature. Modern miracles we readily
ascribe to their true cause; to fraud, credulity, superstition, interest. The
rules of historical evidence are the same in all centuries. Why then should we
hesitate to impute ancient miracles to the same cause, and thus to remove
them altogether out of the historical record of the Church?

To conclude his study, Middleton drew a parallel with more recent
history. 'There is not', he wrote,

> in all history one miraculous fact so authentically attested as the existence
> of witches. All Christian nations whatsoever have consented in the belief
> of them and provided capital laws against them, in consequence of which
> many hundreds of both sexes have suffered a cruel death. . . . Now to deny
> the reality of facts so solemnly attested and so universally believed seems
> to give the lie to the sense and experience of all Christendom . . . yet the
> incredibility of the thing prevailed, and was found at last too strong for all
> this force of human testimony; so that the belief in witches is now utterly
> extinct and quietly buried, without involving history in its ruin, or leaving
> even the least disgrace or censure upon it.[119]

Recognition of the unity and regularity of Nature had destroyed belief in
witchcraft. How could it fail to destroy belief in miracles too?

Predictably, Middleton's *Free Inquiry* raised a storm. From every professorial chair, every pulpit, the denunciations rang out, and the pamphlets flew
from the presses. John Wesley was about to set off on a missionary journey
to Holland when the scandalous book came to his hands. Urged on all sides
to demolish the infidel, he postponed his journey and spent three weeks on
'that unpleasing employment'.[120] It happened that David Hume was at that
time returning to England from Italy. He had just published his work on
Human Understanding, and was looking forward, in particular, to the reception of the 'Essay on Miracles' which it contained, and which he confidently
expected to be 'useful as long as the world endures'. He was sadly disappointed. 'I had the mortification', he afterwards wrote, 'to find all England in
a ferment on account of Dr Middleton's *Free Inquiry*, while my performance
was entirely overlooked and neglected.'[121] Middleton himself remained
unbowed by the storm. He congratulated his assailants on the honours and
preferments which they had gained by attacking him, openly professed his
own deist views, and looked forward to the time 'when we may be allowed to

laugh without offence at the pious frauds of the ancient Fathers and add the stories of their miracles' to those other numerous impostures – 'those oracles, auguries, divinations, magic, witches' – which, in the past, had successively 'triumphed over the senses and reason of men'.[122] Meanwhile he was collecting other hitherto-suppressed papers for publication. He was determined now to go out with a bang; and he invited his chosen executor – his friend and physician Dr Heberden – to come and hear 'what new heterodoxies I have been meditating and sketching out since we last met'.[123]

'The *Free Inquiry*', wrote Macaulay, 'is Middleton's masterpiece. He settled the authority of the Fathers for ever with all reasonable men.'[124] But now that his blood was up, Middleton was not going to stop at miracles: he would go on and storm the last redoubt of orthodoxy, the prophecies. Twenty-five years ago, the credit of the prophecies had been gravely shaken by Collins;[125] but the clergy, wise in their generation, had known how to deal with that challenge. According to Horace Walpole, they 'artfully stifled all mention' of Collins' book, and saw to it that the orthodox view was publicised. The most successful publicist was Thomas Sherlock, whose six sermons on the subject were regularly reprinted, with successive improvements, which wafted him upwards through successive bishoprics. Middleton, as we have seen, had been friendly with Sherlock until 1737, when Sherlock kept him out of the Mastership of the Charterhouse. Thereafter he was a mortal enemy; but as Sherlock was a close friend of Lord Hervey, it would have been imprudent to attack him. Now, however, Hervey was dead, and in 1749, when Sherlock signalised his promotion to the bishopric of London by publishing a new edition of his work, Middleton saw his chance. With one and the same blow, he could complete the rout of orthodoxy and savour a long-deferred revenge.

The task was not difficult, for Sherlock had evaded rather than refuted the challenge of Collins. Altering the accepted definition of prophecy, he had abandoned Moses and the major Prophets, whom Collins had discredited, and had postulated a new system going back from Moses to Adam. In Middleton's phrase, he resolved 'to quit that field to his adversary, and to take shelter in his antediluvian scheme'. Unfortunately, the antediluvian scheme only raised greater difficulties, since it necessarily presumed the historical truth of the Book of Genesis. Middleton had very little difficulty in showing that Moses and the Prophets were essential to the whole system of Christianity as professed by Christ, St Paul and the Evangelists, and he made merry with Sherlock's antediluvian alternative. So, having swept Sherlock somewhat unceremoniously out of the way, he restored the field to Collins, whose book (says Horace Walpole) 'was now received and extremely read, by which Dr Middleton wounded the Church more than by his own book'.[126]

Six months after publishing his *Examination of the Bishop of London's Discourse on Prophecy*, Middleton died. He was active to the end, preparing for publication not only his replies to his critics but also the various specialised essays which he had written, but hesitated to publish, in his years of discretion. After his death, Dr Heberden examined these manuscripts and saw most of them through the press.[127] But there were some manuscripts which he decided not to publish. The suppressed second Letter to Waterland remained suppressed: it had been superseded by the *Free Inquiry*. A Latin treatise on miracles 'of a decidedly heterodox kind' was also suppressed – on the advice, it is said, of Lord Bolingbroke, who, however, first contrived to take a private copy of it. What became of that copy, we do not know.[128] A treatise on 'the inefficacy of prayer' was prudently burnt.

When Middleton died, his friends lamented the failure of his worldly career. 'A greater instance of neglected merit', wrote one of them, 'was never known.'[129] Even the orthodox thought that such neglect had been a mistake. If only he had been made Master of the Charterhouse, exclaimed one of them, perhaps he would never have written those last pernicious treatises. But because of those treatises, he died famous, or at least notorious. By his rigorous intellectual method, and his irresistible style, he had destroyed all the external supports of Christianity, leaving it to fend for itself in secular history. God had not revealed himself through Moses, or foretold his plan of salvation through the Prophets, or authenticated its fulfilment by granting to His Church a 'standing power' of miracles. All these claims were, at worst, clerical imposture, the means of clerical tyranny and persecution; at best, decorative myth. Theology, in fact, was now extinct: dissolved in history.

It is true, Middleton had not denied the essentials of Christianity; the divine mission and authenticating miracles of Christ and his Apostles. As he piously, and rather tentatively, expressed it, 'the history of the Gospel I hope may be true, though the history of the Church be fabulous'.[130] But how rational was his pious hope? Stripped of its external support, of the historical flying buttresses which had sustained it for so many centuries, how long could the central fabric stand? Did it not rest merely on the narrow base of assertion, already undermined? Was it not left there, an isolated precarious stack rising naked above the rubble, upright only because Middleton's explosive reasoning had not yet touched it?[131] In the face of his own logic, Middleton's elaborate excuses for his own fundamental orthodoxy are at best negative. They rest not on his own reasoning, but on its voluntary restraint.

In the first five years after his death, Middleton's accumulated heterodoxies, old and new, were published, and it became possible to form a comprehensive view of his philosophy. He was an avowed rationalist. No certainty, he believed, was to be obtained on any subject except by reason; by which he meant not deductive reasoning, reasoning from first principles, but inductive reasoning, from experience. Newton, not Descartes, was his avowed model.[132] But Middleton went beyond Newton in applying his method not only to the physical world but also to theology. He would not allow any exemption to the Bible or the Jews. 'The case', he wrote, 'is the same in theological as in natural enquiries: it is experience alone, and the observation of facts, which can illustrate the truth of principles.' And what was in fact revealed by such observation, by 'the testimony of facts, as it is presented to our senses, in this wonderful fabric and constitution of the world?' Was it not the unity, the power and the Providence of God? How absurd and vulgar, he exclaimed, to suppose that God needed the trivial miracles recorded, at second and third hand, by weak and silly men – 'the ecstasies of women and boys and the visions of interested priests' – in order to instruct mankind, when all the time He had revealed Himself, and set himself 'continually before our eyes, in the wonderful works and beautiful fabric of the visible world'. For the essence of religion had been revealed long before the Gospel was published. It had been set out by 'all the principal sages of Antiquity'. Cicero, in particular, had given 'a short abstract of it'. 'Our doctors', Middleton added, 'perhaps will look with horror on all this, as rank deism.'[133] They did indeed.

However, Middleton was not a systematic deist, for he allowed both the limits of reason and even a certain scope for revelation. Beyond the reach of reason, he argued, the human mind could only speculate. Speculation could never be conclusive, and it could be very absurd; but at least, so long as it was not hardened into orthodoxy or enforced by persecution, it was harmless, and he himself was happy to discuss any theory. He was, in fact, in the strict sense of the word, 'a free-thinker'. At one time he proposed to break his isolation at Cambridge by founding a corresponding club 'for the discovery and defence of truth in every branch of science, without prejudice, regard to party, or any interest whatsoever' – a revival in eighteenth-century England of Cicero's Tusculan disputations. Such a club, he thought, could be very useful for civil and religious liberty. But could it be realised, except perhaps 'in the new colony of Georgia, under the auspices of the hero Oglethorpe?'[134] He doubted it, and in the end contented himself with a regular evening session in the Cambridge coffee-house: the only hour, he said, that he regularly spent outside the domestic felicity of his own house.[135]

In the area of mystery beyond the reach of reason, Middleton allowed only provisional conclusions based on probability. Here too he felt himself in good company. This was the doctrine of the New Academy in Greece, the school to which Cicero adhered. What was good enough for Cicero was good enough for Middleton. He too, he declared, was 'a mere academic, humbly content to take up with the <u>probable</u>', 'to pursue the faint track of probability', 'which, to an Academic, of which sect I profess myself, is all that is to be expected from any enquiry where our sense cannot decide'.[136] Whither the faint track of probability led him in these high matters, Middleton prudently did not say; but it certainly did not lead to the doctrines which would have been enforced by Dr Waterland.

Did it even lead to Christianity? So far there is nothing to suggest that the religion of Christ had any advantage over the religion of Cicero. Indeed, Middleton seems to prefer that of Cicero. At least there were no Waterlands in pagan Rome. The high priests of its religion, the augurs, were cultivated political grandees – Lucullus, Pompey, Caesar, Cicero himself. These men did not of course believe the fabulous theology over whose ritual they presided: indeed, in their private discussions they 'made no scruple to laugh at the folly of it'. But they recognised that the fabulous rites and worship were 'the best calculated to promote the general good and prosperity of the republic', and so, like all 'the best and wisest of the heathens', they not only complied with them, 'but thought it a duty and point of morals to comply, taking them to be useful'.[137] Clearly Middleton had no distaste for paganism *per se*. It was not on account of the paganism in it, which he had demonstrated, that he disliked the Roman Catholic Church; his complaint was rather that the Church, while retaining the innocent rites of paganism, had infused into them an intolerant spirit and caused them to serve an oppressive government. As he put it, 'My aversion to popery is grounded, not only on its paganism and idolatry, but on its being calculated for the support of despotic power, and inconsistent with the genius of free government.'[138]

The only religious system which Middleton openly endorsed on intellectual grounds was that of deism. He never gave explicit support to any exclusively

Christian doctrine, or even allowed it the benefit of probability. No one could suppose that such doctrines as the Incarnation, the Resurrection or the Trinity were 'probable'. How then, we naturally ask, was he able to insist, and to insist with some urgency, that he was a Christian? For to the end of his life he protested – though always in general terms – that he was not an infidel, that he did not doubt the mission or the miracles of Christ, or the inspiration of the Bible. The difficulty of reconciling these claims with his expressed philosophy inevitably brought upon him the charge of insincerity: for how, it was asked, could so acute a mind have failed to perceive the necessary implications of his own reasoning?[139] And yet, when we read his own writings, with their sometimes passionate defence of his own belief, it is difficult to impute to him conscious hypocrisy. At least he was no more insincere than the numerous contemporary clergymen who admitted the force of his arguments but refused to accept their logical conclusions.

In his last months, Middleton began to compose an 'Apology' for his life and writings. The work was not finished, perhaps because of his death;[140] but the fragment repeats and resumes the constant burden of his previous attempts at self-justification. In it he declares that the prime motive of his life has been his desire to resist the growth of infidelity, which had been quickened, not stayed, by the stupidity and the 'haughty and overbearing temper' of the orthodox. This had been the purpose of his first *Letter to Dr Waterland*, in which, in order to win the ear of the critics, he had made such concessions of style and substance as reason required and the convention of anonymity permitted. However, the attempt, he admitted, had failed; he had been defeated by the clamour and animosity of 'the bigoted part of the clergy', which had pursued him even when he had taken refuge in the *Life of Cicero*. And yet, in all his writings, he protested, he had only sought to defend not particular Churches or men, but 'the sum and substance of religion itself . . . and to reduce the controversy to one general question concerning the superior excellence of revelation to natural religion, when considered as a rule of life and manners, and which of them is the best calculated for the benefit of society and the support of government'.

'The benefit of society and the support of government . . .' Here, surely, is the explanation of the apparent inconsistency of Middleton's position. Middleton was not a religious man. He had no sense of awe or devotion, except in the presence of Nature, of 'the wonderful fabric of the world'. He had no feeling of sin, no need of redemption, no tragic sense of the world. But he recognised that deism was not enough. It might satisfy 'the wiser sort', but it could not, by itself, provide a means of social control. That required the additional force of revelation; and for that purpose Middleton would support, or at least do nothing to undermine, revelation. His aim, as he once wrote to Hervey, was to reconcile religion with reason, or, 'where that cannot be', to bring them 'as nearly together as possible'.[141] In the areas where that could not be, revelation could come in.

There were two such areas. One was the mission of Christ. Middleton's reason had dissolved the entire cosmological context of Christianity, but the simple moral teaching of Christ, he believed, was a social necessity which must be inculcated by an established Church; and this in turn needed the assurance, or the myth, of a divine origin. Therefore Middleton was prepared to concede a special status to Christ as the articulator of the moral law. That law was expressed in the Gospels. Although even the Gospels must not be taken literally (for the Evangelists were not always inspired), Middleton was prepared to take them on trust. Thus reduced to its own limits, Christianity was socially useful, politically harmless, and compatible with free thought: 'if to live strictly and to think freely, to practise what is moral and to believe what is rational, be consistent with the sincere profession of Christianity, then I shall always acquit myself like one of its truest professors'.[142]

The second area in which Middleton allowed revelation was the interrelated doctrines of the immortality of the soul and of posthumous rewards and punishments. These doctrines also were judged necessary to society, but could not be proved by empirical reason. It is true, the best of the ancient philosophers had inclined towards them; but other philosophers disagreed with them and such speculative opinions could not command assent. The best of all the ancient writers was, of course, Cicero; and Middleton was at pains to show that he had held the correct view: that is, he believed 'as much as weak reason was then able to teach poor mortals: the probability of an Immortality', leaving to revelation 'the glory of establishing its certainty'.[143] Thus revelation was welcomed by Middleton in order to confirm the speculative views of the pagan Cicero, and to fortify the Church as a pillar of the social order.

An established Church, claiming divine authority and appealing to posthumous judgment, but preaching only moral and social virtues and allowing complete freedom of thought – such was the religious ideal of Conyers Middleton. It was an ideal which, by now, he thought, it should be possible to realise. The way had been prepared, intellectually, by the deists, politically by the Glorious Revolution of 1688 and the Protestant Succession. Unfortunately, even under the whig ascendancy, the forces of reaction were reasserting themselves. The high churchmen – 'and no age', he wrote, 'had higher' – were seeking to reimpose a compulsory orthodoxy, to establish a monopoly of patronage, and to 'fetch us back again into all the absurd notions and arbitrary principles from which the Revolution had in great measure set us free'.[144] They were denouncing free thought as a threat to 'the peace of the Church: that is, to the power and repose of rich and lazy prelates',[145] and by their authority in the universities they were blocking scientific and moral improvement. There were times when Middleton could be radical in his demands for reform of the structure which gave these men their power. 'An ecclesiastical constitution not to be altered', he wrote to Hervey, 'is a contradiction to Protestantism and to liberty, and can produce no other peace than what we see in popish countries, that of slaves'; and he urged his whig patrons not to be afraid of action. Had not Queen Elizabeth dissolved the whole frame of the Church in defiance of the whole clergy? Why then should a whig government be deterred by the clamour of a mere party in the Church, 'when the laity are apparently on the other side'?[146]

It was the same with the universities: they too needed a thorough reform – abolition of obsolete statutes 'which neither can nor ought to be kept', alteration of courses, and the prospect of public careers for university men.[147] Not that Middleton himself was radical. 'Those slumberers in stalls', he wrote, 'suspect me very unjustly of ill designs against their peace; for although there are many things in the Church that I wholly dislike, yet I know too well the use and force of a national establishment to wish even the reformation of it by rash or violent means'.[148] He was a true whig – a convert to whiggism who really believed the doctrines in which his patrons, being hereditary whigs, merely acquiesced.

Middleton's utilitarian concept of religion, his belief that it could be defended by reason, and his unpopularity with the high-church establishment, brought him into contact and temporary agreement with another clergyman even more controversial than himself: a man, moreover, who, in the generation after his death, would be the most formidable opponent of his influence. At this point, therefore, we may turn aside to observe their brief and somewhat paradoxical association. The clergyman in question was that vigorous literary adventurer who was to become, for a time, the dictator of the Republic of Letters, William Warburton.

It was in the mid-1730s, when Middleton had retired bruised from the fray, that Warburton projected himself into it. A crude, ambitious, thrusting lawyer's clerk turned country parson, of great mental vigour and equal self-confidence, he had acquired a miscellaneous stock of learning, uncontrolled by education or scholarship, and he was resolved to force his way upwards by the alternate methods of flattery and effrontery. At present, he was still largely dependent on flattery; but, like other clergymen, he also saw in the deist controversy a means of self-assertion and self-advancement. Observing that the deists were gaining ground among the laity while orthodoxy was still essential in the Church, he hit on the idea of reconciling the two by proving that natural reason, so far from undermining orthodoxy, could be made – at least if wielded by a resourceful and overbearing polemicist – to reinforce it. With this aim, he published, in 1736, a book entitled *The Alliance between Church and State*, which proved that the most rational form of religion was a national episcopal Church established by law and protected by religious tests: in other words, the model of the Church of England.[149] He then sent a copy of this work to Middleton.

Middleton was in need of friends. This was the time when he was seeking, by discretion, to recover credit with the orthodox clergy. He was therefore pleased to be courted by another clergyman who, like himself, professed to combine religion with reason. A friendly correspondence ensued. Warburton visited Middleton in Cambridge; learned subjects were discussed; common enmities were savoured; and at the beginning of 1738 Warburton sent to Middleton the first instalment of his own *magnum opus*: a rambling, pretentious work entitled *The Divine Legation of Moses*.[150] The thesis of the book was that since belief in the immortality of the soul and in a system of rewards and punishments after death was essential to a well-ordered society, and since Moses had not prescribed these essential beliefs to the Jews, the defect must have been made good by a private assurance of divine support. Thus reason (or at least the reason of Warburton) proved that Moses was inspired after all, and by this somewhat fanciful hypothesis the great system of Christian cosmology, which the deists had almost toppled, could be shored up again.

Reading the friendly correspondence between Middleton and Warburton, and Middleton's comments on it to Lord Hervey, we soon see that Middleton had scant respect for Warburton as a scholar and Warburton had little understanding of Middleton's true position.[151] But Warburton needed scholarship and Middleton needed support, and they drew together in self-defence against the undiscriminating bigots of orthodoxy. Middleton could see that they differed fundamentally from each other, but was by nature tolerant;

Warburton was intolerant but did not, at first, see. Warburton even hailed Middleton as an ally against the free-thinkers, which brought down upon him the rage of the *Miscellany* and the expostulations of bishops Sherlock and Hare; but he stood his ground and the friendly correspondence continued.

However, in 1741, all was changed. In that year, in the new edition of his *Letter from Rome*, Middleton ventured to reply to certain objections which Warburton had made in the fourth book of his *Divine Legation*. The objections had been public; the reply was courteous; but Warburton was never a man to accept public criticism, especially when it was, as in this case, unanswerable. Moreover, in his *Life of Cicero*, published in the same year, Middleton politely dissented from Warburton (as he had already done in correspondence) on the question of Cicero's views about a future life. He did not indeed name Warburton; but Warburton recognised the allusion and regarded it as an unpardonable 'liberty', deserving punishment. Thereupon the correspondence ceased altogether; and three years later Warburton publicly dissociated himself from Middleton.[152] By that time he had found a new and more valuable patron in Alexander Pope, whose deist views he had contrived to reconcile with orthodoxy. From that moment, he never looked back. A literary reputation, a valuable legacy, a rich wife and a bishopric would be the ultimate results of that fortunate association. Thereafter flattery was unnecessary. Warburton had arrived, and a truculent literary dictatorship was about to begin.

The consistent purpose of Warburton, apart from the mere enjoyment of power, was to destroy the deists with their own weapons: to prove, by a parade of learning, that orthodoxy was rational; and if his reasoning was questioned, to beat down or silence the questioners by abuse or authority. For this purpose, he drew into dependence upon himself a claque of minor writers who wrote to his dictation, and acted as a kind of literary bodyguard, prepared to applaud his works and assassinate his opponents. The chief of these, 'the Warburtonian' *par excellence*, was his 'prim sycophant', Richard Hurd, whom he discovered in 1749, the year in which Middleton's *Free Inquiry* was published.

To destroy deism and restore orthodoxy by reason entailed a counterattack against Middleton on all the three fronts on which he had advanced: the authority of Moses, the prophecies and the miracles. Warburton conceived that he had restored the authority of Moses by his great work, *The Divine Legation*. Of this work new parts, and new editions, continued to come out at regular intervals, with ever-expanding footnotes in which, as a contemporary wrote, 'offenders by the dozen were whipped at the cart's tail'. In 1749 he turned his attention to the miracles. In his *Julian*, an immediate reply to Middleton, published in 1750, he attempted to show that, although many of the early miracles were spurious, one at least – and one, for his purposes, was enough – was genuine.[153] All that he in fact showed was that he claimed, like the pope, the right to designate miracles at will. Finally, in 1768, at the age of seventy, having exhausted his own strength in maintaining his literary empire, he handed over to his janissaries the defence of the prophecies. He endowed an annual series of 'Warburton Lectures' on that subject, and appointed, as his first lecturer, not unexpectedly, his own familiar toady, now his archdeacon, Hurd.

It was at this moment that a new character entered upon the stage: Edward Gibbon.

Gibbon's acquaintance with Middleton's work had begun early. In 1752, two years after Middleton's death, he had gone, as an undergraduate, to Oxford. It was then not long, he would afterwards write,

> since Dr Middleton's *Free Inquiry* had sounded an alarm in the theological world; much ink, and much gall, had been spilt in the defence of the primitive miracles; and the two dullest of their champions were crowned with academic honours by the university of Oxford. The name of Middleton was unpopular, and his proscription very naturally tempted me to peruse his writings and those of his antagonists. His bold criticism, which approaches the precipice of infidelity, produced on my mind a singular effect.

The effect was indeed singular. Middleton, as he himself tells us, had written his *Free Inquiry* in order to check 'the late growth of popery in this kingdom'; but his method had been to show that the miracles of the early Church rested on no better authority than those of modern Rome: a two-edged argument, which could be used to validate the latter miracles as well as to invalidate the former. This perverse but logical inference was made by the young Gibbon, and so, as he afterwards put it, 'at the age of 16, I bewildered myself in the errors of the Church of Rome'.[154]

But if Middleton, by a perverse route, at first led Gibbon to Rome, later he led him out from Protestantism to deism. If we follow Gibbon's intellectual history, at every stage we find the name, or the trail, of Middleton. In his first work, his *Essai sur l'étude de la littérature*, begun in Lausanne and published in England in 1761, he cites Middleton's *Free Inquiry* as one of the 'fine monuments of an enlightened age'.[155] On his return to Lausanne, to begin his Grand Tour, in 1763, he reread Middleton in French and commented on the French reviews of his work.[156] This was the time when Voltaire was reading and annotating the English deist writers and, above all, Middleton.[157] Arrived in Rome, Gibbon felt the same sentiments which Middleton had expressed a generation before, almost in the same language.[158] Back at his father's house in Hampshire, we again find him reading the works of Middleton.[159] At that time he was making a systematic study of the evidences of Christianity.[160] When in doubt, he consulted 'my friend Dr Middleton' and was immediately put right.[161] Thus, by 1770, Gibbon was master of the evidence and felt himself qualified to enter the fray, even – as Middleton himself had done – against the reigning oracle. This meant, at that time, against the tyrant of literature Warburton and his acolyte Hurd.

In 1770 Gibbon published, anonymously, his first work in English. It was a formidable criticism of that part of *The Divine Legation* which, we are told, had given the greatest satisfaction to its author;[162] the hypothesis that Virgil, in the sixth book of the *Aeneid*, had presented an allegory of the initiation ceremony of the Eleusinian mysteries. Two years later, when Hurd published his Warburton Lectures on prophecy, Gibbon wrote a long letter to him, again anonymously, presenting cogent arguments to show that the Book of Daniel could not be admitted as prophecy, having been written not in the seventh but in the second century B.C. Some of these arguments had already been put forward by Anthony Collins in 1725, but it seems that Gibbon did not know Collins' work.[163] Hurd replied civilly, but without meeting Gibbon's objections. He did not discover the identity of his correspondent until after Gibbon's death.[164]

In both these cases – both against Warburton and against Hurd – Gibbon was certainly right. But why, we naturally ask, did he write these anonymous works? His biographers, without exception, either ignore them completely or explain them as eccentric expressions of personal frustration.[165] But if we see them against the intellectual history of their time, their significance is surely clear. They announce the final phase of the deist controversy: the counter-attack against 'the Warburtonians' who had sought, by shoddy and pretentious scholarship, to reverse the irreversible victories of Middleton. Even their anonymity, which Gibbon afterwards regretted as cowardly, is then explained. That too was in the deist tradition. Toland, Collins, Tindal, Middleton had all, at first, written anonymously. So had David Hume. It was one of the accepted rules of the game.[166]

Six years after his critique of Warburton, four years after the letter to Hurd, Gibbon published the first volume of the *Decline and Fall*. If its historical explanation is inspired by Montesquieu, its attitude towards religion, from beginning to end, is that of Middleton. The human necessity of religion, the inherent tolerance of polytheism, the duty of the citizen to conform to the established cult, its utilitarian social function, are all emphasised at the beginning. 'The various modes of worship which prevailed in the Roman world were all considered by the people as equally true, by the philosopher as equally false, and by the magistrate as equally useful.' Like Middleton, Gibbon relies on 'the admirable work of Cicero, *de Natura Deorum*', and he remarks, with evident approval, that 'Socrates, Epicurus, Cicero and Plutarch always inculcated decent reverence for the religion of their own country and of mankind'.[167] At the end of the volume, Gibbon turns from paganism to Christianity. The Roman Empire, he writes, had now been invaded by a 'pure and humble religion', 'fitted to inspire the most rational esteem and conviction'; but this new religion had come attended by miracles and announcing itself as the fulfilment of a divine plan and of ancient prophecies. This miraculous apparatus was at the time a necessary accompaniment in order 'to attract the curiosity, the wonder and the veneration of the people', but Gibbon does not expect his readers to accept a literal interpretation which 'is repugnant to every principle of faith as well as reason'. Rather, he assumes, they will protect their rational faith by interposing that 'ample veil of allegory' which the most learned of the Fathers have 'carefully spread . . . over every tender part of the Mosaic dispensation'.[168]

So much for the prophecies. Then we come to the miracles: those miracles which, 'after obtaining the sanction of ages, have been lately attacked in a very free and ingenious enquiry' – that is, of course, by the *Free Inquiry* of Middleton. Fortunately, says Gibbon, 'the duty of an historian does not call upon him to interpose his private judgement in this nice and important controversy'. So he merely remarks on the difficulty of reconciling 'the interest of religion with that of reason', touches lightly on a few curious details, and then, in that wonderful passage of sustained irony, ceremoniously deplores 'the supine inattention of the pagan and philosophic world' which, during the age of Christ and his Apostles, failed altogether to notice the 'innumerable prodigies' which were taking place around them: 'the lame walked, the blind saw, the sick were healed, the dead were raised, demons were expelled, and the laws of nature were frequently suspended for the benefit of the Church'.[169]

The last two chapters of Gibbon's first volume raised a storm of protest, which seems genuinely to have taken Gibbon by surprise. As he afterwards wrote, 'the name of Gibbon was become as notorious as that of Middleton'.[170] And indeed, precisely at this time, the name of Middleton was acquiring a new notoriety. For in 1777 Augustus Hervey, 3rd earl of Bristol, the second son of Middleton's friend, decided to allow the publication of some of his father's letters to Middleton on the Roman Senate. For this purpose he allowed the rector of Ickworth, Dr Thomas Knowles, to examine the whole correspondence.[171]

Now the cat was let fairly out of the bag. To no man had Middleton expressed himself more freely than to Hervey. When Dr Knowles read those uninhibited letters which, for the past generation, had been hidden away at Ickworth, he was deeply shocked. He copied out the most damaging extracts and carried them to Cambridge (his old university). His friends there saw to it that 'they were multiplied so as soon to be dispersed all over the nation'.[172] So the orthodox could read, with a pleasant thrill of disapproval, that Middleton had sought the company of the dreadful Chubb in Salisbury, that he was 'squeamish' in his Christian studies, that he blamed himself for his 'ugly assent and consent' to the Thirty-Nine Articles, that he was more proud of his scepticism than of his faith, etc., etc. When Middleton's friend William Cole read these extracts, he was outraged. Middleton had always seemed to him exemplary in his morals, his Anglican conformity, his Christian professions. He had been so regular in his church-going, so decent in his observances, so respectable in his invariable gown, cassock and square cap. Now he seemed quite a different person: a rake, a sceptic, an infidel . . .[173] But in fact there was no need for surprise. There was nothing in these extracts which could not equally be found in Middleton's published works;[174] but being so widely disseminated, without their protective context, they provided the orthodox with new weapons against him. It was on the evidence of these extracts that Leslie Stephen, a century later, would describe Middleton as a 'covert' enemy of Christianity and 'one of the few divines who can fairly be accused of conscious insincerity'.[175]

It was against this background that Gibbon resolved, in 1778, to hit back against the clerical critics of the two famous chapters of the *Decline and Fall*.

So, in his devastating *Vindication*, he suspended his customary 'grave and temperate irony', and struck out. He now ranged himself firmly and defiantly on the side of Middleton. 'As the works of Dr Middleton may be found in every library', he wrote, 'so it is not impossible that a diligent search may still discover some remains of the writings of his adversaries';[176] and again, 'a theological barometer might be formed, of which the cardinal' – i.e. Baronius – 'and our countryman Dr Middleton should constitute the opposite and remote extremities, as the former sunk to the lowest degree of credulity which was compatible with learning, and the latter rose to the highest pitch of scepticism in anywise consistent with religion'.[177] How far Middleton's views were consistent with religion is a nice question. The answer to it depends on our definition of religion.

All through his life Gibbon maintained his position, which, in respect of religion, was identical with that of Middleton. Like Middleton, he confessed that he 'was attached to the old pagan establishment' and saw the maunderings of the Christian Fathers as a sad decline from the philosophy of Cicero.[178] But he was not an infidel – like Middleton he strongly resented 'the invidious name of unbeliever'.[179] He was a deist, who repudiated revelation but believed that 'the God of Nature has written his existence on all his works and his law in the heart of man'.[180] But he was also an English deist who, unlike the French deist Voltaire, respected 'the religion of his own country, and of mankind'. For the English deists were heretics within the Church rather than enemies outside it. Gibbon did not, of course, take his material from them. He always went back to the original sources and used his own judgment. But his attitude was theirs. He was, in a sense, the last of the deists as well as the first of the modern historians, subsuming, in his new historical synthesis, the material supplied by Middleton.[181]

Subsuming Middleton's work, Gibbon also transcended it, and thereby drove him out of fashion. For another generation Middleton's perfect style preserved him: at least it preserved his *Life of Cicero*; but in the pious nineteenth century, which had silently absorbed so much of his work, he lost his general appeal. However, in his own college in Cambridge he had one great devotee. Macaulay read all his works with close attention and was clearly fascinated both by them and by him. Again and again, in his own writings, he returned to Middleton, whose character he did not admire but whose works delighted him. 'No man in English literature', he wrote, 'had a clearer and more just understanding, or a style which more exactly and agreeably expressed his meaning.'[182] His own set of Middleton's published works is sprinkled with marginal notes, sometimes – when prudence overcame him – in the decent obscurity of the Greek language. Sometimes he was critical of Middleton's scholarship, sometimes of his evasions. Why, he asked, did Middleton not follow his own reasoning to the limit – that is, blow up the miracles of Christ as well as those of the Church? Or, if he was unwilling to do that, and wanted preferment in the Church, why did he not, like any rational man – like Macaulay himself – conform and shut up? Macaulay never had much sympathy with the dilemmas, or the compromises, of more sensitive men. But on other occasions he was enthusiastic: Middleton was, after all, a robust, free-thinking whig, and in some respects his voice still needed (and needs) to be heard. In 1843, when Newman and his Oxford friends were putting the clock back and reviving, with infantile credulity, the miracles of the third and fourth centuries, Macaulay could exclaim, 'the times require a Middleton'.[183]

CHAPTER 6

David Hume, Historian

As a historian, who now reads David Hume? As a philosopher, he is one of the immortals, but his *History of England*, to which in his lifetime he owed greater fame, sits neglected on the shelves of English country houses and is sold as a job lot in country sales. And yet, for over sixty years, Hume dominated the interpretation of English history. He was the first of 'philosophical historians'. Voltaire praised him as a historian such as could only write in a free country. Gibbon regarded him as 'the Tacitus of Scotland' (and Tacitus, he once wrote, was the only writer who lived up to his idea of a 'philosophical historian'); when he read him, he admitted, he put down his own pen in despair of imitation; and when he had completed the first volume of *The Decline and Fall of the Roman Empire*, the labour of years seemed to him rewarded by an approving letter from Hume. For the next sixty years whig historians fretted beneath the apparently permanent empire of Hume. Finally, Macaulay set out, consciously, to dethrone him. Hume, he wrote, was 'an accomplished advocate' who, 'without positively asserting much more than he can prove,' emphasised the facts which supported his cause and slid lightly over those which did not. Some would say that this was a perfect description of Macaulay. At all events, in Victorian England, Macaulay's advocacy prevailed. Hume went out of fashion. His facts – it is the fate of all historians – were overtaken; his philosophy was declared to be mere political prejudice; only his graceful style was allowed to remain; and literary style, it is generally agreed, cannot carry a reader through eight volumes of history which is presumed, from the start, to be partisan and inaccurate.

But, in fact, is Hume's historical philosophy mere political prejudice? Is it likely that a philosopher of the quality of Hume suspended his intellectual power when he wrote history? Is it likely that Gibbon (who called himself a whig) and Voltaire (who was certainly not a tory) were gulled by a mere 'advocate'? Hume's political essays, which lie at the back of his *History*, are of recognised importance – far more important than those of Macaulay, which lie at the back of his. Now that Macaulay has sunk to a lower level, and is recognised as a skilful historical advocate preserved by his compelling narrative style, we may fairly look past him to the greater man whose lesser work he pushed off the bookstalls; and we may ask what was the intellectual content of that work which excited Voltaire and Gibbon, and how Hume's philosophy expressed itself in it. This is what has here been done by Mr Giuseppe Giarrizzo, the able and learned young Italian student of the English eighteenth century, who is already known for his work on Conyers Middleton and on Gibbon.[1]

As a historian, we all know, Hume was a tory. His letters, his autobiography, reveal his growing toryism. When he began his *History* he respected the standard work of his whig predecessor Rapin; but as he wrote (and he wrote, says Giarrizzo, even to the end, with Rapin in his hand), his opinions hardened. Rapin, he discovered, was 'totally despicable'. When his first volume was published, the whig world of 1754 treated it with cold contempt, and the only compliments and encouragement which he received were from the archbishops of Canterbury and Dublin – which, remarked 'the Great Infidel', 'seem two odd exceptions'. The archbishop of Canterbury even sent Hume a standing invitation to stay at Lambeth Palace, which greatly diverted him. 'You would do very well at Lambeth', the tory James Boswell told him on receiving this information, 'you would give them good politics and they would give you good religion.' As time passed, the tory bias in the *History* increased. And in his last years, as he corrected later editions, he applied himself to 'soften or expunge many villainous whig strokes which had crept into it'. To the earliest volume – the volume on the reigns of James I and Charles I – he made a hundred alterations, 'all invariably to the tory side'.

But if Hume was undoubtedly a tory, what was a tory in the last years of the 'whig ascendancy' of the eighteenth century? Since the reign of Queen Anne there had been no tories in power and non-Jacobite toryism, out of contact with practical politics, had dissolved into private grumbles. There was the toryism of rustic Squire Westerns who hated the Hanoverian 'court', and there was the toryism of high-church parsons who failed of promotion under a whig establishment; but Hume can hardly be accused of personal sympathy with these classes. There was the journalistic toryism of Bolingbroke; but Voltaire and Hume, though they both owed something to Bolingbroke, entertained little respect for his ideas: he was, as Gibbon wrote, *petit philosophe*. And anyway, Hume did not regard himself as a pure tory. Before 1745 his political views were those of an 'independent whig'. Even in 1748, when he was already contemplating historical writing, he defined himself as 'a whig, though a very sceptical one'. He was a whig as to things, a tory as to persons, he wrote in 1756. And looking back at his *History*, after it was finished, he lamented 'the plaguy prejudices of whiggism with which I was too much infected when I began this work'.

Thus Hume's *History* is the work of a man feeling his way out of 'sceptical' whiggism into 'philosophic' toryism. This gradual conversion was a complex process, developing partly out of his philosophical ideas, partly out of the politics of his time; and the deepening study of history, which it inspired, also confirmed it. Like Robertson and Gibbon, his partners in what Gibbon called 'the triumvirate of British historians', he was deeply influenced by Montesquieu, from whom he accepted the idea of an organic society; but even before reading Montesquieu he had ranged himself, by implication, against whig doctrines when he opposed Locke and insisted on the long-term validity of 'custom', rather than 'reason', in human affairs. Tracing them through the *Treatise*, the two *Enquiries* and the *Essays*, Giarrizzo shows the gradual crystallisation of these concepts in Hume's political and historical philosophy; but he also shows how this crystallisation was precipitated by certain external influences. One of these influences was general: Hume's life and upbringing in Scotland. Another was particular: the last Jacobite revolt against the Protestant, Hanoverian succession in Britain, 'the Forty-Five'.

The Scottish background of Hume, and indeed of 'philosophical history' generally in Britain, is obviously of great importance. How was it that the intellectual life of England was regalvanised by a country which, in the previous century, had been of ludicrous barbarity? Clearly the phenomenon must be explained, at least in part, by changes in the social structure of Scotland since the Union of 1707. But the science of sociology, which owes so much to the Scottish thinkers of the eighteenth century, has never been applied to this native problem, and all we can do is to note the fact. Because he was a Scot, Hume looked on English history from outside. He had standards of comparison which the too insular English whigs lacked. Their general theories might look well enough in isolation; but against Scottish experience they crumbled. In Scotland property was protected against the prerogative of the crown; the

Protestant religion was established in a bishopless, puritan form; there had been zealous 'whig' noblemen as in England; but where was the liberty which, in England, was ascribed to these causes? Where, for that matter, was civilisation? The Scots may boast of having produced the Scottish Enlightenment, but the fact remains that all its great figures took pains to dissociate themselves from their own literature and associate themselves with England. They took courses in 'de-Scoticisation' and pounced, with malicious pleasure, on the 'Scoticisms' which they detected in one another's works. But while repudiating the barbarism of their national past, they could not overlook its comparative significance in their study of social history. English historians had overlooked it, and consequently they had gone wrong. They had ascribed the universally envied liberty and prosperity of Hanoverian England to causes which were either imaginary, being based on too restricted evidence, or, if real, had produced very different results in other lands.

From his own observation of England and Scotland, and from the logical consequences of his philosophical principles, Hume found himself gradually drawn to conclusions very different from the established whig orthodoxy. That mankind was fundamentally the same in all times and places, so that a science of politics could be deduced from history, and that progress could be traced and its machinery explored, were commonplaces of the eighteenth-century philosophers. But why was it that this progress had occurred in England but not in Scotland? The whigs spoke of the original contract and the victory of their party and principles. But Hume saw no evidence of such a contract, no possible basis for imagining it outside English history, and his whole philosophy tended to reduce the credit of intellectual principles. Custom seemed more important to him than principle. Society, he believed, advanced through the sophistication of its organic structure and the 'revolutions of the mind' which accompanied such sophistication, not through the victory of this party or that; there was a 'natural history' of human societies as of human beliefs; and the central organ of a progressing society was a tough, continuous, flexible authority, held in place and made to function freely by the existence of other organs. The most important of these other organs, he came to believe, was an independent, intermediate class, between the crown and the unthinking people; and this class he identified, regardless of particular principles, with the prosperous, traditional gentry.

Looking at British history, Hume saw that in Scotland, in effect, there was no such class; and it was because there was no such class that there was, for practical purposes, no liberty. In England, on the other hand, that class had been the essential motor of progress. Under the Stuarts, it had sustained and – when free from outside pressure – contained the crown. But under the Hanoverians, he believed, and especially under Walpole, it was being slowly undermined by the immense growth of that whig invention, the National Debt, which was creating, out of its ruin, a new élite of tax-farmers and fund-holders without either independence or traditional, customary authority. This interpretation was already halfway to toryism – of a kind. But the tories of the Walpole era were not yet eligible as the makers of progress. They were tainted with Jacobitism. That, for Hume, was too much. And so, in the 1740s, he would still openly proclaim himself, though with increasing reservations, a 'whig'.

However, in the middle of the 1740s, a spectacular event eased Hume's conversion to avowed toryism. The Hanoverian succession, which seemed so securely established, was suddenly challenged and nearly overthrown. A handful of Scottish Highlanders, 'the bravest, but still the most worthless' of British subjects, overran Scotland, occupied its capital and advanced to within 125 miles of London. The most admired political system in the world trembled before the assault of 5,000 northern barbarians. When the shock was over, all parties in Britain were determined that no such thing should happen again. One step taken to prevent it was the abolition, in 1747, of the feudal jurisdiction of the Scottish nobility. Another was the repudiation by the English tories of the last relics of their Jacobite loyalty. Both these events were important in the development of toryism in general and of Hume's historical toryism in particular.

The feudal jurisdictions of the Scottish nobility had already aroused English interest in the time of the puritan republic. It was thanks to these powers that Scottish armies had been raised to invade England in the Stuart cause in 1648 and 1651, and the republic had therefore resolved, at one blow, to destroy the social basis of the Stuart cause in Scotland and emancipate a Scottish 'middle class', or the beginnings of it.[2] But the restored Stuarts had brought back the abuse, and they were wise in their generation: for it would serve them again after their second fall. In 1740 the abolition of the feudal jurisdiction was demanded on the grounds that they had caused the 'wicked and unnatural' Jacobite rebellion of 1715 and would cause another.[3] After the shock of 1745 the lesson was learned. Hume himself was deeply interested in this structural change in Scottish society which at once ended Jacobitism and opened the way to a new intermediate, independent class in Scotland. It was on this subject that he opened a correspondence with Montesquieu, whose *De l'Esprit des lois*, published in 1748, strengthened the base of his increasingly 'tory' philosophy; and when he came to write the history of Anglo-Saxon England, he would turn to this subject for an apt illustration. Scouting the (whig) idea that the Anglo-Saxon Witenagemot was a guarantee of liberty, he would remark: 'the Highlands of Scotland have long been entitled by law to every privilege of British subjects; but it was not till very lately that the common people could in fact enjoy these privileges'. When writing of Cromwell he did not, however, mention that the first emancipation had come from the usurper whom, like all his contemporaries, he failed to understand.

The emancipation of toryism from its Jacobite taint, the discovery of Montesquieu – these are successive stages in the removal of Hume's 'whig' scruples, the release of his fundamentally 'tory' philosophy. In 1748, in his *Essay on the Protestant Succession*, he based the claim of the Hanoverian dynasty not on whig doctrines, but, in effect, on its continuity with the old, pre-Hanoverian system which the 'factions' of the Stuart kings and the whigs had needlessly convulsed but which had now settled down under new management. About the same time he decided to realise an old plan, implicit in his political thinking: to illustrate his philosophy by writing a new history of England from the beginning to his own time.[4] According to the official whig interpretation, the English constitution was 'a regular plan of liberty', drawn from Anglo-Saxon origins and preserved against royal encroachment by the whig party, the defenders of property. Hume would show that there was no such constitution – the historic constitution of England was 'an inconsistent fabric' whose provisions were 'neither fixed nor regarded'; that liberty arises not from an inviolate constitution, or the pressure of a party, but from economic change, the creation of a strong monarchy and a strong middle class of gentry in alliance with it, and the revolution of manners which accompany such changes; and that political faction and religious enthusiasm, so far from advancing, had positively retarded progress. In particular, he would show that the great enemies of English liberty had been the very people who had carried the defence of private property against the crown, and of Protestantism against the episcopal Church, to its farthest extent, and among whom there had been no solid, independent 'tory' party but only a frontal opposition between a 'Jacobite' Stuart court and a 'whig' opposition: his own Scotland.

In the first volume the challenge was thrown emphatically down. Rapin had declared that England had never been less flourishing than under James I. Hume reversed the statement. Never before that reign, he wrote, had there been 'a more sensible increase . . . of all the advantages which distinguish a flourishing people'. With Clarendon, against the puritan writers, he asserted the prosperity of the 'despotic' years of Charles I; with Clarendon, against Hobbes, he argued that 'mixed monarchy' was a viable system. James I and Charles I, looking at the surface or at false foreign analogies, had mistaken it; but they could have been corrected. The structure of English society contained the means of correction. This was shown in 1660 and again in 1688. There was no need, in the 1640s, of civil war. The convulsions of those years were caused, not by any inherent necessity but by the disastrous introduction of religious fanaticism and a foreign army: the fanaticism and the army of Scotland.

Throughout his history Hume treats Scotland with unfailing contempt. To him it is a barbarous country which was only rendered capable of progress in 1707, perhaps in 1747. His earliest judgment is of the 'imperfect, or rather fabulous annals which are obtruded on us by the Scottish historians'; his latest refers to the attempt of the whig hero, the earl of Argyll, who, at the time of Monmouth's revolt, attempted to raise Scotland also against James II, and with equally disastrous consequences. 'It was in vain', comments Hume, 'that Argyll summoned a nation so lost to all sense of liberty, so degraded by repeated iniquities, to rise in vindication of their violated laws and privileges. The greater part of those who declared for him were his own vassals: men who, if possible, were still more sunk in slavery than the rest of the nation.' Between these two judgments, the character of Hume's Scotland remains constant. In the Middle Ages it is beneath notice; in the sixteenth century it is rather 'a confederacy, and that not a close one, of petty princes than a regular system of civil polity'; and with the Reformation there 'commenced in Scotland that cant, hypocrisy and fanaticism which long infested that kingdom and which, though now mollified by the lenity of the civil power, is still ready to break out on all occasions'. Against Knox, whose 'political principles . . . were as full of sedition as his theological were of rage and bigotry', and against the Calvinist preachers generally, who introduced into Scotland 'the whole tyranny of the Inquisition, though without its order', Hume extolled that 'amiable princess', Mary Stuart, as a woman of French culture who had the misfortune, in her new kingdom, to be 'surrounded with a

factious turbulent nobility, a bigoted people and insolent ecclesiastics'.[5] And
when the Scots, in 1640, invaded England and sent their preachers to impose
their primitive doctrines on the advanced society whose divisions they were
exploiting, Hume excels himself in his sardonic account of their 'holy rhetoric
. . . delivered with ridiculous cant and a provincial accent, full of barbarism
and ignorance'.

To Hume, Scotland is the *reductio ad absurdum* of the whig philosophy.
His own positive 'tory' philosophy is represented by the history of England
which, from the time when the third estate arose to independence and allied
itself with the traditional power of the crown, followed a very different
course: a course of orderly progress which, but for the interruptions of whiggish and Scottish faction, might have been more orderly still. For liberty and
progress depend on authority, continuity, social cohesion; they are slow
growths, requiring 'such improvement in knowledge and morals as can only
be the result of reflexion and experience, and must grow to perfection during
several ages of settled and established government'; and without such a
structural basis mere constitutional guarantees are like 'the seeming liberty,
or rather licentiousness, of the Anglo-Saxons' under which 'the great body
even of the free citizens . . . really enjoyed much less true liberty than where
the execution of the laws is most severe, and where subjects are reduced to
the strictest subordination and dependence on the civil magistrate'.

So Hume evolved his sociological toryism. Ironically, even as he evolved
it, the balance between England and Scotland was being changed. In the late
1750s, with the rise to power of Chatham, and even more with the accession
of George III in 1768 and the emergence of the radical John Wilkes in the
early 1770s, Hume saw a return of 'faction' comparable, in his eyes, with the
struggles which, in the last century, had precipitated the 'dangerous and
unnecessary' Civil War. On the other hand, the new tories, the 'King's
Friends', of whom he counted himself one, were driven back upon a Scottish
base and were violently attacked by the English whigs, not only as servile flat-
terers of prerogative but as Scots: the true descendants of those Scots who,
in the days of the later Stuarts, had been 'lost to all sense of liberty', 'sunk in
slavery'. Faced by this recrudescence of 'faction', this national hatred, Hume
became more tory than ever. He saw the continuity of English history threatened by the English whigs and championed by the Scottish tories. In these
years his private letters assume a new tone – a tone almost of embitterment.
He will never return to England, never cross the Tweed; England is 'sunk in

stupidity and barbarism and faction'; freedom has outrun itself – 'so much liberty is incompatible with human society'; and he hopes, notwithstanding his age, to see 'a public bankruptcy, the total revolt of America, the expulsion of the English from the East Indies, the diminution of London to less than a half, and the restoration of the government to the king, nobility and gentry of this realm. To adorn the scene, I hope also that some hundreds of Patriots will make their exit at Tyburn, and improve English Eloquence by their dying speeches.' These were the years when Hume, in revising his *History*, was expunging the 'villainous whig strokes' that had crept in. In a fit of disgust with 'the licentiousness of our odious Patriots', he even struck out the words 'and happy' in the passage in which he had traced to the revolution of 1688 'that singular and happy government which we enjoy at present'. But at this point he had second thoughts; at the last moment he wrote to the printer and had the words restored.

It would be as unfair to judge Hume's historical philosophy by these explosions as it would be to judge them by Macaulay's summary verdict. That philosophy, as Giarrizzo has shown, was not the propaganda of a partisan. It was rooted in Hume's moral and political philosophy, as already shown in his *Treatise* and his *Essays*, and deepened by his reading of Montesquieu and his own experience. Its conclusions can be questioned. Would the social progress which was ultimately made possible by the Reformation really have been achieved without the 'enraged and fanatical reformers'? Would the English liberty which amazed Montesquieu and Voltaire really have been secured if Charles I had met no resistance except from the gentle pressures of English society? The answer to such questions cannot be assumed. But at least Hume, in placing the machinery of progress firmly into a social context, looked at history more profoundly than Macaulay, and now that the obliterating shadow of Macaulay has passed by, he deserves to reappear. Besides, he could write. A writer whose faultless, ironic style struck despair into the heart of Gibbon should not be allowed to die.

CHAPTER 7

The Idea of *The Decline and Fall of the Roman Empire*

W E ALL TEND to simplify, perhaps to dramatise, our mental development. In retrospect, the slow processes of the mind are disguised, sometimes even obliterated, by the dramatic moment of discovery, or conversion. St Augustine's *tolle lege*, Newton's apple . . . intellectual history is full of such episodes which immortalise, though they may not explain, crucial stages in the transformation of thought. In the historical philosophy of the Enlightenment there is one such moment, and it too has been immortalised by retrospective isolation. 'It was at Rome, on 15th October 1764', Gibbon wrote in his autobiography, 'as I sat musing amidst the ruins of the Capitol, while the barefooted friars were singing vespers in the Temple of Jupiter, that the idea of writing the decline and fall of the city first started to my mind . . .'[1]

Those who (like myself) regard *The Decline and Fall of the Roman Empire* as the greatest historical work in our language must always be thankful for that dramatic moment. What would have happened, we may ask, if Gibbon had lacked that unforgettable experience? What would he then have written, if he had written any great work, in the next twenty years of his life? He himself has told us of his earlier projects: the projects which, up to that moment, had occupied his mind. He had conceived of English subjects – Richard Coeur de Lion, the baronial wars against Henry III, the life of Sir Philip Sidney, or of Sir Walter Ralegh. He had thought of Italian subjects too: of the French invasion of Italy in 1494 and the rule of the Medici in Renaissance Florence. He had also pondered long on another subject which fascinated him: the history of the liberty of the Swiss. How fortunate, we may now say, that he did not waste his genius on these subjects in which later scholarship would inevitably have overtaken him, as it has overtaken the historical works of Gibbon's revered contemporary masters, David Hume, the historian of England, and William Robertson, the historian of Scotland, of Charles V and of America! Who now reads those works, those 'well turned periods' of Robertson, those 'careless inimitable beauties' of Hume, which first inspired the young Gibbon with ambition, then caused him, as he tells us, 'to close the book with a mixed sensation of delight and despair'? And would not the same fate (we may ask), however unjust, have overtaken Gibbon too, had he confined himself to those medieval or modern subjects which had successively engaged his mind while he 'bumperised', in the barren years 1760–62, with his rural neighbours in the Hampshire militia?

Fortunately he did not. Early in 1763, while he was still beholding, 'in a dark and doubtful perspective', the 'splendid subject' of Medicean Florence, the affairs of Europe were suddenly transformed. The long war, the Seven Years War with France, was over; all America north of Mexico was British – for a time; and with the disbandment of the militia, temporary captain Gibbon could at last extract from his father, temporary major Gibbon, the fulfilment of that old promise: a tour of the Continent. With his mind still unsure, he crossed the Channel. He visited Paris and mixed, in the salons of the great, with the philosophers of the French Enlightenment – Diderot and d'Alembert, Helvétius and Holbach. He revisited Lausanne, the place of his education, and there settled down, in more luxurious circumstances, for several months. At Lausanne he made two new friends. One was John Baker Holroyd, afterwards Lord Sheffield, whose 'long and active friendship', as he wrote in his will, he could never repay. Modern admirers of Gibbon may say the same; for it is to Lord Sheffield that we owe the preservation and publication of Gibbon's autobiography and other papers. The other was William Guise, the son of a Gloucestershire baronet. Afterwards Guise, Gibbon and Holroyd would all sit together in Parliament. And it was with Guise that Gibbon now completed his continental tour, going on from Switzerland into Savoy, over the Alps to Austrian Milan, to Medicean Florence, to papal Rome.

With his mind still on the Medici, Gibbon lingered long in Florence. He visited the memorials of their rule and admired the products of their patronage. But then came Rome and that famous moment in the ruined Capitol. It was a moment of inspiration, never to be forgotten. Mr Arnold Toynbee, who, I fear, does not much like Gibbon or the Enlightenment in general, has described it rather grudgingly as the sole moment of inspiration ever experienced by Gibbon. This is one of the points – there are others – on which I venture to dissent from my distinguished compatriot.[2] I believe that

Gibbon's intellectual life was full of excitement, and that this experience in Rome, far from being a solitary flash, suddenly sparked off by an immediate occasion, was merely one episode in a long process of fermentation. In fact I suspect that Gibbon himself, in retrospect, may have dramatised that experience and, in so doing, over-simplified – at least to us who do not live in the eighteenth century or recognise all his allusions – the origin of his life's work. That work, I shall suggest, had deeper origins. It was not, I believe, merely the realisation of a sudden idea, of a momentary accidental inspiration. It was something far greater, and to his contemporaries far more significant, than that. It was the fulfilment of the historical ambitions and questionings of a whole generation.

But before coming to that genial subject, let me dispose of a more immediate issue. The modern enemies of the Enlightenment sometimes represent its thinkers in general, and Gibbon in particular, as cold, unimaginative creatures. This view began, I suppose, with the romantic movement. 'Gibbon's style is detestable', wrote Coleridge sourly, 'but his style is not the worst thing about him', etc., etc.[3] But of course such a view is a travesty of the truth. Certainly Gibbon, and most of his friends, disapproved of public 'enthusiasm'. 'My temper', he tells us, 'is not very susceptible of enthusiasm, and the enthusiasm which I do not feel I have ever scorned to affect. But' – he goes on (for the generalisation is only introduced to lead to the exception) – 'at the distance of 25 years I can neither forget nor express the strong emotion which agitated my mind as I first approached and entered the eternal city. After a sleepless night, I trod, with a lofty step, the ruins of the Forum; each memorable spot where Romulus stood, or Tully spoke, or Caesar fell, was at once present to my eye; and several days of intoxication were lost or enjoyed before I could descend to a cool and minute investigation.'[4] This is not the language of frigidity; nor is the excitement merely retrospective: Gibbon's letters to his father from Rome fully confirm the exaltation of that time. Nor, indeed, is this the only evidence of such emotion. Again and again, whenever we look below the polished – the six-times-polished – surface of the *Autobiography*, or even below the august, coruscating prose of the *Decline and Fall*, we discover warmth and movement. 'I sighed as a lover, I obeyed as a son': how often has that phrase been quoted to indicate the low temperature of Gibbon's emotions! And yet, when we look at the raw materials of the *Autobiography*, at the intimate papers which Lord Sheffield caused to be shut away from profane eyes for a whole century,[5] how different, how much more impassioned, the whole affair of Gibbon's romance with Suzanne Curchod appears! The man who, at the age of sixteen, had been swept from the tepid formalism of the established Anglican Church, the Church of Porteous and Hoadly, into the warm delusions of popery as seen through the golden prose of Bossuet and the majestic poetry of Dryden; the man who, reconverted, and faced by the marvellous, outrageous, newly rebuilt baroque abbey of Einsiedeln, flaunting its costly enchantments 'in the poorest corner of Europe', found himself animated by the spirit of the old Swiss reformers; the man whose humanity was revolted by being carried over the Alpine passes by human porters, *'mes semblables'*, and who saw, in every gilded moulding in the palace of Turin, 'a village of Savoyards ready to die of hunger, cold and poverty';[6] the man who, in the last year of his life, when he could scarcely move without pain, hurried from Lausanne to London, skirting the armies of the French Revolution and the European coalition, within earshot of the French cannonade, in order to be with the suddenly widowed Lord Sheffield, was certainly not a cold, torpid soul; nor could I ever agree with Mr Toynbee in describing the eighteenth century, that century of new sensibility, and the Enlightenment, that movement of heightened humanity, as a mere 'weary lull' of exceptionally low temperature in the long, fevered decline of the West.

Gibbon's enthusiasm is, I believe, constantly discernible, even in his writings; and if we search more deeply in those writings, or more widely in the intellectual world around him, we can, I think, detect the successive stages of illumination which were brought together in the idea with which I am concerned: the idea of the *Decline and Fall*. The major stages, I shall suggest, were three. First, there was Gibbon's introduction to the new philosophy of the eighteenth century in Lausanne. Secondly, there was his discovery – an intoxicating discovery – of the great teacher of the new historians of the eighteenth century: Montesquieu. Thirdly, there was the general preoccupation of his age with the problem – 'the great problem of the 18th century' as an Italian scholar has called it[7] – of the later Roman Empire and the Middle Ages. Only against this larger background, only as the culmination of this slower process, does Gibbon's Roman experience, I suggest, acquire its full significance.

For the first of these stages – for Gibbon's introduction to the new philosophy – we must go back eleven years, to his early exile from England: to that sudden, shameful removal from the premature liberty and laxity of unreformed Oxford to the straitened lodgings, mean diet and strict supervision of a Calvinist minister in Switzerland. How little Gibbon's father, that amiable, indolent, feckless Tory squire, can have dreamed of the consequences of his impulsive act! A widower, without much interest in education, he had dumped his inconvenient son, out of 'perplexity rather than prudence', at Oxford. The result had been disastrous. The boy had become a papist. That, of course, was a fate worse than death, and it provoked Edward Gibbon senior into action. So, once more out of perplexity rather than prudence, he dumped his son elsewhere – further from temptation, further from popery, further from home. That done, he could return to Hampshire, mingle freely with the highest and lowest society, for which (as his son remarked) he was equally fitted, enter his horses for the local races, and sink, quiet and content, into the glutinous web of debt. And yet for the young Gibbon the consequences of this abrupt removal were enormous: how enormous we can hardly envisage unless we compare the intellectual condition, in the 1750s, of England and Switzerland.

The European Enlightenment, admittedly, owes much to England. The Englishmen Bacon, Locke and Newton were its prophets; the English Revolution of 1688 was its political starting-point; the English deists were its midwives. But in England itself, by 1750, these forces were spent. The great thinkers of the last century had become totem figures; the last of them, Newton, had died in majestic orthodoxy, carefully concealing his own heretical past. The whig revolutionaries had become a new establishment, an aristocracy fixed in complacent postures of ancestor worship. The deist controversy was played out. David Hume, in his letters, never ceased to lament the intellectual sterility of England in his time, 'so sunk in stupidity and barbarism and faction that you may as well think of Lapland for an author'. Only Scotland and America, he thought, produced writers of English; the only work of literature produced in England in the last generation, he wrote, was '*Tristram Shandy*, bad as it is'.

We may think this verdict unjust – Gibbon himself, that enthusiastic admirer of Fielding's *Tom Jones*, would certainly have thought it unjust – but there is no doubt that it was Hume's true opinion. When the first volume of the *Decline and Fall* broke the spell, Hume confessed to Gibbon his amazement. 'Your country-men', he wrote, 'for almost a generation', had so given themselves up to 'barbarous and absurd faction', and so neglected all polite letters, that 'I no longer expected any valuable production ever to come from them.'[8] The English literary scene was dominated, in that generation, by Dr Johnson; and what Johnson and his obedient biographer thought of the

Enlightenment, we know. To them Voltaire was a coxcomb, Hume and Gibbon were poisonous infidels, Rousseau should be transported to the Plantations, Robertson was damned as a Presbyterian, and Adam Smith (according to that model of polite table manners, Dr Johnson) was not only as dull a dog as he had ever met but 'a most disagreeable fellow' whose wine, at dinner parties, 'bubbled in his mouth'.[9]

But if England, in those years, seemed to have lost touch with the Enlightenment which it had once inspired, how different was Switzerland! What Holland had been in the seventeenth century, Switzerland had become in the eighteenth. It was the haven to which philosophy had fled from English indifference, French censorship, Italian persecution. Thither the greatest of eighteenth-century Italian historians, Pietro Giannone, had fled from the long arm of the Church – until that long arm hooked him out again and stuffed him into a Savoyard dungeon to languish and die. There Montesquieu had published his greatest work. There Voltaire had finished and published his most ambitious historical study, his *Essai sur les moeurs*. This vigorous intellectual life of Switzerland had its centre among the liberal 'Arminian' ministers of Geneva and Lausanne. After a long struggle, these liberals had defeated the old die-hards of the Word and inaugurated, with the new century, a new era of freedom. It was they who welcomed Giannone and corresponded with Voltaire. One of them, Jacob Vernet, a minister of Geneva, was a personal link between Giannone, Montesquieu and Voltaire. Another, Daniel Pavillard, a minister of Lausanne, was Gibbon's tutor. And it was through them and their philosophic teachers – Jean-Pierre de Crousaz, Jean Leclerc and Jean Babeyrac – that Gibbon would find his way to the European, and even the English, writers who had never been commended to him in tory Oxford: to Grotius and Pufendorf, Chillingworth and Bayle, Locke and Tillotson. Through them also he would discover the great philosophic historians: read Giannone, devour Montesquieu, call on Voltaire.

Switzerland, it is not too much to say, introduced Gibbon to the eighteenth-century Enlightenment. It also introduced him to some of the great works of seventeenth-century scholarship which had equally been ignored in Oxford. For some of the best seventeenth-century scholars, those who had most influence on Gibbon, were either Swiss, like the legal historian Jacques Godefroy and the numismatist Ezechiel von Spanheim, or French Huguenots who belonged to the Calvinist International, whose capital was in Geneva, like Jacques Basnage, the historian of the Jews, and Isaac de

Beausobre, the historian of the Manichees. He would say as much himself. 'Such as I am in genius or learning or manners', he wrote, 'I owe my creation to Lausanne: it was in that school, that the statue was discovered in the block of marble'; and again, 'if my childish revolt against the religion of my country had not stripped me in time of my academic gown, the five important years, so liberally improved in the studies and conversation of Lausanne, would have been steeped in port and prejudice among the monks of Oxford. Had the fatigue of idleness compelled me to read, the path of learning would not have been enlightened by a ray of philosophic freedom'[10] – the philosophic freedom which, from Switzerland, had reanimated the subject which Gibbon, from his earliest years, had resolved to pursue: history.

Above all, at Lausanne Gibbon discovered Montesquieu. This was the second of the three great experiences I have mentioned. It was the greatest single inspiration of his years of study. Whenever Gibbon mentions Montesquieu, we sense the note of excitement. Above all other books, he tells us, 'my delight', in those Lausanne years, 'was in the frequent perusal of Montesquieu, whose energy of style and boldness of hypothesis were powerful to awaken and stimulate the genius of his age'.[11] Before leaving Lausanne, Gibbon would begin his first published work, his *Essai sur l'étude de la littérature* (for all this time he preferred to write in French, not English), in which he would hail Montesquieu as the true guide (and Tacitus as the true example) for a philosophic historian. Even the style of that essay, he would afterwards write, was corrupted by the too faithful imitation of Montesquieu. And nearly thirty years later, in his last volume, he would pay a final tribute to that early master whose work, for the last forty years, he said, had been the greatest stimulus in historical enquiry.[12]

What was the lesson which Gibbon learned from Montesquieu? Briefly, it was that human history is not a mere pageant of dramatic (or undramatic) events, nor even a storehouse of noble (or deterrent) examples, but a process, and a process governed, in its detail, not by a divine plan, as the 'universal historians' of the past – the Protestant Ralegh, the Catholic Bossuet – had thought, but by a complex of social forces which a 'philosophic historian' – that is, a historian who looked behind mere events for fundamental ideas, causes and connexions, who saw 'the chief use of history' (in Hume's words) as the discovery of 'the constant and universal principles of human nature' – could isolate and describe. Geography, climate, economic resources – these lay at the very base of history; institutions, laws, religion – these, conditioned

by them but developing their own momentum, created in turn new and
subtler forces to whose interwoven pattern human behaviour was subject.
'Men are governed by many things', wrote Montesquieu: 'climate, religion,
laws, maxims of government, examples of things past, customs, manners;
from all which is derived a general spirit'; and this 'general spirit' he strove to
illustrate by thousands of examples, deductions, aphorisms in his great work,
published in 1748, the work which we can see as the foundation of the
modern science of sociology: *De l'Esprit des lois*.

Gibbon, of course, was not the first historian to read *De l'Esprit des lois*.
Already, in 1749, within a year of its publication, David Hume, passing through
Savoy, had been captivated by it. He had at once opened a correspondence
with Montesquieu; he had had part of Montesquieu's book published in
Edinburgh; and he had decided to become a historian himself. Hume's *History*,
which began to appear in 1754, was the application to English history of
Montesquieu's principles. A few years later another Scotsman, William
Robertson, applied them to Scottish history too. All the great Scotsmen of that
generation – Adam Ferguson, Lord Kames, Adam Smith, John Millar –
professed themselves disciples of Montesquieu, whose works were repeatedly
reprinted in Scotland. For we are now in the great era of the Scottish
Enlightenment: an enlightenment which, as in Switzerland, had followed the
defeat of Calvinist bigotry. William Robertson himself, minister of the Kirk,
Moderator of its General Assembly, friend of Hume, admirer of Voltaire, was
the leader of the liberal clergy of Scotland, just as the clerical friends of
Giannone and Voltaire – the Vernets, the Turrettini, the Tronchins – had led
the liberal clergy of Switzerland. Thanks to such men Gibbon could refer to the
'strong ray of philosophic light' that has 'broke forth from Scotland in our own
time', and could appreciate particularly those tributes which came to him, in
London, from 'the northern part of our island, whither taste and philosophy
seem to have retired from the smoke and hurry of this immense capital'.[13]

They had indeed. In those very years the 'immense capital' of London
bowed before the Great Cham of English literature, Dr Johnson: Johnson
who did not look northwards to Scotland with veneration, but who, again
unlike Gibbon, felt a comfortable glow on approaching the spired and clois-
tered orthodoxy of Oxford. It is interesting to observe Johnson's recorded
remarks on history: they show that to him, and to his circle, the new 'philosophical history' which had triumphed in Scotland meant absolutely
nothing. History, to Johnson, was mere mechanical compilation in which

'there is but a shallow stream of thought' and 'all the greatest powers of the human mind are quiescent'. He never mentioned Montesquieu, boasted of having never read the 'infidel' Hume, put the hack-work of Goldsmith above 'the verbiage of Robertson', and praised as 'the first of historians' the now-forgotten author of what Gibbon would call 'a partial and verbose compilation from Latin writers, 1,300 folio pages of speeches and battles', devoid of any 'tincture of philosophy and criticism'.[14] 'The part of an historian', Gibbon once wrote, 'is as honourable as that of a mere chronicler or compiler of gazettes is contemptible.' It is obvious that to Johnson this distinction did not exist. However ennobled by dignity of language or moral commentary, history to him was essentially chronicles or gazettes.

But if Montesquieu had pointed the way, and Hume and Robertson had illustrated it, what subject should Gibbon, now that he had been inspired by these examples, choose for his own? Here let me interpose a general point. All great historians, whatever their subject, respond to some extent to the demands of their age. Many of them have been directly inspired by a present crisis. Such were Thucydides, Machiavelli, Guicciardini, Clarendon. Others have turned to a carefully chosen chapter of past history in order the better to interpret their own age. Thus Paolo Sarpi, the greatest of seventeenth-century historians – 'that incomparable historian' as Gibbon called him – looked back to the Council of Trent in order to explain the resistance of Venice to papal aggression in his own time. Similarly the nineteenth-century English whigs – and their French disciples like Guizot – would see the justification of their present politics in the Glorious Revolution of England in 1688. It was this second category into which the 'philosophic historians' of the eighteenth century fell. To interpret their own times, times not of crisis but of new Enlightenment, they looked back into previous centuries. They saw the history of humanity in a long perspective; and they asked themselves a series of questions about the past. Above all, they asked questions about the declining Roman Empire, the Dark and Middle Ages of Europe.

Why did they ask these questions? Their predecessors of the seventeenth century did not. To their predecessors Antiquity and the Middle Ages looked quite different. In the seventeenth century Antiquity, to churchmen, was the age of pagan error from which Europe had not declined but risen; and if the humanists, as admirers of Greece and Rome, admitted the decline, they could not yet detect the signs of recovery. To them Antiquity was a heroic age which the degenerate modern could only admire, not judge. But with the eighteenth

century, which began with the victory of the 'moderns' over the 'ancients', a
new attitude was possible. A revolution had happened in the minds of men.
Europe, they felt, had grown up; it was no longer in tutelage either to the
Church or to the ancients; and the moderns, in Basil Willey's phrase, 'across
the vast gulf of the monkish and deluded past', could 'salute the Ancients from
an eminence perhaps as lofty as their own'. From such an eminence they
could judge; over such a distance they could compare. They could measure
progress in the past and infer progress to come. And why, they asked, had this
progress happened? Why had it not been continuous? Why had the high civilisation of Antiquity not led directly to the high civilisation of modernity, but
foundered in that dark, intermediary millennium? And finally, since that had
happened once, might it perhaps happen again? Could the new Antonine Age
of the eighteenth century, this wonderful new century of 'light and freedom'
so slowly and painfully achieved, also perhaps founder in a new age of
monkish darkness and 'gothic' barbarism?

To answer these questions – even to pose them – would have been impossible in the seventeenth century; but they haunted the new 'philosophic historians' of the eighteenth. Listen to the earliest of them, Giannone – the great,
unfortunate Giannone whose work so deeply influenced both Montesquieu
and Gibbon. In his autobiography – which cannot have influenced either of
them, since it only saw the light a century later – Giannone describes his
preoccupation with this theme. As a young law student in Naples, he says, he
studied the legal codes of Theodosius and Justinian – and of course, like
Gibbon, he used and revered 'that stupendous work', the commentary on the
Theodosian code by the Swiss Protestant Jacques Godefroy – 'not as ends in
themselves, but as effective means to understand the origins and changes of
the Roman empire, and how, from its ruins, there arose so many new rulers,
laws, customs, kingdoms and republics in Europe'.[15] Later, the same question
was posed by the English patron of the European philosophers, Lord
Bolingbroke. 'Would you not be glad, my lord', he wrote, in his fifth *Letter on
the Study of History*, 'to see, in one stupendous draught, the whole progress of
that government' (he was referring to the government of Rome) 'from liberty
to servitude, the whole series of causes and effects, apparent and real, public
and private . . .? I am sorry to say it', added the fallen minister, who perhaps
generalised too widely his own catastrophe, 'this part of the Roman history
would be not only more curious and more authentic than the former, but of
more immediate and more important application to the present state of

Britain.'[16] Meanwhile one of Bolingbroke's French friends had already offered one answer to the problem. In his book *Considérations sur la grandeur des Romains et de leur décadence* Montesquieu gave his views on the subject; and Montesquieu's Scottish disciples all took up, in different ways, the same unsolved – still unsolved – problem. As one of them, Dugald Stewart, wrote, 'it was indeed a subject worthy of their genius; for in the whole history of human affairs no spectacle occurs so wonderful in itself, or so momentous in its effects, as the growth of that system which took its rise from the conquests of the barbarians. In consequence of these, the Western parts of Europe were overspread with a thick night of superstition and ignorance which lasted nearly a thousand years; yet this event, which had at first so unpromising an aspect, laid the foundation of a state of society far more favourable to the general and permanent happiness of the human race than any which the world has hitherto seen.'[17]

That Gibbon, the greatest historical disciple of Montesquieu, should have taken up this challenge seems, in retrospect, almost inevitable. In his earliest work, his *Essai*, we see him groping towards it. Those modern themes which haunted his mind never caused him to suspend his classical studies. Indeed, it was while in camp with the Hampshire militia, and while thinking of modern topics, that he turned seriously to the study of Greek and made Homer 'the most intimate of my friends'. When he set out for Italy, still apparently intent on Medicean Florence, the books which he took with him were not Renaissance chronicles but ancient classics and modern antiquaries: books on the geography, the roads, the architecture, the coinage of Rome. Was this, we may ask, as we read the amazing catalogue of his travelling library, really the prospective chronicler of the Medici, or of the liberty of the Swiss, and not rather, even now, even before his Roman experience, the historian of the decline and fall of the Roman Empire?

And yet what historian could face, all at once, so huge a subject? Giannone had contented himself with a geographical fragment of it: he had studied the social consequences of the Church in the kingdom of Naples only. Hume had shown what could be done in one brilliant essay: his essay on the populousness of ancient nations, which reversed the orthodoxy of the humanists and of Montesquieu himself, is a landmark in the new methods of history. Robertson had swept over the whole period from Antiquity to the Renaissance in two long, masterly sketches: his introductory chapters to the histories of Charles V and of America. How much simpler it must have seemed to Gibbon to follow the example of these revered masters: to detach another manageable portion rather than tackle the whole gigantic problem! So, at first, he followed where they had led. His first subject, the French invasion of Italy, was inspired by Giannone;[18] the English subjects were suggested by Hume; Medicean Florence had been foreshadowed to him by those earlier masters, the Renaissance founders of 'philosophic history', Machiavelli and Guicciardini, who, as he would write, 'were justly esteemed the first historians of modern languages till, in the present age, Scotland arose to dispute the prize with Italy herself'.[19]

And then there was that other tempting subject, the liberty of the Swiss. That too was a living issue, a chapter in the rise of Europe from feudal barbarism to modern enlightenment. Switzerland, like Holland afterwards, had broken away from the feudal and clerical domination of the Habsburgs and the Vatican. As a result, it had become the receptacle of all those European heretics who had challenged the tyranny of their native traditions: of Erasmus, of Calvin, of Bucer, of Castellio, of Sozzini, of the English republicans, of the French Huguenots, of the Vaudois of Savoy, of the philosophers of the eighteenth century. What a splendid subject for a 'philosophic historian' who himself owed his philosophy to Lausanne! In 1762 Gibbon wrote of it with enthusiasm, but then seemed to turn sadly away. 'The materials', he wrote, 'are inaccessible to me, fast locked in the obscurity of an old barbarous German language of which I am totally ignorant, and which I cannot resolve to learn for this sole and peculiar purpose.' Like his contemporary and supporter, the great Greek scholar Richard Porson, Gibbon thought that life was too short to learn German – especially since he could read Mosheim in Latin and Winckelmann in French. It is never too short to learn Italian; so he turned back to Florence and the Medici and set out on his famous journey: the journey to which so many Northerners have owed their ultimate inspiration: the journey to Italy.

Thus all the subjects which in turn occupied Gibbon's mind can be seen as elements in the great problem which exercised the historians of the eighteenth century. Even in Rome, Gibbon's sudden vision was not of the whole problem, but of another element in it. What he saw was, as he makes quite clear, the decline and fall not of the empire but of the city of Rome. For if Medicean Florence was the patroness of the new ideas which would lead Europe out of gothic barbarism back to classical models and a new enlightenment, and if Swiss liberty was to provide the laboratory for the development of those ideas, could not the same long process be illustrated, perhaps more dramatically, in the medieval history of Rome itself, in the continuity and yet change of that eternal city, where the old temple of Jupiter had become the church of the Zocolanti, where the mole of Hadrian had become the papal prison, and where the insolent palaces of Renaissance popes looked down upon the ruined Coliseum whence they had been quarried? To Gibbon's romantic – yes, romantic – spirit, those crumbling arches and grass-grown amphitheatres that we still see in the drawings of Piranesi presented an epitome of the whole process which so fascinated his contemporaries: the process which had since been reversed from such small beginnings as the merchant republic of Florence and the liberty of the Swiss.

So the seed of a new subject was planted in Gibbon's mind. And yet, when transferred to the cool climate of Hampshire, that seed somehow did not germinate. His mind returned to Switzerland, that Switzerland to which he owed so much: his intellectual formation, the friends of his life – Georges Deyverdun, Lord Sheffield, the de Severy family – and to which he himself would return to spend his later years. In 1767, after again considering Medicean Florence, he came to a decision. He would write the history of the liberty of the Swiss. In his friend Deyverdun he had a translator from the German; 'my judgment as well as my enthusiasm', he writes, 'was satisfied with the glorious theme'; he planned its range, wrote the first book, and submitted it to the historical master whom he most revered, David Hume.

Hume's only objection was that it was written in French. He assumed that Gibbon had chosen French as the international language of today; but what, he asked, about tomorrow? 'Let the French triumph in the present diffusion of their tongue', wrote the junior negotiator of the Treaty of Paris, the first Scotch founder of Canada. 'Our solid and increasing establishments in America, where we need less dread the inundations of barbarians, promise a superior stability and duration to the English language.'[20] This answer of Hume clearly made a deep impression on Gibbon. As Mr Bond has pointed out, the ideas, even the phrases in it, reappear in the *Decline and Fall*.[21] Perhaps it decided Gibbon to write his great work in English. But Gibbon's immediate reply is interesting for another reason. 'I write in French', he explained, 'because I think in French and, strange as it may seem, I can say, with some shame but with no affectation, that it would be a matter of difficulty to me to compose in my native language.'[22] It is a reminder – one among many – that one of the greatest of English writers, though he 'gloried in the name of Englishman', though he described himself proudly as 'an Englishman and a whig', and though he sat in the English Parliament, was always, intellectually, not English but European.[23]

So three years after his experience in Rome, Gibbon was still thinking of old subjects. He had not yet envisaged the decline and fall of the Roman Empire. He had forgotten, or suspended, his project of the decline and fall – what fall anyway? – of the city. And meanwhile he was reading, as always, the Greek and Latin classics, studying, like Giannone and Montesquieu, the laws and institutions, the geography and topography and climate of the lower empire, the Dark and Middle Ages, until gradually, fed by that copious nutriment, the buried seed grew into a new idea. He decided not merely to take another detail from the problem of his age, to cut off another manageable slice of it, but to seize, as none had yet dared to seize, the whole problem. The decline and fall of the city was transformed into the decline and fall of the empire. That vast subject, 'of whose limits and extent', as he admitted, 'I had yet a very inadequate notion', could be made to stretch from Antiquity to the Renaissance, from Europe through Arabia to China. It would subsume Gibbon's own early interest in the Middle and Far East, in the revolutions of China and Central Asia, Islam and India – an interest which links him, once again, with Montesquieu, and which caused Dr Johnson contemptuously to repeat the gossip that Gibbon, at Oxford, had been converted to Mohammedanism. It would extend Giannone's study of the social power of the Church from Naples to all Europe. It would apply the sociological ideas of Montesquieu to the rise of Christianity. It would deepen the sketches of Robertson on the progress of medieval Europe, embrace the debates of Voltaire, Robertson and Hume on the character of feudalism, the transformation of society, the significance of the crusades.

Byzantine history, by itself, might seem to Gibbon – as modern Byzantists complain of him – a mean subject. But, as he observed, 'the fate of the Byzantine monarchy is passively connected with the most splendid and important revolutions which have changed the face of the world' – the revolutions which, together, raised Europe from barbarism to civility. In such a study, on such a scale, Gibbon could illuminate far more effectively than Montesquieu the great problem of the failure of Antiquity; in his thirty-eighth chapter, in his 'General Observations on the Fall of the Roman Empire in the West', he would face the troubling question whether modern civilisation too might fail; and in the last chapter of all he would fulfil his old ambition and finish his work with the history, over those 1,300 years, of the city of Rome. Little had he thought in 1764 'that this final chapter must be attained by the labour of six quartos and twenty years'. But now that it had been attained, his mind went back to that original impulse and ascribed to it, perhaps, a new clarity: 'it was among the ruins of the Capitol that I first conceived the idea of a work which has amused and exercised near twenty years of my life, and which, however inadequate to my own wishes, I finally deliver to the curiosity and candour of the public'.[24]

With those words Gibbon, sitting, late at night, in his summer-house in Lausanne, ended his great work. Then – for how can one resist this final quotation from the *Autobiography*?

> after laying down my pen, I took several turns in a *berceau*, or covered walk of acacias, which commands a prospect of the country, the lake and the mountains. The air was temperate, the sky was serene, the silver orb of the moon was reflected from the waters, and all Nature was silent. I will not dissemble the first emotions of joy on recovery of my freedom and, perhaps, the establishment of my fame. But my pride was soon humbled, and a sober melancholy was spread over my mind, by the idea that I had taken an everlasting leave of an old and agreeable companion, and that whatsoever might be the future date of my history, the life of the historian must be short and precarious.[25]

Short and precarious it might be; it had already been long enough to bring together and to answer, in one majestic work, the problems which had exercised all the greatest historical minds of that most inquisitive, most penetrating, most inspiring of generations, the generation of the Enlightenment.

Gibbon and the Publication of *The Decline and Fall of the Roman Empire,* 1776–1976

In 1976 WE celebrate the bicentenary of – among other events – the publication of the first volume of *The Decline and Fall of the Roman Empire.* That publication, as is well known, created an immediate sensation. It was a *succès de scandale.* In this lecture, if I speak briefly of that sensation, it is in order to look past it and see what I believe is far more important and has been far less generally recognised, then or now: the revolutionary historical philosophy which, in that year, almost unnoticed in the noise of sectarian battle, moved in to command the field.

Yes, almost unnoticed. For who, in eighteenth-century England, either among those who welcomed the new book, or among those who attacked it, showed any appreciation of its true character, its real novelty? (I say 'England' advisedly, for Scotland, of course, was different.) Those who praised Gibbon's work, at the time, praised it for its style. Some also – like Porson and Coleridge – deplored its style.[1] Horace Walpole, the arbiter of contemporary taste, thought there was nothing new in it except the style.[2] Even in our century, Lytton Strachey, a literary man of the 1920s, dogmatically stated that the foundation of Gibbon's work was its style: 'the style once fixed, everything else followed'.[3] What rubbish! Reading such judgments, I am inclined to agree with that learned but tart Italian scholar, Signor Giarrizzo, who exclaims against 'the trite and vulgar judgments and insipid chatter' of most Anglo-Saxon writers on Gibbon.[4]

If Gibbon's contemporaries extolled him mainly for his style, they attacked him mainly for his 'infidelity'. This entrancing style, they protested, was used to recommend the most pernicious doctrines. The book had scarcely been published when the outcry began. In the same letters in which Gibbon purred with satisfaction at the success of his book, he had to add that already he could hear the ominous sound of parsons 'sharpening [their] goose-quills'.[5] The book, he told his stepmother, had been 'very well received, by men of letters, men of the world and even by fine feathered Ladies: in short by every set of people except perhaps by the clergy who seem (I know not why) to shew their teeth on the occasion';[6] and to his Swiss friend Deyverdun, after similar self-congratulation, he added, 'But now let us consider the other side of the coin and respect the means by which Heaven has seen fit to humble my pride. Would you ever suppose, my dear Sir, that anyone would have carried injustice so far as to attack the purity of my faith? A cry has been raised against me by bishops, and by a number of ladies respectable both for years and enlightenment. They have presumed to maintain that the last two chapters' – that is, the famous chapters fifteen and sixteen on the rise and establishment of Christianity in the Roman Empire – 'are nothing less than a satire against the Christian religion: a satire all the more dangerous because it is disguised by a veil of moderation and impartiality; and that the emissary of Satan, having long beguiled the reader by a very agreeable narrative, insensibly leads his footsteps into an infernal snare. You will appreciate, Monsieur, the full horror of all this, and will understand that I shall maintain only a dignified silence in the face of my enemies.'[7]

'An agreeable narrative ... an infernal snare ...' This was the standard charge. It could be heard even in 'the Club' – that convivial and intellectual society founded by Sir Joshua Reynolds and made famous by Johnson and Boswell. It was precisely at this time that Boswell recorded a conversation on the subject with Johnson. 'We talked of a work much in vogue at that time, written in a very mellifluous style, but which, under pretext of another subject, contained much artful infidelity. I said it was not fair to attack us thus unexpectedly; he should have warned us of our danger, before we entered his garden of flowery eloquence, by advertising "spring-guns and man-traps set here".' Boswell then remarked that the author (whom he is careful not to name) was an Oxonian who had turned papist and then become an infidel, and 'I did not despair yet of seeing him a methodist preacher'. Johnson replied that he believed that he had also once been a Mohammedan, but he doubted whether there would be any further changes: 'now that he has published his infidelity, he will probably persist in it'.[8]

Such was the reaction of the *literati*. Soon the parsons' goose-quills would be briskly scribbling. At first Gibbon kept to his resolve and maintained a dignified silence. But ultimately he was provoked to reply by the assault of a

young man from Balliol College, Oxford, eager to draw attention to himself.
Like Johnson and Boswell, young Mr Davis accused Gibbon of seduction: of
'betraying the confidence and seducing the faith of those readers who may
heedlessly stray in the flowery paths of his diction, without perceiving the
poisonous snake that lurks concealed in the grass'.[9] But unlike Johnson and
Boswell, Davis sought to document this grave charge by allegations of inca-
pacity and dishonesty as a scholar. This provoked Gibbon and he decided,
reluctantly, to reply at once to all his critics. He suspended his work on the
Decline and Fall and wrote that splendid work, the *Vindication*.[10]

The effect was devastating. Never, in literary history, has there been such
a rout. Under that sustained and deadly fusillade, all Gibbon's clerical critics
were laid prostrate, and now they are only remembered as the unpitied
victims of their own temerity. Having discharged his shot, Gibbon recased
his weapon and never took it out again. There was no need. The battle was
over. He could go on with the next volumes of the *Decline and Fall*.

This decisive battle is famous in literature, but it has, I believe, distracted
attention from Gibbon's true achievement as a historian. Its very finality has
given it a false significance. It has been seen as a frontal battle: as if a fanatical
tribe of Old Believers had gathered in some spiritual Thermopylae to block
the advance of the well-armed infidel and had been mercilessly mown down,
leaving him free to enter and waste at will the undefended Thessaly of ecclesiastical history. But this was not so, and Gibbon knew it was not so. He knew
that his adversaries were not defending a vital pass: they were harassing him
on his flanks with assegais and blowpipes. Their attacks were irritant but
irrelevant, and his *Vindication*, to him, was a necessary but unwelcome puni-
tive diversion. As he himself put it on setting out, 'And now let me proceed
on this hostile march over a dreary and barren desert, where thirst, hunger,
and intolerable weariness, are much more to be dreaded, than the darts of
the enemy'; and, on his return, 'a victory over such antagonists was a sufficient humiliation'.[11]

What was Gibbon's real purpose, from which he was temporarily diverted
by these lateral incursions? It was not to write a sceptical history, as Voltaire
might have done, as Voltaire had done. Gibbon disliked Voltaire, regarding
him as an anti-Christian 'bigot, an intolerant bigot' who 'insulted the religion
of nations'.[12] It was not to challenge the Church, or its historians. He had
great respect for many Church historians, and was contemptuous of the
'lively' philosophers of France who presumed to snipe at them. His purpose

was much more positive than this. It was to create an altogether new kind of history, to put historical study on a new base, to give it a new philosophical dimension. His great Scottish contemporaries could see this. Consequently, there was no outcry in Scotland. The Scottish literary establishment was dominated by the 'philosophers' of Edinburgh: David Hume, William Robertson, Adam Ferguson, Adam Smith. From them came nothing but praise – although Robertson was a Presbyterian clergyman and Moderator of the General Assembly of the Kirk. Gibbon greatly appreciated this praise which came to him 'from the northern part of our island, whither taste and philosophy seemed to have retired from the smoke and hurry of this immense capital'.[13] But in England there was no one who even understood what he was doing. Why should they, when England had no native tradition of historiography, and Gibbon himself, intellectually, was not an Englishman?

It is easy for us to forget the poverty of English historiography before Gibbon; but it was a truism at this time. Gibbon himself would refer to 'the old reproach that no British altars had been raised to the muse of history'. In 1754 David Hume had remarked on it. 'It is well known', he wrote, 'that the English have not much excelled in that kind of literature'; in fact, he could find no good historian since the Elizabethan William Camden.[14] Three years earlier, Dr Johnson had observed the same phenomenon and had sought to explain it by a curious argument, unflattering to our branch of study. The English, he wrote, had shown great abilities in other departments of literature and therefore it could not be supposed that they were incapable of writing history; but the writing of history was so easy and so unexacting an occupation, there was in it so thin a stream of thought, that it offered no challenge to strenuous minds. That there was any philosophy in history, Johnson did not allow; that was mere 'colour' with which the historian afterwards decked out his patiently but unimaginatively assembled facts. To find a good English historian, Johnson, like Hume, went back to Elizabethan times. He found him in Richard Knolles, whose *General History of the Turks* (1603), he said, was unrecognised only because of the extreme dullness of the subject.[15]

This observation of Johnson was not unnoticed by Gibbon. In a footnote to his great work, he touched lightly on Johnson's praise of Knolles' *General History*, and added, somewhat contemptuously, 'I much doubt whether a partial and verbose compilation from Latin writers, thirteen hundred folio pages of speeches and battles, can either instruct or amuse an enlightened age, which requires from the historian some tincture of philosophy and criticism'.[16]

In this little exchange, we see the confrontation of two worlds. To the conservative Johnson, history was a branch of literature – an inferior branch in which imagination was not required and 'all the greatest powers of the human mind are quiescent'.[17] That was the humanist orthodoxy of the time. But to Gibbon, history had a much higher place. It was a branch of 'philosophy', of thought. The tradition to which he looked back was quite different. It was not the humanist tradition – indeed, it was anti-humanist – and its pedigree was not English. As he himself wrote, its first modern practitioners were the great Florentine historians of the sixteenth century, Machiavelli and Guicciardini, and it remained an Italian monopoly 'till, in the present age, Scotland arose to dispute the prize with Italy herself'.[18] To this foreign tradition Gibbon had attached himself in 1753 when, after a brief and disastrous career at Oxford, ending abruptly with his conversion to Catholicism, he was removed to be reconverted and re-educated by a sound Protestant minister in Lausanne.

What had Gibbon's intellectual formation been before that? Formally, he had hardy been educated at all. Two years at Westminster School, continually broken by illness, two years of neglect at Oxford. His reading had indeed been voracious. 'Many crude lumps of Speed, Rapin, Mezeray, Davila, Machiavel, Father Paul, Bower, etc. passed through me like so many novels, and I swallowed with the same voracious appetite the descriptions of India and China, of Mexico and Peru. Before I was sixteen, I had exhausted all that could be learned in English, of the Arabs and Persians, the Tartars and the Turks.'[19] So, at sixteen, he had arrived at Oxford 'with a stock of erudition that might have puzzled a Doctor and a degree of ignorance of which a school boy would have been ashamed'.[20] For this vast private reading was undirected, unsystematic, without method. Then, in Lausanne, it had been, for the first time, articulated. He there acquired a new method, a new philosophy, which enabled him to organise and wield that formless erudition.

Gibbon always recognised his debt to Lausanne. Lausanne had denationalised him, cut him off from his own countrymen. Even after two years in the militia, and nine in Parliament, he was never fully at home in England, and he would return, for his last ten years, to Lausanne. But, intellectually, Lausanne had made him, 'Whatsoever have been the fruits of my education', he would afterwards write,

> they must be ascribed to the fortunate shipwreck which cast me on the shores of Leman Lake. . . . If my childish revolt against the Religion of my

country had not stripped me in time of my academic gown, the five important years, so liberally improved in the studies and conversation of
Lausanne, would have been steeped in port and prejudice among the
monks of Oxford. Had the fatigue of idleness compelled me to read, the
path of learning would not have been enlightened by a ray of philosophic
freedom: I should have grown to manhood ignorant of the life and
language of Europe, and my knowledge of the world would have been
confined to an English cloyster.[21]

For Lausanne, not England, had formed him. 'Such as I am in Genius or
learning or in manners, I owe my creation to Lausanne: it was in that school,
that the statue was discovered in the block of marble.'[22]

Above all, in Lausanne Gibbon had discovered the writer who was to be
the greatest single force in his intellectual life: the writer who was to be as
important to the historians of the later eighteenth century as Herder or Marx
would be to those of the nineteenth and twentieth; who had first given to
narrative history the new dimensions of social context and relative ideas;
who, though ignored in England, had inspired the new generation of Scottish
writers, from the 'philosophic historian' William Robertson to the 'political
economist' Adam Smith. This was the founder of the new science of sociology: Montesquieu.

Without Montesquieu, we may confidently say, there would have been no
Gibbon. Writing of his Lausanne days, Gibbon describes his discovery of
Montesquieu. 'My delight', he says, 'was in the frequent perusal of Montesquieu
whose energy of style, and boldness of hypothesis were powerful to awaken
and stimulate the genius of the age.'[23] His first work, his *Essai sur l'étude de la
littérature*[24] – that marvellously precocious work, begun at the age of twenty,
which looks forward from the literary scholarship of the eighteenth century
to the *Altertumswissenschaft* of the nineteenth – was impregnated with the
matter and (as he himself confessed) deformed by the style of Montesquieu.
Throughout the *Decline and Fall*, homage – by now a more critical homage – is
paid to Montesquieu.[25] And in his last volume, Gibbon, citing once again
Montesquieu's great work, *De l'Esprit des lois*, remarks that 'in the forty years
since its publication, no book has been more read and criticised; and the spirit
of inquiry which it has excited is not the least of our obligations to the author'.[26]

Genius does not rise in isolation, though it may sometimes seem to do so.
It arises from the competition of peers. Gibbon, intellectually isolated in

England, belonged to a recognisable European and Scottish intellectual group, and he addressed himself to a problem that exercised all the members of that group, using methods familiar to them all, and derived by them from Montesquieu. That problem, the new problem which preoccupied the eighteenth century, was the problem of progress in history.

Before the eighteenth century, men had not thought in terms of progress. They had looked back for their models – back to the Apostolic Age in religion, back to classical Antiquity in literature, history, ideas. The idea that the past could be transcended did not occur to them. But at the beginning of the eighteenth century this modesty had been overcome. Men began to admire the moderns, to realise that, recently, they had made great steps forward. This recognition of the fact required some investigation of the means. How had it happened? And if it was possible, why had it not been continuous? How was it that the great civilisation of Antiquity had somehow stopped progressing and had foundered in a thousand years of gothic barbarism? Although Europe had now, somehow, climbed out of the gulf, it was important to analyse the process and thus, if possible, to correct those faults in the mechanism which had led to its previous interruption. Otherwise, how could one be sure that the same fault would not recur, and the whole process be reversed again?

The problems posed by the decline and fall of the Roman Empire exercised many minds in the eighteenth century – far more than we now remember – and they looked to history for an answer. The great Neapolitan historian Pietro Giannone, Montesquieu himself, all the disciples of Montesquieu, were exercised by it. If we always think of it in connexion with Gibbon, that is not because he was alone, but because he eclipsed all others. He mobilised his incredible range of scholarship and used it to answer their question.

In the rest of this lecture I wish to describe, very briefly, Gibbon's 'philosophic' answer to the problem and thereby to show, incidentally, that his treatment of religion – which created such an outcry in England – had nothing to do with personal 'infidelity' but was simply a necessary element in his essentially sociological method. For just as Montesquieu, in his philosophy, so Gibbon, in his history, argued that society, institutions and ideas were interdependent. Both believed that particular values, and sets and priorities of values, corresponded with particular social structures and political systems. Consequently, great religious changes both entailed and consecrated great social changes. Religious ideas could not be studied in a social vacuum. They were connected – intimately and actively connected – with social progress or decline. This novel philosophy could hardly be understood in the England of Johnson and Boswell, Horace Walpole and John Wesley, which was quite unprepared for it and easily shocked by it. Therefore, when it was first published, English critics seized on such superficial aspects or detachable details of it as they could at once grasp or resent. They were dazzled by the style, or they cried out against the 'infidelity'.

What then was Gibbon's novel philosophy, his particular interpretation of progress and decline? At the very beginning of his first volume he gives some indication of it. Unfortunately, even here, his views have been widely misunderstood and misrepresented. They have been misrepresented, in spite of the plain evidence of his own words, by those who credit him with the view that the age of the Antonine emperors – that is, the five emperors from A.D. 96 to A.D. 180 – was the happiest of human history, the irrecoverable zenith from which mankind had since fallen away.

In fact, this is not what Gibbon believed, or wrote. What he wrote was that, 'if a man were asked to fix the period in the history of the world, during which the condition of the human race was most happy and prosperous, he would, without hesitation', point to that period.[27] He would indeed: it was the truism of the time. Gibbon is but repeating, in almost identical words, a phrase in Francis Bacon's *Advancement of Learning* 170 years before.[28] But does he endorse that truism? No, he does not. From the very beginning, his praise of the Roman Empire is qualified. He does not admire even its founder, Augustus. For Gibbon, unlike Voltaire, is not impressed by benevolent despots. As a disciple of Montesquieu, he looks past individual rulers and sees, in the very structure of the Roman Empire and in the distinctive 'spirit' which was generated by that structure and consecrated it, the seeds of its decay.

For what is the form of society which leads to progress, and what is the 'spirit', the system of values, necessary to create and animate that form? In Gibbon's view, the first condition of progress is the free circulation of goods and ideas; this freedom in turn requires an open, plural society; and such a society both fosters and depends upon an independent public spirit, that spirit of 'civic humanism', of participation in public affairs, which Machiavelli had called *virtù*. Now it was precisely these qualities which the Roman Empire, from the beginning, had stifled. 'That public virtue', writes Gibbon, 'which among the ancients was denominated patriotism, is derived from a strong sense of our own interest in the preservation and property of the *free* government *of which we are members*. Such a sentiment, which had rendered the legions of the republic almost invincible, could make but a very feeble impression on the mercenary servants of a despotic prince.'[29] And at the end of the three chapters in which Gibbon describes the Antonine Empire, he emphasises 'two peculiar circumstances' which made its subjects, potentially at least, 'more completely wretched than the victims of tyranny in any other age or country'. These two circumstances lay in the memory of past freedom and the universality of present power.

'The division of Europe into a number of independent states', Gibbon wrote, '. . . is productive of the most beneficial consequences to the liberty of mankind.' Thanks to it, the heretic, the nonconformist, could always find a new base, and so ideas and experiments, however unacceptable to present power, could not be stifled. But the monopoly of the Roman emperors was absolute. There was no practical alternative, no escape:

> The slave of imperial despotism, whether he was condemned to drag his gilded chain in Rome and the senate, or to wear out a life of exile on the barren rock of Seriphus, or the frozen banks of the Danube, expected his fate in silent despair. To resist was fatal, and it was impossible to fly. On every side he was encompassed by a vast extent of sea and land, which he could never hope to traverse without being discovered, seized, and restored to his irritated master. Beyond the frontiers, his anxious view could discover nothing, except the ocean, inhospitable deserts, hostile tribes of barbarians, of fierce manners and unknown language, or dependent kings, who would gladly purchase the emperor's protection by the sacrifice of an obnoxious fugitive. 'Wherever you are,' said Cicero to the exiled Marcellus, 'remember that you are equally within the power of the conqueror.'[30]

So, at the very beginning of Gibbon's work, the ruling theme is set out, and as we read his philosophy emerges. Looking back through history, Gibbon sees the essential conditions of progress not in great political systems but in the cultivation of science. 'The history of empires', he had begun his first work, 'is that of the miseries of mankind: the history of the sciences is that of their splendour and happiness.'[31] By science, he meant useful science, experimental Baconian science, directed to the understanding of nature and the improvement of human life.

What then is the political system which favours progress? To Gibbon, progress is intimately linked to urban freedom and self-government. It was the free cities of Europe, he insists, not the empire of Rome, or any other empire, which transmitted civilisation through the Dark Ages. Indeed, the Roman Empire, by its centralisation of power, its erosion of independent urban life, and its suppression of political freedom, was the enemy of progress. Even a good emperor – a Trajan or a Marcus Aurelius – could not reverse this fatal process, which, in the fourth and fifth centuries, under the dynasties of Constantine and Theodosius, would ultimately become ruinous. For it was not the Germanic conquerors – 'those innocent barbarians' – who destroyed the civilisation of Antiquity: 'if all the barbarian conquerors had been annihilated in the same hour', Gibbon wrote, 'their total destruction would not have restored the empire of the West'. It was the empire itself which in its blind, and ultimately defensive, bureaucratic centralisation had caused the organs of progress to become atrophied so that, in the end, 'the stupendous fabric yielded to the pressure of its own weight'.[32]

Thus the empire, by the momentum of its own monopoly, destroyed itself. After its fall, the organs of freedom, which it had stifled, could not be revived. Neither the imperial institutions of Byzantium nor the new feudalism of the Germanic kingdoms allowed it. But gradually, as feudalism weakened, the cities of Italy and the West began to revive and re-create those lost institutions. Moreover, the crusades, those aggressive imperialist ventures of the feudal order, hastened its decline. In a memorable passage, Gibbon describes this process. 'The iron weight of the martial aristocracy', he writes, had hitherto crushed 'every hope of industry and improvement', but now

> the estates of the barons were dissipated and their race was often extinguished, in these costly and perilous expeditions. Their poverty extorted from their pride those charters of freedom which unlocked the fetters of the slave, secured the farm of the peasant and the shop of the artificer, and gradually restored a substance and a soul to the most numerous and useful part of the community. The conflagration which destroyed the tall and barren trees of the forest gave air and scope to the vegetation of the smaller and nutritive plants of the soil.[33]

So, after the 'stupendous fabric' of the bureaucratic Roman Empire, the 'gothic edifice' of military feudalism also sank under its own weight, and the organs of freedom, in spite of the crimes, follies and misfortunes of which history is the register, were able to recover their strength. Thanks to them, the last three centuries had seen the recovery of civilisation, and now, Gibbon thought, the danger of regression was past.

For modern Europe was not like the Roman Empire. It was a plural society: 'one great republic whose various inhabitants have attained almost the same level of politeness and cultivation'. There were now no barbarians left who could press it from outside – only 'the remnant of Calmucks or Uzbecks' who 'cannot seriously excite the apprehensions of the great republic of Europe'. In America, there was a growing European population: 'whatever may be the changes of their political situation, they must preserve the manners of Europe: and we may reflect with some pleasure that the English language will probably be diffused over an immense and populous continent'.[34] We are reminded that Gibbon himself – so un-English was his mind – had nearly written his great work in French. He had been dissuaded by the man whom he admired most in the world, David Hume, who had pointed out that, with the defeat of France in the Seven Years War, English, not French, would now be the language of the New World.[35]

So Gibbon gave a confident answer to the great problem of his time. Since progress was the product of science, and since science and the useful arts were irreversible in a world of free competition, and since Europe, unlike the Roman Empire, was a plural society where such competition could not be stifled by a single repressive central authority, a reversion to barbarism was impossible. There might be local regression; there might be public crimes and follies; there might be natural disasters; but the danger of the total failure of civilisation was inconceivable, at least in the foreseeable future. The arts which Europe had discovered or invented, and which were the essential motor of progress, had been diffused over the globe; 'they can never be lost. We may therefore acquiesce in the pleasing conclusion that every age of the world has increased, and still increases, the real wealth, the happiness, the knowledge, and perhaps the virtue of the human race.'[36]

We pause; we reflect; we wonder. Is it true? Is science always beneficent? Cannot human crime and folly misuse it to fatal effect? Will the civilised world always be divided in healthy competition? May not circumstances change? May not that pluralism be lost in a new monopoly of empire which will stifle the hard-won progress of the past? Are there no barbarians but Kalmucks and Uzbecks? Is there not a barbarian precariously pent up within each apparently civilised man? Every historian who seeks to generalise tends to extrapolate. He looks for the present in the past and sees both past and future in the present. At the close of his life Gibbon himself may have had doubts. Had he foreseen, not merely the fact, but even the possibility of the French Revolution? However, if we remember his implied conditions, we may accept his generalisations, which have not yet been disproved. By the next century, his philosophy could digest even the French Revolution.

I have tried to summarise Gibbon's general philosophy. It is an interpretation of the social mechanics of progress and decline in history; and it is within this general philosophy, not divorced from it, that we should see his treatment of religion. For Gibbon, obviously, could not evade the problem of religion. Christianity, like any other religion, was a set of values related to social structure and political form. The question he faced was: how did the rise and establishment of Christianity, its victory over classical paganism, its gradual acquisition of social power throughout the empire, affect the social process which he was describing? What was its effect in the contest between 'public virtue' and despotism, free competition and monopoly?

Essentially, this was a social question. It was unconnected with the truth or falsity of any particular doctrines; and Gibbon pleased himself with the idea that he could answer it without causing offence. At least, he thought, his answer would not offend the Protestant Church of his own country to which he conformed. For although he had long ago suspended his religious enquiries, he acquiesced 'with implicit belief' in the agreed tenets of the Christian Churches. Such conformity, he believed, was the duty of the philosopher: did not the best of the pagan philosophers, Socrates, Epicurus, Cicero and Plutarch, always inculcate 'decent reverence for the religion of their own country, and of mankind'?[37] 'The satirist may laugh, the philosopher may preach', he would afterwards write, 'but reason herself will respect the prejudices and habits which have been consecrated by the experience of mankind.'[38]

In fact, Gibbon's sociology of the early Church does not affront any Christian doctrine, or at least any Protestant practice; but it does imply that the early Church positively accelerated the decline of the Roman Empire. It did so, he maintains, thanks to two grave defects. First, by the mere fact of its establishment under the later empire, it acquired an organisation which reflected, and aggravated, that of the empire. In other words, a centralised, monopolist, parasitic state was reinforced by a centralised, monopolist, parasitic Church. Secondly, it positively repudiated, by its teaching and practice, that 'public virtue' which he saw as the motor of progress. Both these defects were carried to a fatal extent in that institution, unknown to the Apostolic Age, which, in Gibbon's words, had 'counterbalanced all the temporal advantages of Christianity': monasticism.[39]

How carefully Gibbon always chooses his words! Nothing, he implies, could counterbalance the spiritual advantage of Christianity. He allows that it has temporal advantages. But these admitted temporal advantages are, he believes, nullified by monasticism where it exists. For monasticism at once both intensifies the economic parasitism of an endowed monopoly and, by precept and example, undermines that 'active virtue' which had created and animated the great civilisation of Antiquity.

On both these issues, Gibbon's own views are strong. He detested the immobilisation of resources, in mortmain or treasure. He would not even allow his own library to be preserved as a monument to himself: he wished it to be broken up and sold for the use of active scholars.[40] He looked with indignation on the magnificent baroque abbey of Einsiedeln, newly rebuilt in 'the poorest corner of Europe',[41] and on the royal palaces of Turin, sustained by oppressive corvées on Savoyard peasants.[42] And he could see without horror the accumulated treasures of the Byzantine Church, at a time of national peril, taken from the temples in which they inculcated a dazed devotion, and 'most wickedly converted to the service of mankind'.[43]

He was even more contemptuous of the withdrawal from active life preached by the early Church and practised by its monks. In particular, he poured his scorn on the anchorites, those 'ascetics who obeyed and abused the rigid precepts of the gospel', those 'unhappy exiles from social life', 'the monastic saints who excite only the contempt and pity of a philosopher', not only by their credulity, their superstition, their 'horrid and disgusting' aspect and ridiculous mortifications, but because, by withdrawing into solitude, they 'impaired the strength and fortitude of the Empire'. At a time when the fate of civilisation hung in the balance, 'the clergy', says Gibbon, 'successfully preached the doctrines of patience and pusillanimity; the active virtues of society were discouraged; and the last remains of the military spirit were buried in the cloister'.[44]

These are the ways in which the early Church, according to Gibbon, at once redoubled the burden and reduced the strength of the empire. Thereby, he believed, it contributed to its ruin. In this belief he was consistent and firm. 'I believed', he would afterwards write, 'and . . . I still believe, that the propagation of the gospel and triumph of the Church are inseparably connected with the decline of the Roman Monarchy.'[45] But sometimes Gibbon surprises us by positively praising the Church or the clergy; and it is instructive to observe these occasions. For once again they illustrate the central theme of his philosophy: a belief in active civic virtue, resistance to social oppression, dissemination or advancement of industry, science, and wealth.

Read, for instance, his notable tribute to Pope Gregory the Great, whose antique Roman patriotism re-created the virtue of Rome and gave to the city, deserted by its distant Byzantine overlords, a new lease on life. 'Like Thebes, or Babylon, or Carthage, the name of Rome might have been erased from the earth', he says, 'if the city had not been animated by a vital principle, which again restored her to honour and dominion.'[46] Later, he similarly praises the popes of the eighth century, thanks to whom he can say that although the temporal rule of the popes 'is now confirmed by the reverence of a thousand years . . . their noblest title is the free choice of a people whom they had redeemed from slavery'.[47] Similarly, where the Church supported the cause of humanity – as in opposing gladiatorial contests in the Roman Empire or in alleviating the lot of the poor in feudal Europe – he would commend it. Even monasticism would be praised when it earned its keep by scholarly or other labour. Gibbon would never mention the 'Benedictine workshop' of the monks of St Germain-des-Prés without genuine veneration.[48]

But these are exceptions. Generally, he believed, the Church had stifled progress because, being adopted and adapted into the bureaucratic later empire, it had added its weight, and its blessing, to a despotic and centralised system – indeed, to a series of such systems – which had fatally injured the organs of freedom and progress. In a casual footnote – and how much of his philosophy is contained in his apparently casual footnotes – Gibbon gives a neat summary of his views on the successive phases of European social history. 'Within the ancient walls of Vindonissa', he observes, 'the castle of Hapsburg, the abbey of Königsfeld, and the town of Bruck have successively arisen. The philosophic traveller may compare the monuments of Roman conquest, of feudal or Austrian tyranny, of monkish superstition, and of industrious freedom. If he be truly a philosopher he will applaud the merit and happiness of his own time.'[49]

It is in this context too, I believe, that Gibbon's attitude to the Byzantine empire must be seen. Byzantinists generally disapprove of Gibbon. They detect in him a continuous distaste for Byzantium – a political system, they assure us, which for a thousand years maintained itself, and the residue of Greco-Roman culture, against its enemies from the north and east. True enough; and yet, Gibbon might answer, what had become of that culture? Is it not, in all those thousand years, dead? Where is Byzantine literature, Byzantine thought? The Arab conquerors, like the Roman conquerors long before them, like the European Renaissance long afterwards, took over Greek science, Greek philosophy, and made them live again. In Byzantium they remained pickled, dead – dead because the animating spirit which had produced them was extinct. Ancient literature, ancient thought, had been the product of ancient virtue. It could not survive the extinction of that virtue.

Such, I believe, was Gibbon's general philosophy – a philosophy of progress as demonstrated by the history of 2,000 years. It was an all-embracing philosophy, and its treatment of the Christian Church, as a social organism generating the 'spirit' of successive political and social systems, was an integral and necessary part of it. But it was also a novel, indeed a revolutionary, philosophy. It was therefore eminently capable of misinterpretation, especially by the English literary establishment, with its narrow humanist conception of history as a mere branch of literature. How was Gibbon to put it across?

The tactics he adopted were not new. In order to protect himself from the charge of 'infidelity', he made use of the old distinction, which, in the previous century, had served Francis Bacon and other old investigators: the distinction between 'first' and 'second' causes. The first cause of all things was, of course, the inscrutable Will of God which it was impertinent in men to question; but there were also, in the mere machinery of history, 'second causes', secular causes, which God permitted to operate and which men might study without sin. In this instance, Gibbon somewhat ostentatiously allowed that the first cause of the rise and establishment of Christianity was of course its truth, and then went quickly on to examine the secondary cause of which God had deigned to avail himself for the fulfilment of His Will.[50] Gibbon seems to have believed that this device would serve his turn. He flattered himself, as he afterwards wrote, 'that an age of light and liberty would receive without scandal, an enquiry into the *human* causes of the progress and establishment of Christianity'.[51]

Alas, he was wrong. His hero David Hume saw the future more clearly than he. 'When I heard of your Undertaking (which was some time ago)', Hume wrote to Gibbon on 18 March 1776, 'I own I was a little curious to see how you would extricate yourself from the Subject of your last two Chapters. I think you have observ'd a very prudent Temperament; but it was impossible to treat the Subject so as not to give Grounds of Suspicion against you, and you may expect that a Clamour will arise.'[52] Hume had been warned by his own experience. He may also have considered that profound truth, that it is not what you say that matters, but the tone of voice in which you say it; and the tone of Gibbon's voice did not entirely carry conviction. When the clamour arose, Gibbon, as he tells us, was taken by surprise: 'Let me frankly own', he afterwards wrote, 'that I was startled at the first vollies of this ecclesiastical ordnance.' He was also pained, and later expressed his regret: 'Had I believed that the majority of English readers were so fondly attached even to the name and shadow of Christianity; had I foreseen that the pious, the timid and the prudent would feel or affect to feel with such exquisite sensibility; I might, perhaps, have softened the two invidious chapters, which would create many enemies, and conciliate few friends.'[53] I believe that both his surprise and his regret were genuine. Perhaps he had been *naïf.* Insulated by his foreign education and his social life among philosophers and men of the world, he had never felt, or had forgotten, the bigotry which still smouldered under the smooth surface of English life.

A few years after the publication of his work, when Joseph Priestley, the radical Unitarian chemist of Birmingham, sought to draw him into controversy, Gibbon refused absolutely to be drawn, and particularly resented 'the invidious name of *unbeliever*' which Priestley had applied to him.[54] He was not in fact an unbeliever: he was a deist. But he had profounder reasons for regretting that controversy which had exploded on the publication of his first volume. It had set criticism on a wrong track and thereby distorted his achievement.

Now, surely, we can recognise that achievement. It was not purely critical or purely literary or purely scholarly. It was historical. Indeed, it was a revolution in historical philosophy: a new kind of historical interpretation, an interpretation of the whole historical process in which social structure and ideas assumed a coercive and dynamic force. None of his contemporary critics had seen this; but after they had died out, their world-view of history could never be restored, and their successors, however much they might hate Gibbon for destroying it, had to admit the revolution which he had caused.

Perhaps the best, because the most reluctant, witness to this is Thomas Carlyle. Carlyle's whole mind was basically antithetical to that of Gibbon. He was brought up in unquestioning peasant piety by strict Presbyterian parents in Dumfriesshire. Then, at the age of twenty-two, he read Gibbon and the mould in which his whole historical philosophy had been formed was shattered: so shattered that the philosophy itself could never be reconstituted, and Carlyle spent the rest of his life trying, not very successfully, to find another divine plan in history: by arbitrarily deifying such improbable human heroes as Oliver Cromwell and Frederick the Great.

Carlyle hated Gibbon for having shattered the comfortable, unquestioning philosophy in which he had been brought up. On the other hand, he recognised that Gibbon's work was irreversible: it must stand. The consequent ambivalence of his attitude towards Gibbon comes out very clearly in his letters. There he would protest that Gibbon's style was 'flowery – his sarcasms wicked – his notes oppressive, often beastly'. Hume, Robertson, Gibbon, 'the whole historical triumvirate', he wrote, 'are abundantly destitute of virtuous feeling, or indeed of any feeling at all. I wonder what benefit is derived from reading all this stuff.' And yet at the same time he found himself reluctantly seduced by the range and depth, the strength and subtlety, of what he called 'the most strong-minded of all historians'. Gibbon, he concluded in a letter to his future wife, Jane Welsh, had to be read, and read through: 'there is no other tolerable history of those times and nations, within the reach of such readers as we are; it is a kind of bridge that connects the antique with the modern ages. And how gorgeously does it swing across the gloomy and tumultuous chasm of those barbarous centuries! Gibbon is a man whom one never forgets – unless oneself deserving to be forgotten: the perusal of his work forms an epoch in the history of one's mind.'[55]

CHAPTER 9

Gibbon's Last Project

IN GIBBON'S LITERARY career there is a certain recurrent syndrome. Before he started work on *The Decline and Fall of the Roman Empire* he had toyed with various topics quite unrelated to that subject, all of them in early modern history: the life of Sir Walter Ralegh, the French invasion of Italy in 1494, Medicean Florence, the history of the liberty of the Swiss; and he wrote occasional specialised pieces. But all the time he was reading and thinking about the Roman Empire, which finally took over and dispersed these phantoms.

Then, in 1781, when the first three volumes of his great work had been published – when he had despatched the Roman Empire in the West and pronounced its epitaph – he contemplated stopping there. He had fulfilled his 'first undertaking to the public'; the work which he had published was complete in itself; should he really go on for another thousand years to the fall of Constantinople? Life was uncertain; he was (he frequently said) 'lazy'; why not rest on his fame and take his ease? So, for a time, he took it. For a year he indulged himself, reading the Greek classics. But then the urge to write, to read for a purpose, to resume the enjoyable routine of composition, reasserted itself, and he set off again. He quickened his pace, widened his field, and carried the story to the conclusion which he had originally intended.

In 1788, when he had published those last three volumes, had enjoyed his triumph in England, and had gone back to Lausanne, the old syndrome returned. His fame was now secure. His life in Lausanne was very agreeable, where he was, as Maria Holroyd reported, 'king of the place'. So, from now on, he would be his own master and, once again, take his ease. 'You may possibly hear', he wrote to his stepmother, 'that Mr Gibbon has undertaken some new history. Be persuaded, if I know his intentions, that after six weighty quartos, he now reads and writes for his own amusement, though I will not answer for what those amusements may one day produce'. So he returned to the Greek classics and toyed with various projects. Perhaps a seventh volume supplementary to the *History*? But no: that idea soon evaporated. So why not a series of *Historical Excursions*, forays into various fields? That led to the beginning of one such excursion, a study of 'the antiquities of the House of Brunswick', which, however, was never finished. And then there were the *Memoirs*, of which the various drafts were now being successively composed only to be laid aside or replaced.

Meanwhile another phantom floated before his mind. Why not a collection of essays on the lives and characters of 'the most eminent persons in arts and arms, in Church and state, who have flourished in Britain from the reign of Henry VIII to the present age?' For this project the faithful Sheffield was mobilised and received his instructions. 'It is essential', Gibbon told him, 'that I be solicited and do not solicit'; so, 'in your walk through Pall Mall you may call on the bookseller . . . and after some general questions about his edition of Shakespeare etc., you may open the "British Portraits" as an idea of your own, to which I am perfectly a stranger. If he kindle at the thought and eagerly claim my alliance, you will begin to hesitate: "I am afraid, Mr Nicol, that we shall hardly persuade your friend to engage in so great a work. Gibbon is old, and rich, and lazy. However, you may make the tryal, and if you have a mind to write to Lausanne . . . I will second the application".' But what if the bookseller were not to kindle, but to remain cool? In that case, Gibbon instructed Sheffield, 'you will be still colder'.

Sheffield dutifully performed his part, but the 'machiavellian ploy' (as Jane Norton has called it) did not succeed. Mr Nicol did not kindle, and the phantom 'British Portraits' evaporated. However, a new phantom soon replaced it. It was a phantom which had hovered before Gibbon's mind for twelve years, but now it became material. It would be embodied in the person of John Pinkerton.

John Pinkerton, when he first thrust himself into the literary limelight, bore a somewhat questionable character. A young Scotchman, he had come to London, like so many of his aspiring countrymen, to make his name; and under varying but transparent disguises he soon made it. His first publications had included a selection of allegedly ancient Scottish ballads, some of which he had in fact written himself. He was following the fashion set by James Macpherson's *Fingal*, in whose authenticity he then believed, though he would afterwards revise his opinion.[1] He also published an *Essay on*

Medals, which showed a more genuine antiquarian interest. But the book which launched his fame, or notoriety, was his *Letters of Literature*, published in 1785, under the pseudonym Robert Heron (Heron being his mother's maiden name). Pinkerton, by then, was aged twenty-seven.

The book was a success – of a kind: a *succès de scandale*; but it secured him a valuable patron. Horace Walpole was delighted by it, and was flattered when he was suspected of having written it. He was also attracted by Pinkerton's book on medals, of which he was a collector. When Pinkerton heard of Walpole's interest, he called on him personally and was well received. Walpole became his patron, invited him often to Strawberry Hill, and helped his career by securing his entry into public and private archives.[2] Other readers of the book were less impressed. They were outraged by Pinkerton's presumption or made merry over his absurdity.

For Pinkerton presented himself as an arbiter of literary taste, a severe censor of the ancient classics, a radical reformer of the English language. His proposed linguistic reforms excited particular hilarity. English words, he declared, were made unnecessarily harsh and rough by their consonantal endings, and he proposed that they be softened by the addition of harmonious vowels borrowed from Greek and Italian. This proposed reform, whose merits he demonstrated with copious but farcical examples, brought him much ridicule. As Charles Lamb wrote, 'luckilissime this proposalio of the absurdissimo Pinkertonio was not adoptado by anybodyini whateverano'.[3] Perhaps Pinkerton did not mean it to be taken seriously, but he never explained himself. If it was a joke, it misfired.

Pinkerton showed his presumption further in two 'letters' on Virgil, whose reputation he undertook to demolish. Virgil, he allowed, had an agreeable Latin style and some skill in 'the mechanical part of poetry', but that was all, and it was not enough to justify his reputation – indeed any reputation, for he had 'not the most distant pretence to any attribute of a poet': his *Eclogues* were 'beneath all contempt', and his *Georgics* – 'the best poem of the best poet' as Dryden had called them – were 'the very essence of absurdity'. In short, he was a 'tinsel poet' who wrote meretricious trifles to please his patron, Maecenas, a man of no taste or judgment. So that did for him. In another 'letter' Pinkerton similarly demolished Hume's *History of England*, the unchallenged historical classic of the time. Pinkerton dismissed it as 'a mere apology for prerogative, and a very weak one'. These were only some of Pinkerton's ventures in literary and historical revision.

To Horace Walpole, with his superficial whig prejudices, his unconventional literary tastes and his weakness for 'historic doubts', these sallies gave no offence, but to Gibbon they could only appear as a shocking heresy by a very silly fellow. Virgil was Gibbon's favourite poet, whose works he read again and again. He idolised Hume, and read his *History of England* 'with mingled delight and despair'. And his opinion of Pinkerton can hardly have been improved by Pinkerton's remarks, in the same book, on his own work. Discussing the first three volumes of the *Decline and Fall* – all that had been published at that time – Pinkerton declared that the style was 'rather incorrect and even sometimes puerile'; that in his later chapters Gibbon was apparently bored and certainly boring; and that his concluding 'General Observations on the Fall of the Western Empire' were 'more worthy of an old woman who has been frightened into hysterics by a sixpenny history of the sack of Rome by Alaric than of a man of science'.

After such a beginning one would hardly suppose that Pinkerton would find in Gibbon a patron and a friend. However, Gibbon was a magnanimous man; he respected real scholarship; and he soon discovered that Pinkerton, for all his arrogance and eccentricity, which he would never shed, and which would ultimately alienate Walpole, was a real scholar: indeed, the most original of Scottish antiquaries, the first, after Fr Thomas Innes in 1729, to put the early history of Scotland on a solid base: a base not only of authentic manuscript sources but also of iconography, coinage, costume, literature. In the years immediately after his unfortunate *Letters of Literature* Pinkerton published a series of works on these subjects: *Ancient Scotish Poems* (this time genuine, from the Pepys manuscripts in Cambridge) in 1786; A *Dissertation on the Origin and Progress of the Scythians or Goths* in 1787; *An Enquiry into the History of Scotland Preceding the Reign of Malcolm III* (i.e. until 1056) in 1789. All these books were acquired by Gibbon. In 1790 he published his Latin Lives of the Scottish saints of which 100 copies were printed, for subscribers only. Gibbon was one of the subscribers. This last work was a valuable document: it would be reprinted, with a translation, a century later.

These works, published in 1786–90, were just too late to be read by Gibbon while he was writing his last three volumes. Had they come a little earlier, they could have saved him from serious factual error concerning the dark age of Scotland. For Gibbon had allowed himself to be guided, on that subject, by 'two learned Highlanders' (as he termed them), James Macpherson, the 'translator' of Ossian, and the Rev. John Macpherson, minister of Sleat in Skye: two impostors who, while pretending independence of each other, had secretly collaborated in order to sustain their own fictions.[4] In his *Enquiry* Pinkerton touched on Gibbon's error – but this time more lightly. Among those writers who had repeated the false tradition asserted by those 'truly Celtic' impostors, the two Macphersons – men 'more ignorant in our age than Geoffrey of Monmouth in his' – he found himself obliged to include, 'I tremble to say, Gibbon', who, 'instead of bestowing even the slightest examination on the subject, has been led by the Macphersons, whose little local designs his large mind could not even suspect'. The little local designs of the Macphersons were, of course, to construct a historical context for the Caledonian Ossian. However, Pinkerton atoned for his criticism of Gibbon's particular error by general praise: he now cited, as his own historical mentors, Gibbon and Montesquieu, and referred to their example to justify his own use, and later his own edition, of the *Lives of the Saints* as sources of secular history.[5]

Pinkerton would not have been Pinkerton if he had not carried some of his theories, even now, to extremes and made new enemies with each new work. One of his theories, which posterity has not endorsed, was that the Picts – or 'Piks' as he preferred to call them – of Caledonia were by origin not Celts but Goths, who, he supposed, had sailed to eastern Scotland from Scandinavia by way of the Orkney Islands. This theory enabled him to express, with his customary vehemence, a racial theory which had become an obsession with him. The Goths, he maintained, were a creative *Kulturvolk*, barbarous indeed, but capable of being improved into modern Lowland Scotchmen, while the indigenous Celtic inhabitants of Scotland and Ireland, 'the riff-raff of O's and Macs', lacked this capacity altogether: they were subhuman, mere 'cattle', designed by nature to be an intermediary species between man and beast, and should have been cleared out of the country as useless rubbish five centuries ago. Understandably, this did not go down well in Scotland; but Pinkerton, well established in Kensington, had no intention of returning even to 'Gothic' Lowland Scotland.

When did Gibbon discover, and begin to appreciate, Pinkerton – John Pinkerton the genuine scholar as distinct from 'Robert Heron' the presumptuous literary critic? Evidently not before his visit to England in 1787–88 to oversee the publication and enjoy the triumph of the last three volumes of the *Decline and Fall*. During that visit he could have caught up with English publications and literary gossip, but it does not seem that even then he had taken any interest in this serious critic of his work. The first evidence of such an interest comes in a letter which Gibbon wrote to his London bookseller and friend Peter Elmsley in February 1789. By that time he had been back in Lausanne for six months.

In this letter Gibbon asked Elmsley to obtain for him certain books, including the Latin history of the Orkney Islands by the seventeenth-century Danish scholar Thomas Torfaeus, and he adds, 'has Robert Heron (I forget his real name) published his Lives of the Scottish saints to which I am a subscriber?' This suggests that Gibbon was re-examining Scottish history – perhaps in connexion with the supplementary volume to the *Decline and Fall* which he was then considering. But apparently he had not yet fixed Pinkerton as Pinkerton in his mind: to him he was still the Robert Heron of the *Letters of Literature*. However, the interest in the Orkney Islands, combined with the reference to the 'Lives of the Scottish saints', suggests that Gibbon had now read Pinkerton's *Dissertation*, which had been published in 1787, and of which he possessed a copy (though we do not know when he acquired it). Moreover, in this same year, 1789, Pinkerton published his *Enquiry*, and Gibbon, who obtained a copy, was greatly impressed by it. It was, he would afterwards tell Pinkerton, 'the only work which had given him precise and authentic ideas on the early history of Scotland'. Lord Sheffield confirms this: Gibbon, he records, always mentioned this book 'with applause'.[6] Evidently Gibbon was not offended by the reproof to himself that it contained, and accepted the correction.

That established Pinkerton in Gibbon's mind as an *érudit* in early Scottish history, where he himself, as he now realised, had gone seriously astray. But meanwhile Pinkerton had advanced on a wider front. Throughout 1788, under yet another pseudonym, Philistor, he had published, in *The Gentleman's Magazine*, a series of twelve 'Letters to the People of Great Britain on the Cultivation of their National History'. In these letters he deplored the lack of interest which British scholars had shown, for nearly a century, in their own historical records. How different from France, Italy, Germany, Denmark! How different even from Russia, 'where literature was unknown until the present century!' What we need, he wrote, is not new historians but accurately printed archival sources, not philosophy but erudition: 'a cold German, whose erudition is boundless, who collected the most minute facts, and who has not even fancy enough to form one conjecture, is worth a thousand ingenious dabblers whose light is a mere *ignis fatuus* and only dazzles to mislead'. So he called for the publication of the authentic sources of British history, properly collated and edited, using modern techniques, particularly for the dark period before the Norman Conquest; for was it not 'a mortifying reflexion' that Englishmen thought the history of their own country of no account 'till it became a prey of Norman ravagers'? And by 'British' Pinkerton meant British, not just English. Irish history, he remarked, was in a particularly bad way – no available sources before Tighernach in 1088 except lives of the saints (valuable though these can be); in consequence of which Irish history, owing to 'the extreme folly of Irish dabblers in antiquity', is 'never mentioned but with laughter'. The Irish, of course, were Celts.

So Pinkerton pressed not only for the publication of sources, as in Germany by Leibniz, in Italy by Muratori and in Denmark by Langebek, but for the professional training of the historians who should use them. He wanted courses in history at the universities. 'Professorships of English history in Oxford and Cambridge, Irish history at Dublin, Scotch at Edinburgh, might be of service, if the places became not mere sinecures, as not unusual.' There should be dissertations, libraries, professional associations. All this, of course, required financial support, patronage, as abroad: patronage by the crown, the aristocracy, the great. Without such patronage, nothing could be done.

Were these 'letters' read by Gibbon? If so, did he know that 'Philistor' was Pinkerton? There is no evidence either way. The first 'letter' was published in February 1788, and five of them had appeared before Gibbon left England for Lausanne in July. Gibbon would surely have read *The Gentleman's Magazine* while in England: it was edited by his friend, the printer and antiquary John Nichols, whom he described as 'the last, or one of the last, of the learned printers of Europe'. On the other hand, we know that the August number of *The Gentleman's Magazine*, which contained an article of special interest to him, about the Gibbon family, did not reach him in Lausanne till February 1792: a four-year delay. All we can say is that Gibbon in his surviving papers shows no sign of having read the 'letters' at the time of their publication, and that Pinkerton, when he wrote to Gibbon in 1793, assumed that he had not.

However, intellectually, their interests were clearly converging. For Gibbon too had long deplored the lack of any modern scholarly edition of the sources of English history comparable with the great continental ventures. In 1781, in the third volume of the *Decline and Fall*, citing (as he often would) the great work of 'Dom Bouquet and the other Benedictines' who, between 1738 and 1767, had published the sources of French history up to 1060, he had remarked

that 'such a national work . . . might provoke our emulation'.[7] It was an observation which he would often repeat; and now, composing his *Memoirs*, he
referred again to 'the Benedictine workshop' of St Germain-des-Prés which he
had visited in 1763 and whose productive industry he contrasted with the sterile
indolence of 'the monks of Magdalen' and the sinecurist professors of Oxford.
On that subject he agreed entirely with the implied strictures of Pinkerton. And
then there was Muratori, for whose sake he had visited the ducal museum at
Modena and who had been his 'guide and master' through the 'darkness of the
Middle Ages'. Pinkerton, as 'Philistor', had explicitly cited the examples of
Muratori and Leibniz as models. Now, in 1790, Gibbon was preparing his
'historical excursion' on 'the Antiquities of the House of Brunswick' for which
his two main authorities were Muratori for the Italian and Leibniz for the
German ancestry of the dynasty. He already possessed the *Antichità Estensi*, as
well as the other works of Muratori; now he wrote to the librarian of the duke
of Brunswick asking him to find a copy of Leibniz's *Origines Guelficae* for the
German side.

So the stage was set for the final convergence and collaboration. The
action began in 1793. By the end of January in that year all the successive
'visionary designs' which, as Gibbon put it, had 'floated in my head' had
dissolved. The 'Historical excursions' had stalled; the work on the house of
Brunswick was at a standstill; the supplementary volume of the *Decline and
Fall* had been forgotten. Of the *Memoirs*, as Gibbon wrote to Lord Sheffield,
'little has been done, and with that little I am not satisfied. They must be
postponed.' It was at this point that he asked Sheffield to dangle the bait of
the 'British Portraits' before Mr Nicol. But Mr Nicol had not risen to it.
Then, in May, Gibbon set out from Lausanne for another visit to England, to
stay with Sheffield in London and Sussex. Six weeks later he made his first
contact with Pinkerton.

According to John Nichols, the learned printer, Gibbon was introduced to
Pinkerton by Horace Walpole.[8] No doubt Gibbon made preliminary
enquiries through his friends, and Walpole would be an obvious informant.
But Pinkerton states clearly that Gibbon was still a stranger to him in July
when he suddenly received, through George Nicol the bookseller, an invitation to meet him at Nicol's shop in order to discuss the new venture. The
invitation was couched 'in the most flattering terms', and Pinkerton was
bowled over by it, as well he might be, after his early indiscretions.[9] When
they met, Gibbon praised Pinkerton's work highly, particularly his *Enquiry*

which, he said, had induced him to think of Pinkerton as his coadjutor; and he set out his plan. Pinkerton was delighted: it seemed the realisation of his dream – the dream of 'Philistor', whose 'letters' Gibbon had now read. From the language used by both men it is clear that they took to each other at once. Gibbon had found his ideal editor, Pinkerton his ideal patron; for Gibbon's name would surely bring in the financial sponsorship which such a venture required. They evidently liked each other personally too. Pinkerton was charmed by Gibbon's civility and Gibbon was pleased by the thought that he could help a real scholar to live down an unfortunate reputation. As he wrote to Pinkerton, the execution of the project would not only fill a public need but also 'wipe away those early prejudices and personal animosities which you have been perhaps too careless of provoking'. Pinkerton accepted the reproof. 'Too true', he commented: 'Peccavi.'[10]

Between July and November Gibbon and Pinkerton held 'several conversations' in which the details were worked out. Nicol, who was equally enthusiastic, urged that no time be lost. He also wanted Gibbon to be the editor, but Gibbon declined: his residence abroad, he said, made that impossible. But he agreed to sponsor and design the work, to give advice and assistance in detail, and to contribute to the cost by ordering at least six sets. He also undertook to write a preliminary prospectus, a general preface to the whole series, and a particular preface to each volume. For this purpose he planned, on his return to Lausanne, to read all the medieval English chronicles in order: 'a labour', wrote Pinkerton, 'which he mentioned with pleasure as the last and most favourite occupation of his life'. This new enterprise, he said, was the only plan which he had seriously meditated since completing the *Decline and Fall*, and as he still hoped for twenty years of existence, he looked forward to its completion. In the end he agreed also to be named as 'conjunct editor' since that would improve the sale of the volumes.[11]

Meanwhile he drafted the prospectus which was to be published, together with a second prospectus by Pinkerton, in January 1794. In this document he again compared his project with the work of the French Benedictines and Muratori, and he named Pinkerton as his chosen editor. He praised Pinkerton's scholarly works – his *Essay on Medals*, his *Dissertation*, his *Enquiry*, which, he candidly admitted, had 'rectified my old opinions', and his Lives of Scottish saints, which had scattered some rays of light over a dark age. He recognised that there might be some prejudice against him – 'the impulse of a vigorous mind' having urged him 'to write and print before his taste and judgement had attained their maturity' – but all that was now past: 'repentance has long since propitiated the mild divinity of Virgil . . . he smiles at his reformation of the English tongue'. By such juvenile explosions, 'the volatile and fiery particles of his nature have been discharged and there remains a pure and solid substance endowed with many active and useful energies': 'the Goths still continue to be his chosen people but he retains no antipathy to a Celtic savage'. In short, he had all the qualities required for the task: he was 'one of the children of those heroes whose race is almost extinct' and who could carry out such a work single-handed. He could be the English Muratori.

The prospectus having been drafted, Gibbon arranged to meet Pinkerton again late in November 1793, but then he had to put him off, for he was in the hands of the surgeons, undergoing his second operation within a few weeks. However, he invited Pinkerton to call on him immediately after the operation. Pinkerton probably did so, for soon afterwards we find him in correspondence with Thomas Astle, the Keeper of the Records in the Tower, to whom he gave an up-to-date summary of the plan as agreed in 'repeated conferences' between them. The work was to be 'a splendid republication of all the ancient English historians, down to the year 1500, in one chronological body, with prefaces, notes, indexes, maps, and other illustrations': twelve folio volumes in all, 'on the plan of Bouquet's French historians'. There would be an ordinary edition at thirty guineas and a larger de luxe edition at fifty guineas, and those who subscribed to the latter were to form a committee to manage the funds as 'special patrons of the work'. Astle, in his reply, expressed his admiration for 'Mr Gibbon's gigantic plan', adding, 'I agree with him that you are the most proper person in England to execute it.'[12] However, within a month Gibbon was again in need of surgery, and after a third operation he died, on 16 January, the very day on which his prospectus was to be published. Lord Sheffield, his executor, found the draft among his papers and printed it, describing it as 'a sketch interrupted by death'.

'My good friend Gibbon is dead', Pinkerton wrote to his friend Lord Buchan, a Scotch antiquary no less eccentric than himself, 'and his plan has perished with him.' For the plan, Pinkerton had always insisted, was Gibbon's alone and only his patronage could have carried it through: 'I must repeat', he had told Gibbon from the start, 'that all our hopes of success depend on your name alone.' Indeed, after Gibbon's death, Pinkerton questioned whether even that support would have sufficed: 'I doubted its success even with his name'; 'I never hoped for success in a design which government alone could carry into execution. It was solely his own project and has expired with him.' The great difficulty, of course, was the cost. The Maurists had had the revenues of the Benedictine Order behind them. They could also count on a captive market: all the monasteries in France were instructed to purchase their publications. Muratori was supported by his prince, the duke of Modena.[13] But Gibbon had intended to rely on private subscriptions which, with his death, could not be assumed. So the ambitious plan was dropped, and Pinkerton returned to the purely Scottish antiquarian interests which still entitle him to remembrance.

Gibbon's death obviously shattered Pinkerton and it put an immediate stop to their common venture, but it was not the only cause of its failure. There was also another distraction. By 1794 Britain was at war with revolutionary France, and afterwards with Napoleon. That long war inevitably pushed the medieval chronicles of England into the background: their potential patrons were otherwise occupied. But it did not entirely stifle the project; and sure enough, when final victory was in sight, it revived – and so, briefly, did Pinkerton.

In August 1814, with Napoleon defeated and exiled to Elba, Pinkerton's spirits rose again. Gibbon was dead, but might not other patrons, might not government itself, now take up the project? So he prepared a new campaign. He wrote a new prospectus, caused a hundred copies to be printed, and solicited the support of Lord Grenville, the former whig prime minister. The plan, he explained, was still the same, even though it had been interrupted by 'the unexpected death of Mr Gibbon and the lengthened war of twenty-one years', and he himself, 'the editor proposed by Mr Gibbon', was 'still anxiously desirous to carry it into effect'. Lord Grenville was sympathetic, which was encouraging. Meanwhile the subject became topical, because Lord Sheffield was preparing a third volume, and a new edition, of Gibbon's *Miscellaneous Works* in which he was about to print Gibbon's draft prospectus. He wrote to Pinkerton asking for any relevant information, and Pinkerton, in reply, touched lightly on the new opportunity. Gibbon's 'last great work', he wrote, 'would not have expired with him if a war of twenty-one years had not engaged the whole attention of those distinguished characters who could alone promote such an expensive design. At present, it is hoped, it might be resumed with some prospect of success, and among our monuments of triumph this literary temple might be erected to the ancient glory of our country.'[14]

Sheffield obligingly published Pinkerton's letter, but unfortunately the publishers did not respond. 'Notwithstanding the powerful encouragement of Lord Grenville', Mr Longman wrote to Pinkerton, his partners foresaw so much trouble that 'they have declined to engage with you'. Undeterred, Pinkerton went higher still. He drew up a memorial to the prince regent himself. 'The late celebrated Mr Gibbon', he wrote, 'had projected, in conjunction with the memorialist, the publication of all the ancient English historians in one regular series, they being now scattered in various dissimilar collections'; and once again he set out the plan. But once again he was doomed to disappointment. The prince regent, it seems, though a judicious patron of learning, was not impressed. Pinkerton's petition evidently received no reply.[15]

That was the end of the project as far as Pinkerton was concerned. Perhaps, in his case, there was a special reason for its failure, and the trouble which Mr Longman's partners foresaw may have been connected with the personal circumstances and character of the proposed editor. For Pinkerton, no longer young, was now in financial straits and his attempt to revive the project may even have been a gesture of desperation. By the end of that year his creditors were pressing him and his days of learned literary work and correspondence were over. He disappeared from the scene and we last hear of him in Paris, 'a very little and very thin old man with a very small, sharp, yellow face, thickly pitted by the smallpox and decked with a pair of green spectacles'. He died in 1825, aged sixty-seven, in Paris where he had lived his last years, as Sir Walter Scott would write, 'in exile, in obscurity and, we fear, in indigence'.[16]

So we take leave of Pinkerton; but not of Gibbon's project with which he had been so briefly involved. For even while his attempts to reanimate it were being rejected by a new generation of patrons, it was not allowed to die. The persons who sought to revive it after the end of the war were different, but the scheme which they promoted was recognisably continuous with it. Indeed, there was a personal link with Gibbon himself. That link was supplied by George John Spencer, 2nd Earl Spencer.

Lord Spencer was well known in his time as a patron of scholarship, a bibliophile and a statesman. He had been carefully educated: his father had engaged as his tutor Sir William Jones, the famous orientalist, who was also a classical scholar, lawyer and poet. Jones was a close friend of Gibbon, who praised him in the Decline and Fall. He was also an admirer of Pinkerton.[17] In 1778, when Spencer, then Lord Althorp, was twenty years old, Jones proposed him as a member of 'the Club'. Jones' letter to him describing the company which he was inviting him to join is a well-known document in the history of that society.[18] At the Club, Spencer must have become familiar with Gibbon. In 1783, when he succeeded to the earldom and the family estates, he began to reorganise and improve the great library at Althorp, making it 'the richest private collection in Europe'. Two years later, Lord and Lady Spencer came to Lausanne, and Gibbon saw them 'almost every day at my house or their own during their stay of a month'. Lady Spencer also had cultivated tastes and was the friend of literary men. When in England, Gibbon was 'in the habit of visiting Althorp' where he would occasionally 'have a resolute intellectual conflict' with the Italian librarian, Mr Ocheda. During his last visit to England in 1793, he stayed at Althorp from 20 October to 6 November – precisely the time when he was engaged in planning his project with Pinkerton. On his return to London, he dined twice with Lady Spencer's father, Lord Lucan. His last social engagement, unfulfilled owing to his death, was to be a dinner with Lord Lucan.

In view of their close friendship and the intellectual interests of Lord Spencer, who was a founder and first president of the Roxburgh Club and served for forty years as a trustee of the British Museum, it seems inconceivable that 'Mr Gibbon's gigantic plan' was not discussed between them during that fortnight at Althorp, or that Spencer was not keenly interested in it. But after Gibbon's death any such interest must have been suspended. In that very year, Spencer became first a privy councillor, then ambassador in Vienna, then first lord of the Admiralty. He held this last post for over six years – six very dramatic years during which Britain's naval supremacy in the world was secured by the successive victories of Nelson. Indeed, it has been said that 'for him, more distinctly perhaps than for any other English administrator, may be claimed the title of "organiser of victory" '. In these circumstances his literary and historical interests must necessarily have been suspended.

When peace had returned they were resumed. In resuming them, Spencer was assisted by an antiquary whom he had patronised and who was to him what Pinkerton had been to Gibbon. This was Henry Petrie, who had been introduced to Spencer by his bibliographical adviser, Thomas Frognal Dibdin. Spencer used Petrie's services and encouraged his researches, and about 1816 – that is, after Pinkerton's applications had been rebuffed or ignored – they revived Gibbon's project. In 1818 a meeting of noblemen and gentlemen interested in historical literature and conscious of the inadequacy of all previous attempts was convened in Spencer House, Lord Spencer's house in London, to consider the publication of the English records. This informal body agreed that 'no association of individuals, however zealous or liberal', could be expected to carry through such a project and decided to recommend it, through the prime minister, Lord Liverpool, to the government. The proposal now made was for a complete collection of the annals and other historical documents of British history from the beginning to the death of Henry VII in 1509. This was precisely the plan set out by Gibbon and Pinkerton. The model suggested was also theirs: the *Recueil des historiens des Gaules et de la France* of Bouquet. The editor proposed was, inevitably, Petrie, who in the meantime, in 1819, had been appointed, on the recommendation of Lord Spencer, as Keeper of the Records in the Tower, and who was now invited to draw up a detailed plan.

In 1822 Petrie's plan was forwarded to the government by the Commissioners for Public Records, who dwelt, as Gibbon and Pinkerton had done, on 'the reproach under which this country lay in the estimation of other nations' for its backwardness in the publication of its records, and reiterated the name of Bouquet. The proposal was put to the House of Commons and approved. A humble address was thereupon presented to the king, and George IV, who as prince regent had ignored the personal request of Pinkerton, now, as king, accepted the same request from his Parliament. So, in 1823, 'this great national work' was begun. It was recognised by all whose memory went back thirty years as the realisation of the last project of Gibbon.[19]

Petrie's work on the documents was delayed by personal and administrative accidents, but when he died in 1842 he left his first volume – a large folio volume containing documents from the earliest times to the Norman Conquest – almost complete. It was published in 1848, entitled *Monumenta historica Britannica*, and dedicated to Queen Victoria. An introduction by Petrie's pupil and successor Thomas Duffus Hardy traced the story of the project back to Gibbon. Then Hardy himself took over the project, and indeed transformed it. Under his energetic direction the project gathered momentum, and from 1858 the great 'Rolls Series' of chronicles and memoirs began to appear: no fewer than sixteen volumes in that first year and a total of 237 volumes in the forty years from 1858 to 1897. So the reproach of other nations was at last wiped away. 'Mr Gibbon's gigantic plan', frustrated by his sudden death, postponed by the Napoleonic Wars, but kept alive by his friend Lord Spencer, had at last, a century after his death, yielded a harvest far beyond his dreams. Poor Pinkerton had been left nowhere, remembered only for his eccentricities – those eccentricities which Gibbon had hoped, by this project, to redeem. And yet he too was a pioneer. As an eminent Scottish contemporary wrote of him, he was 'the most sensible, I might almost say the only sensible, writer on Scotch antiquities'.[20] Gibbon, whom he had presumed to correct, recognised that. By his researches he had broken what has been called 'a chain of error in Scottish history'. He also looked forward. In his 'letters' of Philistor he had set out the scheme of historical teaching, research and publication which has since become general; and time has proved him right when he wrote that such a scheme as he envisaged could be executed, in Britain, by government alone.

CHAPTER 10

The Romantic Movement and the Study of History

THE INTERESTS OF John Coffin, in whose memory this lecture was founded, were evidently various. They included literature, philosophy, history. Today it is the turn of history. But it seemed to me, when I sought for a title, that, in order to commemorate him, I should not be too austerely historical: that I should examine before you some aspect of history which partakes also of literature and philosophy; and for this reason, I have chosen as my subject, or at least for my title – for it is a great mistake to give away too much in a title – the Romantic Movement and the Study of History.

Every age has its historical philosophy, and such a philosophy is seldom, if ever, the work of historians only. Historians follow each other along professional grooves, refining their predecessors' techniques; but they do not create new philosophies. These are brought in from outside, either by the immediate impact of events or from more general intellectual revolutions. The new science of Machiavelli underlay the 'civil history' of the seventeenth century. The new sociology of Montesquieu made possible the 'philosophic history' of the eighteenth century. I am concerned today with the external intellectual force which made the next great historical change: which changed the philosophy of the eighteenth-century historians – Hume, Robertson, and Gibbon – into the philosophies of their nineteenth-century successors – Macaulay, Michelet, Ranke.

I say, 'the external intellectual force', for of course there were external nonintellectual forces too. Most obvious of all was the impact of events. In the last years of the eighteenth century Enlightened Europe was convulsed, first by the French Revolution, then by the French conquest. In those convulsions the ideas of the past century were damaged beyond repair. When the goddess Reason was set up as the idol of a sanguinary dictatorship and French

'Enlightenment' was carried over the continent by military force, the charms of both quickly faded. In England, in Germany, in Spain, old native traditions, even superstitions, acquired a new force, a new respectability. Man did not live, it was discovered, by reason alone. The old, customary organs of society, the old established beliefs, which had seemed so contemptible to the rationalists of the *Encyclopaedia*, now acquired a new dignity. The greatest of English whigs, Edmund Burke, became the European prophet of a new conservatism: the conservatism of a society which must protect its living organs against the frivolous surgery of fashionable or interested theorists. In his last years, the greatest of eighteenth-century historians, who had never accepted the radicalism of the *Encyclopaedia* – for, like Burke himself, he was a disciple of Montesquieu – would hail Burke's *Reflexions on the French Revolution* as 'an admirable medicine against the French disease. I admire his eloquence, I approve his politics, I adore his chivalry, and I can even forgive his superstition.'[1] And the greatest of nineteenth-century historians would declare that the historical studies of his time had developed 'in opposition to the tyranny of Napoleonic ideas'.[2]

But if the immediate convulsions of Europe caused men to appreciate anew the previously insulted traditions of their own society, another movement, independent in its origins, invested those traditions with a positive, romantic glow. Already, in the middle of the century, that movement had begun. It began, or at least one great stream of it began, in Scotland. In 1760 James Macpherson, a man of questionable morals both in literature and in politics, published his *Fragments of Ancient Poetry Collected in the Highlands*, the precursor of his more famous fabrication, the *Fingal* of 'Ossian'. In 1765, in England, Thomas Percy established a less brilliant but more lasting fame with his *Reliques of Ancient English Poetry*. With these two works, a new fashion was launched: a romantic cult of primitive society, primitive literature; and it was this cult which, transformed by political events unimagined in the 1760s, would help to create a new historical philosophy.

At first, the reaction of historians to this new literary or philological fashion had been cool. To a disciple of Voltaire, the Dark and Middle Ages were dark indeed. They were the ages of gothic barbarism and superstition and nothing that came out of them could have any virtue at all. Even to a disciple of Montesquieu, such literature, however interesting for the light that it shed on the society which produced it, was of no intrinsic value; and anyway, was it authentic? 'Something of a doubtful mist still hangs over these Highland traditions', wrote Gibbon, 'nor can it be entirely dispelled by the most ingenious researches of modern criticism. But if we could, with safety, indulge the pleasing supposition that Fingal lived and that Ossian sung, the striking contrast of the situation and manners of the contending nations might amuse a philosophic mind.'[3] 'I see', Hume wrote to him on reading these words, 'you entertain a great doubt with regard to the authenticity of the Poems of Ossian. You are certainly right in so doing.'[4] In his private conversation, Hume was more outspoken. He would not believe in the authenticity of Ossian, he said, though fifty bare-arsed Highlanders should swear to it.

So spoke the voice of reason in 'the full light and freedom of the 18th century'. But as the full light faded and the ordered freedom dwindled, the artificial glow and the anarchical liberty of the past appeared more attractive. Ossian, that thin, tawdry figment of the Highland *débâcle*, might excite the smile of Gibbon, the ridicule of Hume, the rage of Johnson, but abroad his fortune was fabulous. He would become the inspiration of Herder,[5] the idol of Germany. Napoleon himself would carry the book as his *bibelot* on his campaigns: it was to him, he would say, as Homer had been to Alexander, Virgil to Augustus; and at Malmaison his empress would decorate her elegant new palace with Ossianic *bric-à-brac*, busts of the mythical Highland poet, paintings of his ghost welcoming in Elysium the heroes of her husband's wars. Meanwhile, in a more modest way, Bishop Percy too was enjoying his posthumous triumph. His *Reliques of Ancient English Poetry*, having also inspired Herder in Germany, fell into the hands of a Scotsman more influential even than Macpherson: Walter Scott.

Macpherson and Scott, the Highlander and the Lowlander of Scotland, these are the makers, direct or indirect, of the new romanticism which would change the character of historical study. At first it may seem parochial to say this; for, after all, romanticism had many sources: why then should we deduce it from this private northern spring? But in fact, this is not, I think, too gross a simplification. Scotland, in the eighteenth century, was one of the intellectual capitals of Europe. The direction of its energies might change, but the power behind them was the same. The same social chemistry which released, in one generation, the genius of Hume and Adam Smith, formed, in the next, as its secondary product, the genius of Scott. Nor was Scott in any way parochial. Rooted though he was in the Scottish Border, whose every valley and stream, castle and peel-tower he knew so well, he was a cosmopolitan, a European too. We should not forget that long before he became known in Europe, years before he decided to abandon the law for literature, Scott had studied not only Ossian (whom he had the taste to despise) and Percy (whom he revered), but the romantic literature of Europe; that he learned Italian to read, every year, Ariosto and Boiardo; that he pored over Bartholin and studied Old Norse in order to read the Scandinavian sagas;[6] and that, as a young lawyer in Edinburgh, he learned German in order to enjoy the poets of *Sturm und Drang*: that his earliest published works were translations of Bürger's poems and Goethe's *Goetz von Berlichingen*.

But for all his cosmopolitan range, Scott was also intimately wedded to his own country. He was a Scotsman, and a Borderer. Indeed, this local loyalty lay at the base of his cosmopolitanism. The Scottish Enlightenment, like every era of enlightenment, had its social foundations. Its great writers – Hume, Robertson, Ferguson, Adam Smith – directed their minds to the progress of society not merely because they had read Montesquieu, but because their own society provided them (as English society did not provide Englishmen) with a case history for the application of Montesquieu's social laws. They saw before them, simultaneously, the old static, introverted society of pre-Union Scotland and the new transforming energies released by the renewed post-Union contact with the world. The dynamics of progress were visible before them,[7] and they delighted in that progress. A generation later Scott looked more nostalgically at the same process. For him, the old society, whose relics had seemed barbarous to his predecessors, had acquired, in retrospect, a new charm. Just as Macpherson had idealised the vanishing tribal society of the Celts and turned Hume's 'bare-arsed Highlanders', 'the bravest but the most worthless' of men, into romantic heroes, so Scott was captivated by the archaic Border society of which, by now, only the memory survived. For centuries the Borders, on the Scottish side, had been a closed, static, almost fossil society. A few grandees, enriched by the patronage of the English court, might live magnificently in their heavy, bizarre castles; but beneath them the gentry, generation after generation, lived on, the same ritual, predatory life, within their closed, traditional circle. Then, with the Union of 1707, came the change. First by trade with England, then by service in England, finally – and most of all in Scott's own time – by the vast patronage of India, the circle was broken. Like the Highlands after Culloden, but more gradually, the Borders became an 'open society'; and each area in turn found the poet who would romanticise its dissolving past.

It was in his childhood, at the farm of Sandy-knowe, near Smailholm tower, that Scott discovered his romantic attachment to the Border country.

It was under an Oriental Plane-tree in a garden at Kelso that he read Percy's *Reliques*; and Percy and Goethe (says his son-in-law) were to be the inspiration of his whole life. It was under the influence of Percy that he would study the ballad literature of Northern Europe and set out, as a young lawyer, every year, on his 'raids' into Liddesdale, sometimes on horseback with his friend Shortreed, sometimes with his wife by phaeton – the first wheeled carriage ever to penetrate those rural valleys – in quest of those popular ballads which he would publish in 1802 as *Minstrelsy of the Scottish Border* – 'the well', as Carlyle called it, 'from which flowed one of the broadest rivers'. At the same time he was exploring the Highlands too, visiting old survivors of the Jacobite days before Culloden, studying the vanishing manners of Highland society, 'wasting his great talent', as his shocked old Presbyterian tutor complained, collecting 'ancient ballads and traditional stories about fairies, witches and ghosts',[8] and writing those original poems – *The Lay of the Last Minstrel, Marmion, The Lady of the Lake* – so unreadable today, which gave him his first fame. Before he had ever written a novel, Scott had eclipsed the two founding fathers of the romantic revival. He was at once the new Percy of his country, the new Ossian of his time.

Ballad literature, to the student of it, is inseparable from history: it is the direct expression of a historical form of society which often has no other documents. In collecting the ballads of the past, Scott was re-creating and illustrating a vanished or vanishing society, and thereby, indirectly, becoming its historian. Nor was it only by such collection that he showed his historical interest. All his life he read history, re-created history, published the materials of history. Historians use his compilations still: his *Sadler State Papers*, his *Somers Tracts*, his reissues of arcane Stuart pamphlets. He founded the Bannatyne Club to publish Scottish antiquities. At one time he planned 'a *corpus historiarum*, or full edition of the chronicles of England, an immense work', to rival the great collective work of the Benedictines of St Maur – a work for which Gibbon had once sighed and encouraged the Scottish historian Pinkerton to undertake.[9] But this vast enterprise remained a dream. It was not, perhaps, beyond Scott's powers – after all, Scott's edition of Dryden, in eighteen volumes, thrown off between poetry, essays and an active life in the law, was good enough to be reprinted *in toto* a century later – but ultimately Scott was not that kind of historian. If he had been, he would by now be forgotten. For all his accuracy of detail, he was not a scholar: he was an imaginative historian who used his evidence not to document but to re-recreate the past. As Carlyle wrote in his journal, on learning of Scott's death, 'he knew what *history* meant; this was his chief intellectual merit';[10] and he found his perfect medium when, after so many preliminary ventures, he produced, from 1814 onwards, his great historical novels, with their marvellous fusion of living persons and a reconstructed past: *Waverley, Guy Mannering, Old Mortality, Rob Roy, Heart of Midlothian . . .*

Above all, *Old Mortality*. What a wonderful work that is! What historian has ever so captured the character of pre-Union Scotland: of the fanatical Cameronians, of John Graham of Claverhouse, of the royalists and Episcopalians and 'indulged ministers' of the 'killing times'! Who that has once read it can ever forget the murder of Archbishop Sharp on Magus Moor, or Lady Margaret Bellenden and her Tower of Tillietudlem? It was a real work of scholarship as well as imagination, the first novel – as Lockhart remarks – in which Scott had to reach back beyond the date of human memory and recon-struct, from books alone, an unremembered past age.[11] And how well he reconstructed it! The professional historians did not like it. The Rev. Thomas McCrie, the learned biographer of John Knox and Andrew Melville, a strict dissenting Presbyterian, protested that Scott had libelled the Covenanters, and thundered away in the *Edinburgh Christian Instructor*. 'Spare not the vile Tory of an author!' the Christian editor adjured him; and he spared not. *Old Mortality*, wrote McCrie, was full of 'gross partiality and injustice . . . disfig-ured with profaneness . . . unjustifiable in any book, but altogether inexcusable in one that is intended for popular amusement'. Scott's greatest historical disciple, Macaulay, would afterwards present a very different picture of Claverhouse, as a man 'rapacious and profane, of violent temper and obdurate heart', rightly detested 'with a peculiar energy of hatred' by Scotsmen throughout the world. But time has vindicated the novelist, not the historians. The fanatical Covenanters are fanatics still, in spite of Dr McCrie and the long, dreary line of Kirk hagiographers. Macaulay's portrait of Claverhouse was exposed as a caricature by Paget and can never be restored.[12] Scott, whose imagination saw past the mere literary evidence, who envisaged the whole, compact, articulated society of Scotland in its years of crisis, and who looked daily on the portrait of Claverhouse,[13] saw, here at least, better than both.

In 1814, when Scott began to publish his novels, the public events of Europe had conspired to provide him with an audience. The nations were now in arms against Napoleon; Burke, not Voltaire, was the political philosopher of the day; and historians were eager to describe, not the mechanics of progress, which so easily led to revolution, but the robust vitalising spirit which fortified and preserved the legitimate organs, institutions, and traditions of the past. Moreover, in the countries of Europe – and particularly in Germany, which had never yielded to the 'philosophy' of the Encyclopaedists – the same romantic quest for reliques of ancient poetry had ended not only in the discovery of such poetry but in the creation, through it, of a new historical philosophy.

For in Germany, too, Percy as well as Ossian had his disciples. The greatest of them, of course, was Herder: Herder the philosophic founder of cultural history, the prophet of romantic nationalism, who saw the primitive poetry of every nation as the direct expression of its distinguishing soul, the repository of its autonomous history; and who, in his famous collection of national songs, *Stimmen der Völker in Liedern*, published in 1778–79, included many translations both from Ossian and from Percy's *Reliques*. But if Herder first proclaimed the new doctrine in Germany, and made out of it a new philosophy of history, it was not he who applied that philosophy. That was done, first of all, not by philosophers or historians but by classical philologists; and the new ballads which they discovered or invented came not from Germany but from ancient Greece and Rome.

First there was Friedrich Voss, whose translation of Homer into German hexameters in the 1780s and 1790s so excited his contemporaries. Then there was F.A. Wolf, who, by his exact philological scholarship on the Greek text, so dissolved the unity of Homer that it has never been restored. To Wolf, the creator of 'the Homeric question', the *Iliad* was not, as it had been to all his predecessors, the majestic artefact of one great blind poet: it was a later construction, pieced together, like Macpherson's *Ossian*, out of numerous old Greek 'lays'; lays exactly comparable with the popular ballads now published by Percy and Herder. Wolf's exciting doctrine was published in 1795. A few years later its historical implications were drawn out and applied by the most revolutionary historian of the nineteenth century. This innovator was the lifelong friend of Voss, the devout disciple of Wolf: the North German scholar-banker, Barthold Georg Niebuhr.

Like Scott, Niebuhr was a Borderer, strongly attached to his childhood home. He was brought up in Dithmarschen, on the Danish border, among the historic recollections of an ancient peasant republic whose stubborn conservative resistance against the dukes of Holstein was commemorated in popular ballads. All his life Niebuhr remembered Dithmarschen and its solid rural independent conservatism. All his life he was interested in ancient popular poetry. He translated a modern Greek folk song and proposed to translate the newly published Serbian ballads.[14] He regarded the recently discovered *Nibelungenlied*[15] as the greatest of poems. In Latin literature he despised Virgil as a feeble, artificial court poet. Even Ennius, the rude father of Latin poetry, seemed to him too aristocratic, too literary; for was there not evidence that, before Ennius, the primitive Roman republic, like the autonomous republic of Dithmarschen or the oppressed peoples of the Balkans, had possessed still ruder and therefore better ballads which Ennius, with his Greek metres, had driven out of memory? Then, in a moment of inspiration, 'a sudden flash of light', sparked off by Wolf's treatment of Homer,[16] Niebuhr saw a new solution to an old problem.

That problem concerned the sources of early Roman history. The only continuous native literary evidence for that history was the work of Livy. But what evidence, men asked, had Livy himself used? The official records of Rome had been destroyed in 389 B.C., when the city was taken by the Gauls. How then could Livy narrate, in such detail, events two and three centuries even before that date? Already in the late seventeenth century the Dutch scholar Perizonius had raised this question and had suggested an answer: Livy had drawn his matter from popular 'lays' transmitted orally from generation to generation.[17] But Perizonius had no direct knowledge of such 'lays'. He wrote before Ossian was known or Percy had published, or the *Nibelungenlied* had been recovered. His suggestion was therefore a hypothesis only. But now, exclaimed Niebuhr, the hypothesis had been put 'on firm ground' by the happy discoveries of the philologists. 'For us the heroic lays of Spain, Scotland, and Scandinavia have long been a common stock; the song of the Nibelungs has already returned and taken its place in literature; and now that we listen to the Serbian lays and to those of Greece, the swan-like strains of a slaughtered nation; now that everyone knows how poetry lives in every people' (the words might be taken straight from Herder), until art stifles it, 'the empty objections' made to Perizonius' theory 'no longer need any answer': the case is self-evident.[18] Having reached this conclusion, Niebuhr looked again at Livy, and under that smooth, milky text his eye divined, and his critical scholarship disengaged, the very form and structure, the titles, even the words of a whole cycle of lays; and from those lays, in turn, he deduced the character of the society which created them: the popular, conservative republic of Rome.

Niebuhr's achievement – his imaginative use of exact critical methods to revise the history of the past – inspired all the historians of the nineteenth century, even those who rebelled at the dogmatism of his conclusions. He was the father of constructive historical *Quellenkritik*. His method, one English historian wrote, was like 'Ithuriel's spear' at whose touch falsehood was transformed to truth.[19] But he also did, more scientifically, in his historical writing, what Scott had done in his novels. Both used a new insight to reconstruct, out of hitherto neglected material, the vanished context of formal history. Implicit in the work of both was a new historical philosophy. Unlike the classical 'philosophic historians', they saw the successive ages of the past not as mere stages in the history of progress, whose value lay in their relevance to the present, but as self-sufficient totalities of human life, valid within their own terms, demanding from the historian neither praise nor blame but sympathetic, imaginative re-creation. Such re-creation required effort. The historian must breathe the atmosphere of the past, think in its mental categories. He may not, like the 'philosophical historians' of the Enlightenment, insulate himself in his library in London or Paris, Edinburgh or Lausanne. Voltaire, for all his universal claims, had never stepped down from his eighteenth-century elevation. Even Gibbon, for all his submerged romanticism, had never visited any part of that Byzantine Empire whose millennial history he had written. No nineteenth-century historian would dare to show such sublime insouciance. The reality of the past, the historical value of its spontaneous, popular expression, its local temporal colour, would be respected alike, though with different emphasis, by radical and conservative, whig and tory: Michelet and Carlyle, Macaulay and Ranke.[20]

Consider the greatest of conservative historians, perhaps the greatest of all historians in the nineteenth century, Leopold von Ranke. At first it might seem difficult to discover romanticism in this austere, dispassionate scholar. Technically, indeed, Ranke was a disciple of Niebuhr. Niebuhr's book, he wrote, was the first German historical work to excite him by opening new historical horizons, and time only increased his respect for that 'magnanimous spirit', that 'great Master of Antiquity'. At the age of ninety Ranke would still look back on Wolf and Niebuhr as 'our classics, who illuminated my youthful steps'.[21] In his own rigorous *Quellenkritik* Ranke proves the truth of this claim. But it was not only a critical spirit that Ranke shared with Niebuhr. He too was a conservative, revolting, in historical scholarship as in politics, against the tyranny of French ideas; and he too looked to native popular literature as the authentic, direct expression of autonomous societies or past ages.

At first Ranke, like so many lesser historians,[22] was seduced by that universal enchanter, Sir Walter Scott. In his autobiography he tells us how, in those years, Scott's novels were being read all over Europe, and were inspiring sympathy with past times. He too read and was excited by them. Admittedly, the excitement did not last. *Quentin Durward* broke the charm. Scott's Louis XI and Charles the Bold, Ranke discovered, did not tally with those of Commines and other contemporary writers, and he decided to pursue truth, not romance. So 'I turned altogether away and resolved, in my work, to avoid all imagination, all poetry, and keep firmly to the facts'.[23] In his first published work, at the age of twenty-nine, he declared this resolution. His aim, he then wrote, was not to judge the past, but simply to show it 'wie es eigentlich gewesen'.[24] Nevertheless, this rejection of romance was not absolute. A few years later it was to return, in a new form: direct, as Scott himself had received it, from a popular source.

In 1827, at the age of thirty-two, Ranke went to Vienna and there gained access to the Venetian *Relazioni* preserved in the *Hofbibliothek*. The Keeper of the Library, at that time, was Jernej (Batholomäus) Kopitar, a Slovene who was interested in the popular literature of the South Slavs. Fifteen years earlier, Kopitar had been Metternich's censor of Slavonic languages and in that capacity had opened and read letters written in Slavonic. By this unusual method of patronage he had discovered, in Vienna, a Serbian *émigré* who was seeking to revive the half-forgotten Serbo-Croat language. Kopitar had sought out and encouraged his victim, who, thanks to that encouragement, became the greatest figure in the literary history of Yugoslavia, the re-creator of its language, the collector and publisher of its historic ballads, Vuk Stefanović Karadžić. Through Kopitar, Ranke met Vuk himself, and Vuk showed him all his documents concerning the recent Serbian revolt, which he had witnessed. Ranke was fascinated by them. The historian who had turned away from the romantic novelist, from the editor of *The Minstrelsy of the Scottish Border*, found himself entranced by 'the most learned of all Serbs', the editor of the *Pesnarica*.

When Ranke discovered Vuk, he forgot or postponed his work on the Venetian *Relazioni*. He decided, with Vuk's aid, to write a history of the Serbian revolt. Every day the two men sat together at a table going through Vuk's papers, and Vuk told Ranke about the Serbian ballads which he had collected and which another common friend in Vienna, Wenzeslaw Hanka, had translated into German. The result of their collaboration was Ranke's

History of the Revolution in Serbia, which appeared in 1828 and contained a chapter on Serbian popular culture and Serbian ballads. It was read by Niebuhr who declared that that little book was 'the best that we have in our literature' (*das vortrefflichste was wir in unsrer Literatur besitzen*). When this verdict was reported to Ranke he was delighted: it was, he wrote, 'an antidote to all calumny'.[25]

Ranke never forgot Vuk, or his debt to him – though his biographers and critics do not think it worth mentioning. To him, Serbian history and Serbian ballads were as significant as the history and ballads of Dithmarschen had been to Niebuhr. Fifty years later he would recall how 'my unforgettable friend Vuk' would come very day, stumping with his wooden leg up the stairway in Vienna, to bring to the historian a new supply of Serbian records, Serbian ballads, Serbian reminiscences.[26]

So much for Ranke. Now let us turn from the greatest of conservative historians to the greatest of whigs. No two contemporary historians could be more opposite from each other than Ranke and Macaulay. They had a common tradition, of course. Both were heirs of the Enlightenment. But they inherited different parts of that tradition. Ranke inherited its universal spirit, from which, however, he abstracted its driving motor of progress, believing (like Herder) in the autonomy of the past and the equal right of all cultures: every age, as he put it, was 'immediate to God'. Macaulay believed intensely in that motor and drove it fast, respecting no such rights. History, to him, was 'emphatically the history of Progress', and the past only mattered, in the last analysis, in so far as it illustrated that process. As Ranke complained, Macaulay constantly summoned the past before the bar of the present to be judged and condemned. And yet Macaulay, like Ranke, was deeply influenced by the new spirit – though, once again, with a difference. While the conservative, academic Ranke turned away from the warm but dangerous imagination of Scott to the exact criticism of Niebuhr, the whig politician Macaulay, while moving within the same field, moved in the opposite direction. He was first captivated, then disillusioned by Niebuhr; but for all his whiggism, and his almost pathological hatred of the Stuarts, he never ceased to be a disciple of the romantic Jacobite tory, whose politics, ideas, and way of life he uniformly deplored, Sir Walter Scott.[27]

Macaulay, like Ranke, was a young man when Scott's novels were conquering the world and, like Ranke, he was captivated by them. He also saw that they provided new opportunities to the writer of history, and in 1828 he said so. In that year he published, in the *Edinburgh Review*, an essay on 'History'. It is not a profound essay, and he did not afterwards include it in his collected essays;[28] but it contains, for our purpose, an interesting passage. It is the passage in which he discusses the qualities of the ideal historian.

It is interesting to compare Macaulay's profession of historical faith, at the age of twenty-eight, with that which Ranke had published four years earlier, at the age of twenty-nine. There is nothing here of austere objectivity, of the natural rights of the past. And yet the past was not to be entirely subordinated to the present. It might be indulged in inessentials. Like an 'autonomous' republic under the firm rule of Muscovite orthodoxy, it might at least keep its quaint local costumes, its country dances, its dialect, its cheeses. The ideal historian, says Macaulay, should not confine himself to formal narrative, but should enliven his account of public events by interspersing in it 'the details which are the charm of historical romances'. Then, after telling the story of the apprentice of Lincoln who made, for the cathedral, out of fragments rejected by his master, a stained-glass window so fine that 'the vanquished artist killed himself from mortification', he goes on: 'Sir Walter Scott, in the same manner, has used those fragments of truth which historians have scorn-fully thrown behind them, in a manner which may well excite their envy. He has constructed out of their gleanings works which, even considered as histo-ries, are scarcely less valuable than theirs. But a truly great historian would reclaim those materials which the novelist has appropriated': he would blend Clarendon with *Old Mortality*, Hume with *The Fortunes of Nigel*.

About the same time, Macaulay told his sister about his own historical method. 'My accuracy as to facts', he said, 'I owe to a cause which many men would not confess. It is due to my love of castle-building. The past is in my mind soon constructed into a romance.' Then he went on to describe how, on his solitary London walks, he constantly envisaged the scenes of the past: how every detail was visually imagined, every building exactly reconstructed, every place accurately peopled. 'I seem to know every inch of Whitehall. I go in at Hans Holbein's gate, and come out through the matted gallery. The conversations which I compose between great people of the time are long and sufficiently animated: in the style, if not with the merits, of Sir Walter Scott's.'[29] This same quality, this visual identification and localisation of past history, is shown in a comment which Macaulay made a few years later about Virgil: 'I like him best on Italian ground. I like his localities; his national enthusiasm; his frequent allusions to his country, its history, its antiquities, and its greatness. In this respect he often reminded me of Sir Walter Scott.'[30]

In the same years in which Macaulay was thus borrowing the historical method of Scott, he found his way, through the translation of Hare and Thirlwall, to the revolutionary work of Niebuhr. Though not, like some of his friends, 'Niebuhr-mad', Macaulay recognised at once that 'the appearance of the book is really an era in the intellectual history of Europe'.[31] He was particularly delighted with Niebuhr's idea of a cycle of Roman lays – lays which, even more than his favourite passages of Virgil, would obviously cling to Italian ground. But as yet Macaulay had not visited Italy. When he did go to Italy, in 1839, on his return from India, he was disillusioned with Niebuhr – the bold whig could not endure that timid conservatism, the dogmatist that rival dogmatism[32] – but the lays were still vivid in his mind, and when he saw the castellated hills and historic lakes of Tuscany, as romantic to a classical scholar as the river Tweed and Cheviot hills to a Borderer, a new project formed in his mind. Niebuhr and Scott, the Roman lays and the Border ballads, were suddenly fused together. Niebuhr, with his usual confidence, had already declared the exact subject of those lays: 'the history of Romulus, the story of Horatius, the destruction of Alba, above all "the lay of Tarquinius", culminating in the truly Homeric battle of Lake Regillus'. This last, wrote Niebuhr confidently, was the greatest of all, and 'should anyone ever have the boldness to think of restoring it in poetical form', he should cast it in the form of its only worthy rival, the *Nibelungenlied*.[33] Macaulay had that boldness. He wrote his *Lays of Ancient Rome*. They were the very lays which Niebuhr had named. In his preface he paid his tribute to Niebuhr. But the style of his poems was not that of the *Nibelungenlied*: it was that of the poems of Sir Walter Scott.

Thereafter Macaulay settled down to his great *History*, and sought to realise the ideal which he had set out in 1828. That whole work is indeed deeply influenced by Scott – not of course in its intellectual direction, but in its method and incidental illustration: its skilful use of local colour, trivial anecdote, and popular literature. No modern critic, that I know of, has mentioned this intimate dependence of Macaulay on Scott; but once mentioned, it is obvious, and contemporaries, who knew their Scott, quickly recognised it. In Ireland, Scott's old friend Maria Edgworth was still living at Edgworthstown, in County Longford. She it was who, by her Irish stories, had first inspired Scott to write his Waverley novels. Now, at the age of eighty-two, she read a presentation copy of Macaulay's first volume. Only one complaint qualified her delight: 'there is no mention of Sir Walter Scott throughout the whole work', even in places where it seemed impossible to avoid paying so obvious a tribute.[34] In England, a more critical commentator was another old friend of Scott, J.W. Croker. 'We suspect', he wrote, 'that we can trace Mr. Macaulay's design to its true source – the example and success of the author of Waverley. The historical novel, if not invented, at least first developed and illustrated by the happy genius of Scott', had taken 'a sudden and extensive hold of the public taste.' The press, since his time, had 'groaned with his imitators'. 'We have had served up in this form the Norman conquest and the Wars of the Roses, the Gunpowder Plot and the Fire of London, Darnley and Richelieu'. Harrison Ainsworth had just published 'a professed romance' on Macaulay's historical villain James II. 'Nay, on a novelist of this popular order has been conferred the office of *historiographer* to the Queen.'[35]

What was the quality, in Macaulay's writing, that proved, to these critics, the influence of Scott? First of all, there was Scott's great innovation, local colour. I have mentioned Macaulay's strong sense of 'locality', the association of events with places: a sense which he appreciated in Virgil and explicitly associated with Scott. In all his own writing he showed this sense – in his Indian essays as in his Italian 'lays' – and he gratified it fully in his *History*. When writing his *History*, Macaulay did not sit continuously in his library. He travelled abroad. He visited not only the archives but the scenes: the marshlands of Sedgemoor, the town of Torbay, the battlefields of Flanders, Scotland, Ireland. He saw with his own eyes Londonderry and the Boyne, Glencoe and Killiecrankie, and peopled them, as he had long ago peopled Whitehall and Hampton Court, with their historic actors. In so doing, he gave life to the past even if – since Macaulay's vices are never very far from his virtues – he could not resist the temptation to reiterate, every time, the vast improvement which 'whig' progress had brought to the marshes and towns of the West Country, the bogs of Ireland, and the waste Highlands of Scotland.

Moreover, Macaulay drew this life from the same sources as Scott: from the neglected informal, popular literature of the time. He had no patience with those who talked of 'the dignity of history'.[36] Like Scott, he was a great browser in bookshops, a voracious reader in the byways of literature. He read comedies and farces, lampoons and satires, broadsheets and went through the Pepysian ballads in Magdalene College, C: dug out the unindexed Roxburghe Ballads in the British Mus the success of *Lilliburlero* to illustrate the unpopularity of

Protestant Ireland, and a bogus ballad planted upon him 'in a most obliging manner' by a clergyman at Morwenstow to illustrate the popularity of Bishop Trelawney in Cornwall.[37] In this way he realised his old ambition to reclaim for history 'those materials which the novelist has appropriated'.

A dangerous ambition! we may exclaim, as we look back at a century and more of romantic historiography: as we read the purpler passages of Carlyle, Froude, and Freeman, Motley, Prescott, and Parkman; as we think of the long decline of what the French called *histoire Walter Scottée* into the 'tushery' of Victorian novelists and those local pageants which were organised by Louis-Napoleon Parker and ridiculed, but not killed, by J.H. Round. How much better, we may think, is that other, opposite product of the romantic movement in history, the austere, self-denying spirit of Ranke, who sought to sever the past from the present, to avoid not merely modern prejudice but even imagination and poetry, and to pursue only an unattainable objectivity! How much better still, we may conclude, are the pre-romantic historians, the enlightened, 'philosophical' historians of the eighteenth century, who, since they did not deaden the past by severing it from the present, had no need either to embalm it in the cold, stately mausoleum of German conservatism, or to jerk it into spurious life by imposing on it their synthetic colours and ventriloquial sounds! Both Ranke and Macaulay, by their romantic borrowings – the one by his almost sterilised conservatism, the other by his distorting vitality – may be said, like the romantic movement in general, to have put the clock of European thought not forward but back. Has not Ranke been accused of having, by his passive, academic 'objectivity', contributed indirectly to the rise of that German Nazism to which Carlyle, by his romantic hero worship, directly pointed the way? Did not Macaulay, by his compelling narrative, by his decorative romantic detail superimposed on a purely political study, distract historians from that profounder analysis which the disciples of Montesquieu had made possible but which was only resumed, a century later, by the disciples of Marx?

So we may say; but to what purpose? Genius is not responsible for the botcheries of its imitators, nor should we judge new ideas by their distorted consequences. No great movement is pure; advance in any one field is often purchased by retreat in another; and every new gospel introduces a train of superstitions, sometimes grosser than those which it has displaced. Ideas are to be valued not by their incidental corruptions, but by their permanence, their power to survive those corruptions. If we are to judge the contribution of romanticism to historical study, we should try to isolate what was permanent in it, and view it at its best.

The historiography of the Enlightenment, at its best, had been animated by 'philosophy'. The eighteenth-century historians looked back and saw a new meaning in the past. They saw history as a process, and a process, moreover, of improvement, of 'progress'. Thereby they gave to its study a new value, not merely moral and political, but intellectual and social. But if they thus penetrated to the inner meaning of history, they did so, too often, by overlooking its human content. The men of the past entered their story only indirectly, as the agents or victims of 'progress': they seldom appeared directly, in their own right, in their own social context, as the legitimate owners of their own autonomous centuries. The romantic writers changed all that. Seeing the doctrine of progress converted from a gospel of humanity into a slogan of conquest, they cast it aside and tried to look on the past direct. Whether, like Ranke, they altogether rejected the concept of progress as merely distorting their new vision, or, like Macaulay, adjusted their new vision in order to embellish that concept, they resolved, at all costs, to make the past live. As Carlyle wrote of Sir Walter Scott, who is the real hero of this lecture (but I did not dare put him in the title lest his very name should frighten away the audience), he first showed 'the old life of men resuscitated for us. . . . Not as dead tradition but as palpable presence, the past stood before us.' Scott's historical novels, said Carlyle, 'have taught all men this truth, which looks like a truism, and yet was as good as unknown to writers of history and others, till so taught: that the bygone ages of the world were actually filled by living men, not by protocols, state-papers, controversies, and abstractions of men'.[38] That surely is a permanent truth which, however it may be corrupted, historians can never afford to forget.

CHAPTER 11

Lord Macaulay: *The History of England*

firefly

Whig History

Lord Macaulay is unquestionably the greatest of the 'whig historians'. By the clarifying brilliance of his style, and his compelling gift of narrative, he won an instant and apparently effortless success in the nineteenth century. The interpretation of English history which he gave became the standard interpretation for nearly a century: so universally accepted that we hardly realise the novelty which it once contained. Admittedly, that interpretation has now become unfashionable. But it can never be altogether rejected. Much of it – both in factual scholarship and in general interpretation – has become part of the permanent acquisition of historical science. The severest critics themselves are generally unaware of the extent to which they depend on the achievement of their victim. In order to appreciate that debt it will be useful to begin by considering the interpretation of English history before Macaulay stamped it, indelibly, with his imprint.

For 'whig history' is essentially English. In its crudest form it is the interpretation imposed on the English past by an English political party in search, at the same time, of both a historical pedigree and a political justification. This is not to deny that the thesis may also be true, or that it may also be applicable to other countries. In fact, the whig theory of history has foreign as well as English origins. It owes much to the French Huguenots and even more (including the name 'whig') to the Scots. There are continental historians – the French Protestant statesman-historian F.P.G. Guizot is an obvious example – who can be described as 'whigs'. But it is in England that the continuous 'whig' party was developed and in England that the consistent whig theory of history was elaborated. It was also to English history that it was most naturally applied. A 'whig' interpretation of Europe is conceivable; but it could never be expressed with Macaulay's brilliant clarity. The pattern would not admit the simple antitheses which are possible, and perhaps justified, in the special English circumstances. Macaulay himself was well aware of this. He was, he once wrote, 'as much puzzled as pleased' by the success of his *History* abroad, 'for the book is quite insular in spirit. There is nothing cosmopolitan about it.'[1]

Whig history, then, is insular history. It is also Protestant history. Indeed, its Protestantism is inseparable, in origin, from its insularity: for it was the revolt from Rome, in the sixteenth century, which caused historians – not only in England or Scotland – to look for a national history, independent of that universal Roman Church which had been served and extolled by the monkish chroniclers of the past. But these earliest national, Protestant historians, if they had dissociated the history of their countries from foreign 'despotism', had not, at that time, supplied it with any secular ideology. If they were Protestant, they were not yet republican or 'whig'. In some countries they might be. In France, for instance, the Huguenot writers soon discovered that national Protestantism could only be secured in opposition to the Valois monarchy; and so, after the Massacre of St Bartholomew in 1572, they discovered that the ancient constitution of France was not monarchical but oligarchic. The same discovery was made in Scotland, after the deposition of Mary Queen of Scots. Buchanan's *History of Scotland* (1582), like Hotman's *Franco-Gallia* (1573), seeks to justify aristocratic revolt against monarchy by appeal to an ancient 'Protestant' tradition, and for this reason both would be reprinted by the English whigs of the seventeenth century. But in Elizabethan England the new national Protestant historiography had no reason to be antimonarchical. Far from it. Since the Protestant Revolution had been made and was preserved by English sovereigns, not against them, its historians looked back and saw the national Protestant tradition maintained by the English monarchy. While Hotman and Buchanan cried up the 'whig grandees' of ancient France or legendary Scotland, the hero of their English colleagues was not the English baronage, who extorted Magna Carta from King John, but King John himself. In view of the bad name which King John would acquire among the later whigs, this may seem ironical. But we must remember that King John stood up (for a time) against the most imperious of medieval popes. He was thus a precursor of those other 'despotic' but national Protestant monarchs, Henry VIII and Queen Elizabeth.

That was all very well in Tudor times. But when the Stuarts came from Scotland to rule over England, the terms of the formula soon changed. In seventeenth-century England, as in sixteenth-century France and Scotland, the national Protestants found themselves in opposition to the crown. So, when they looked back into history, they discovered that the English, like the French and Scottish, constitution had always been essentially aristocratic. It was the monarchy, but a 'mixed monarchy'. Sir Edward Coke, the great champion of the English common law, discovered a continuous parliamentary constitution going back to the ancient Britons. More cautious antiquaries were prepared to settle for the Anglo-Saxons. In the course of the seventeenth century, while the English parliamentary classes fought, with differing weapons, against successive Stuart kings, their antiquaries built up a historical 'myth' according to which the English monarchy had always been implicitly contractual. Even the rude fact of the Norman Conquest had not interrupted this good old Anglo-Saxon tradition, for William the Conqueror (they said) had accepted and perpetuated the existing constitution. And this constitution had been preserved intact ever since. It had been guaranteed by the common law, strengthened by Magna Carta, guarded by Parliament; and those kings who had sought to break the contract had found themselves resisted, even deposed. Such had been the fate of Edward II in 1327, of Richard II in 1399; such would be the fate of Charles I in 1649, of James II in 1688. Of the 'Tudor despotism' of the sixteenth century, these historical theorists did not find it convenient to speak.

All through the seventeenth century this 'whig' theory of the ancient contractual constitution of England was improved by antiquarian research, political struggle, and philosophical speculation. Royalists, high Anglicans, 'tories' resisted it on all fronts; but they resisted in vain. The 'Glorious Revolution' of 1688, followed by the Hanoverian succession in 1715, inaugurated the period known in English history as the 'whig ascendancy': the triumph of the whigs in politics, in philosophy, and in historiography. In the early years of the whig ascendancy the first complete and up-to-date history of England was published. It was, and would long remain, the classic whig history. Its author, Paul Rapin de Thoyras, was a French Huguenot who had served William of Orange as a soldier in Ireland and had then been employed as a tutor in the household of William's Dutch favourite, William Bentinck, earl of Portland. He wrote it in Wesel, in Germany, in the French language, and published it in Holland in 1723.

Rapin wrote mainly for foreigners. He set out to explain, to bewildered Europeans, how it was that England, after a century of external impotence and internal faction, had suddenly appeared, powerful and united, as the arbiter of Europe; and he explained it by accepting and expounding, with great clarity and moderation, the official whig thesis, *viz* that England, alone in Europe, had contrived to preserve the old free constitution which had once been the common property of the 'barbarian' conquerors of Rome but which, elsewhere, had been lost. His explanation, solidly based on new documents published by the order of the English whig government and edited by the whig historiographer royal, Thomas Rymer, was widely accepted. Rapin's work was translated and continued in England, respected by tories as well as by whigs, and enthusiastically praised by Voltaire. For our purposes it is important because it is the classic expression of the pre-Macaulay 'whig' interpretation of English history, and the difference between Rapin and Macaulay is the measure of the novelty of Macaulay's 'whig' history.

Not that the innovations were entirely Macaulay's own work. The greatest innovator was a man whose name is seldom mentioned by Macaulay but whose work is always in his mind – a man whom he regarded as his greatest intellectual enemy, but to whom he was deeply, if indirectly, indebted – David Hume. For it was David Hume, the 'tory' historian of England, who, by totally destroying the 'whig' history of Rapin and advancing a completely new philosophy of history, imposed on the new generation of English whigs the need to think again.

Hume's *History of England* was published in the years 1754 to 1761, the last years, as it happened, of the 'whig ascendancy'. When he wrote, few of his readers could remember anything but whig rule and the whig establishment was sunk in doctrinal complacency. That complacency, in the historical field, he completely shattered. He himself came to history from outside the closed whig world, first, because he was a Scot (and it was difficult to find much virtue in Scottish whiggism), secondly, because he had begun as a philosopher, not as a historian. Moreover, as a philosopher, he had – like Gibbon – been captivated by Montesquieu, the great transformer of historical philosophy. Thus influenced, Hume was able to look at history in a new way, and the new way in which he looked at it made the old whig thesis (and the old tory thesis, too) permanently obsolete.

Hume did not believe that sacred 'constitutions' were the guarantee of 'liberty'. To him all constitutions were relative, and effective liberty was the result not of constitutional forms but of social and economic progress and 'sophistication of manners': the same 'liberal' constitution which might guarantee 'liberty' in a mature society (like England) might merely perpetuate faction and oppression in an immature society (like seventeenth-century Scotland). In fact, Hume devalued all 'constitutional' ideas and measured the virtue of government by the extent to which the established forms permitted economic and social progress or 'utility'. By this criterion many authoritarian systems were better guarantees of 'liberty' than many ancient anarchical 'constitutions'. In his *History*, Hume expressed these ideas with exquisite wit in an irresistible style; and he deployed his wit most mercilessly at the sacred cows of the official whig faith: at the virtuous Anglo-Saxons, at the medieval barons, at the whig 'patriots' of the seventeenth century.

For half a century after the publication of Hume's work, the whig historians raged impotently at it; but they were quite unable to set up again the shattered Humpty-Dumpty of Rapin. The 'new whigs' at the end of the eighteenth century – the political party which, after a generation in the wilderness, was at last to capture power in 1830 – needed a new historical philosophy; and that historical philosophy had to incorporate the permanent content of Hume's work. That permanent quality was its dynamism. Rapin had represented liberty as an ancient inheritance of which the whigs were the hereditary guardians. Hume had represented it as a continuing capacity for social improvement. For the immutable legacy of our ancestors he had substituted the new idea of social progress.

The fusion of Hume's historical philosophy with whig politics was the work, essentially, of Scottish whig writers, who worked under the social patronage of the disconsolate English whig aristocrats, nursing their wounds and preparing their next campaign in the London home of their leader, Charles James Fox. This was Holland House, in which Fox lived as the uncle and guardian of the young Lord Holland, who afterwards continued his patronage. Intellectually the ablest of these new whig writers was John Millar, a radical disciple of Hume, who for forty years was professor of law at Glasgow University, and who dedicated his *Historical View of the English Government* to Charles James Fox. Millar had a great influence on Scottish whiggism and it was his disciples who, in 1801, founded the *Edinburgh Review*, soon to be the intellectual organ of the English whig party. Charles James Fox himself was among those who sought to re-establish whig history.

In his political eclipse, he decided to write a history of the English Revolution of 1688 in order to vindicate the whig party from the aspersions of Hume. In 1800 and 1801, during the brief Peace of Amiens, he carried out some research in the French archives and prepared his material; but he completed only a fragment, which was afterwards published by his nephew Lord Holland. His work was taken over by another Scottish whig, who was also a *protégé* of Holland House, and who was to have a great influence on Macaulay, Sir James Mackintosh.

Mackintosh's plan was more ambitious than that of Fox. Like Fox, he was determined to re-establish, against Hume, the historical pedigree of the whig party. He was also, like Millar, imbued with Hume's philosophy. But he proposed to go further than Fox. Having been deeply impressed by the French Revolution, which he at first welcomed for its liberal promise, then repudiated for its radical performance, he was concerned to show that true whiggism not only secured English liberty and progress in 1688 but also saved England from the bloody revolution which had overtaken France and Europe from 1789. He therefore planned to write a history of England from 1688 to 1789. In order to equip himself financially for this task, he accepted the lucrative post of Recorder of Bombay and spent the years 1804 to 1811 in India. On his return he became a member of Parliament; and when the whigs returned to office in 1830, he was appointed a member of the Board of Control for India. But although, in those years, he collected a vast mass of material (which now fills forty bound volumes in the British Museum), he wrote little; and when he died in 1832, he too left only a fragment of his History. That fragment, which began with the accession of James II in 1685 and ended with the settlement of the crown on William III in February 1689, was published in 1834 as *History of the Revolution in England in 1688*.

Thus by 1834, although the whigs had recovered political power, English historiography was still dominated by the 'tory' Hume. And yet successive whig writers had believed that, even out of Hume's historical philosophy, a new whig interpretation of history could be constructed. The basic materials for such a history lay to hand. Vast manuscript collections – those of Fox and Mackintosh – were available to Holland House. The theory was already presented – by Mackintosh and others – in the *Edinburgh Review*. All that was needed was a historian with the energy and literary power to complete what Fox and Mackintosh had merely begun. It was this opportunity that was seized by Macaulay.

Thomas Babington Macaulay

Macaulay was born in 1800, at Rothley Temple in Leicestershire, the home of his uncle Thomas Babington, after whom he was named. His father, Zachary Macaulay, was a Scottish Highlander by birth, who had gone to Jamaica at an early age and devoted the rest of his life to the abolition of the slave trade. He was a pious evangelical and one of the members of the 'Clapham Sect' – practical evangelicals who sought to reform social abuses in general and to abolish slavery in particular. Like most other members of his group, Zachary Macaulay was a tory. Many of them were also Quakers. Macaulay's mother was the daughter of a Quaker bookseller in Bristol. These biographical details may be of some interest for Macaulay's own intellectual development, of which we know very little; for although Macaulay always respected his father and his father's philanthropic work, he emphatically rejected the political and religious world in which he had been brought up. He was educated at an evangelical school before going to Cambridge, and we know that he arrived at Cambridge a tory; but when he first appeared as a writer, a few years later, his views were absolutely fixed, and fixed for life. He was a whig. Moreover, he not only rejected his family toryism: he also, in his writings, expressed consistent contempt for Highlanders and Quakers; he was completely without religious sense, being a conventional conformist, expressing amused disdain for all kinds of nonconformity; and if he never ceased to be liberal, and to hate the institution of slavery, he would speak with contempt of professional 'negrophils'. Nor can Zachary Macaulay have felt altogether happy at his son's later devotion to Holland House and, in particular, to Lady Holland: for Lady Holland was the daughter of a West Indian planter and brought to her husband a West Indian plantation, worked by slaves. She would refer to Macaulay's father, somewhat contemptuously, as 'a great saint, Zachariah, and the bitterest foe to all West Indian concerns'.[2]

It thus seems that Macaulay's whiggism may have been part of a general reaction against his family circle, and this, in turn, may account for its intensity. But whiggism, it seems, was not his first or direct reaction from the toryism in which he had been brought up. There had been an intermediate conversion. For a short time, while an undergraduate at Trinity College, Cambridge, Macaulay had been a radical. He was converted to radicalism by a fellow-undergraduate, Charles Austin, a well-known Cambridge converter. But although he remained a lifelong friend of Austin, Macaulay quickly rejected radicalism, and afterwards attacked both radicals and radicalism as violently as he would attack tories and toryism. He had settled for aristocratic, political whiggism. This he first showed in 1822, when he won an annual college prize for an essay on William III, prince of Orange and king of England.[3] William III, the maker of the 'Glorious Revolution' of 1688, the founder (however involuntary) of the whig establishment, was to remain Macaulay's lifelong hero. From this time on, we may say that his views were fixed. Age and practice might sophisticate the expression of them, but their substance, even in detail, would never change.

However, if Macaulay became, and remained, an uncompromising whig, it was a whig of a special kind. He was a 'new whig', a whig of the party which, in his own words, had been 'purified' in the reign of George III; which had been inspired by Burke, led by Rockingham, and sustained in opposition by Fox; and which had now retreated into the aristocratic citadel of Holland House. Moreover, among those aristocratic whigs, Macaulay, who was not at all aristocratic (his 'want of pedigree', wrote Lady Holland, was a serious handicap in 'that most aristocratic assembly', the English House of Commons),[4] was distinguished by what we may call his Scottish inheritance. He had absorbed the 'utilitarian' philosophy which had made Hume a tory, which had been made whig by Adam Smith, Millar and Mackintosh, and which was now the philosophy of the *Edinburgh Review*. Macaulay's rejection of political utilitarianism – the utilitarianism of the radicals – did not entail a rejection of utilitarian ideals: indeed, Macaulay, in the crude materialism of his concept of progress, is sometimes positively vulgar. What Macaulay rejected was the idea that material progress could be attained or preserved by the direct political action of a 'democratic' party, lacking political experience and relying on academic theories or paper constitutions. Entirely unphilosophical in his outlook, entirely empirical in his politics, he despised theory and theorists – even the great whig theorists meant little to him – and trusted implicitly in the continuing political capacity of a practised liberal, historically educated ruling class. Progress, defined in utilitarian terms, would, he believed, be far more painlessly achieved, and far more securely based, under the leadership of whig magnates than by the direct action of political pedants. In the past, English 'whigs' – whether so named or not – had been more successful than English republicans, English 'Levellers', or French Jacobins. In the present, and for the foreseeable future, they would be more successful than English 'utilitarians', French 'socialists', or American 'democrats'. This was the lesson of history.

Once fixed in these views, Macaulay was eager to assert them, and from the time when he left Cambridge, he proposed to himself a life of politics and literature. Success in both fields was not long in coming: indeed, throughout his life, Macaulay suffered from instantaneous success in every field – in politics, in oratory, in prose, even in poetry. In 1825 he published, in the *Edinburgh Review*, his long essay on Milton. This was a trenchant, uncompromising expression of the whig view, and at once attracted notice. Other articles in the *Edinburgh Review* followed, including (in 1829) a violent diatribe against the radical 'utilitarians', and especially their prophet, James Mill. By means of these two essays, the one excoriating the tories, the other the radicals, Macaulay recommended himself to the aristocratic whig leaders, and, in particular, to his father's friend Henry Petty-Fitzmaurice, 2nd marquis of Lansdowne. Lord Lansdowne was the son of a famous father, a whig prime minister who had been the friend and patron of radical thinkers and who had sent his son to study at Edinburgh University together with Brougham, Jeffrey, Horner, and Sydney Smith, the founders of the *Edinburgh Review*. In 1830 Lansdowne offered Macaulay the representation of his 'pocket' parliamentary borough of Calne, Wiltshire. Macaulay was duly elected, and thus entered Parliament at the beginning of the long-delayed whig triumph. Next year his speech in support of the Reform Bill made him famous. A few weeks later he received the highest mark of social favour that any young whig could hope for: he was invited to Holland House. In the same year he received also a political reward. He was made secretary of the Board of Control for India.

Macaulay joined the Board of Control just at the time when Mackintosh was vacating it by death. He already knew Mackintosh in Parliament and had been noticed and befriended by him. Two years later he was to follow Mackintosh's example again. In 1833 the constitution of the East India Company was changed and a supreme council for India was set up. In 1834 Macaulay was offered a seat on this supreme council. The term was for five years; the salary £10,000 a year. Like Mackintosh, Macaulay calculated that such a post would enable him to save enough money to finance a life of literature thereafter. In fact, he stayed in India for only three and a half years, but in the course of his residence there he made a permanent mark on Indian administration, for he took a prominent part in founding the educational system of India and ensured that English, not any of the Indian languages, should be the language of instruction. He also set up and presided over the committee which devised the criminal code for India. At the same time he continued to read and write. His reading, largely in the classical languages, was immense, and thanks to his phenomenal memory he rarely forgot anything that he had once read. His writing was still for the *Edinburgh Review*. It was in India that he wrote his famous essay on Bacon, which reveals at once the strength and the limitation of his mind. But a more important essay, at least for our purpose, is his long review of the posthumous fragment of Mackintosh's *History*.

In this essay, which appeared in the *Edinburgh Review* in July 1835, Macaulay expressed once again the new whig philosophy. He also took the opportunity to make another violent attack on radical doctrines, as expressed by Mackintosh's editor, William Wallace. The attack was so violent that Macaulay was nearly forced, on his return, to fight a duel with Wallace. But the interest of the review lies largely in its implications. In writing it, Macaulay must have been acutely aware of the void which first Fox, then Mackintosh, had sought, and failed, to fill; and this awareness happened to coincide with a great void that had suddenly opened in his own life.

At the beginning of January 1835 Macaulay received news from England of the death of his younger sister, Margaret. It was a terrible blow: 'what she was to me', he wrote at the time, 'no words can express. . . . That I have not utterly sunk under this blow, I owe chiefly to literature.' 'Literature', he wrote twelve months later, 'has saved my life and my reason. Even now, I dare not, in the intervals of business, remain alone for a minute without a book in my hand.' And he added that he was 'more than half determined', on his return to England, 'to abandon politics and to give myself wholly to letters: to undertake some great historical work which may be at once the business and the amusement of my life'.[5] With Mackintosh's fragment before his eyes and this resolution in his mind, it could hardy be doubted what that great historical work would be. Macaulay would write what Mackintosh had meant to write: the whig history of England from 1688 until recent times. 'I do not believe', he would afterwards write, 'there is in our literature so great a void as that which I am trying to supply. English history from 1688 to the French revolution is even to educated people almost a *terra incognita*.' And on another occasion he wrote that he was determined not to 'fritter away' his powers 'like poor Mackintosh'.[6]

In order to carry out this project, Macaulay resolved to return to England at the first opportunity. In the summer of 1838 he was back in London. However, he did not at once devote all his energies to his new tas'

Immediately after his return, he made a tour of Italy; he continued to write essays for the *Edinburgh Review*; and he returned to the House of Commons, this time as member for Edinburgh.

All these diversions took up his time and some of them added significantly to his literary output. He was active in Parliament, where he delivered some famous speeches. 'Whenever he rose to speak', Gladstone would afterwards write, 'it was a summons like a trumpet-call to fill the benches.' His speech on the proposed Copyright Act of 1841 was an oratorical triumph: Macaulay carried the majority of the Commons to his side and killed the proposal. He also held high political office as secretary at war in Lord Melbourne's government from 1839 to 1841. The essays which he wrote between 1839 and 1842 include the two most widely published of all his essays, those on Clive and Warren Hastings: the fruit of his Indian experience. And meanwhile, as a result of his Italian visit, he had entered – and conquered – a new field: that of poetry. In 1842 he published his *Lays of Ancient Rome*.

Macaulay's *Lays of Ancient Rome* are more important than they might seem for his historical work. The idea of writing such poems was supplied to him by the work of the German historian B.G. Niebuhr. Niebuhr's *History of Rome* began to appear in English in 1828. It was reviewed in the *Edinburgh Review*, and at once caused great interest in England. Macaulay himself, at first reading, regarded it as marking 'an era in the intellectual history of Europe'. What particularly excited historians was Niebuhr's interpretation of early Roman history, as represented by Livy. Niebuhr argued that Livy had no authentic historical sources for so remote a period, and that his formal narrative was in fact based on traditional ballads or 'lays'. Macaulay afterwards lost faith in Niebuhr – especially on discovering that he was an abject conservative in politics – but the idea of such old Roman 'lays' remained in his mind. There it was fertilised by contact with another strong interest which Macaulay shared with many other nineteenth-century historians: his interest in the writings of Sir Walter Scott.

Macaulay had always been an admirer of Scott. He knew his poems by heart and, in his historical work, consciously imitated Scott's method of writing: his use of description, of local colour, or popular tradition or ephemeral literature. A good historian, he wrote in an early essay,[7] should not confine himself to battles, sieges, negotiations, politics; he should also 'intersperse the details which are the charm of historical romances'. In this way, he added 'Sir Walter Scott . . . has used those fragments of truth, which historians have scornfully thrown behind them, in a manner which may well excite their envy. He has constructed out of their gleanings works which, even considered as histories, are scarcely less valuable than theirs. But a truly great historian would reclaim those materials which the novelist has appropriated.' Macaulay's skill in such reclamation is obvious to all readers of his work, and the pervasive influence of Scott in Macaulay's *History* was at once remarked by critics as different as Maria Edgeworth and John Wilson Croker.[8] The theory of Niebuhr attracted Macaulay because it suggested, once again, the interdependence of history and ballad literature: it gave him the idea, of which he often spoke, of 'restoring to poetry the legends of which poetry had been robbed by history'. So when he travelled in Italy, the scenes of ancient Roman history had on him the same effect which the scenes of the Scottish Border had had upon Scott: they inspired him to re-create the ballads which the Roman historian (according to Niebuhr) had also recognised as the legitimate material of history.

Macaulay's *Lays of Ancient Rome*, once again, was an instant success, and Macaulay, as always, was pleased, not to say complacent, at their success. But he did not allow this new literary interest to distract him from his main purpose. Even while he was in Italy, and acquiring the local colour for his poems, he was thinking of his *History*. 'As soon as I return', he wrote, 'I shall seriously commence my *History*'; and he sketched its plan. By beginning in 1688 and continuing, if possible, to 1830, he would be able to incorporate, and to connect, the triumphs of the old whigs, who made the Glorious Revolution and secured the Hanoverian succession, and of the new whigs, who, after the loss of the American colonies, set out on the long struggle for parliamentary reform. Between these two revolutions, which he would portray in detail as 'the revolution which brought the crown into harmony with Parliament and the revolution which brought Parliament into harmony with the nation', he would dispatch 'more concisely' the intermediate events, necessary only to prove the essential continuity of the whig party. From 1838 onwards he was at work on his programme, modifying it as he studied more deeply – for instance, he soon realised that he must start before 1688 in order to 'glide imperceptibly into the full current of my narrative'.[9] After 1842, when he had dispatched his *Lays of Ancient Rome* and basked, for a time, in the applause, he contracted his dispersed activities in order to concentrate exclusively on his *History*.

In 1843 he agreed to publish his collected essays. Here his hand was forced by American piracy: inaccurate versions were already circulating widely, and

Macaulay agreed, somewhat reluctantly, to supply an authorised text. His essays, like everything else that he wrote, at once became a best-seller. After that, he wrote only two major essays: one on William Pitt the elder, Earl of Chatham, which summarises, in mature form, his interpretation of eighteenth-century English history; one on the French Jacobin Bertrand Barère, which illustrates, once again, his hatred of political radicalism. Both these essays were published in 1844. Next year, Macaulay wrote to Macvey Napier, the editor of the *Edinburgh Review*, that he could undertake no more such articles. He would work exclusively on his *History*.

At the same time, he detached himself as far as possible from politics, which he now definitely subordinated to literature. He had been out of office anyway since the fall of the whig government in 1841. On the return of his party to power in 1846, he accepted the office of paymaster-general. This was a comparative sinecure which would give him what he wanted: 'leisure and quiet more than salary and business'. He did not speak much in Parliament, and he lost the support of the electors of Edinburgh, who accused him of caring 'more for his *History* than for the jobs of his constituents'. In consequence of this apparent indifference, he lost his seat, and with it his office, in the general election of 1847. He remained out of Parliament for the next five years, refusing all proffered seats. In 1852 the Edinburgh whigs turned back to him and invited him to stand. He refused; but they nevertheless elected him to Parliament. For the next four years he attended Parliament, but he spoke rarely. He never held political office again. In 1856 he applied for the Chiltern Hundreds – that is, retired from Parliament. During these years, and indeed for the rest of his life, he was absorbed in the *History* which he was determined to leave as his monument.

In writing his *History*, Macaulay had certain advantages over his predecessors. First of all, he had their work. Fox's fragment, indeed, did not carry him far, but Mackintosh's work, though also a fragment, was, so far as it went, a solid and original piece of historical research, and a comparison of it with Macaulay's first volumes shows Macaulay's continuous reliance on it: he often repeated Mackintosh's words, and he sometimes adopted his errors. But even more valuable to him than the finished work of Fox and Mackintosh was their raw material. The transcripts which Fox had made were supplied to Macaulay by Lord Holland; the huge manuscript collection of Mackintosh was put at his disposal by Mackintosh's son. These magnificent collections saved Macaulay a great deal of labour, especially at the beginning of his work.

Thanks, in part, to them, Macaulay was able to publish the first two volumes of his *History* in November 1848. These two volumes coincided exactly, in scope, with the work of Mackintosh. They carried the story down to the deposition of James II.

As with his first essay, as with his first speech, as with his first poems, the success of these first volumes of the *History* was instantaneous. Macaulay had intended that it should be: his work was 'to have a permanent place in our literature', and his confidence was well based. He was sure of his thesis – the whig thesis. There was merit, no doubt, he wrote in his journal, in the great 'philosophical historians' of the eighteenth century, Hume, Robertson, Voltaire, and Gibbon, 'yet it is not the thing. I have a conception of history more just, I am confident, than theirs.' He took great trouble over his style: 'how little', he exclaimed, 'the all-important art of making meaning pellucid is studied now! Hardly any popular writer except myself thinks of it.'[10] And he was determined to be not only pellucid but also 'amusing', readable: 'I shall not be satisfied unless I produce something which shall for a few days supersede the last fashionable novel on the tables of young ladies.'[11] But even he had hardly reckoned on the scale of his success. Thirteen thousand copies were sold in four months. 'Of such a run', he wrote in his diary, 'I had never dreamed.' It was exhilarating; but it was also sobering. It made him feel 'extremely anxious about the second part. Can it possibly come up to the first?' For now he had to deal with the uncharted field of the reign of William III.[12]

Faced with this challenge, Macaulay made even greater efforts. Three months after the publication of the first volumes he recorded in his diary that he had decided 'to change my plan about my *History*'.

I will first set myself to know the whole subject: – to get, by reading and travelling, a full acquaintance with William's reign. I reckon that it will take me eighteen months to do this. I must visit Holland, Belgium, Scotland, Ireland, France. The Dutch archives and French archives must be ransacked. I will see whether anything is to be got from other diplomatic collections. I must see Londonderry, the Boyne, Aghrim, Limerick, Kinsale, Namur again, Landen, Steinkirk. I must turn over hundreds, thousands of pamphlets. Lambeth, the Bodleian and the other Oxford libraries, the Devonshire papers, the British Museum, must be explored, and notes made: and then I shall go to work. When the materials are ready, and the *History* mapped out in my mind, I ought easily to write on an average two of my pages daily. In two years from the time I begin writing, I shall have more than finished my second part. Then I reckon a year for polishing, retouching and printing.[13]

On this system he worked methodically, first obtaining a general under-standing of the period – 'the reign of William III, so mysterious to me a few weeks ago', he wrote in June 1849, 'is now beginning to take a clear form' – then studying each particular episode and sketching his first account of it, while the impressions were fresh, 'at a headlong pace'. Afterwards he wrote out the revised version in a regular 'task' of six pages a day. His aim was perfect clarity: 'the great object is that, after all this trouble, they may read as if they had been spoken off, and may seem to flow as easily as table-talk'.[14] No one can deny that he achieved this result: for full effect, Macaulay's work ought to be read aloud.

The result was another well-deserved success. At the end of 1855, when his third and fourth volumes were published, bringing the story down to the Peace of Ryswick in 1697, they were even more successful than their predecessors. In ten weeks 26,500 copies were sold, and eleven weeks after publication Macaulay received from his publisher a record-breaking cheque for £20,000.

From then on, Macaulay's reputation was not only insular: it was world-wide. His work was translated into almost every European language, and even Persian. In America its sale – a pirate sale – was surpassed only by that of the Bible. He received numerous foreign honours. He was praised by Ranke, nominated to the Institut de France by Guizot. But his work was by no means finished; a long stretch still lay ahead of him; and his health was by now seri-ously impaired. In 1852 he had suffered a heart attack and, as he said, 'became twenty years older in a week'. If he were to complete, or even continue, his work, he would be obliged to contract his life still further. He therefore gave up his seat in Parliament, accepted from the whig prime minister Lord Palmerston a peerage as Lord Macaulay of Rothley Temple and, giving up his bachelor apartments in the Albany, bought the lease of a spacious villa, Holly Lodge, in Kensington. It was in a suitably whig quarter, for his next-door neigh-bour was the whig duke of Argyll and Holland House was hard by. There he settled down in comfort, with four men-servants to supply his needs, and, in the intervals of entertainment, continued to read and write. But he never completed his work. Illness diminished its tempo, and by 1857 he had contracted his original ambition. He no longer hoped to reach the American

Revolution or the 'new whigs' of the late eighteenth century. 'I now look forward', he wrote, 'to the accession of the House of Hanover as my extreme goal.'[15] In fact, even that goal was beyond his reach. He did not, himself, publish another volume. He died on 28 December 1859, and was buried in Westminster Abbey.

At his death, Macaulay's papers passed to his surviving sister, Hannah, to whom he had always been devoted. She had accompanied him to India and had there married Charles Edward Trevelyan, who was afterwards a distinguished public servant in both England and India. She now edited and published the last chapters of his manuscript. They appeared in 1861 as the fifth volume of the History, which they carried down to the death of William III in 1702. The rest of Macaulay's papers remained in the hands of the Trevelyan family, who, for a hundred years, have been the hereditary custodians, even high-priests (if a whig high-priest is conceivable), of Macaulay's fame.

After Hannah Lady Trevelyan's edition of Volume V of the History came the excellent biography of Macaulay written by her son, Macaulay's nephew, Sir George Otto Trevelyan. This was based on Macaulay's papers, which Trevelyan edited with a certain benevolent partiality towards his uncle. Afterwards Sir G.O Trevelyan, by writing The History of the American Revolution, supplied, in some sense, the originally intended conclusion to Macaulay's work. The more immediate conclusion, to which Macaulay himself had afterwards restricted his ambition, was supplied by Sir G.O. Trevelyan's second son, George Macaulay Trevelyan, regius professor of history and Master of Trinity College, Cambridge, with his three-volume History of the Reign of Queen Anne. By his History of England in the 18th Century, G.M. Trevelyan may also be said to have supplied the 'more concise' connecting link which Macaulay had envisaged.[16] In 1962, on the death of G.M. Trevelyan, Macaulay's papers passed to Trinity College, Cambridge.

The History of England

Thus in the end Macaulay, like his predecessors Fox and Mackintosh, only completed a fragment of the work which he had set out to do. But, in fact, no one can regard The History of England as a fragment. It is a solid work filling, in the original edition, five volumes. It has a clearly defined theme: the history of the revolution of 1688 and the reign of William III which effectively consolidated that revolution. By its forward and backward glances – its long introductory chapter and its frequent illustrations from later periods – it gives Macaulay's interpretation of the whole course of English history. And in so doing, it expresses, with absolute clarity, the new, modernised 'whig' thesis. If Macaulay's immediate purpose was to destroy the long dominion of Hume's 'tory' history, he certainly succeeded where Fox and Macintosh had failed. From the moment of its publication, his *History* replaced that of Hume as the canon of historical orthodoxy in England: replaced it so completely that it is difficult now to see past its long and apparently effortless triumph. This is the measure of Macaulay's victory. It could hardly have been more complete even if he had finished his work and carried it down to the victory of the new whigs in 1830.

Today Macaulay has gone the way of Hume, into historical perspective. The whig thesis is no longer exciting, no longer irresistible. Parts of it have been accepted and are regarded as truisms; parts have been exposed, with damaging effect, to that persistent light of criticism which, in the noonday of whig triumph, was so easily outglared. Macaulay's qualities were always obvious. With his dogmatic character, his rhetorical style, his 'pellucidity', he never left his readers in doubt, never even suggested that doubt was a permissible state of mind. In his own time, he carried them with him by the obviousness of his merits. Today, it is his faults which are more obvious. If we are to assess his permanent contribution to historical study, it will therefore be best to begin by admitting his obvious faults, some of which are the inescapable by-products of his merits.

Macaulay owed his success, in part, to the absolute clarity of his views and his style. This clarity proceeded from his own conviction. From the age of twenty-two, as far as we know, his convictions were fixed: he never changed his mind. And because his convictions were strong and clear, he tended, when faced with the evidence on any subject, instantly to range it in accordance with them. He did not, of course, do this crudely. His mind was both powerful and liberal. He had a marvellous understanding of political realities, which his own political experience naturally improved. His wide reading in all kinds of literature, classical, modern, and ephemeral – ballads, plays, novels, and sheer trash – enlarged his vision. He was no doctrinaire but an exceptionally well-read man of the world. Nevertheless, whatever concessions he would make, however elevated or sophisticated his expression of it, his judgment was always influenced by his convictions; and however liberal and rational these convictions might be, they were overpowering. They caused him to make dogmatic judgments in fields where he was unqualified to speak and would never stoop to learn. To the modern reader, the dogmatism of his comments, in such fields, can be even more offensive than their ignorance or insensitivity.

These fields which Macaulay so brusquely invaded include the fields of literary criticism, art, and human psychology. In spite of his vast reading, and his obvious pleasure in it, Macaulay's appreciation of literature was severely limited. He read the classics voraciously, but indiscriminately, and his comments are rather those of a schoolmaster awarding marks than of a catholic or sensitive critic. He admired no poetry written since the early poems of Scott and reckoned that his own *Lays of Ancient Rome* was better than anything written in the rest of the decade: years which (as David Knowles reminds us) saw the publication of the early works of Tennyson, Browning, and Matthew Arnold.[17] Of pictorial art he understood even less. In Italy he swept through the galleries, distributing confident priorities but showing no appreciation at all. Of music he knew nothing. Dining at Windsor Castle, he once recorded that 'the band covered the talk with a succession of sonorous tunes. "The Campbells Are Coming" was one.' 'This', says his nephew, is the only authentic instance on record of Macaulay's having known one tune from another.'[18] Of religious sense he had none, though he delighted in the worldly details of theology. And yet on all these subjects 'cocksure Tom', as his contemporaries called him, did not hesitate to lay down the law. His literary essays, when they touch literature itself, are worthless (as he himself afterwards admitted).[19] His descriptions of art, architecture, music are of a frigid, conventional pomposity, if they are not positively absurd. Queen Mary is laboriously ridiculed for her 'frivolous and inelegant' taste in china: she admired the 'hideous' and 'grotesque baubles' of Ming porcelain. If the English country gentry of the late seventeenth century attempted to decorate their houses, says Macaulay, they only achieved 'deformity'. But the suburban or seaside villas of the Victorian middle class are always given the highest marks. Whenever Macaulay wishes to emphasise the material progress which 150 years of whiggism have brought to the English towns, he cannot forbear to mention the 'long avenues of villas, embowered in lilacs and laburnums', the 'gay villas peeping from the midst of shrubberies and flower-beds', the 'villas multiplying fast, each embosomed in its gay little paradise of lilacs and roses'.

This philistinism, which can be so infuriating to the reader of Macaulay, springs directly from his philosophy. He saw history as the history of progress, and progress as material progress. In one of his earliest essays he had looked forward to a materialist millennium in the twentieth century, when villas would crowd up to the top of Ben Nevis and Helvellyn, 'machines constructed on principles yet unknown' would be in every house, and there would be 'no highways but railroads, no travelling but steam'. This same spirit of complacent materialism runs through his whole work. It is the new content which the 'Scottish' school had injected into whiggism to excite the nineteenth-century middle classes and to depress us who face the consequences of its realisation. But even if we dislike it, we have to recognise that Macaulay, in thus emphasising it, did isolate and define an important element in historical change.

Moreover, in isolating and defining material progress, Macaulay attached it – as he attached everything – to political action. He did not, like Hume, see progress as distinct from politics. To him, progress needed a constant political motor. In his own time he saw that the whig party could be that motor; and having once seized on this formula, he generalised it. He projected it both forwards and backwards in time. He saw the whig party of the seventeenth century as the direct precursor of the whig party of the nineteenth century, constantly pursuing, under the same social leadership, the same ultimate ends. Equally, the same party, he thought, would achieve the progress of the twentieth century. That the whig party might dissolve and that material progress might be achieved through the programme of European 'socialism' or American 'democracy', or English 'toryism', seemed to him quite impossible. The very thought of such ideas provoked him to omniscient scorn.

It is easy to expose Macaulay's errors about the future – his confident predictions that 'democracy' would reduce America 'to the state of Barbary or the Morea'.[20] Historians are often wrong about the future. But what about his interpretation of the past? Here he may well have been right. His thesis is not in itself absurd. But even here he may equally have been wrong. In spite of superficial appearances, in spite of the continuity of names, it is perfectly possible that the seventeenth-century whigs and the nineteenth-century whigs were different parties, pursuing different aims, in entirely different circumstances. It is possible that the seventeenth-century whigs never thought of 'progress', even if they accidentally forwarded it. It is also possible that the circumstances of the two periods were so different as to preclude comparison: that any connection between them could only be accidental, the connection of names, not things. Such was the view of the greatest historian of Macaulay's time, Leopold von Ranke, who held that every age was 'immediate to God' and must be studied from within, on its own terms, in its own right. But Macaulay, though he reviewed Ranke's Lives of the Popes and once met Ranke at breakfast (it was a very unsuccessful breakfast),[21] never sought to understand either the method or the philosophy of the German school. If he had, he would no doubt have dismissed Ranke, like Niebuhr, as an abject tory.

This refusal to admit the autonomy of the past, this insistence that the past must be judged in relation to the present, and is responsible to the present, is fundamental to Macaulay's historical interpretation and is the cause of some of his historical errors. Macaulay once wrote – in his essay on Ranke, although not with reference to Ranke's ideas – that 'a Christian of the 5th century with a Bible is neither better nor worse situated than a Christian of the 19th century with a Bible. . . . The absurdity of literal interpretation was as great and as obvious in the 16th century as it is now.' Such a view, which implies that there is no difference in 'intellectual climate' between one age and another, may well seem grotesquely unhistorical to us who live in the post-Rankean age. In Macaulay, who looked back to the eighteenth-century Enlightenment and had never breathed the atmosphere of Göttingen, it was more venial. But it explains the summary judgments which he too easily pronounced on the statesmen and thinkers of the past, his tendency to set them in the dock and (as Ranke himself expressed it) to borrow his tone from the proceedings of the criminal courts. To Ranke, there was no dock in which the past could be put: one generation was outside the jurisdiction of another.

And once they were in the dock, how did the men of the past fare at the hands of the judge? With his clear mind, his complete understanding of his own historical law, and his absolute certainty, Macaulay never wavered in his judgment. It was not an unconsidered judgment. Macaulay would survey all the facts, take past convictions into consideration, allow extenuating circumstances, and then, in his own favourite word, 'pronounce'. But judgment, once decided, was firm. There was no qualification. Ignorance of the law – that is, of the newly enacted, retroactive whig law of history – excused no one. If a man was found to be a 'tory', however virtuous, he must be sentenced, and even his admitted virtues were somewhat suspect. On the other hand, a good whig record could excuse the same faults which, in a tory, merely aggravated his crime. And once the sentence was 'pronounced', there could be no reconsideration, no reversal, no appeal.

Macaulay's double standard of judgment is incontestable. It is entirely political. It is applied to evidence: the same sources are treated as authentic when they ascribe vices to Marlborough, 'Jacobite libels' when they ascribe other vices to William III. It is applied to persons. James II's liaison with the plain but intelligent Catherine Sedley was disreputable profligacy; William III's liaison with the plain but intelligent Elizabeth Villiers was an excusable lapse: she 'possessed talents which well fitted her to partake his cares'. When Charles II accepted money from France, no words of condemnation are strong enough for such 'degradation', such 'complacent infamy'. When the whig hero Algernon Sidney did exactly the same, his action is described as 'indelicate', and even that adjective is quickly smothered in excuses: the censure, as J.W. Croker wrote in his review of Macaulay's first volume, is 'so light as to sound like applause'.[22]

Macaulay's injustice to persons is not solely dependent on their political choice. It may equally arise from their political doubt, from their refusal to choose. Confident himself, he had no patience with the hesitations of others. Political and unspeculative himself, he had no patience with the unpolitical and the speculative. Complex and divided personalities were ruthlessly simplified by him: caricatured as a bundle of contradictions and cast contemptuously aside. Archbishop Cranmer, hesitating in his pursuit of religious truth and the political means of ensuring it; Archbishop Sancroft, hesitating to adjust his sworn beliefs to the revolution which was necessary to preserve them – these men are castigated in outrageous terms. Even those whose convictions were clear and consistent obtained no benefit of their consistency unless its framework was obvious to Macaulay and recognised by him. Francis Bacon and William Penn were such men. They were not tories; they were not divided or hesitant personalities; but they did not fit neatly into Macaulay's categories. The whole context of their thought was different. They breathed a different 'intellectual climate'. But Macaulay did not admit such differences. Consequently, in his pages, they pay the price. Since the artist is intellectually incapable of portraying them, they are caricatured.

Moreover, these and such caricatures, in Macaulay's pages, are compounded by repetition. Once he had made up his mind about any man (and he made it up very quickly), all later evidence automatically adjusted itself in support of that conclusion, and every episode, thus interpreted, served to aggravate the original charge. Thus Macaulay very early made up his mind about John Graham of Claverhouse, Viscount Dundee, the Jacobite commander in Scotland, and about John Churchill, the great duke of Marlborough. Already in 1838, before he had even begun to work on his

History, he had – in his essay on Sir William Temple – consigned them both to 'the deeper recesses' of Dante's Hell. So, when he came to write his *History*, he approached every episode in which they were concerned with an absolute certainty that it would show them in an odious light. By the time he had interpreted the episode, it generally did; and although his interpretation was often grossly erroneous, it served to blacken their prospects still further when they next appeared in court.

Many are the historical characters whom Macaulay, having once decided to condemn, pursued through his *History* (as Croker wrote concerning his persecution of Marlborough) 'with more than the ferocity, and much less than the sagacity, of a bloodhound'.[23] Perhaps the most outrageous – and also the most interesting – of such pursuits is his vendetta against William Penn, the second founder of Quakerism. It is interesting because it shows not only the lengths to which Macaulay would go in denigration but also, by its consequences, the absolute irreversibility both of his own judgment, even when he was demonstrably convicted of error, and of whig opinion, so long as it was held enthralled by the new orthodoxy which he had established.

Why did Macaulay hate Penn? Partly, no doubt, because he hated Quakers. Quakers, by definition, were unpolitical, which to Macaulay was a fault. But Penn aggravated this fault by nevertheless becoming involved, however acci-dentally, in political action. He was thus not only wrong-headed but *naif*. All this might well have been excused had Penn been involved on the whig side. But Penn was a personal friend of James II, and his very refusal to become involved in politics made him, in effect, an accomplice of the king. Even if Macaulay's animosity was not sharpened by a distaste for his parents' Quaker friends, there was enough material here to prejudice him against Penn; his prejudice was sharpened by a gross error of identification which Macaulay took over from Mackintosh; and thereafter every incident in which Penn appeared was misinterpreted in order to fit, and to aggravate, the character thus ascribed to him. By the time he had finished with him, Macaulay had represented Penn as a man who (in Paget's words) 'prostituted himself to the meanest wishes of a cruel and profligate court, gloated with delight on the horrors of the scaffold and the stake, was the willing tool of a bloodthirsty and treacherous tyrant, a trafficker in simony and suborner of perjury, a conspir-ator, seeking to deluge his country in blood, a sycophant, a traitor, and a liar'.[24] In fact, every one of Macaulay's particular charges can be proved to be false.

Two attempts were made during Macaulay's lifetime to correct his libel of Penn. The first was by the Quakers themselves. Immediately after the publication of Macaulay's first volume, a new edition of Thomas Clarkson's *Memoirs of William Penn* was published, with a new preface by W.E. Forster, factually refuting the charges. About the same time, a deputation of Quakers called on Macaulay to persuade him of his error. Macaulay looked forward to the encounter with confident glee: 'The Quakers', he recorded, 'have fixed Monday at eleven for my opportunity. Many a man, says Sancho, comes for wool and goes home shorn.' On Monday they duly came. Complacent as ever, Macaulay described the visit. 'Then the Quakers, five in number. Never was there such a rout. They had absolutely nothing to say . . .' As Sir Charles Firth says, if the Quakers 'had absolutely nothing to say' it was presumably because they were not allowed to speak.[25]

In an attempt to secure a public hearing, Forster's preface was published separately, and in 1851 W. Hepworth Dixon published a new *Life of Penn* with a whole chapter refuting Macaulay's charges. Macaulay paid not the slightest attention, and in 1856 a new edition of the first volumes of his *History* confidently repeated the libels. This roused the indignation of a new critic, this time a strong whig: John Paget. In 1858 Paget published a scholarly pamphlet entitled *An Enquiry into the Evidence Relating to the Charges Brought by Lord Macaulay against William Penn*. Next year Paget similarly exposed Macaulay's no less glaring errors concerning the duke of Marlborough, the Massacre of Glencoe, and the Scottish Highlands. All these were published in Macaulay's lifetime. In 1860, after Macaulay's death, Paget showed that Macaulay had similarly libelled Viscount Dundee. All these essays Paget collected and published in 1861 as *The New Examen*. But just as Macaulay had ignored the criticism made during his life, so the whig establishment ignored it after his death. The *Edinburgh Review* dismissed Paget's book with contempt, hardly deigning to notice 'so very inaccurate a performance';[26] Trevelyan, in his biography, never mentioned Paget or allowed it to appear that Macaulay was in error on any subject; and *The New Examen*, having fallen stillborn from the press, was never reprinted till 1934, when Sir Winston Churchill, hearing from Lord Rosebery of this rare and unknown book, stimulated a new edition in defence of his ancestor.

How could Macaulay be guilty of such gross errors, such shocking injustices? It is clear from his own language that he genuinely believed that he was right. And yet the evidence against him, which was shown to him, is absolutely unanswerable. Mere prejudice is not a sufficient explanation for this psychological problem. The most natural explanation lies in the combination of political prejudice with an extraordinary memory.

Macaulay's memory was indeed a prodigy – and a prodigy of which he was undoubtedly vain. Numerous stories are told about it. He knew the whole of *Paradise Lost* and the whole *Pilgrim's Progress* by heart. He could take in at a glance, and retain in his mind, a whole printed page; and too often he discharged it again in his conversation. 'He should take two table-spoonfuls of the waters of Lethe every morning', said Sydney Smith. But this great gift had its disadvantages. Macaulay would remember the pattern in which he had arranged the evidence, and which he had imprinted on his mind, rather than the evidence itself; and he would unconsciously refer back not to the evidence but only to the pattern. As Gladstone wrote, 'the possessor of such a vehicle as his memory could not but have had something of an overweening confidence in what it told him'.[27] Macaulay's memory did not often let him down. He seldom forgot a fact. Unfortunately, he seldom, if ever, detached a fact from the pattern in which, and through which, his memory had preserved it.

It is impossible to ignore Macaulay's gross personal injustices. They are the major blemish in all his work. But having made this admission, it is important to recognise that these injustices are limited. They damage only his treatment of persons, of human motivation: an area in which Macaulay, with his psychological insensitivity, was always weak. They do not affect the value of his work as narrative of events, as political analysis, as historical explanation; and it is in these fields that his greatness lies. A minor historian would have been forgotten long ago, had he committed errors as gross as those of Macaulay. Macaulay, in spite of his errors, remains one of the great historians.

In order to appreciate this, it is necessary first to consider Macaulay's originality. Macaulay may not have been the first to advance what we may call the 'whig-utilitarian' historical thesis – i.e. the thesis that the substance of history is material progress and that such progress can be attained through the application of particular political principles – for this thesis is implicit in the work of some of his Scottish predecessors, such as Millar and Mackintosh. But he was certainly the first to express this thesis in a consistent and persuasive historical form. He was able to do this not only by the clarity of his ideas and the literary force of his writing, but also by his originality as a technical historian. Hume, whom he replaced, may have been a profounder historical philosopher; but the superiority of Macaulay in mere historical scholarship – in the range of his sources and in his own mastery of them – makes Hume seem, by comparison, an amateur.

Of course, there are admissions to be made. Behind Macaulay always stands Mackintosh. Macaulay's first two volumes rest heavily on Mackintosh; and even after Mackintosh's *History* had ceased, Macaulay still relied on Mackintosh's vast manuscript collections, which supplied many of his needs down to 1702. Since Macaulay himself never got beyond 1702, we may say that he never completely emancipated himself from Mackintosh, who still supplied the bulk of his foreign transcripts. But the fact remains that, for the period of the reign of William III – a particularly complicated period since William was the head, and England the principal power, of a European coalition – Macaulay was a pioneer; and he was a pioneer because he used a range of material infinitely greater than had been used by any of his predecessors. When Macaulay wrote that the reign of William III, as he approached it, was 'mysterious', he was stating a general truth. Nobody, till then, had elucidated it. Macaulay was the first to do so; and he did so from a wide range of sources, printed and manuscript, literary and historical, public and private, British and foreign. To supplement Mackintosh's collection, he obtained transcripts of national archives from Paris and The Hague; he paid a personal visit to the archive of Venice; and he acquired, through Guizot, the whig statesman-historian of France, copies of Spanish archives from Simancas. On the other hand, he made little use of Italian and no use of German or Austrian sources.

In this widened use of sources Macaulay was helped, of course, by external facts. Since the French Revolution, there had been a general opening of the archives of Europe. Macaulay profited by that fact, just as other historians would do: indeed, the historians of the German school – in particular Ranke – would apply a far more professional technique to a far wider range of the documents thus made available. To historians like Lord Acton, who was himself trained in the German school, Macaulay was both amateur and insular. Even non-historians like Gladstone recognised the great gulf which separated Macaulay from the new German pioneers of historical method and source-criticism.[28] But for all the gaps which posterity can find in his range of sources, and in his use of them, compared with his predecessors, Macaulay was himself a professional.

Macaulay also improved on his predecessors by the scale of his study. He may have been (as he himself admitted) insular, in that he saw European problems from a purely English point of view; but at least he was the first historian to study the revolution of 1688 and its aftermath as a British, not a purely English, revolution. Everyone knows that the revolution of 1688, though it was precipitated by purely English affairs, was not stabilised till it had been extended to Ireland and Scotland; and that the result of that extension was not merely to secure the benefits of the revolution in England: it was also to transform the government and society of Ireland and to join Scotland with England in the United Kingdom. But English historians have customarily treated this extension of the revolution as a mere military operation, as if Ireland and Scotland were simply the theatres in which the victory of William III over James II was completed. This, no doubt, was William's own view, and the view of the English statesmen of the time. But Macaulay, as a historian, looked deeper than they. Himself a Scotchman who, through the Union, had become a British statesman, aware of the unceasing importance of Ireland in British affairs, he recognised that each country had distinct problems, which the revolution might either settle or inflame; and his analysis of these problems is one of the most valuable parts of his work. He did for the Glorious Revolution of 1688 what nobody, even now, has done for the Puritan Revolution of 1640 to 1660: he saw it as a social and political revolution whose progress and consequences were equally important to all three kingdoms.

In the technique of presentation, too, Macaulay was an innovator. He marks an important stage in the transition from the 'philosophical' historians of the Enlightenment, whose work he continued, to the 'romantic' narrative historians of the nineteenth century, who imitated him. Like his 'philosophical' predecessors, he believed that the significance of the past lay in its relation to the present. Like them, he saw history as the record of 'progress' – progress, in his view, not towards 'freedom', but, by means of freedom, to ever-greater prosperity. But equally, his view of history was coloured by the new romanticism which separated the past from the present in order to give it, in spite of its continuity, a distinctive colouring.

Macaulay's romanticism is admittedly of a very qualified kind. He openly despised those who, in his own time, affected to prefer the past to the present. He insisted that romanticism itself was a luxury, dependent on material progress: the beauty of wild scenery, as in the Scottish Highlands, could only excite pleasure when roads and inns, industry and public order, had made it safe to travel there. But however relative, his romanticism was genuine. It was not only as the incidental poet of the *Lays of Ancient Rome*: it was in his convictions as a historian that he was deeply influenced, like so many other nineteenth-century historians, by Sir Walter Scott. Indeed, we may say that Macaulay's historical philosophy is a synthesis of the eighteenth-century idea of progress and the nineteenth-century cult of the romantic past. We may add that he was able to achieve this synthesis because English history – unlike German or French history – itself combined essential progress with the superficial forms of the romantic past. Macaulay dwells with equal emphasis, as occasion allows, on the external pageantry of former times and the thread of progress which makes the inner reality of the present time so much better; and the revolution of 1688 seemed to him particularly glorious in that it contrived to secure them both: to preserve the antique forms of a static, feudal, Christian monarchy around the substance of a progressive, secular, materialist state.

This 'relative romanticism', this romanticism of form combined with a materialism of substance, shows itself in Macaulay's literary method. He was the first great historian to make use of local and temporal 'colour'. The eighteenth-century historians had never sought to capture the atmosphere of the past. They had not judged it necessary to travel, except for the general purpose of broadening the mind. Robertson wrote of the European empire of Charles V, of America and of India, without ever leaving Britain. Gibbon wrote the whole history of the Byzantine Empire without ever visiting any part of that empire. Macaulay was far more 'modern'. Wherever possible, he visited the sites which he was to describe in his *History*. He followed William III's progress through Ireland, inspected Londonderry, Limerick, the Boyne. He went to Scotland to visit the passes of Killiecrankie and Glencoe. He travelled abroad almost every summer to look at cities, fortresses, battlefields. And when he looked at them, his imagination peopled them with their historic inhabitants. He had, as he once told his sister, a love of such 'castle-building' whereby 'the past is in my mind soon constructed into a romance'. He even composed imaginary conversations, 'long and sufficiently animated, in the style, if not with the merits, of Sir Walter Scott's'. To such 'castle-building' he ascribed his 'accuracy as to facts'.[29] To the same castle-building we may ascribe his inaccuracies as to persons. There are historical dangers, as well as literary advantages, in 'recapturing' the supposed 'atmosphere' of the past.

In order to recapture that atmosphere Macaulay relied heavily on literature. The literary reserves on which he could draw were formidable. Poetry, plays, pamphlets, satires, lampoons, ballads, novelettes, farces – all the residue of his enormous, promiscuous reading lay ready to hand, accurately labelled, in his preservative memory and could be drawn upon at will to illustrate the social habits and popular opinions of the time. This wide range of illustrations renders his writing direct, vivid, and cogent; but the method has its dangers, too. Literature, after all, is not life: it is a heightened version of life; life itself is duller, more prosaic. Satire and drama, particularly, are by definition a caricature of reality. It may be legitimate to use such literature as evidence of opinion – to illustrate the rivalry between the Old and New East India Companies by a quotation from Nicholas Rowe's comedy *The Biter*, and the mania for speculation by a scene in Shadwell's *Stockjobbers* – but it is not legitimate to use it, without careful reservation, as evidence of historical fact or personal character. Macaulay was never a man of careful reservations. Consequently, some of his most entertaining or most damaging passages can be discredited as resting not on historical fact but on literary exaggerations. Just as he illustrates the character of Marlborough from Jacobite libels and that of Jeffreys from whig tirades, so he caricatures the country clergy by accepting the evidence of stage parsons and the society of the Scottish Highlands by relying on chosen passages from exasperated or satirical foreigners. This is a danger into which other, later historians have fallen. The late R.H. Tawney, for instance – as politically committed a historian as Macaulay – tended to illustrate the 'acquisitive society' of early seventeenth-century England from Jacobean comedy. But the dangers inherent in a historical method do not invalidate the method itself, and by his command and use of literature for historical purposes Macaulay undoubtedly gave a new, if somewhat perilous, depth to the art of the historian.

In all these respects Macaulay, in his own time, was an innovator. But his most permanent contribution to the study of politics – what makes his *History*, in spite of all its blemishes, so difficult to fault – is his unerring grasp of political reality. Uninterested in abstract ideas, insensitive in his approach to persons, Macaulay had nevertheless an unfailing appreciation of political situations. Himself a politician, who had lived through the excitement of the parliamentary struggle for reform and had enjoyed personal experience of government both in England and in India, he understood the pressures of politics, the need and the moment of action. And since, unlike Hume, he believed that material progress was essentially linked to political action, and that effective politics depended not on academic blueprints or new constitutions, but on empirical skill serving an enlightened general philosophy, this understanding of the scope and limits of political action was an essential part of his historical philosophy. That philosophy might lack depth, but it was never caught without an answer. The historian could see, at any moment, what ought to have been done; and he often said so, with irritating self-assurance.

Again and again, in his *History*, Macaulay declares his faith in political action rather than political theory, as the means of progress. The key to history is politics; and politics is not a philosophical but an empirical science. The politician is an engineer, not a mathematician. He must indeed have some knowledge of the philosophy of government, just as the engineer must be versed in the philosophy of equilibrium and motion; 'but as he who has actually to build must bear in mind many things never noticed by D'Alembert and Euler, so must he who has actually to govern be perpetually guided by considerations to which no allusion is to be found in the writings of Adam Smith or Jeremy Bentham'. Constitutions, political manifestos, are not to be admired for their philosophical profundity, for their intellectual symmetry. They are not to be examined 'as we should examine a chapter of Aristotle or of Hobbes'. They are to be considered 'not as words but as deeds. If they effect that which they are intended to effect, they are rational, though they may be contradictory. If they fail of attaining their end, they are absurd, though they carry demonstration with them.' Consistently with this doctrine, Macaulay, in his *History*, while describing the political conduct of Sunderland and Godolphin, Somers and Montagu, totally ignores the great work which, for all Europe, was to provide the philosophical basis of the Glorious Revolution, the two *Treatises on Government* by John Locke; and in his practical Indian statesmanship he was not inhibited by the whig doctrines which he had learned to apply to English history.

If Macaulay's key to history is politics, equally his key to politics is history. The problems of government, he insists, are not philosophical, nor can we ever explain political results by examining political motives or 'the principles of human nature'. The explanation of political action is to be sought in the history of political action. History is 'that noble science of politics which is equally removed from the barren theories of the utilitarian sophists' and from mere political expediency.[30] The best politicians are those who have studied history and the best historians are those who have taken part in politics – especially in whig politics. So Macaulay extols Fox and Mackintosh as historians because 'they had spoken history, acted history, lived history': the very fact that they had been politicians gave them, according to

Macaulay, 'great advantages over almost every English historian who has written since the time of Burnet'.[31] The choice of Bishop Burnet, in this context, may seem odd to us, when Macaulay might have cited Bolingbroke or – even more aptly – Clarendon, who not only fulfilled all the necessary conditions but expressed, in his attack on Hobbes and in his essay on other historians, the very views of Macaulay. But then Burnet was a whig; Bolingbroke and Clarendon were tories.

Macaulay's acute political sense, his recognition of the scope, the limits, and the timing of political action, is indeed his greatest contribution to historical writing. It never failed him. As S.R. Gardiner, the historian of seventeenth-century England, wrote, 'his judgment of a political situation was as superb as his judgment of personal character was weak'.[32] He not only appreciated, instinctively, the exact balance of political forces at any given moment; he also saw how great political problems should be faced and solved. It might or might not be true that only the historic whig party could carry out such solutions, but the solutions which he proposed – whether as a historian, for the settlement of Ireland, or as a statesman, for the education of India – were not only based on a vast historical knowledge and inspired by a genuine belief in material progress: they were also unquestionably right. Perhaps Macaulay's greatest achievement, as a historian, was not merely his success in temporarily capturing historical interpretation for his political party, or even his incorporation of the utilitarian philosophy in the historical process, but his reassertion – a reassertion since made on behalf of other political parties – of the primacy of politics in that process, as the essential motor even of social change.

This is not an obvious quality. No virtue, in a historian, is obvious, except style. History is too subtle a process to be firmly seized or summarily decided. Consequently Macaulay's virtues are much less apparent than his faults, which are faults precisely for this reason: they are the result of too instant apprehension. These faults appear at their worst in Macaulay's *Essays*, where there is less room for the emergence of subtlety. But in the long haul of the *History*, although the particular judgments are identical, the deeper virtues become gradually apparent, as almost everyone who has become familiar with it agrees. It is no doubt for this reason that Lord Acton, who hated Macaulay, regarding his philosophy as 'utterly base, contemptible and odious', nevertheless made a remarkable, and otherwise unintelligible, distinction between the *Essays* and the *History*, between Macaulay in haste and Macaulay at a more reflective pace. The essays, he wrote, were 'flashy and superficial', 'only pleasant reading, and key to half the prejudices of our age. It is the *History* (with one or two speeches) that is wonderful. He knew nothing respectably before the seventeenth century. He knew nothing of foreign history, or religion, philosophy, science, or art. His account of debates has been thrown into the shade by Ranke, his account of diplomatic affairs by Klopp. He is, I am persuaded, grossly, basely unfair. Read him therefore to find out how it comes that the most unsympathetic of critics can think him very nearly the greatest of English writers.'[33]

CHAPTER 12

Thomas Carlyle's Historical Philosophy

Thomas Carlyle was much more than a historian. He was man of letters, moralist, political preacher, prophet. Before turning to history, he wished to be a poet, began a novel and tried to write philosophy. Three times, before he was forty, he applied for professorial chairs: in aesthetics, moral philosophy, astronomy; but never in history. In the end, however, it was as a historian that he made his name. His three most substantial works – *The French Revolution* (1837), *The Letters and Speeches of Oliver Cromwell* (1845), and *The Life of Frederick the Great* (1858–65) – were historical. For it was history, he came to believe, which was the necessary demonstration of all the other arts and sciences. 'The only poetry', he once wrote, 'is history.' The present, he declared, is but a thin film between the past and the future. History is philosophy in action, the theatre of politics and morality, the explanation of the world.

It was through his historical philosophy too that he exercised so great an influence in his time, challenging all the reigning orthodoxies. No one could ignore it. Some of the most original minds of the time were carried away by it. Marx and Engels – up to a point – endorsed it. Other historians adopted it. Two disciples of Carlyle – Charles Kingsley and his brother-in-law J.A. Froude – held the regius chairs of history in Cambridge and Oxford respectively. And its long-term effect was even more surprising. Little though Carlyle himself could have guessed it, he was pointing the way forward to some of the darkest experiences of the twentieth century.

The orthodoxy which he challenged was the whole tradition of 'philosophic history' as established by Montesquieu and his disciples in the eighteenth century. The greatest representatives of that tradition had been, in historical writing, Gibbon, and in political economy, Adam Smith. Thanks to these men, the motor of history had been moved down from heaven to earth, from the Providence of God to the structure of society, and history itself had been changed from a divine drama whose key lay in scriptural prophecy to the material progress of humanity, made intelligible by the rules of social science. By the end of the eighteenth century, this tradition, in spite of the protests of the clergy, was well established. Refined by the Scottish school of political economists, given force by Bentham and his Scottish disciples, it was published through the *Edinburgh Review* and would soon be accepted as the basic orthodoxy both of the whig party and of their utilitarian rivals: the advocates of liberal political institutions and economic *laissez-faire*.

Of course, the advance of this philosophy had not gone unchallenged. The Providence of God did not retire without a fight. Late in the eighteenth century, John Wesley would chastise the infamous Scottish historian who had explained the conquest of America without any reference to Divine Providence. But it was not by preaching that the new science could be shaken or stopped. The real shock was to come from external events, and particularly from one great event which, as great events generally do, took all the philosophers by surprise: the French Revolution.

By 1815 the shock of the French Revolution had been absorbed in Britain and the whigs at least knew how to explain it: it was because the French had never had a rational whig revolution in the past (Macaulay would afterwards explain) that they had suffered from an irrational radical revolution in more recent times. British writers could afford this complacency because Britain had after all defeated Napoleon and its own institutions had remained intact throughout the storm. But in conquered and liberated Germany the reaction was more radical. There a whole school of historians was formed whose basic principle was frontal opposition to those 'enlightened' French ideas which, it was thought, had led to the 'revolutionary doctrines' so disastrous in Europe. This was explicitly stated by the founder of the school, Leopold von Ranke, who was born in 1795, five years before Macaulay and in the same year as Carlyle.

Ranke and Macaulay were able men from educated middle-class homes. They drew, each in his own country, on a newly established intellectual tradition: Ranke on the philosophy of Herder and Goethe, Macaulay on that of the *Edinburgh Review*. Carlyle was quite different. He was a man of genius brought up in Scotland, indeed, but far from the fashionable ideas of 'enlightened' Edinburgh. His home was in rural Dumfriesshire; his peasant parents were pious members of the strictest of Calvinist sects; and his earliest ideas were deeply rooted not in the rich alluvial soil of the Scottish Enlightenment but in the barren intellectual rock upon which that soil had been recently and perhaps superficially spread: in the irreducible Cameronian fanaticism of the seventeenth century. No breath of eighteenth-century scepticism, no whiff of modern philosophy, had penetrated those quiet valleys or tarnished their pre-diluvian fundamentalist faith; and it was in that faith that he was brought up, by parents who wished – it was the common ambition of Scottish peasant parents – 'to see him wag his head in a pulpit'.

At home in Ecclefechan, at school in Annan, Carlyle's faith remained intact. Even at Edinburgh University, he was repelled, not seduced, by the fashionable doctrine of the place. It was not till he was twenty-three, teaching in a school in Kirkcaldy, that he began to doubt. His doubts were not about the metaphysical world: he would always be a metaphysician. Nor were they about the Calvinist doctrine of predestination and election: in that he would continue explicitly to profess his belief. They were about the historical truth of the biblical revelation and the historical function of the Church. They were inspired, above all, by the discovery of Gibbon's *Decline and Fall of the Roman Empire*.

At Kirkcaldy, Carlyle read the whole of Gibbon straight through – twelve volumes in twelve days – with a kind of horror-struck fascination which finds expression in wildly inconsistent judgments. Sometimes he expresses hatred and disgust: hatred alike of Gibbon's style, matter, philosophy. But on other occasions he would express his 'high esteem' for this 'most strong-minded of historians'. 'Gibbon', he wrote, 'is a man whom one never forgets – unless oneself deserving to be forgotten: the perusal of his work forms an epoch in the history of one's mind.'

Certainly Carlyle never forgot Gibbon. He would read his work again, right through, at the end of his own life. And certainly his first reading of it formed an epoch in the history of his own mind: though he repudiated it, it is the only great work of history of which he would ever speak with respect. For it was Gibbon who, effectively, liberated Carlyle as a historian. 'Those winged sarcasms', as he would afterward describe them, 'so quiet and yet so conclusively transpiercing and killing dead', shattered the fundamentalist mould in which hitherto the history of the world had, for him, been so comfortably enclosed. Intellectually, Carlyle was now set free from his ideological prison. And yet the liberation was not complete. With his deep peasant conservatism and his profoundly religious spirit, he could not accept such liberty. He could not accommodate himself either to a world without divine justice or to an interpretation of history without a divine purpose. The world, as he saw it, needed both: particularly the world which he saw around him in Edinburgh and in Annandale in 1819.

For we are now in 1819, in the lean years after the victory over Napoleon, the years in which the peasantry and artisans of Scotland were near to starvation: 1819 itself was the year of the radical rising in Edinburgh and the suppression of 'the Radical War' at Bonnymuir, the Scottish Peterloo. To Carlyle, who genuinely sympathised with the poor, and who had a strong sense of the organic unity of society, it seemed that revolution was in sight: that the French Revolution had not been destroyed with Napoleon; that its roots were still living and would sprout anew; and these roots would never be destroyed by mere political treatment. For he did not share the view, so complacently expressed by both whigs and radicals, that society could be inoculated against revolution by political liberalism or democratic institutions. On the contrary, its disease, he thought, would only be aggravated by 'the dismal science' of 'political economy', with its doctrine of *laissez-faire* and Devil-take-the-hindmost, which was the ultimate achievement of the complacent Scottish Enlightenment.

From 1818, when he read Gibbon at Kirkcaldy, until 1821, Carlyle lived in a state of deep despair, exaggerated by the chronic constipation, and the unbounded egotism, which, throughout his life, made him so difficult a companion. He was poor, but he hated the teaching, which – apart from occasional hack-writing for David Brewster's *Encyclopaedia* – was his only means of earning money. His secure ideological world had been destroyed, and he could see no alternative system around which it could be reconstructed. He indulged in orgies of self-pity. Then, in 1821, he recovered his spirits. Having reached the bottom of depression, he resolved, by an effort of will, to climb up again: out of scepticism and perplexity he would discover a new certainty thanks to which, and within which, he would feel free. The end of life, he decided, was not thought but action. Action resolved doubt. Action – even violence – provided it was in defence of 'reality', provided it was 'sincere', could not be wrong. The essential thing was to see through 'shams' to 'reality' and then act, knowing, as he would put it later, that 'the Eternal Providences do rule, and the great soul of the world is just'.

The new philosophy was worked out in the six years which Carlyle and his recently married wife spent in her inherited farm of Craigenputtock in

Dumfriesshire. It was finally published as *Sartor Resartus*, an extraordinary work whose personal names, irrelevant digressions and metaphors sufficiently indicate the mental and physical constipation behind it. Its picture of the world was described in images of ingestion, digestion, fermentation, obstruction, explosion, dung. But to Carlyle this work – the only original work that he would ever write – was of immense significance. It was, he said, the illumination for which the world had been waiting for 1,800 years, a metaphysical system to replace what he would afterwards call 'the rotting carcase of Christianity'. He was the first man since Christ to see through the outward vesture to the heart, the reality, of the world. This reality was set out, in *Sartor Resartus*, by his imaginary *alter ego*, the German professor Teufelsdröckh, 'Devil's Dung'. This was the popular German name for the laxative drug *asafoetida*; and, indeed, Carlyle described the book itself as a purge to produce 'new secretions' from 'the pudding stomach of England'.

Carlyle believed that his philosophy had been inspired by the German writers whom he was then studying and, in particular, by Goethe. But Carlyle took from Goethe only what he wanted: there is an immense difference between the serenity and maturity of Goethe's ideal and the explosive philosophy of Carlyle; and Carlyle's reverence for Goethe was rather for having shown him, in *The Sorrows of Werther*, how to escape from intellectual despair than for pointing in a particular direction. Goethe, said Carlyle, 'had travelled the steep rocky path before me – the first of the moderns'. He too had been driven almost to despair by 'the blind strength of a soul in bondage'. But he had found his way out of it and had shown that way to Carlyle too: 'the sight of such a man was to me a Gospel of Gospels, and did literally, I believe, save me from destruction outward and inward'. This was what lay behind Carlyle's message in *Sartor Resartus*: 'Close thy Byron, open thy Goethe'; in other words, bid farewell to romantic despair, and begin again with an organic philosophy of life.

Sartor Resartus expressed Carlyle's philosophy of the world: a philosophy in which the moral unity, and moral purpose, of the world, threatened with dissolution by the scepticism and the 'mechanical' philosophy of the eighteenth century, was reconstructed on a new, non-Christian but still metaphysical base. The world itself, he insisted, was a divine work, a great miracle, a living, unitary, harmonious system; man was part of the miracle, a microcosm of that macrocosm; and the history of the world, and of man, was, by a necessary consequence, the working out of the divine plan. That plan was not the Christian model deducible from the Scriptures, but even less was it the amoral,

Newtonian (or post-Newtonian) model of the eighteenth-century deists – 'an absentee God sitting idle ever since the first sabbath, at the outside of his universe, and seeing it go'. It was a secularised, but still moral, version of the Christian, Augustinian, Calvinist system. Divine justice had created the world, and divine justice regulated it – but not smoothly. Like the children of Israel in the wilderness, men were continually backsliding – worshipping idols, that is, 'shams', 'quackeries', the conventions of the past which had grown into fetishes – and needed periodic correction. So, when the accumulated and petrified 'shams' had become an intolerable affront to divine justice, a great and terrible conflagration would break out, an apocalyptic *Götzendämerung*, in which they would all be violently consumed, and on the *tabula rasa* thus created, a new order, corresponding with 'reality', could be built. One of the advantages of this cosmic theory, to Carlyle, was that it solved the great problem of his age: the French Revolution. As he would afterwards put it, 'truly, without the French Revolution, one would not know what to make of an age like this at all'.

Closely related to Carlyle's catastrophic theory of history was the theory of the 'great man', the 'hero'. For 'Great Men', he wrote in *Sartor Resartus*, 'I have ever had the warmest predilection. . . . Great Men are the inspired (speaking and acting) Texts of that divine Book of Revelations . . . by some named History.' And the greatest of great men were those who orchestrated the grand drama of destruction and regeneration. Such men, 'heroic God-inspired men', 'God-intoxicated men', were natural kings; they ruled by divine right – that is to say, they needed no other title than their own claim – and men turned to them naturally by that instinct for 'hero worship' which was immanent in man – was indeed one of the 'organic filaments' which ensured that the new era of 'reality' was born, like a phoenix, out of the holocaust of 'shams'.

In this Pentateuchal view of history, there was no room for any consideration of anything so commonplace as human institutions. In all his writings, Carlyle showed the greatest contempt for institutions. These, he maintained, were merely 'mechanical' devices. But the motor of history, he insisted, was not 'mechanical' but 'dynamical'. The greatness of nations lay not in external, secondary forces, 'checks and balances of profit and loss', but in 'the inward primary powers of man'. Take, for example, the crusades. The crusades had been deplored by the Enlightenment as a movement of lunatic fanaticism and imperialist aggression; but Carlyle thought differently. To him they were a great and noble expression of the human spirit. And how were they set in motion? Not by committees, or subscription dinners, or political compromise:

'only the passionate voice of one man, the rapt soul looking through the eyes of one man; and rugged steel-clad Europe trembled beneath his words and followed where'er he listed'. Similarly, in modern times, the French Revolution was 'a dynamic not a mechanic force. It was a struggle, though a blind and at last an insane one, for the infinite divine nature of right, of freedom, of country'. All this was written before 1834, when Carlyle and his wife left the solitude of Craigenputtock for a new life in the literary world of London.

Thus before he had written any work of history, Carlyle had acquired a distinctive historical philosophy, and that philosophy, though reached by a different route, resembled that of his German contemporaries. Like them, he rejected the idea of progress and the whole philosophy of the Enlightenment. Like them, he recognised the autonomy of the past. Like them, he saw the universe as a great organism with an inner unity and vitality, suffused with divine power. Like them, he believed in *Weltgeschichte*, 'world history', as the working out of a 'World Plan'. Like them or some of them, he believed that this plan required the emergence, from time to time, of 'great men' to ensure its execution. In most of these respects he resembled his exact contemporary Ranke.

But if there were resemblances, there were also differences. To Ranke, the Prussian conservative, world history was an orderly, self-regulating process which the historian could serenely 'contemplate', even admire. To Carlyle, the Scottish radical, it was an uneven process, in which long periods of dull, torpid ingestion were periodically corrected by glorious expulsive evacuations. Perhaps the difference can be traced to the different religious traditions in which the two men had been steeped when young. Ranke had been brought up as a Lutheran, the descendant of a long line of Lutheran parsons, obediently consecrating the powers that be. Carlyle had been brought up as a Calvinist, the descendant of those irreducible Cameronian fanatics who had defied every established power and resolutely maintained that everyone except themselves was eternally damned.

This difference of philosophy, the difference between an almost sycophantic Lutheranism and a fiery, radical, messianic Covenanting Calvinism, extended also to style. The style of Ranke was smooth, dry, without life or character, the style of an obsequious, punctilious, Prussian functionary. Carlyle's style – his 'piebald, entangled, hyper-metaphorical, style of writing' as he described it – was very different. His friend John Sterling once protested against that extraordinary style, 'as amazing as if the Pythia on her tripod had struck up a drinking song, or Thersites had caught the prophetic strain of Cassandra'. But Carlyle would accept no discipline. That style was to him the necessary form for his revolutionary message. 'The whole structure of our Johnsonian English', he replied to Sterling, was 'breaking up from its foundation'; and in a revolutionary age, 'revolution there is visible as everywhere else'.

Such being his historical philosophy, it was natural that Carlyle should turn, for his first historical work, to the French Revolution. Not only was this the great historical challenge of his time; he also believed that it was not yet over; the grand finale was still to come. This last stage had begun in 1830, with the fall of the restored Bourbons in France and its reverberations throughout Europe. Carlyle was convinced that the revolution would spread to England: William IV, he declared confidently, would be the last British king. The whigs, coming at last to office in 1830, might think they could forestall it by parliamentary reform; their radical allies might put their trust in new democratic institutions. But Carlyle had no such belief. Nor, indeed, did he really wish to avert revolution. With his psychopathic love of violence, he positively wanted it.

So, in *The French Revolution*, begun in 1834 and completed in 1837, he set out to place that revolution in its true, metaphysical context: to show that it was not (as the English whigs argued) the consequence of political errors in the past, nor (as Ranke would suppose) the escape of energy through a safety-valve in the perfect mechanism of world history, but the delicious sanguinary reassertion of divine justice. Moreover, that justice was not merely eschatological. It was social. Almost alone of contemporary British historians of the revolution – the high tory Croker is the other exception – Carlyle saw that it had a social dimension. Divine justice was directed against an indolent epicurean élite who, by exploiting the unrewarded labour of a starving peasantry, had been able to indulge the luxury of 'enlightened' philosophy. For the 'prime mover' in the revolution, he wrote, was not political or intellectual, not the resentment and ideas of 'philosophical advocates, rich shopkeepers, rural *noblesse*', but 'hunger and nakedness and nightmare oppression lying heavy on 25 million hearts'; and therefore no well-balanced political systems, no nicely drafted resolutions – no deliberations of the National Assembly or perfect constitutions of the *abbé* Sieyès – could have averted it. The revolution itself was needed, to burn up the 'shams' of the past and replace them by a new 'reality'. How that reality could be restored, whether it had in fact been restored, Carlyle did not say. His theme was the revolution: it ends with the 'whiff of grapeshot' which cleared the way to the personal dictatorships of Napoleon.

Theoretically, Napoleon should be the hero of *The French Revolution*. In fact, he is not. In fact, there is no hero in the book. Mirabeau dies, Danton is guillotined. Napoleon only appears in the wings: he never assumes the heroic stature which Carlyle's theory seems to require. At first sight this is odd; but perhaps there is an explanation. We shall return to seek it shortly. Meanwhile it is enough to say that Carlyle's immediate concern was with the collapse of an old order, not the creation of a new: a collapse which he expected to see any moment now in England – 'now', he wrote in 1839, the year after publication, 'is *our* French Revolution' – and the hero, in such revolutions, did not appear at the beginning: he needed time to emerge.

The publication of *The French Revolution* made Carlyle famous. Its vivid, metaphorical style, its rapid narrative, its power to re-create events, as if one were in the midst of them, carried away its earliest readers. This was a new kind of history, living history, in a new, living language. To read it, even today, is a great literary experience. Whether it explains the revolution, or any historical problem, is of course quite another matter. To a historian, reading it today, it must seem an inspired historical retrogression, a denial of all the progress made in historiography since the Renaissance. It takes us back to John Knox's *History of the Reformation in Scotland* – a work which, incidentally, Carlyle would puff, thirty years later, as 'a glorious old book' worthy to be read by every student at Edinburgh University – if not to the Books of Samuel, Kings and Chronicles. Or, if we prefer, we may describe it, with J.A. Froude, as 'an Aeschylean drama, composed of facts literally true, in which the Furies are seen once more walking on this prosaic earth and shaking their serpent hair'.

In the years after the publication of *The French Revolution* Carlyle exploited his success. He poured out articles and books and gave popular lectures, in all of which he used the past to shed a new and disturbing light on the present. It was these works, above all, which gave him his great influence; and although their force may now be spent, we must surely respect writings which inspired such men as G.H. Lewes, John Sterling, John Ruskin, James Anthony Froude. What inspired them was the restoration, in a world perplexed by doubt and threatened with social dissolution – in the decade of Newman's apostasy and the Chartist revolt – of belief in human free will. Carlyle had himself known that doubt and that fear, and now he not only proclaimed his triumph over it but called in the past to give depth and weight to his message. In his biography of Carlyle, Froude has vividly described Carlyle's significance to himself and his contemporaries. 'The present generation', he wrote, 'which has grown in an open spiritual ocean, which has got used to it and learned to swim for itself, will never know what it was to find the lights all drifting, and compasses all awry, and nothing left to steer by but the stars.' In these circumstances the doctrine of the hero who prevailed over doubt, and acted in the serene conviction that his sincerity guaranteed the support of Providence, could give a new meaning to life; and it was a comfort to discover that history endorsed, or could be made to endorse, that view.

The burden of all Carlyle's writings of the 1840s was the same. Politically they were concerned with 'the condition of England'. All around him, at that time, Carlyle could hear serious men offering their remedies for that dangerous condition. Conservatives urged a return to tradition, a revival of Christianity; whigs pressed timely political reform; radicals looked beyond reform to a perfect system of democracy. All these voices were impatiently shouted down by Carlyle. Religion? Coleridge, with his 'spectral Puseyisms' and 'vain phantasmal moonshine', was at best 'a mass of the richest spices putrefied into a dunghill'. Newman had the mind of a half-grown rabbit. Keble was an old ape. Whiggism? Macaulay was 'a sophistical ambitious young man of talent . . . irremediably commonplace'. Radicalism? John Mill, once a friend, would soon be discarded as 'essentially made of sawdust', 'a silly logic-chopping engine, a thing of mechanized iron'. To Carlyle, all these remedies were futile because they were 'mechanical', external to man. What was needed was a 'dynamical' remedy, a change in the outlook of men, a new generation of men inspired by a new prophet, ready to be led by a new hero. Perhaps the prophet and the hero would be one and the same man.

Whence was such dynamism to spring? Not from the suffering poor themselves. As a good Calvinist, Carlyle despised the unregenerate populace, and the idea – that cant of Enlightenment – of the rights and natural goodness of man. 'All democracy', he told Mill in 1840, was 'a mere transitory preparation' for a new aristocracy. For essentially he believed in an aristocracy; but it must be an effective aristocracy, ruling and leading the people, a Calvinist Elect. Such an aristocracy had once been in England. Looking back into English history, he admired the ruthless feudatories of the Norman kings – that 'martial aristocracy' whose 'gothic edifice' had seemed so horrible to the philosophers of the eighteenth century. But what hope was there of the modern aristocracy? The Scottish aristocracy had always been irredeemably bad: 'a selfish famishing unprincipled set of hyenas, though toothless now, still mischievous and greedy beyond limits'. The irresponsible French aristocracy of the *ancien régime* had been the cause of all the trouble. The English aristocracy was better, and indeed, as time passed, and he was cultivated by it, Carlyle developed a snobbish respect for it. Unfortunately English aristocrats spent too much of their time preserving, shooting and consuming partridges, or in patronising the opera and 'what they call art, poetry and the like' and 'wasting themselves in that inane region'. Still, they were not altogether lost: they were worth preaching at; perhaps they would learn from history.

So, in his writings of these years, Carlyle, like Macaulay, invoked history to reinforce a political philosophy. But whereas Macaulay, an heir of the Enlightenment, saw history as progress, Carlyle rejected that whole concept. We must see the past, he insisted, not 'through the medium of Philosophic History', but in its own context, with the eye of sympathetic imagination. Then we shall find in the Middle Ages not gothic barbarism but an organic society and see – for instance – the Norman conquerors of England not as 'vulturous irrational tyrants' but as 'true royal souls, crowned kings as such'. For the past was not necessarily worse than the present simply because it lacked political freedom, or democracy, or newspapers, or parliaments, or 'spectral Puseyism', or diseased Methodist introspection. This was not different from the philosophy of the Germans: of Herder and of Ranke, who saw every age as immediate to God and sought to understand it not by comparing it with the present but by seeing it in its own context, 'wie es eigentlich gewesen'.

To demonstrate this, 'and from the Past, in a circuitous way, illustrate the Present and the Future', Carlyle took up the recently published medieval Latin chronicle of Jocelyn of Brakelond, and used it to portray the life of a twelfth-century monastic community which had fallen into insolvency and decay, but which, through the energy and practical leadership of a strong new abbot, recovered its function in a real, cohesive, responsible, though medieval, society. Abbot Samson was the hero of the chronicle, as also of Carlyle's *Past and Present*. He pulled his demoralised community together, restored its finances, chased away the 'harpy insatiable horseleech Jews' on whom it had become dependent, and reconstituted it as a living social organism. Out of this story comes a picture of the past which seems superior, within its own context, to the divided and tortured present. Of course, Carlyle allowed, the Middle Ages were not to be revived in the nineteenth century. The Catholic religion, monasticism, feudal institutions were now dead, and any revival of them – neo-gothic architecture, Anglo-Catholic ritualism, etc – was a mere sham. But in their own context these institutions had been 'real' and therefore better than the modern system of shameless materialism and pitiless *laissez-faire*; as Carlyle then, reverting from the past to the present, proceeded to show, to some tune.

Meanwhile he was preparing his next great work of history. From the French, he had moved to the English Revolution. Not, of course, to the Glorious Revolution of 1688: that, with its cold Dutch hero and its institutional achievements, he was content to leave to the whigs, and to Macaulay, who was already working on it. Carlyle's English revolution was the Puritan Revolution of the 1640s, which produced no institutions at all, but did produce a hero: Oliver Cromwell.

Carlyle had long been interested in the age of Cromwell, but his plans for writing on it had varied. He had contemplated an essay, a book and, at one time, a drama: history was always, to him, something of a drama – a high, Aeschylean tragedy. In the end it was a compilation. He had begun it in 1838, immediately after the publication of *The French Revolution*. It appeared in 1845 as the *Letters and Speeches of Oliver Cromwell*.

Carlyle's *Cromwell* is an extraordinary work. Formally, it is not a work of history but a collection of documents held loosely together by an uneven narrative, and themselves interrupted by the running commentary of the editor. The narrative has all the virtues of *The French Revolution*: the vivid imagination, the sense of actuality and participation, the bold imagery; but also all the faults: the over-dramatisation, the highly personal judgments, the rhetorical interruptions, the grotesque egotism. Carlyle was never patient of other writers, but his impatience was now pathological. He abused all his authorities, while quietly appropriating their material, and then trumpeted his own labours and his own originality: how he alone had traversed 'the inarticulate rubbish continent' of Rushworth's *Collections*, waded through the 'shoreless lakes of ditchwater and bilgewater' in Thurloe's *State Papers*, mastered 'the pamphletary chaos' of the Thomason Tracts; how he first had discovered unknown manuscript texts (which in fact he had taken from printed books) and authenticated newly discovered documents (which in fact were palpable forgeries); and how his own patient scholarship had at last cleared passages hitherto overlaid by 'the accumulated guano of human stupor', 'the obscene droppings of an extensive owl-population' – that is, previous commentators – or 'trampled down for two centuries by mere bison and hoofed cattle' – that is, previous editors. But even more repellent, to a modern reader, is the incessant theme of his commentary: contempt for every rival or critic of his hero, for every effort to institutionalise the victory of the Parliament, and vulgar worship of personal power.

It is sometimes said that Carlyle's philosophy changed between his earlier and his later work: that the former – in particular, *The French Revolution* – showed tolerance and understanding while later he 'went mad' and succumbed to the uncritical cult of the hero. No date is given for this change, and indeed it would be difficult to substantiate it, for wherever it is placed, chronology defeats it. No doubt Carlyle's attitude did harden with time. But his philosophy did not change: all its essential elements are there from the beginning. The convulsive theory of history, the contempt for institutions, the uncritical worship of the hero who is guided by his instinct alone, being in touch with 'the eternal verities' – all these had been spelt out by him in his writings at Craigenputtock, before he came to London and began *The French Revolution*. If there is a difference between *The French Revolution* and *Cromwell*, it is simply that the former did not provide Carlyle with a ready-made hero, while the latter did.

It was while he was at work on his *Cromwell* that Carlyle delivered his famous series of lectures on 'Heroes and Hero-worship' in which he defined his ideal of the hero and, incidentally, showed why Cromwell did, and Napoleon did not, fulfil that role. The hero, Carlyle there insisted, is not merely a man of action: heroism is indivisible, and the true hero 'is a hero at all points' – he can be poet, prophet, sage, warrior or ruler; but his highest role is when he is ruler, for then he is 'the summary for us of *all* the various figures of heroism'. As such, he is, at first, a destroyer, 'the indispensable saviour of his epoch – the lightning without which the fuel never would have burnt'. But afterwards he reveals his constructive character. Once the 'shams' have gone up in smoke, and the immediate agencies of destruction – 'all this of liberty and equality, electoral suffrages, independence and so forth' – have been shoved on to the fire after them, then the hero emerges as the man of order: 'he is here to make what was disorderly, chaotic, into a thing ruled, regular'. So 'some Cromwell or Napoleon is the necessary finish of a sans-culottism'. However, when the test is applied, Napoleon fails. He lacked 'sincerity': indeed, there was 'a portentous mixture of the Quack in him', and this element of quackery ultimately prevailed. Not content with his proper, heroic function of 'bridling-in that great devouring, self-devouring French Revolution', taming it so that it became 'organic', he 'took to believing in Semblances: strove to connect himself with Austrian dynasties, Popedoms, with the old false Feudalities which he once saw clearly to be false'. Your hero should not make any such synthesis with the past. The value of history, to Carlyle, lay not in its continuities, but in its violent interruptions, its 'Phoenix-death-birth'.

How different was Cromwell! Originally Carlyle had shared the traditional view of Cromwell as a bold, bad man: 'brave, yet cunning and double withal, like some paltry pettifogger. He is your true enthusiastic hypocrite, at once crackbrained and inspired, a knave and a demigod'. But as he came closer to his subject, he changed his view. Soon he was positively admiring Cromwell's brutality; in *The French Revolution* he incidentally praised him for personally shooting and killing, in front of his army, a sergeant who sought to present a Leveller petition: 'Noll was a man fit for such things.' By 1840 Cromwell had become 'one of the greatest souls ever born of English kin'. By 1845 he was a hero 'bathed in eternal splendours', in direct contact with 'reality' and the 'elemental powers'.

Thereafter it is plain sailing. Cromwell's rivals could be dismissed with contemptuous epithets, and if they spoke, their voices could be drowned by diversionary noises. On the other hand, when Cromwell spoke, all profane voices must be silenced, and his words accompanied only by regular bursts of applause and a continuo of revolting sycophancy. Here too, of course, Carlyle was motivated by current politics. Charles I's great minister Archbishop Laud – 'old scarecrow Laud' – had indeed sought to redress the grievances of the poor, but his efforts has been consecrated by Anglo-Catholic ritualism; so he was dismissed as a purblind 'college-tutor, whose whole world is forms': a precursor, clearly, of Coleridge and Southey. The Parliament men who sought to control first Charles I, then Cromwell, by means of laws and institutions, were held up to contempt as petty legalistic pedants – like the modern whigs who believed in the efficacy of parliamentary suffrages and Reform Bills. The Levellers, with their abstract new models of government – 'their Agreement of the People – their Bentham-Sieyès constitutions: annual parliaments', etc. – these, of course, are the precursors of modern Radicals. Only Cromwell himself had no equivalent in modern politics; for the contemporary world had as yet produced – at least in Europe – no man of 'sincerity' who would cut through and cast away the 'shams' of the time, sweep aside parliaments and constitutions, and rule by personal, charismatic, unflinching authority.

'At least in Europe' . . . But might not one be found outside Europe – in a remote land which, like Cromwell's England, had recently been delivered from a corrupt monarchy and 'the enormous bat-wings of the clergy'? While Carlyle was working on Cromwell, he learnt that José Rodriguez Francia, the 'perpetual dictator' of landlocked Paraguay, had died.

Dr Francia – he was a civilian, a doctor of law – had begun his career as secretary to the republican *junta* or directorate of his newly independent country; but in 1814, like Cromwell or Napoleon, he had dispensed with his colleagues and had set up a personal dictatorship which had lasted until his death twenty-six years later. In those years he had built up the machinery of repression, 'hermetically sealed' the frontiers, established a restrictive monopoly over all commerce, and ruled the whole country as his patrimonial estate. Visitors from Europe were fascinated and appalled by Francia's 'reign of terror', which was made notorious by the kidnapping of the French botanist Aimé Bonpland. Bonpland had become famous as the companion of Alexander von Humboldt in his travels through Latin America, during the last years of Spanish power. Afterwards he had returned to the continent and had established a tea-farm there. It was beyond the frontiers of Paraguay, but not beyond the reach of Dr Francia, and Dr Francia regarded it as a threat to his monopoly. So he resolved to suppress it. Suddenly, a troop of raiders invaded the tea-farm, seized Bonpland, and carried him into oblivion in Paraguay. The European Republic of Letters, Humboldt at their head, protested and implored; but in vain. Bonpland simply disappeared and was never heard of again in the lifetime of the dictator. Francia's death in 1840 elicited obituary condemnations in Europe, and they in turn inspired Carlyle to turn aside from Cromwell and offer an obituary tribute to a new, and modern, hero.

To Carlyle, Francia was a man after his own heart. Had he not been destined, like himself, for the Church? Was he not, like himself, 'saturnine', 'atrabiliar', 'subject to terrible fits of hypochondria, as your adust men of genius too frequently are'? Was he not a man of action who had sent useless committees of notables packing? He was the Cromwell of South America, 'a man sent by Heaven', 'a sovereign with bared sword, stern as Rhadamanthus', 'of iron energy and industry, of great and severe labour', 'the one veracious man' who opposed shams and flunkeyism, and therefore deserved a true biographer. In his hatred of European liberalism, Carlyle positively revelled in the severities of Dr Francia in his rough treatment of the innocent Bonpland, his contempt for Bonpland's European champions, his ruthless repression of

dissent, his 'frightful prisons, far up among the wastes, a kind of Paraguay
Siberia, to which unruly persons, not yet got to the length of shooting, were
relegated'. 'Republic of Paraguay, how art thou indebted to the toils, the
vigils and cares of our perpetual Dictator!' Francia, to him, was the great
restorer who burnt up the newly imported 'shams' of republicanism, liberalism, free trade, in that isolated rural society, reimposing, in purer form, its
happy insulation and patriarchal rule. He was the enemy of novelty. 'The
world gets even madder with its choppings and changings and never-ending
innovations, *not* for the better', Carlyle wrote to his wife, protesting at an
improved form of writing paper – for with him, the smallest personal incon-
venience was a symptom of cosmic disturbance: 'my collars too are all
on a new principle. Oh for one hour of Dr Francia!' His lyrical essay on
Dr Francia was published in 1843; then he returned to Cromwell: Cromwell,
who, as he wrote, explicitly comparing him with Francia, 'now first begins
to speak'.

He was beginning to speak, of course, through his prophet Carlyle. And
what were the qualities that were shared by Carlyle's Cromwell and Carlyle's
Francia? They were, above all, 'sincerity', 'veracity', 'reality' – and effective
power. These were held to justify even their most questionable acts. The
most questionable acts of Cromwell were in Ireland. These, Carlyle
admitted, had been the object of 'much loud criticism and sibylline execra-
tion'. But was he not, even then, 'sincere'? Did he not fairly warn the Irish
garrison at Drogheda that, if his terms were refused, he could not leave a man
of them alive?

> They rejected his summons and terms; he stormed the place and,
> according to his promise, put every man of the garrison to death. . . . To
> Wexford garrison the like terms as at Drogheda and, failing them, the like
> storm. Here is a man whose word represents a thing! Not bluster this, and
> false jargon scattering itself to the winds: what this man speaks out of him
> comes to pass as a fact; speech with this man is accurately prophetic of
> deed. This is the first King's face poor Ireland saw; the first Friend's face,
> little as it recognises him – poor Ireland!

If Cromwell was a hero, a prophet of 'reality', it followed of course that
Cromwell's failure, the complete rejection of his work and aims after his
death, was a disastrous reversion to the 'shams' which he had sought to

hod-loads of heavy German fact back to Chelsea, to reconstitute them as a sacred Mount Sinai, bathed in heavenly light, with *der alte Fritz*, like Jehovah, smoking on top of it; but after all, he always groaned while at work: it was part of the process. So, in the end, the crowned Prussian cynic appeared as the hero, the only hero, of the otherwise 'putrid eighteenth century', a 'noble human reality' 'sprung from the head of God Almighty' to be 'a divine revelation to the torpid frivolous children of men', proving 'that there is a Veracity in all things and a Mendacity in Sham-things', etc., etc. Carlyle even contrived to idolise, as 'a rhadamanthine Spartan King', Frederick's dreadful father, Frederick William I. This brutal, boorish tyrant ruled his country by stick and gallows, hanged innocent men without compunction, and forced his eighteen-year-old son to witness the summary execution of his closest friend. Frederick William, Carlyle admits, was indeed 'a very arbitrary king. Yes, but then a great deal of his *arbitrium*, or sovereign will, was that of the Eternal Heavens as well, and did exceedingly behove to be done if the earth would prosper.' After that, there could be no argument.

'All history', Carlyle wrote, 'is an imprisoned epic, nay an imprisoned psalm and prophecy.' If the epic broke from its prison in *The French Revolution*, the psalm and prophecy broke out in *Frederick the Great*. It was a psalm of praise: praise of Frederick, of the Hohenzollern dynasty, of Prussia, of Prussian domination in Germany; and it was a prophecy of a new German Empire in Europe, a 'solid German' Empire to rise on the ruins of 'unsolid revolutionary' France and materialist, mechanical England: an empire to be created by Frederick's methods, by great battles striking 'like a huge war-gong, with long resonance, through the general ear', and heralding 'a universal European war' and 'a new epoch' to come. Thanks to Frederick's Prussia, the heroic Nordic Germans, 'Hyperborean Spartans', 'grim and hirsute' men 'in dim uncertain garniture, of which the buff belts and steel are alone conspicuous', boisterous and beer-drinking, would trample down the fashionable follies of 'emancipation, political rose-water, and friendship to humanity, as we now call it', and if they could get through the 'various child-diseases' of growing nations, their unavoidable but temporary 'measles and Mumps', and particularly 'one of the most dangerous diseases of national adolescence, extremely prevalent over the world at this time', 'the parliamentary eloquence or ballot-box influenza', who can tell what they may not do for world history? A few years later, when Bismarck's lightning wars were crowned by the founding of the German Empire, Carlyle was jubilant. He looked forward, he wrote, to a German domination of Europe for 'another five centuries or so'.

Carlyle's *Frederick the Great* was not well received by English historians. Macaulay, who lived to read only the first volume, noted in his journal that he had never seen a worse book – 'the philosophy nonsense and the style gibberish'. Acton described it as 'a history made up of eccentricities', comparable only with *The Pickwick Papers*. But in Germany, naturally enough, it found admirers. Bismarck wrote personally to Carlyle on his eightieth birthday, praising his great work; the Kaiser conferred on him the Prussian Order, *Pour le Mérite*; and seventy years later, when the last all-German Reich was foundering in total defeat, the same book gave comfort to its leaders as they awaited the end in their underground bunkers in Berlin. Joseph Goebbels read it regularly, and periodically he dropped into Hitler's adjoining bunker to cheer him with choice excerpts. 'The Führer', he recorded in his diary, 'knows the book very well himself. I repeated certain passages of it to him, and they affected him very deeply.'

Again and again in those last days of Nazism, appropriate gobbets from Carlyle's *Frederick* were served up to Hitler and were acknowledged by him to be 'extraordinarily instructive and uplifting'. The climax would come when Goebbels read to Hitler how Frederick, beset on all sides and in danger of final defeat, was saved by 'the miracle of the House of Brandenburg', the sudden death of the czarina of Russia. 'Why should we not hope for a similar wonderful turn of Fortune?' asked Goebbels. Why not indeed? A little later, the sudden death of Roosevelt seemed, briefly, to be the miraculous delivery and Carlyle, from his grave, to have staved off the fall of the Third Reich.

In the intellectual pedigree of Nazism, Carlyle cannot be refused a place. Reacting against the rational eighteenth century, he believed in the insufficiency of human reason and extolled the direct intuitive knowledge of the visionary man. Throughout his life, his mind was dominated by the French Revolution, which he saw as the still-unfinished revenge of divine justice on the Enlightenment of the eighteenth century. 'To me', he wrote in *Frederick the Great*, 'the eighteenth century has nothing grand in it, except that grand universal suicide named French Revolution, by which it terminated its otherwise worthless existence by at least one worthy act – setting fire to its old home and self and going up in flames and volcanic explosions.' But the grandeur of the revolution, for him, did not lie in its ideas: liberty, equality, fraternity. It lay solely in the size and force and noise and stink of the great conflagration in which these ideas too, having served their turn, were happily incinerated. Hating reason, he hated rational discussion, the 'eternal babblement' of parliaments and assemblies. In 1834, on his arrival in London, he watched the burning of the Houses of Parliament with something of the satisfaction with which a German Nazi might have watched the burning, a century later, of the Reichstag. To solve the problems of society he looked not to the arguments of rational men, but to the dynamic, charismatic powers of 'the leader – the true Leader', the Führer. Such a leader drew no authority from the existing laws; those were the 'shams' which it was his function to destroy. The only visible tests of this power are sincerity and success. Cromwell was sincere, a man of his word: he did what he said that he would do to the Irish, as Hitler to the Jews, and he succeeded. Success justified all his methods, as it justified, in Frederick the Great, aggression, fraud, breach of faith. The end justifies the means. Might is right.

Might and right ... the phrase runs like a refrain through Carlyle's works. Might and right, 'these two', we read already in *The French Revolution*, 'are they not one and the same?' 'Might and right do differ frightfully from hour to hour', he wrote in *Chartism*, 'but give them centuries to try it, and they are found to be identical'. 'Mights ... do in the long run, and for ever will, in this just universe ... mean Rights.' The power of the hero is automatically just, even if it be used for conquest; the conquered, by definition, deserve to be conquered, and so they too have only the right to obey; which is for their good. The strong man is, by definition, the just man. The Norman kings, being conquerors, were just and wise. The Irish should have recognised Cromwell as their hero-king. The Partition of Poland was 'Heaven's justice', a salutary extinction of Anarchy not 'worth dwelling on in History'. And since the weak are a legitimate prey, the strong may solve their own problems at their expense. For the answer to the social problems of the master race is not Malthusian restraint or 'Benthamee formulas, barren as the East wind', but heroic leadership and conquest of *Lebensraum*; the leadership of 'Attila and his Huns' against 'foul old Rome', of Hengist and Alaric conquering and enslaving inferior peoples. For slavery too is a right, just like mastery: the Nigger has 'the right ... to be *compelled* to work', and talk of his emancipation is 'rose-pink cant' tossed up by 'the deep froth-oceans of benevolence', 'Fraternity', 'Exeter Hall-philanthropy': what Hitler would call *Humanitätsduselei*.

When Hitler wrote, in 1924, that once in many centuries the political philosopher and the statesman might converge in one man who would then be able to end an old age of history and begin a new, he was not inspired by Carlyle: he was inspired by a purely German school of thinkers of which Carlyle was, as it were, a foreign corresponding member; but he was uttering the pure doctrine of Carlyle. And when Hitler himself, in that role, undertook to solve the problems of his country by eliminating an ineffectual parliamentary democracy, destroying obsolete institutions, and creating a new, charismatic leadership which would unite all classes in the realisation, under the guidance of Providence, of ancient, hitherto frustrated aims, he was acting the part of Carlyle's hero. He was, in fact, a unique synthesis of Carlyle's Cromwell and Carlyle's Frederick the Great: like the former, a usurper who destroyed the 'shams' of the past and created a new, ideological leadership; like the latter, a cynical realist of unbreakable willpower in politics and war. Like Carlyle, Hitler believed in 'dynamism', 'the triumph of the will', the force of inner human strength over 'mechanical' institutions, the right of the hero to arbitrary, not legal, power. He too blamed Napoleon for renouncing his 'world-historical' role in order to compromise with the 'shams' of the past. This does not necessarily mean that Carlyle would have approved of all that Hitler afterwards did, but it serves to remind us that those Germans who listened to some parts of Hitler's message, while overlooking others, were not necessarily more foolish or more wicked than those Englishmen who, like Froude and Kingsley, Lewes and Ruskin, were carried away by what they accepted of the message of Carlyle.

So much for Carlyle's contribution to political philosophy. What of his contribution to the study of history? I have said that he put the clock back. The great achievement of the eighteenth-century historians had been to bring the explanation of history down to earth. Carlyle and his German contemporaries, including Marx, with whom he has much in common, put it firmly back into the stratosphere. Not into the will of a Judaeo-Christian God, but into a World Plan, a Hegelian dialectic, a metaphysical Providence. This is not incomparable with technical advance. Ranke's smug concept of *Weltgeschichte* animated him in introducing new techniques of documentary study; the Hegelians gave a great impulse to intellectual, the Marxists to economic and social history. But Carlyle's revolt against the eighteenth century was accompanied by no technical advance as a historian. Technically, as intellectually, it is a regression; which is no doubt why, as a historian, he left so few disciples.

Of the two regius professors whom I mentioned at the beginning of this essay, Kingsley was a historical novelist, not a historian, and Froude's undoubted virtues as a historian – his range, his energy, his archival industry – were rather vitiated than improved by the inheritance of Carlyle: the respect for power, the hero worship of Henry VIII. These men, like the other disciples of Carlyle, had been inspired by his moral philosophy: his refusal to be enervated by intellectual doubt, his conviction that action was the answer to such doubt, his belief that the course of history is directed not by purely mechanical causes but by an immanent divine justice, and that it is within the power of man, single-handed, to sustain and implement that justice when it is betrayed by human corruption. Such a doctrine was not, in itself, ignoble. It inspired reformers like Shaftesbury before vindicating British imperialism and, later, German Nazism. But it did not forward the understanding of history.

However, after all this, one great virtue remains. Carlyle's insistence on the power of the human will, on the necessary function of imagination, of 'wonder', was a valuable corrective to the increasingly impersonal presentation and interpretation of the Scottish 'philosophic historians' after Hume. This was what made him an ally of Macaulay, whom he so hated, in common admiration of Scott, whom both of them imitated as a writer and despised as a man. To Carlyle, as to Macaulay, Scott was a man of perverted values: he wrote daily 'with the ardour of a steam-engine' in order to make £15,000 a year 'to buy upholstery with it' and 'cover the walls of a stone house in Selkirkshire with knick-knacks, ancient armour and genealogical shields'. But he recognised in him a historian who did not merely chronicle or analyse but transported himself, in imagination, into the past, lived in every moment that he recounted, and thereby made the past too live. Scott's son-in-law and biographer returned the compliment: Carlyle, he said, 'had more power of putting life into the dry bones than anyone but Scott'.

To reanimate dry bones can be as dangerous in history as in politics, but now that we have escaped the dangers, we can afford to admire the spectacle. Perhaps it is the surest sign of Carlyle's genius that we read him still, and are interested in him still, although his ideas are totally discredited. Even in the rich and varied landscape of Victorian England, he stands out, like some great volcanic cone (he would himself have appreciated the metaphor), once active and terrible, spouting lurid flame and dense rolling clouds of smoke and ash, now a grim, forbidding feature covered, as far as eye can see, with nothing but barren black lava, impressive even when extinct.

CHAPTER 13

Jacob Burckhardt

How does a historian qualify to be a mastermind? Not by mere professional competence: he must, of course, be professionally competent, but he must also rise above that modest virtue. He must be a general historian, and something of a philosopher. The great historians have always realised that history is not particular but general: that it is a continuum which cannot be understood in one age alone, and that the present, which is also a part of that continuum, is relevant to the past. Therefore they have always been conscious of the public problems of their own times: many of them, indeed, personally involved in them. There are dangers, of course, in such involvement: too often the committed historian becomes insensibly a propagandist and is shown, by a later generation, to have transformed the past by seeing it in contemporary terms. The great historian must survive that danger. His philosophy must be one which does not date. It must survive the criticism of later generations and be found illuminating even in a new and radically different age.

By this criterion Jacob Burckhardt certainly qualifies for inclusion in this series of lectures. He was not a committed public man like most of the great German historians who outshone him in his lifetime. He was an academic historian who taught, and was content to teach, in a provincial university in his native Switzerland. Though his range was vast, he did not write contemporary history: the historical books which he wrote for publication were on Greek civilisation, on the later Roman Empire, and on the Italian Renaissance. In his time, he was best known as an art historian: a title which he would have rejected but which still clings to him in works of reference. His most widely read book was his *Cicerone*, a guidebook to Italian art. Later, his book *The Civilisation of the Renaissance* became famous, although not in the form in which he had written it. It was only after his death that some of his lectures on history in general and on his own times were published. But, like the German historians, he was profoundly influenced by the public events of his lifetime. Only, unlike them, he was not blinded by those events. He did not jump on the bandwagon of German unity, Prussian power, or see the hand of Divine Providence in the creation of the German Empire. Indeed, he revolted against all these ideas and returned to Switzerland in order to attach himself to an older German tradition which his German colleagues, he believed, had distorted.

Burckhardt's implicit dialogue with the great German historians of his time is essential to the understanding of his historical thought; for his ideas were nourished in the same intellectual soil although they grew afterwards in a different direction. That soil was the philosophy of the German Enlightenment, of Winckelmann, Herder and Goethe, of that wonderful generation which, having come to maturity before the French Revolution, had been able to dissent from the complacent narrowness of the French *philosophes* without troubling themselves too much with the problem of political power.

For the German Enlightenment was the enemy of the French Enlightenment. How Herder hated the arrogance of those French philosophers who saw themselves as the prophets of progress and reason, the enemies of ancient superstition, the teachers and emancipators of Europe! No, exclaimed Herder, man is more than dry reason, and civilisation than Parisian salons. Progress, the superiority of the present over the past, is a chimera, the slogan of French cultural imperialism. The past is as valid, within its own terms, as the present. Every age is its own justification: who are we to condescend to the men who wrote heroic poetry and built great cathedrals? *Kultur*, the organic totality of intellectual, spiritual and artistic life, in the individual as in society, is more important than this narrow 'reason', and literature and art, which are the living expression of that totality, are to be judged by their authenticity, not by the artificial canons of modern taste. Such was the essential doctrine of the great Germans of the late eighteenth century. It was a doctrine particularly acceptable in a country whose only unity was provided not by politics – politics only divided and weakened it – but by culture: which was saved from being a mere geographical expression by its newly discovered greatness as a *Kulturvolk*.

That was all very well before the Napoleonic conquests, but after 1815 the position was very different. German culture had indeed survived that terrible shock, and its mere survival, to some, was proof of its vitality. The defeat of

Napoleon, it could be argued, had shown that the ancient traditions of Europe were not merely the obsolete relics of a feudal past, for had they not prevailed over 'enlightened' French imperialism? However, it had been a damned close-run thing, and victory, it had to be admitted, had not been achieved by ideas alone. After 1815 the *Kulturvolk* of Germany had to recognise that it could only compete in the harsh world of modern politics if it had the protection of a powerful state: if, from a *Kulturvolk*, it became a *Kulturstaat*. These views were echoed loudest in the German state which had contributed most to the victory and which now, as its reward, had become a powerful kingdom, dominating North Germany from Königsberg to the Rhine: Prussia.

It was against this background that the school was formed which was to dominate German historical writing for over a century, from the earliest works of Leopold von Ranke, in 1825, to the last work of Friedrich Meinecke, in 1948. The best of these historians never forgot the philosophy of the German Enlightenment. They believed that history was the history of culture, that culture was indivisible, organic, that the past was to be respected on its own terms, not judged by the present: that, as Ranke put it, all periods are equal in the sight of God. But they also, increasingly, saw the power of the state not as an irrelevancy (as it had been in eighteenth-century Germany) but as an essential part of the same organism, the protective carapace which society created out of its own substance, and which was therefore no less valid, no less autonomous, than the culture which it protected. Thus, if differing forms of culture were all equally valid and not to be criticised by absolute standards, so were differing states. States too, like culture, followed their own rules, their 'reason of state', which was thus legitimised, and not to be criticised from a standpoint of morality or natural law. These doctrines were easily accepted by liberal men in the early days after 1815 when the Prussian state was liberal. By the 1860s the situation would be somewhat different. The Prussian state had then ceased to be liberal. But by then the ideas were fixed. They had become an orthodoxy whose only effective challenger, among German-speaking historians, was Jacob Burckhardt.

Burckhardt was a native of Basel, a member of one of the old patrician families of the city. As he was destined for the Protestant Church, he began his university studies – classical studies and theology – at Basel; but he soon shed his theological beliefs (though remaining profoundly religious in spirit). He was captivated by the ideas that came from Germany, the ideas of Herder and Goethe; he longed to escape from the stuffy atmosphere of Basel – a provincial city sadly sunk from its greatness in the age of Erasmus; and in 1839, at the age of twenty-one, having taken his degree in theology, and made a brief, exciting visit to Italy, he found his way to the newest and most famous university of Germany, Wilhelm von Humboldt's university of Berlin.

There were giants in Berlin in those days. They included the great classicist August Boeckh and the historians Ranke and Droysen. Ranke was by now the oracle of the new German historical school: his recent essays idealising the state and the orderly, self-correcting balance of power had made him popular with the Prussian government. Droysen, a younger man, had made his name by his history of Alexander the Great and his 'Hellenistic' successors. He was indeed the inventor of the concept of a Hellenistic age, a Hellenistic culture. But he was also something else: the discoverer of the demiurgic 'great men' of history. To him, Alexander was the 'great man' whom Divine Providence had called forth to implement its 'Theodicy'; for had he not, by conquering and hellenising the East, prepared the ground in which Christianity would spread? This 'Macedonian' theme would soon become very popular with Prussian historians, for obvious reasons.

When Burckhardt first arrived in Berlin, he was enchanted by it. The whole intellectual life of the place excited him. 'My eyes', he wrote to a friend at the time, 'were wide with astonishment at the first lectures which I heard by Ranke, Droysen and Boeckh. I realised that the same thing had befallen me as befell the knight in *Don Quixote*: I had loved my science on hearsay, and suddenly here it was appearing before me in giant form – and I had to lower my eyes. Now I really am determined to devote my life to it.' And to his sister:

What can I tell you about Germany? I am like Saul the son of Kish, who went out to look for lost asses and found a king's crown. I often want to kneel down before the sacred soil of Germany and thank God that my mother tongue is German. I have Germany to thank for everything. My best teachers have been German, I was nourished at the breast of German culture and learning, and I shall always draw my best powers from this land. What a people! What a wonderful youth! What a land – a paradise![1]

Burckhardt greatly respected Droysen and regretted his early depar' ⸱e from Berlin to Kiel. He attended Ranke's seminar and afterwards referr him as 'my great master'. But let us not be deceived by formal tributes fact he soon became disillusioned with Ranke as a person – we may that he came to despise him as a snob, a toady of power, a man without conviction. And as time went on he would repudiate him intellectually too: him and Droysen and their whole school. He saw them as the men who had betrayed the ideal of German culture and the historical philosophy of the age of Goethe. He also came to believe that they were politically misguided and intellectually wrong.

The crucial years were the 1840s: that decade of intellectual ferment, of incubation, in which the thought of all our modern ideologues – of Marx and Carlyle and Gobineau and so many others – was hatched. Politically, those were the last years of Metternich's Europe, years in which the revolution was kept at bay, and the balance of power was held, by the unrivalled worldly wisdom, and the immemorial expertise, of the elder statesman of Vienna. Ranke's concept of world history was not unlike Metternich's European system, only on a more sublime, a more metaphysical level. High in the clouds, a bloodless, Lutheran God, whom Eternity had drained of all identifiable properties, calmly regulated the providential machinery – a touch here, a readjustment there – so that all temporary oscillations were corrected and the great engine of *Weltgeschichte* could proceed on its course, ensuring that, in the end, seen *sub specie aeternitatis*, all would be for the best in the best of possible worlds.

Burckhardt did not share this view. To him as to Herder, the life of the peoples of Europe was not their politics, or their religion, but their total culture, and a system which merely balanced politics and religion in order to preserve the *status quo*, without expressing and protecting the living culture behind them, was, in itself, worthless. The question which he asked was therefore: did Metternich's system express or protect the culture of Europe? And his answer was: no, it did not. That culture had indeed been threatened by the revolutionary imperialism of France, and the other powers of Europe had indeed defeated France; after which they had indeed restored the old political system. But they had not restored the organic society which Napoleon had destroyed, nor had they finally defeated the revolutionary forces which he had harnessed to his imperialist aims. The restoration of 1815 was therefore not a real restoration. It was merely the artificial imposition of a brittle crust which would hardly contain the next outbreak of the still-active force beneath. In 1842 Burckhardt expected that next outbreak. He still looked forward, he said, to 'frightful crises'; but he added, hopefully – for he was still young, still hopeful – that mankind will survive them and Germany will then perhaps achieve its golden age.[2] Then, in 1846, when he was back in Basel, working as a journalist, he witnessed the civil war of Switzerland, the sectarian war of the *Sonderbund*: a premonitory symptom soon to be merged in the universal outbreak of revolution in 1848.

The revolutionary years 1846–52 crystallised Burckhardt's historical philosophy and marked his decisive break with the German historians. It was a break on both sides, a great divide. After the failure of the revolution in Germany, the German historians forgot any liberal views they may have held and invested their hopes and actions (for most of them were active in politics) in the authoritarian Prussian state. The German *Kulturvolk*, they declared, could not now be welded into a viable state by its own efforts. Like ancient Greece, it must be united by a 'Macedonian' military monarchy. It required a Philip or an Alexander, a 'great man' who would assume the burden of history and force the pace of beneficent historic change. It was in those years that Droysen ceased to write about Alexander and Macedon and began instead his immense fourteen-volume work on *The History of Prussian Policy*.

So, when Bismarck came to power, the classically and historically trained intellectuals of Germany were ready for him. They could welcome him as the necessary agent of *Weltgeschichte*. Nor would they demur at his methods, his *Realpolitik*. Why should they? The state, they had already decided, was the organ of a culture which could not be judged, and it had its own morality, which also could not be judged. On this, philosophers and historians were agreed. The state, Hegel had said, was the march of God on earth. The state, Ranke had written, was a living being, a spiritual substance, a thought of God. The state, wrote Droysen, was 'the sum, the total organism of all ethical communities, their common purpose'; it was a law to itself – a moral law; in following its 'real interests', it could not be wrong.

Against this whole philosophy Burckhardt now declared himself a rebel. He was not a liberal: indeed, he hated the liberals of 1848 – men who, he believed, by their individualism and their patronage of the masses, were the destroyers of culture. 'We may all perish', he wrote to a liberal friend in 1846, 'but at least I want to discover the interest for which I am to perish, namely, the old culture of Europe.'[3] The Rhineland liberals, he wrote in 1848, were merely play-acting under the protection of Prussian garrisons. But he equally repudiated the opportunist conservatism of Prussia which was not defending German culture, as an earlier generation had supposed, but distorting, if not destroying, it; and he was contemptuous of those German historians who could not see, or pretended not to see, that their professed homage to culture had turned insensibly into a blind worship of power.

From 1848 until his death fifty years later, Burckhardt remained in Switzerland. From 1858 he was professor of history at Basel. But he was determined not to be like a German professor. In fact, he made himself as different as he could from a German professor. The German professors were pompous, omniscient, magisterial. Burckhardt affected a deliberate infor-mality, a self-mocking insouciance, a Socratic affectation of ignorance. The German professors were bureaucrats, or satraps, in an academic empire. With their hierarchy of patronage and their organised seminars they trained a professional class. Burckhardt remained an individual, an amateur. His only aim, he once wrote, was not to train 'scholars and disciples in the narrower sense', but to interest his students and make them feel that they could 'appropriate those aspects of the past which appealed to them, and that there might be happiness in so doing'.[4] It was a deliberate breach with the methods as well as with the philosophy of Ranke, an emphatic repudia-tion of the German academic world, to which he could never now be tempted back. He refused offers from Munich, Göttingen, Tübingen. In 1872 he was offered the succession to Ranke himself at Berlin. It was the most famous historical chair in Europe, whereas Basel only had 200 students in all faculties. But he refused to go. 'I would not have gone to Berlin at any price', he wrote: 'to have left Basel would have brought a malediction on me.'[5] As a historian, he once wrote, he wished to study the world 'from an Archimedean point outside events'; Basel was the next best thing.

Meanwhile he lectured and wrote, and the message which he uttered was constant. He was not a historian of state policy, like Ranke and his school; nor was he a historian of art or ideas in a narrow sense. He was a historian of 'culture' in the tradition which had passed from Winckelmann through Herder and Goethe, which had inspired the historians and philologists of the Napoleonic period, but which had now, in Germany, under the pressure of events, been diverted, carrying all its professional virtues with it, into the worship of that supposed organ of culture, the state.

Burckhardt's first work, *The Age of Constantine the Great*, published in 1853, can be seen as a sequel, and a rejoinder, to Droysen's *History of Alexander the Great*.[6] Droysen had seen Alexander as the 'great man', the demiurge who had prepared the ground for the predestined spread of Christianity. If that interpretation were accepted, Constantine's function in the divine plan was also clear: he was the second demiurge, the man who established Christianity throughout that ground. But Burckhardt's approach to this great theme, we soon discover, is very different from Droysen's. Whereas Droysen had subjected the subject to the man, and made the man the agent of a World Plan, Burckhardt reversed the process. His subject was not the achievement of the hero (he detested Constantine), nor even the rise of Christianity (to which he was lukewarm), but the historical change itself: the replacement of one millennial culture by another; and this replacement was not, in his view, a predetermined process. No Providence, no Theodicy, could be discerned behind it. Nor was it necessarily an improvement.

Nor was it a direct confrontation. Christianity, to Burckhardt, did not challenge, or even defeat, paganism: it merely entered into the spiritual vacuum left by the death of paganism. For paganism, to Burckhardt, is not a mere set of beliefs: it is a 'culture', an organic system of life; and that whole system was already dying before Constantine withdrew imperial protection from it and so hastened its collapse. Do we doubt this? Burckhardt examines all the aspects of pagan culture in the third century A.D., the years before Constantine, and everywhere – in art, literature, philosophy – he sees only the shadows of past greatness. So, when the new religion attacked, it met no serious resistance. It was not faced by the great classical philosophies – not even by stoicism, 'the noblest philosophy of defeat' – but only by enfeebled outgrowths from their dying trunks or by barbarous superstitions that had grown up around them. Why was this? He asks: was it because poetry and art are blossoms that must fall before the fruit of science and material progress can mature? Was it . . . but Burckhardt never forces answers to his questions. The failure of ancient civilisation is to him a fact – but also a mystery, and a melancholy mystery. 'Anyone', he concludes, 'who has encountered classical Antiquity, if only in its twilight, feels that with beauty and freedom there departed also the genuine antique life.' What was left of it 'can only be regarded as the lifeless precipitate of a once wonderful totality of being'.[7]

'The lifeless precipitate of a once wonderful totality of being' . . . The phrase is pure Burckhardt: Burckhardt the disciple of Goethe. Hellenism, to him, is not a system of ideas; it is not a set of political institutions; it is not Greek religion; it is not even philosophy, literature or art. It is a 'totality', a living organic whole holding all these things together, and giving them life; and by A.D. 300 that totality is no longer alive and neither art nor literature nor philosophy can express it.

Nor can it be revived by political power or political genius. Had that been possible, surely some of the heroic emperors of the third century would have done it: Alexander Severus, Probus, or, above all, Diocletian. But no: organic decay cannot be corrected by legislation, however enlightened; and so Diocletian failed and his dreadful successor Constantine threw open the gates, and let the new religion, the herald of a new culture, come in. If he had not done so, pagan culture still could not have survived. If its unmanned battlements had not fallen to Christianity, they would have fallen, three centuries later, to Islam.

Such was Burckhardt's interpretation of one great turning-point in the cultural history of Europe. Next year he revisited Italy, and published his guidebook to Italian art *Der Cicerone*. Six years later, in 1860, it was followed by a less successful but ultimately more famous work, *Die Kultur der Renaissance in Italien*, 'The Civilisation of the Renaissance in Italy'.[8]

We take the Renaissance, as a phase of cultural history, so much for granted that we do not realise how many of our assumptions we owe to Burckhardt. For although the word had been used before him, it had been used in a far more limited sense. It was *la renaissance des lettres*, the redis-covery of that classical literature which had been lost in the neglect and barbarism of the gothic Middle Ages. To Burckhardt, this was far too narrow a concept. To him, the Renaissance is an age, a 'totality of being', like clas-sical Antiquity itself, and the revival of ancient letters is only one aspect of it. For after all, those ancient letters did not merely turn up; they did not merely tumble out of dusty libraries in Western monasteries, or arrive in Italy in the pockets of refugee scholars from Byzantium. They were sought out and fetched; and they were fetched because Italy – the new Italian society – demanded them. If they had not been there, if they had all been destroyed by the barbarians, that society would still have been there, feeding on other nutriment; for it was original, organic, a civilisation. In *The Age of Constantine* Burckhardt had examined the death of one civilisation: now he was exam-ining the birth of another.

For all his love of Italy and its art, Burckhardt did not idealise the Renaissance. He was not an idealist, but a profound, reflective analyst. But like most of the German historians, he proceeded from the spirit to the matter. Always the spirit came first. And what was the spirit of the Renaissance? Seeking to isolate it, Burckhardt discovers a new concept which he was to make peculiarly his own: the concept of an agonistic society, a society of competitive individualism. And whence came that individualism? Looking at Italian society in the fourteenth century and afterwards, he saw that it was dominated by princes who, unlike the feudal princes of the North, owed nothing to tradition, inheritance, consecration: they were illegitimate, usurpers, sometimes *condottieri* who could command no customary loyalty; and they had to keep, by constant exercise of their wits, the unstable power which they had acquired by force or fraud. In other words, the new Italian princes, by their very illegitimacy, were driven to make a virtue of an individualism which had destroyed the fabric of inherited society. The political system which they set up was not organic: it was mere machinery, *lo stato*, the established system, the state. Here, 'for the first time', says Burckhardt, 'we detect the modern political spirit of Europe, surrendered freely to its own instincts, often displaying the worst features of an unbridled egotism, outraging every right and killing every germ of a healthier culture'.[9] Here also we recognise the authentic voice of Burckhardt: his distrust of power, his hatred of that idol of the German historians, the state.

Such, to Burckhardt, was the essential and original character of the Renaissance. It is not an admirable society, especially to a traditional patrician of Basel. On the contrary, it is artificial, immoral, detestable. And yet this agonistic society, by the intensity and ferocity and pace of its life, created masterpieces of art and became a distinct culture – a hectic feverish culture – of its own. Then, effectively, it destroyed itself. The petty states of Italy consumed their strength in furious competition. The petty princes disappeared, or were reduced to conformity. The papacy, which had nearly been secularised by brigand popes, was transformed by the Counter-Reformation and resumed its old theocratic character; and the peninsula, which the unscrupulous rivalry of the princes had nearly handed over to the Turks, sank into a less disastrous dependence on the rival empire of Spain. Only the intellectual and artistic creations remained as the permanent deposit of that complex historical era which Burckhardt had isolated, defined and named.

When he looked back on it, Burckhardt – in the true spirit of Herder – refused to judge. How can one judge a 'totality of being'? Those deplorable politics had been inseparable from that intense cultural vitality. So, as so often, the verdict is suspended. 'The ultimate truth with respect to the character, the conscience and the guilt of a people remains for ever a secret. . . . The people of Europe can maltreat, but happily not judge one another. A great nation, interwoven, by its civilisation, its achievements and its fortunes, with the whole of the modern world, can afford to ignore both its advocates and its accusers. It lives on, with or without the approval of theorists.'[10]

Nevertheless Burckhardt has his heroes in the Renaissance. One of them is Machiavelli. At first, this may surprise us; for was not Machiavelli the most cold-blooded of political realists, the very godfather of that Reason of State which the German historians professed to admire? Yes, Burckhardt would reply; but Machiavelli, unlike the Italian princes whom he despised, though he studied all the mechanics of state power and sought to construct a powerful state, knew that, to be effective, a state needed more than institutional machinery: it must be animated, as the free commune of Florence had been, by a living spirit, by *virtù*, by that intangible force which gives authentic life to a society, but which in the Italy of his time had withered away. Machiavelli, like Burckhardt, was the pessimist who, in a mechanical age, sought to recapture the formative virtue of a society from which it was fleeing, or had fled.

Another hero of Burckhardt is Aeneas Sylvius, the Sienese humanist who became Pope Pius II. The papacy, of course, was the one legitimate monarchy in Italy, a monument of stability in the swirling egotisms around it, and in the time of Pius II it was not yet corrupted by imitating the lay princes. Besides, Pius II had a Virgilian love of the countryside which appealed to Burckhardt, and liked picnics in the mountains: 'He would often hold consistories or receive ambassadors under huge old chestnut trees or beneath the olives on the greensward by some gurgling stream.' And then this agreeable pope had founded the University of Basel: that naturally ensured him high marks from Burckhardt.[11]

Burckhardt's love of Italy and of Italian art sustained him for another seven years. In 1867 he published his third work of scholarship on it, his *Baukunst der Renaissance in Italien*.[12] But then, as in 1848, public events distracted him and forced his thought into new channels. For we are now in those critical years in which the old European balance, so precariously restored after the revolutionary years, was completely shattered by the *Realpolitik* of Bismarck. Three lightning wars in six years and the creation of a new empire, of enormous industrial power, in central Europe could not fail to excite historians – especially in the German-speaking lands.

Most excited of all were the Prussian historians at whose feet Burckhardt himself had once sat. To them, the military victories of Prussia and the foundation of the empire were the realisation of their dream, the corroboration of their philosophy. The liberals of 1848 had failed to unite Germany, failed to convert the atomised *Kulturvolk* into a viable *Kulturstaat*. Now Bismarck had done it. How right Droysen had been to extol Macedon and Alexander and to despise that parochial Athenian windbag Demosthenes! The power of the state, wielded by the 'great man', the agent of destiny thrown up to meet the need in the crises of history – that was the necessary mechanism of historic change. How right Ranke was to emphasise the historic function, and the divine right, of the state, the primacy of foreign policy, the salutary function of war! It is true, Ranke, the old legitimist, had at first been uneasy about Bismarck, but by now he had swallowed his doubts. His disciples had no doubts. War, they declared, was the proper function of the state, its healthy exercise: 'ein frischer fröhlicher Krieg', as the historian Heinrich Leo put it, 'um das skrofulöse Gesindel wegzugegen'; and had not Herder himself extolled the superior culture of the Germanic barbarians whose native vigour was now armed and directed in accordance with the new science of *Weltgeschichte*?

It was in opposition to this gradual perversion of the ideas of Herder and Goethe that Burckhardt had formulated his own views of history – his antipathy to the state and state power, his insistence on the totality of culture, his refusal to identify state and culture, his distrust of the demiurgic 'great men' of history, his rejection of a metaphysical World Plan, Ranke's *Weltgeschichte*, Droysen's 'Theodicy'. Now, in the destruction of the European order, he saw the confirmation of his fears. He could not regard the immense power of the modern industrial state as merely the natural protective shell of the culture behind it. Power, he believed, was separate from culture, could be hostile to it, had a momentum of its own, and was, in itself, evil. The 'great men' of history were essentially wielders of power and therefore to be distrusted. They might indeed be the effective agents of historical change, but the idea that such change was part of a 'World Plan' in which the occasional setbacks were more than compensated by the general advance seemed to him absurd. The laws of history, he insisted, are to be deduced from history itself – and from history in general, not from chosen periods only. And such deduction was best carried out at a distance – from an observation post in Basel, not in the intoxicating atmosphere of Berlin.

It had been Burckhardt's intention, after completing his work on the Renaissance, to write (as he lectured) on the civilisation of the Middle Ages, on the life of those free communes whose extinction had been the political condition of the Italian Renaissance. He never wrote such a work. The events of 1864–71 concentrated his mind, and directed it towards their explanation. Long ago, in 1851, he had planned a course on the Study of History. Now, in 1868, when Bismarck had smashed the Austrian army at Sadowa, set up the North German Confederation, and was already challenging the new French imperialism of Napoleon III, he resumed this old project in a new form. The result was the series of lectures which his nephew Jacob Oeri would publish after his death under the title *Weltgeschichtliche Betrachtungen*.[13]

Those lectures, unsystematic as they are – for Burckhardt hated systems of thought – are the nearest he ever came to a profession of faith. In form, they deal with three essential forces in history which he now distinguished: religion, state and culture; and his particular interest, the force which he himself had introduced into the argument, was culture. To the German historians, all these forces were complementary, interdependent aspects of the same organism. To Burckhardt, they were not: they could be antithetical; and, in particular, culture was often opposed to and oppressed by both state and religion. Throughout the lectures, in which he examined and illustrated the forms and the relationships of these three forces, and in three further lectures, which are outgrowths from the same stem, on 'The Present Crisis of the State', 'The Function of Great Men in History', and 'Good and Bad Fortune in History', he expressed his total dissent from the new German orthodoxy. Both here and in his correspondence he now offered his own very different views on the real nature of culture and on the present and future of civilisation in Europe.

How can one summarise the views of Burckhardt on so wide and deep a subject, expressed, as they generally are, in Aesopian asides, sardonic apophthegms? No writer is such a master of profound but elusive wisdom as this deeply philosophical historian who disclaimed any philosophy, this observer of world history who explicitly disowned 'world-historical ideas'. Nevertheless, as we read his works, the lineaments of his philosophy emerge clearly enough.

First, like all the German historians, he hated the French Revolution; but, unlike most of them, he believed that its practical results had come to stay. The Restoration of 1815, which Metternich and Ranke saw as a real restoration, was to him a mere fiction. The legitimate dynasties, who had been restored, were no longer effective rulers: they continued by permission only. The balance of power, which Metternich had operated and Ranke extolled, was to him a myth, an improper generalisation from the exceptional circumstances of the years before 1848. In fact, he insisted, the effects of the French Revolution were irreversible, and the forces that had made it were continuously at work, as had been shown in 1848: the age of the masses had come. Secondly, he believed that this change was a cultural change, in his sense of that word: that is, that the old totality of European culture, like Hellenism in the third century A.D., had been drained of its vitality and could not sustain itself against the new, purely material culture of the masses, which was no culture at all. This was the goal to which the 'giddy optimism' of the European liberals was leading them. Thirdly, he believed that the state – that amoral state first called into being by those illegitimate princes of Italy and then continuously strengthened by centralising governments, whether autocratic or revolutionary – would never give up the enormous increase of its power which was one of the results of the revolution. The German historians did not object either to its amorality (which they justified) or to its power (which was now German power). But Burckhardt thought differently. Power to him was distinct from culture; it was even the enemy of culture; it was also 'in itself evil'. It had a demonic character, and a momentum of its own.

From these premises Burckhardt ventured to prophesy the future of Europe. His prophecies were less comforting than those of his contemporaries. The old dynasties, the old political systems, he believed, would linger on for a time, but only by permission, so long as prosperity lasted. Perhaps they would adapt themselves to mass rule, become 'Caesarean'. This was what Napoleon III had tried to do, what Bismarck was doing. Bismarck, with his clear political vision, had seen the forces of the future and had forestalled them: he had said, '*Ipse faciam*', and, driven forward by the need to resolve internal difficulties, he had embarked on three wars, 1864, 1866, 1870.[14] But what after Bismarck? And what if prosperity should fail? Power divorced from culture and morality, power based on enormous industrial resources, would then be at the mercy of populist demagogues. Then the old order, hitherto artificially sustained, may be expected to crumble. The old dynasties will be pushed aside, and new dictators, *Gewaltmenschen*, will step in, who will use the overgrown power of the state, so easily transferable from hand to hand, to end the luxury of nineteenth-century liberalism and set up a new form of life. 'I know the modern state', he had written in 1863, 'and when the time comes, it will display its ruthless omnipotence in evident and most practical form.'[15] At present 'we are only at the beginning . . .', he wrote in 1872: 'I have a suspicion which, at the moment, sounds completely mad, and yet I cannot rid myself of it'; and he envisaged the rise, first of all in Germany, of a military industrial state, driven forward to conquest by inner necessity, under demagogic dictators, 'the *terribles simplificateurs* who are going to descend upon poor old Europe'.[16]

And what, in the meantime, of the culture of poor old Europe? That, Burckhardt believed, would be the victim. 'Now comes a monstrous war', he wrote in 1870, 'the State will once again put forth its hand to master culture. . . . Later wars will do the rest.'[17] Perhaps, he observed sombrely, we shall become like the Americans . . . for there is an idea of culture which Burckhardt hates, and which he ascribes to our transatlantic cousins: of art and literature divorced from history, from its historical context and continuity – in order words, from its life – and converted into a form of entertainment for rich *dilettanti*. Americans, he remarks, 'have to a great extent foregone history, i.e. spiritual continuity, and wish to share in the enjoyment of art and poetry merely as forms of luxury'.[18] But culture to Burckhardt – it is the essence of his philosophy – is not detachable from the social forms which produce it. Its total external form is 'society in its broadest sense'. To detach it is to kill it.

What then must the heir of the German Enlightenment do in the new era which is dawning? How is he to preserve culture, the undivided personality, freedom of mind? What indeed except imitate those dissenters of the early centuries who separated themselves from the world, contracted out of society, and nursed their spiritual isolation in the desert. Already in 1853, in *The Age of Constantine*, he had defended the early Christian anchorites without whose example the Church 'would have become entirely secularised and have necessarily succumbed to crass material power'.[19] That was their response to the crisis of their time. Now, in a comparable period of crisis, he looked for a new generation of 'ascetics' who would withdraw from the great cities and their cult of Mammon 'and the horrible luxury to which official literature and art are falling victim'.[20]

Burckhardt's prophetic period was in the years 1868–72, and we cannot fail to note that those years – the years of Bismarck and the founding of the German Empire – were the years in which another famous prophet had joined him as professor in Basel: the young Nietzsche. Much has been written on the relations between Burckhardt and Nietzsche. Here it is enough to say that all the ideas which they have in common – opposition to Hegel and Ranke, appeal to Goethe and Schopenhauer, repudiation of German historicism and 'scientific' history, insistence on the antithesis of state and culture, belief in the inherent evil of power – had been expressed by Burckhardt long before Nietzsche's arrival. The two men were very different: Burckhardt, by twenty-seven years the older, so detached, so sane, so suspicious of philosophy, so elliptical in his language, so ready to leave insoluble questions suspended in mystery; Nietzsche, so strident, so decisive, so suspicious of history, and, in the end, mad. But from beginning to end – from 1870, when Nietzsche was excited by Burckhardt's lecture on Historical Greatness, till 6 January 1889, when he sent a four-page letter to Burckhardt declaring that he would rather be a Basel professor than God, and then disappeared into the darkness of total lunacy – there was a regular exchange of ideas between them, and that exchange, based on a large measure of previous, independent agreement, finds expression in the writings of both.

Particularly it is expressed in the last substantial work on which Burckhardt was engaged in precisely those years. For in 1868 he had decided that his next book would not, after all, be a work of medieval history: instead he would systematically read through 'all Greek and Roman authors' in order to write a work on 'the Spirit of Antiquity' comparable, as he himself said, with his book on *The Civilisation of the Renaissance*. It was an idea which had long tempted him, as it had previously tempted his classical teacher in Berlin, August Boeckh. Now, under the same pressure which had created his *Weltgeschichtliche Betrachtungen* (for the two works, as Werner Kaegi has written, are *Zwillingskinder*, twins), he decided to realise it. Next year, Nietzsche arrived in Basel as professor of classical philology, and at once became a close friend of Burckhardt. In 1871–72 Nietzsche published his first book, *The Birth of Tragedy*. In the same year Burckhardt gave, for the first time, his lectures on *Griechische Kulturgeschichte* to the largest audience he had ever drawn: fifty-four persons from the university.

Between Nietzsche's *Birth of Tragedy*, which caused such a storm in the German classical establishment, and Burckhardt's *Griechische Kulturgeschichte*, which was first published twenty-seven years later, in spite of all differences of form, there is much in common.[21] Both writers sought to discover the 'spirit', the psychological springs, of the Greek character. What excited Burckhardt in Nietzsche's book was the discovery – Nietzsche regarded it as his discovery – of the 'Dionysian' spirit in Greek culture: the idea that the Greek achievement did not spring from a naturally balanced serenity – a view made popular by Schiller – but from a successful attempt to master and ritualise overpowering irrational impulses. Burckhardt incorporated this new idea in his lectures, which Nietzsche attended and urged him to publish, and Burckhardt acknowledged his debt to Nietzsche; but it is difficult to disentangle the debts of one to the other: the 'agonistic' interpretation of culture, which they shared, goes back to Burckhardt's *The Civilisation of the Renaissance,* and many of the ideas which seem to have come from Nietzsche are foreshadowed in the draft of the *Weltgeschichtliche Betrachtungen,* written in the autumn of 1868, before Nietzsche's arrival in Basel. What we can say is that Burckhardt's posthumous *Griechische Kulturgeschichte* and Nietzsche's precipitate *Geburt der Tragödie* were products of the same time and shaped by shared ideas: the ideas which they exchanged, in this period of their closest friendship, in the 'long walks and talks' recalled by Nietzsche.

They also shared the same immediate fate. Each, as it was published, was ritually slaughtered by the great champion of German classical studies, Ulrich von Wilamowitz. Wilamowitz's shrill and savage attack on Nietzsche is notorious. By the time he came to deal with Burckhardt, he had mellowed a little; but he was unsparing. The work, he wrote, should never have been published: for the world of scholarship it had no significance, 'it does not exist'; for it had not taken note of the philological contributions of the last fifty years . . .[22]

Burckhardt had foreseen the attacks that would be made on his work. He had witnessed the reaction to Nietzsche's book, and he knew that his own views would be unacceptable to the same critics. No doubt that is why he was so reluctant to publish them. As he said, to one who tried to lure him into print, 'No, no, a poor outsider like me, who does not belong to the establishment, cannot take that risk: I am a heretic and an ignoramus, and with my questionable views I would be torn to pieces by those *viri eruditissimi.* Believe me, *Je connais ces gens.* I need peace in my old age.' He even denied the existence of the text: that, he said, was a fantasy, or a misunderstanding, of 'poor Dr. Nietzsche' who was now in an asylum.[23] But in fact it is clear that he valued his work, for he ensured that it would be published after his death. It might not have achieved final form; but it represented his considered views. In it he sought to recapture and explain that 'wonderful totality of being' whose dissolution he had described in his first work, *The Age of Constantine,* and to do so when his vision had been sharpened by the revolutionary events of 1868–71 and by the stimulating dialogue with Nietzsche.

The result was a book which did indeed ignore many of the gains of the philologists in the past fifty years, but which gave to the future study of

Antiquity a new dimension and a new direction. As in Renaissance Italy, so now in ancient Greece, Burckhardt sought to explain the 'spirit' which distinguished and animated society by examining both the structure of political life and the psychology which it engendered. In Italy it had been the cut-throat individualism of illegitimate power; here it was the fierce political rivalries of the city-states. But by now, under the pressure of events, he had refined his concepts, and so he applied to the interpretation of Greek history the analytical methods which he had set out in his lectures – the unpublished *Weltgeschichtliche Betrachtungen*. That is, having discovered the 'spirit' of Hellenism in its 'myth' – myth, to him, is the great universal source and strength of civilisation – he follows its response to the changing interrelation of religion, state and culture. Burckhardt did not love the city-states of Greece any more than the illegitimate princes of Italy. Greek political life might be the necessary condition of the Greek genius for freedom, but in action it was fierce, bitter and bloody, and the passions which it fostered had to be transcended, disciplined or sublimated in order that culture could flourish. And that culture, thus conditioned, was not the fresh, spontaneous expression of a genial, rounded personality, as his predecessors had supposed, but sombre and pessimist. Therefore, in the end, the greatest of the Greeks, to Burckhardt, are those who reject or escape from that exacting political loyalty: Pythagoras, who sought (like Burckhardt) to preserve the essential myth – the 'spirit' – of Greece while shedding its unacceptable or trivial formulations, and who founded an ascetic community outside politics; Socrates, the greatest critic, and the greatest victim, of the city-state; Diogenes, 'the genial pessimist', the freest of 'free personalities'. In all of these, to some extent, Burckhardt saw himself: distrust of the state, whatever its form, especially if it enforced a religion of state, and respect for 'anchorites' who withdrew from it, were essential elements in his philosophy.

In the end, distrust of the city-state, and respect for the culture which had transcended it, led Burckhardt to what may seem a paradoxical conclusion: to admiration for Alexander the Great who destroyed it, engulfing the city-states of Greece in a universal 'Hellenistic' empire. This had been the theme of Droysen, before he was diverted from the Macedonian to the Prussian empire. But, as always, Burckhardt went his own way. He would not follow Droysen in his condemnation of the last great defender of Athenian democracy. As in *The Civilisation of the Renaissance*, he refused to be a judge. 'If I have said that Philip of Macedon was the man of his time, and his policy that of the future', he wrote, 'that does not mean that I cast even the shadow of a reproach upon Demosthenes, his political enemy . . . .' Droysen had said that nobody cut a more pathetic figure than Demosthenes, who misunderstood his time, his people, his enemy, and himself. 'No one', retorts Burckhardt, 'cuts a more pathetic figure here than the *vir eruditissimus* Gustav Droysen'.[24] If Demosthenes had preached surrender, like his Athenian adversaries, we would despise him, as we despise them. 'The minority, whether it conquers or perishes, has its part in world history.' Demosthenes may have been historically wrong – the Macedonian Empire may have preserved Greek culture; but we must respect a great man who, like the Titans, went down vainly resisting the inevitable course of history.

Thus in the end, Burckhardt accepted and reinforced the 'Macedonian' theory, and the idea that, in this case, but perhaps only in this case, the state – the Macedonian kingdoms afterwards absorbed by Rome – was the expression and the protector of culture. But this, to him, was merely a historical fact; not, as to Droysen, part of a divine purpose.

Six years after the publication of *Griechische Kulturgeschichte* had been repudiated by the philological establishment, Burckhardt's nephew published its 'twin', the *Weltgeschichtliche Betrachtungen*, in which he similarly challenged the historical establishment. The spokesman of the historical establishment at that time, its Wilamowitz, was Friedrich Meinecke. Meinecke had been young in the days when Bismarck created the German Empire. He had accepted with enthusiasm the historical philosophy of the Prussian school. Now, reviewing Burckhardt's lectures, less ferociously indeed than Wilamowitz, he lamented 'the great gulf which divides his historical outlook from that of his German contemporaries': those contemporaries who saw world history as an orderly process, and the Prussian state, pursuing its reason of state, as the embodiment and realisation of German culture.[25]

For in 1905 the German philosophy of history, and the German 'third humanism' in philology, were firmly entrenched. In 1914, when the German government went to war, the historians and philologists – Wilamowitz and Meinecke among them – sprang to its support, making public speeches and writing articles in which the established orthodoxy was cited and the war presented as a crusade for German culture, the culture of Goethe and Schiller as redefined by Hegel, Ranke and their disciples. All through the war this philosophical orthodoxy was repeated, and even the defeat of 1918 did not shake it; for that defeat, it was agreed, was an undeserved misfortune, not a historical necessity. Even when power in the state was handed to Hitler and German culture was redefined again as racial purity, the doctrine was not disowned. The rise of Hitler did indeed at first disturb Meinecke, as that of Bismarck had at first disturbed Ranke; but like Ranke, he would come round, and by 1940 he was openly exulting in the military victories of Hitler as Ranke had done in those of Bismarck. Historical Necessity, it was admitted, chose surprising instruments, but after an unfortunate interruption it was back on course and working according to plan. All this time the dissenting voice of Burckhardt was heard in Germany only in whispers or silenced by official disapproval. He was regarded as defeatist, parochial, unable to rise to the great events of history; and his *Weltgeschichtliche Betrachtungen* could be republished only in Switzerland: paper for it, in Germany, was not allowed.

However, by 1943 the tide had turned. As the impending defeat of Germany became clear, the established orthodoxy began at last to fail. In the last months of the war Meinecke himself turned to Burckhardt. 'Will Burckhardt triumph over Ranke?' he rhetorically asked; and when all was over, in 1948, at the age of eighty-five, in a famous lecture on 'Ranke and Burckhardt', he declared his conversion. After confessing that all his life he had been guided by Ranke as his 'polar star', he admitted that 'today, we begin to ask ourselves, whether, in the end, we and our successors, as historians, will not look rather to Burckhardt than to Ranke'.[26] At that moment the historical philosophy of Ranke (though not necessarily its scholarly deposit) may be said to have been declared bankrupt, and Burckhardt, the outsider, so isolated in his own time, to have been recognised as a 'master mind'.

Appendix: A Guide to Later Scholarship
John Robertson

Since these essays were written, scholarship in their fields has developed in several directions, many of them foreshadowed by Trevor-Roper. The following, necessarily selective bibliographical notes identify major studies under each of the headings, including books, collections of papers and the occasional significant article. Where appropriate, the headings consolidate the subject matter of the essays, and I have sought to limit overlap between the various headings.

The Writing of History During the Enlightenment

There are still few overviews of historical writing during the Enlightenment, and as scholarship on individual historians grows more sophisticated and complex, the obstacles to writing a fresh synthesis grow larger. A great exception – and an indication of the scale of the obstacles – is John G.A. Pocock's multi-volume study of the intellectual and historiographical contexts in which Gibbon wrote the *Decline and Fall*. Under the general title *Barbarism and Religion* (Cambridge, 1999–), four volumes have appeared to date: *I. The Enlightenments of Edward Gibbon 1737–64* (1999); *II. Narratives of Civil Government* (1999); *III. The First Decline and Fall* (2003); *IV. Barbarians, Savages and Empires* (2005). A fifth volume is imminent, a sixth in prospect. If a general history of Enlightenment historical writing can be written around one pre-eminent historian, Trevor-Roper would have agreed that it must be around Gibbon.

Three very different studies by younger scholars have advanced the understanding of historical writing in Britain: Colin Kidd, *Subverting Scotland's Past: Scottish Whig Historians and the Creation of an Anglo-British*

Identity 1689–c.1830 (Cambridge, 1993); Karen O'Brien, *Narratives of Enlightenment: Cosmopolitan History from Voltaire to Gibbon* (Cambridge, 1997); Mark Phillips, *Society and Sentiment: Genres of Historical Writing in Britain 1740–1820* (Princeton, 2000). For studies devoted to Hume and Gibbon, see below.

On historical writing in Enlightenment France, see Blandine Barret-Kriegel, *Les Historiens et la monarchie*, 4 vols (Paris, 1988–89), and Chantal Grell, *L'Histoire entre érudition et philosophie; étude sur la connaissance historique à l'âge des Lumières* (Paris, 1993). For Germany: Hans-Peter Reill, *The German Enlightenment and the Rise of Historicism* (Berkeley, 1975); Michael C. Carhart, *The Science of Culture in Enlightenment Germany* (Cambridge, Mass., 2007). Interestingly, there is still no overview of historical writing in Enlightenment Italy. (On Giannone, see below.)

The Scottish Enlightenment

Stimulated and provoked – in at least equal measure – by Trevor-Roper's essay, study of the Scottish Enlightenment took off in the 1970s, and has flourished since. He himself published a second essay on the subject, with the same title, 'The Scottish Enlightenment', in *Blackwoods Magazine* 332 (Nov. 1977), pp. 371–88; in this he reiterated and elaborated on his definition of the Scottish Enlightenment as a movement characterised by certain distinctive ideas, rather than 'a mere period of time in the history of Scottish literature'; the emphasis in his explanation of the phenomenon shifted, however, as he gave more weight to the rise of a heterodox 'Arminian' or 'Socinian' tendency within the Scottish Church. Trevor-Roper's impact on Scottish historians was the subject of a splendid exchange between Colin Kidd and William Ferguson in the *Scottish Historical Review* 84 (2005), pp. 202–20 and 86 (2007), pp. 96–112.

Trevor-Roper's approach to the Scottish Enlightenment was offset by that of an independent-minded Cambridge contemporary, Duncan Forbes, who had previously published 'Scientific Whiggism: Adam Smith and John Millar', *Cambridge Journal* 7 (1954), pp. 643–70; although his later published work related mainly to Hume (and is identified under that heading below), his impact on the field went much further. The first to carry forward their insights, and set them in a fresh perspective of his own, was Nicholas Phillipson, whose own paper 'The Scottish Enlightenment', in R. Porter and

M. Teich (eds), *The Enlightenment in National Context* (Cambridge, 1981), has been another reference point for the field.

Two important collections of essays followed: R.H. Campbell and A.S. Skinner (eds), *The Origins and Nature of the Scottish Enlightenment* (Edinburgh, 1982), and I. Hont and M. Ignatieff (eds), *Wealth and Virtue: The Shaping of Political Economy in the Scottish Enlightenment* (Cambridge, 1984). A later, stock-taking collection is Paul Wood (ed.), *The Scottish Enlightenment: Essays in Reinterpretation* (Rochester, N.Y., 2000).

Two monographs by Richard B. Sher have established our current understanding of vital dimensions of the subject: *Church and University in the Scottish Enlightenment: The Moderate Literati of Edinburgh* (Princeton and Edinburgh, 1985); and *The Enlightenment and the Book: Scottish Authors and their Publishers in Eighteenth-Century Britain, Ireland and America* (Chicago, 2006).

Christopher Berry, *Social Theory of the Scottish Enlightenment* (Edinburgh, 1997) set himself to revise and update Gladys Bryson's *Man and Society*. In the study of Scottish social thought he was preceded by Knud Haakonssen, *The Science of a Legislator: The Natural Jurisprudence of David Hume and Adam Smith* (Cambridge, 1981). On the Scots' historical writing, in addition to the books by Kidd, O'Brien and Phillips (previous section above), see David Allan, *Virtue, Learning and the Scottish Enlightenment* (Edinburgh, 1993), a collection of essays edited by S.J. Brown, *William Robertson and the Expansion of Empire* (Cambridge, 1997), and Silvia Sebastiani, *I limiti del progresso: razza e genere nell'Illuminismo Scozzese* (Bologna, 2008) (The Limits of Progress: Race and Gender in the Scottish Enlightenment).

On the Jacobite dimension of the Scottish Enlightenment – one area in which Trevor-Roper's intuitions are less contested than ignored – see Mark Goldie, 'The Scottish Catholic Enlightenment', *Journal of British Studies* 30 (1991).

A comparative study whose findings lent support to Trevor-Roper's assessment of the limitations of Scottish intellectual culture in the late seventeenth and early eighteenth centuries, and to his emphasis on the originality of Hume, is John Robertson, *The Case for the Enlightenment. Scotland and Naples 1680–1760* (Cambridge, 2005).

The flourishing of scholarship has made possible two works for a more general readership, making large claims for the subject's significance in the making of modernity: Arthur Herman, *The Scottish Enlightenment: The Scots'*

Invention of the Modern World (London, 2002), and James Buchan, *Capital of the Mind: How Edinburgh Changed the World* (London, 2003).

Pietro Giannone

Scholarship on Giannone continues to be led by Giuseppe Ricuperati, whose *L'esperienza civile e religiosa di Pietro Giannone* (Milan and Naples, 1970) remains the fundamental study of Giannone's intellectual formation as a historian. Ricuperati has recently supplemented this with two collections of articles: *La città terrena di Pietro Giannone* (Florence, 2001), and *Nella costellazione del' Triregno: testi e contesti giannoniani* (San Marco in Lamis, 2004). An important new contribution to the field is Lia Mannarino, *Le mille favole degli antichi. Ebraismo e cultura europea nel pensiero religioso di Pietro Giannone* (Florence, 1999). On Giannone's significance for the Scottish Enlightenment, Andrew Hook, 'La *Storia civile del regno di Napoli* di Pietro Giannone, il giacobitismo e l'illuminismo scozzese', *Ricerche Storiche* 28 (1998) corroborates and enlarges on Trevor-Roper's suggestions.

Conyers Middleton

No major new work devoted to Middleton has been published since Trevor-Roper completed his essay. Studies bearing on particular aspects of Middleton's life and thought, and on what Gibbon may have owed to him, have been added to the notes at appropriate points. Forthcoming work by John Pocock in Volume V of *Barbarism and Religion*, and by Brian Young, 'Conyers Middleton: the historical consequences of heterodoxy', in S. Mortimer and J. Robertson (eds), *The Intellectual Consequences of Religious Heterodoxy 1600–1750* (Leiden: 2011), will discuss Middleton at more length, and should enhance the impact of Trevor-Roper's essay.

David Hume

Interest in Hume as a historian has risen steadily since Trevor-Roper's essay was published. Vital to this development have been new, accessible editions of the *History*, beginning with the extracts edited by D.F. Norton and R. Popkin, *David Hume Philosophical Historian* (Indianapolis, 1965). Even more valuable, and sadly out of print, was Duncan Forbes' edition of *The History of Great Britain. Vol. I: The Reigns of James I and Charles I* (1754) (Harmondsworth, 1970). The complete *History of England from the Invasion of Julius Caesar to the Revolution in 1688* (1778) is now available in an edition both handsome and affordable by W.B. Todd, published in six volumes by the Liberty Fund (Indianapolis, 1983). The same publishers are also responsible for a similar edition of the *Essays Moral, Political, and Literary*, by E.F. Miller (Indianapolis, 1985); another accessible edition of the *Political Essays* is by K. Haakonssen (Cambridge, 1994).

Giuseppe Giarrizzo's *David Hume politico e storico* (1962) prompted not only Trevor-Roper's review; it also stirred Duncan Forbes, whose review 'Politics and History in David Hume', appeared in the *Historical Journal* 6 (1963). In due course Forbes published his *Hume's Philosophical Politics* (Cambridge, 1975), still the landmark in the field. Further important studies of the relationship between the *Essays* and the *History* were Nicholas Phillipson, *Hume* (London, 1989) and David Wootton, 'David Hume, Historian', in D.F. Norton (ed.), *The Cambridge Companion to Hume* (Cambridge, 1993).

Different perspectives were opened by the works of Kidd, O'Brien and Phillips, mentioned above under 'Historical Writing'. Kidd, *Subverting Scotland's Past* explored the significance of Hume's failure to sustain the ambition of writing a *History of Great Britain*, and his realisation that a continuous narrative could only be written for the *History of England*. O'Brien, *Narratives of Enlightenment* set Hume alongside the other great narrative historians of the Enlightenment, Voltaire, Robertson and Gibbon. Concentrating on historical writing in Britain, Phillips, *Society and Sentiment* saw Hume as one of the first to appreciate that narrative alone was not enough. Hume and his successors recognised that the genre of historical writing needed to be broadened, and sought new ways of combining social and sentimental with political subject matter and analysis.

Younger Italian scholars are now reviving the interest shown by Giarrizzo. Sebastiani's *I limiti del progresso* contains an important discussion of Hume on race, while Daniele Francesconi, *L'età della storia. Linguaggi storiografici dell' Illuminismo Scozzese* (Bologna, 2003) examines the efforts of Hume, alongside other Scots historians, to uphold the possibility of causal explanation in history.

Edward Gibbon

When Trevor-Roper began to write on Gibbon, in the 1960s, only the essays of Arnaldo Momigliano offered English readers another commentary of any scholarly substance. Of these, the most accessible were 'Ancient History and the Antiquarian' and 'Gibbon's Contribution to Historical Method', both in A.D. Momigliano, *Studies in Historiography* (London, 1966).

Slowly, however, the tide has turned, and a sizeable task-force of English-speaking scholars has followed Momigliano and Trevor-Roper in transforming our understanding of Gibbon's achievement. Two contributions stand out. One is David Womersley's new edition of the *Decline and Fall*, published in three volumes (each containing two of the volumes as originally published by Gibbon) by Allen Lane the Penguin Press (London, 1994), subsequently reprinted in paperback. Besides purging the text of the accretions of later, well-meant references and correctives by J.B. Bury and other editors, Womersley's edition contains appendices with deviations from the copy text, Gibbon's marginalia and the text of his *Vindication*. Most valuable of all, it has a Bibliographical Index, identifying all the works cited by Gibbon in his foot-notes. Although the individual volumes are bulky, appreciation as well as study of Gibbon's great work has never been easier or more pleasurable.

The second great achievement of modern Gibbon scholarship has been John Pocock's monumental study of the making of the *Decline and Fall* through its historiographical antecedents, under the general title *Barbarism and Religion*. The four volumes published to date are listed in the first section above; two more are in prospect. The project has been in genesis since 1976, when Pocock first spoke on the subject of Gibbon, and has since been fore-shadowed and (after 1999) accompanied by a series of essays and articles. It is an achievement which might have been calculated to lay to rest for ever the challenge of Giarrizzo.

But other scholars have played a not insignificant part in this growth of Gibbon scholarship. First among them is Patricia B. Craddock, author of the first scholarly biography of Gibbon, in two volumes: *Young Edward Gibbon, Gentleman of Letters*, and *Edward Gibbon, Luminous Historian 1772–1794* (Baltimore and London, 1982, 1989). John Burrow's *Gibbon* (Oxford, 1985) was a short, lively introduction to the man and his work. Several individual monographs have likewise contributed, notably Joseph M. Levine, *The Autonomy of History: Truth and Method from Erasmus to Gibbon* (Chicago, 1999), and David Womersley, *The Transformation of the Decline and Fall of the Roman Empire* (Cambridge, 1988), followed by his study of Gibbon's reception, and response to his critics, *Gibbon and the 'Watchmen of the Holy City': The Historian and his Reputation, 1776–1815* (Oxford, 2002).

Particularly effective in stimulating research on Gibbon and in dissemi-nating new perspectives have been successive edited volumes, each deriving from an initial bicentenary conference. Marking the bicentenary of Gibbon's first volume was G.W. Bowersock (ed.), *Edward Gibbon and the Decline and Fall of the Roman Empire*, initially published in *Daedalus* 105 (1976), subse-quently by Harvard University Press (Cambridge, Mass., 1977). Indicative of the increasing attention to Gibbon, two conferences in 1994 celebrated the completion of the *Decline and Fall*, resulting in: Rosamund McKitterick and Roland Quinault (eds), *Edward Gibbon and Empire* (Cambridge, 1997), and David Womersley, with the assistance of John Burrow and John Pocock, *Edward Gibbon: Bicentenary Essays* (Oxford, 1997) – the volume containing the third of Trevor-Roper's Gibbon essays included above. Of particular note was Peter Ghosh's 'The Conception of Gibbon's *History*', in *Gibbon and Empire*. Italian versions (some enlarged) of the contributions of Girolamo Imbruglia, Guido Abbattista and Edoardo Tortarolo, along with translations of the essays of Womersley and Ghosh, were simultaneously published in Girolamo Imbruglia (ed.), *Ragione e immaginazione. Edward Gibbon e le storiografia europea del Settecento* (Naples, 1996).

As the opening contributors to *Edward Gibbon and Empire* acknowledge, Gibbon's work remains a reference point for ancient historians at work now. While this is not the place to survey modern scholarship on the Roman Empire, readers of Trevor-Roper's essays will enjoy Bryan Ward-Perkins, *The Fall of Rome and the End of Civilization* (Oxford, 2005), a book whose concise-ness alone seems to challenge Gibbon, but whose conclusions, reached on the basis of quite different forms of research, nonetheless endorse his.

Sir Walter Scott

Recognition that Scott was a historian as much as (and at the same time as) a novelist has grown steadily. Those who have contributed to this include David Daiches, 'Sir Walter Scott and History', *Etudes anglaises* 24 (1971), pp. 458–77; P.D. Garside, 'Scott, the Romantic Past and the Nineteenth Century', *Review of English Studies*, new series, 23 (1972), pp. 147–61, and 'Scott and the "Philosophical Historians" ', *Journal of the History of Ideas* 36 (1975), pp. 497–512; D. Brown, *Walter Scott and the Historical Imagination* (London 1979). More explicitly historiographical were Marinell Ash, *The Strange Death of Scottish History* (Edinburgh, 1980), and Colin Kidd,

Subverting Scotland's Past (details above under 'Historical Writing'), esp. ch. 11, 'History and National Identity in the Age of Scott'. Phillips, *Society and Sentiment* explains why Scott became possible. But the most important recent development in Scott scholarship has been the publishing of the Edinburgh edition of the Waverley novels by Edinburgh University Press, under the general editorship of David Hewitt, twenty-four volumes to date (Edinburgh, 1993–2008).

Lord Macaulay

Since Trevor-Roper first wrote the introductory essay printed above, two fine works of late twentieth-century scholarship have provided a much fuller basis for study of Macaulay than Trevelyan's *Life and Letters*: Thomas Pinney's edition of *The Letters of Thomas Babington Macaulay*, 6 vols (Cambridge, 1974–81), and William Thomas's *The Journals of Thomas Babington Macaulay*, 5 vols (London: 2008), with a shrewd introduction. Scholarly studies of Macaulay the historian have not been numerous, but several have been outstanding, including John Clive, *Thomas Babington Macaulay: The Shaping of the Historian* (London, 1973); John Burrow, *A Liberal Descent: Victorian Historians and the English Past* (Cambridge, 1981), part I; and William Thomas, *The Quarrel of Macaulay and Croker* (Oxford, 2000) – the last a work ranging further than the title might suggest. As with Gibbon, an iconoclastic voice has been Peter Ghosh, in 'Macaulay and the Heritage of the Enlightenment', *English Historical Review* 112 (1977), pp. 358–95, an article in which respect for its subject and for fellow-scholars (including Trevor-Roper) is never confused with reverence. On Macaulay's social and political world, read now the splendidly lively (and lengthy) contribution to 'The New Oxford History of England', Boyd Hilton's *A Mad, Bad, and Dangerous People? England 1783–1846* (Oxford, 2006).

Thomas Carlyle

Carlyle the historian continues to baffle students of historiography. One full-length study is J.D. Rosenberg, *Carlyle and the Burden of History* (Oxford, 1985). Otherwise John Clive reprinted two pieces on him, one his Introduction to an abridged translation of Carlyle's *History of Frederick the Great*, the other a review, in his collection *Not by Fact Alone: Essays on the*

Writing and Reading of History (London, 1989). Having earlier navigated around him, John Burrow tackled him in 'Images of Time: From Carlylean Vulcanism to Sedimentary Gradualism' in Stefan Collini, Richard Whatmore and Brian Young (eds), *History, Religion and Culture: British Intellectual History 1750–1950* (Cambridge, 2000). Blair Worden's *Roundhead Reputations: The English Civil Wars and the Passions of Posterity* (London, 2001) contains a chapter devoted to 'Carlyle's Cromwell'.

Jacob Burckhardt

A major study of Burckhardt whose interpretation of his relationship with Ranke is at odds with Trevor-Roper's is Felix Gilbert, *History: Politics or Culture? Reflections on Ranke and Burckhardt* (New Jersey, 1990). By contrast, Lionel Gossman, author of the 600-page study *Basel in the Age of Burckhardt* (Chicago, 2000), aligned his interpretation on this and other points with Trevor-Roper's. But see the characteristic review of this book by Peter Ghosh in *History of European Ideas* 28 (2002), pp. 295–315, an interpretative essay in itself, as well as a guide to other recent scholarship. See also Ghosh's essay 'After Burckhardt: Max Weber and the Idea of an Italian Renaissance' in his *A Historian Reads Max Weber: Essays on the Protestant Ethic* (Wiesbaden, 2008). Among other recent works on Burckhardt the historians are John R. Hinde, *Jacob Burckhardt and the Crisis of Modernity* (Montreal and Kingston, 2000), and T.A. Howard, *Religion and the Rise of Historicism: De Wette, Burckhardt and the Origins of Nineteenth-Century Historical Consciousness* (Cambridge, 2000).

Beyond Enlightenment History

For those who now wish to set Enlightenment historical writing in a grand narrative of historiography, there is John Burrow's masterly *A History of Histories: Epics, Chronicles, Romances and Inquiries from Herodotus and Thucydides to the Twentieth Century* (London, 2007; pb repr. London, 2009).

Notes

Editor's Introduction

1. Manuscript and typescript plans for volumes of essays, the manuscript version dated 4 Dec. 1982: Dacre Papers, Christ Church Library, Oxford. Letter to Noël Annan, 5 Aug. 1994: Conyers Middleton File, Dacre Papers: 3/10.
2. Richard Davenport-Hines, Introduction to his edition of *Letters from Oxford: Hugh Trevor-Roper to Bernard Berenson* (London, 2006), p. xvi. For Trevor-Roper's biography see this Introduction and Davenport-Hines' memoir of Hugh Trevor-Roper in the *Oxford Dictionary of National Biography* (2004), and, best of all, Blair Worden's biographical memoir, 'Hugh Redwald Trevor-Roper 1914–2003', in *Proceedings of the British Academy* 150 (2007), pp. 247–84.
3. *Letters from Oxford*, p. 65: to BB, 4 May 1951.
4. *Letters from Oxford*, pp. 171, 256: to BB, 28 May 1955, 13 Aug. 1958.
5. *Letters from Oxford*, pp. 250–51: to BB [early Jan. 1958].
6. Worden, 'Hugh Trevor-Roper', pp. 262–67. Typescripts deriving from these projects are in the Dacre Papers: 9/7/1–2.
7. Hugh Trevor-Roper, *Religion, the Reformation and Social Change* (London, 1967; 2nd edn 1972), p. 87, observing that the Stuart kings had possessed neither the intelligence of Elizabeth I nor the docility of Louis XIII:

   It was because they had neither, because their court was never reformed, because they defended it, in its old form, to the last, because it remained, administratively and economically as well as aesthetically, 'the last Renaissance court in Europe', that it ran into ultimate disaster: that the rational reformers were swept aside, that more radical men came forward and mobilized yet more radical passions than even they could control, and that in the end, amid the sacking of palaces, the shivering of statues and stained-glass windows, the screech of saws in ruined organ lofts, the last of the great Renaissance Courts was mopped up, the royal aesthete was murdered, his splendid pictures were knocked down and sold, even the soaring gothic cathedrals were offered up for scrap.

   'Religion, the Reformation and Social Change' was first presented to a conference in Ireland in 1961 and published in 1963; the 'General Crisis' essay was first published in *Past and Present* in 1959. For an analysis of Trevor-Roper's response to Weber see Irene Gaddo, *Il piacere della controversia: Hugh R. Trevor-Roper storico e uomo pubblico* (Naples, 2007), pp. 217–60: 'Percorsi di modernità'.
8. 'Notebook: 1963', Dacre Papers: 13/29, pp. 1–3. See also my article 'Hugh Trevor-Roper, Intellectual History and "The Religious Origins of the Enlightenment"', in *English Historical Review* cxxiv, 511 (2009), for a fuller development of this analysis.

9. For an expression of this earlier conviction: *Letters from Oxford*, p. 171: to BB, 28 May 1955.

10. 'Notebook 1963', pp. 10–15.

11. *Ibid.*, pp. 27–33.

12. *Ibid.*, pp. 33–34, 20–23. On the genesis and character of Trevor-Roper's engagement with the problem of the Scottish Enlightenment, see Colin Kidd's evocative discussion 'Lord Dacre and the Politics of the Scottish Enlightenment', *The Scottish Historical Review* 84 (2005), pp. 202–20 – followed by a splendid exchange with Dr William Ferguson, *ibid.* 86 (2007), pp. 96–125. Ever independent, Ferguson, as Kidd implied, was bent on maintaining a feud which did scant justice to his own contributions to Scottish history.

13. Typescripts of the Trevelyan Lectures in a box file in the Dacre Papers; 'Three Historians', *The Listener*, 30 Sept. (Clarendon), 7 Oct. (Hume), 14 Oct. 1965 (Lord Macaulay). Also a folder marked 'Five Historians (Trevelyan Lectures)', Dacre Papers.

14. 'George Buchanan' and 'William Camden', *The Listener*, 15 Sept., 6 Oct. 1966; 'Five Historians' folder, Dacre Papers. In the same year Trevor-Roper published his much longer essay on Buchanan, 'George Buchanan and the Ancient Scottish Constitution', *English Historical Review, Supplement* 3 (1966). See now also the chapters posthumously edited by Jeremy Cater and published in *The Invention of Scotland: Myth and History* (London, 2008).

15. Personal testimony of Quentin Skinner, an observer of the encounter.

16. Giuseppe Giarrizzo, *David Hume politico e storico* (Turin, 1962); reviewed by Duncan Forbes, 'Politics and History in David Hume', *The Historical Journal*, 6 (1963). For some years Forbes had offered a Special Subject at Cambridge on 'Hume, Smith and the Scottish Enlightenment'.

17. 'Edward Gibbon after 200 years', *The Listener*, 22, 29 Oct. 1964.

18. There is a box file of lectures entitled 'Gibbon and Macaulay' in the Dacre Papers. Several of the lectures are dated 1972, but there are also pages of 'over-matter' of later dates. The better to make it available to undergraduates, Trevor-Roper also persuaded Oxford University Press to publish a new edition of Gibbon's *A Vindication of Some Passages in the Fifteenth and Sixteenth Chapters of The History of the Decline and Fall of the Roman Empire*, with a Preface by himself (Oxford, 1961).

19. 'Sir Walter Scott and History', *The Listener*, 19 Aug. 1971.

20. 'Historical Change and Historical Philosophy 1750–1850, Chicago 1973', box file, Dacre Papers.

21. Another was 'The Other Gibbon', in *The American Scholar* 46 (1976–77), on Gibbon's interests before and after he wrote the *Decline and Fall*. It has not been included in this volume, because of overlap with 'Gibbon's Last Project'. Nor has his overview of Gibbon's achievement 'Edward Gibbon's *Decline and Fall of the Roman Empire*', contributed under the rubric 'The Reconsideration of a Great Book', to *The Great Ideas Today* (1981). This became his Introduction to the reissue of the Everyman edition of the *Decline and Fall* in 1993–94.

22. 'The Scottish Enlightenment', *Blackwood's Magazine* 322 (1977).

23. Kidd, 'Lord Dacre and the Politics of the Scottish Enlightenment', pp. 206–7.

24. Respectively in *Catholics, Anglicans and Puritans: Seventeenth-Century Essays* (London, 1987), and *From Counter-Reformation to Glorious Revolution* (London, 1992).

25. 'Carlyle' folder, Dacre Papers; including a letter of thanks for the lecture from Derek Beales, 13 May 1981, and the note from Alan Taylor, dated 26 June 1981, the day of its publication.

26. Box file of lectures, several dated in the 1970s, marked 'Burckhardt', Dacre Papers.

27. To Noël Annan, 5 Aug. 1994, Middleton file, Dacre Papers. This file contains the successive versions of the essay.

28. To G.A. Wells, 13 Dec. 1993, Dacre Papers: 1/1/W.

29. To Alasdair Palmer, 23 Nov. 1986, Dacre Papers: 1/2/30.

30. Locker Madden, head of careers and appointments, University of Aberdeen, in 'Booklist', *University of Aberdeen Newsletter*, July 2003.

31. Giuseppe Giarrizzo, *Edward Gibbon e la cultura europea del Settecento* (Naples, 1954), p. 10.

32. Arnaldo Momigliano, *Studies in Historical Method* (London, 1966).

33. J.G.A. Pocock, 'Historiography and Enlightenment: A View of their History', *Modern Intellectual History* 5 (2008), pp. 83–96; John Robertson, *The Case for the Enlightenment: Scotland and Naples 1680–1760* (Cambridge, 2005).

34. To Gideon Cohen, 18 May 1983, replying to Cohen's letter of 8 May, enclosing a typescript of the letter Cohen had submitted to the *Times Literary Supplement* on 16 Nov. 1982, but which was not accepted for publication: Dacre Papers. Cohen had written the letter in response to Trevor-Roper's long review of Peter Ganz's new edition of the *Weltgeschichtliche Betrachtungen*, *Times Literary Supplement*, 8 Oct. 1982.

Chapter 1: The Historical Philosophy of the Enlightenment

Given as a lecture to the First International Congress on the Enlightenment, held in Geneva in July 1963; published in *Studies on Voltaire and the Eighteenth Century* 27 (1963), pp. 1,667–87. Most of the quotations in this essay were not supplied with a reference in the original published version. Where a reference has been supplied by the editor, it is within square brackets.

1. [Voltaire, *Essai sur les moeurs* (1769), ch. X, in *Oeuvres complètes de Voltaire*, ed. L. Moland, 52 vols (Paris, 1877–83), XI, p. 237; Edward Gibbon, *The History of the Decline and Fall of the Roman Empire* (1776–88), ch. lxx, n. 89, in the edition by David Womersley, 3 vols (London, 1994), III, p. 1,057. See below, n. 13.]

2. [*The Journal of John Wesley*, Tuesday, 28 April 1772, in the edition in four volumes (London, 1827), III, p. 447. On the importance of Wesley's journal in Trevor-Roper's preparation of this essay, see the Editor's Introduction.]

3. [Basil Willey was the author of *The Seventeenth-Century Background* (London, 1934; pb reprint by Penguin, 1962), and *The Eighteenth-Century Background* (London, 1940). I cannot find 'Mr Willey's phrase' in either work, although ch. 1 of the former, entitled 'The Rejection of Scholasticism', makes the point that the seventeenth century explicitly repudiated the thought of the Middle Ages.]

4. Pietro Giannone, *Vita scritta da lui medesimo*, ed. Sergio Bertelli (Milan, 1960), pp. 10–15 [quotation on p. 15; or in *Opere di Pietro Giannone*, ed. S. Bertelli and G. Ricuperati (Milan and Naples, 1971), pp. 19–26. The importance of Giannone's autobiography to Trevor-Roper is also discussed in the Editor's Introduction.]

5. [David Hume to Président de Montesquieu, London, 10 avril 1749, in *The Letters of David Hume*, ed. J.Y.T. Greig, 2 vols (Oxford, 1932), I, pp. 132–38, with an extract from Montesquieu's courteous reply on p. 138, n. 2: Montesquieu to David Hume, 19 mai 1749. The *Philosophical Essays* were the *Philosophical Essays concerning Human Understanding* (1748), later retitled *An Enquiry concerning Human Understanding* (1756). The observation that Hume was instrumental in the translation and publication of two chapters from the *Esprit des lois* in Edinburgh is probably derived from E.C. Mossner, *The Life of David Hume* (Oxford, 1954; 2nd edn 1980), p. 229; but, as with many of Mossner's suppositions, it is unsupported by evidence. The subsequent French correspondent was the abbé le Blanc, in an undated letter to which Hume replied on 22 July 1757: *Letters of Hume*, I, pp. 258–60, with the passage from le Blanc's letter quoted on p. 259, n. 1.]

6. [*The Journal of John Wesley*, Tuesday, 28 April 1772, Sunday, 21 March 1779: III, p. 447; IV, p. 141.] The philosophy of 'Lord Forbes' has now sunk without trace. I suppose Wesley was referring to Duncan Forbes, lord advocate of Scotland, who published several works, on which Sir Leslie Stephen, in the *DNB*, merely states that 'his piety was superior to his scholarship'. James Beattie was a Scotch poet who, 'much to his own surprise', found himself appointed 'by the influence of a powerful friend' to the chair of moral philosophy in Aberdeen. To justify his appointment, he undertook to refute Hume. Hume referred to him as 'that bigoted silly fellow Beattie' [Hume to William Strahan, his publisher, 26 Oct. 1775, *Letters of Hume*, II, p. 301].

7. John Millar, *An Historical View of the English Government* (1787); quoted in William C. Lehmann, *John Millar of Glasgow* (Cambridge, 1960), p. 363.

8. Furio Diaz, *Voltaire storico* (Turin, 1958), p. 170; J.H. Brumfitt, *Voltaire Historian* (Oxford, 1958), pp. 117–19.

9. [William Robertson, *The History of the Reign of the Emperor Charles V*, 3 vols (London, 1769), I, 'A View of the Progress of Society from the Subversion of the Roman Empire to the Beginning of the Sixteenth Century', 'Proofs and Illustrations', pp. 392–93.]

10. Montesquieu, *Mes pensées*, no. 954, in *Oeuvres complètes*, ed. Roger Caillois, Bibliothèque de la Pléiade, 2 vols (Paris, 1949, 1951), I, p. 1,256.

11. Voltaire, *Dictionnaire philosophique*, s.v. 'Histoire', section iv. [*Oeuvres complètes de Voltaire*, ed. Moland, XIX, p. 367.]

12. Michaud, *Biographie universelle*, s.v. 'Mirabeau'; quoted in Robert Shackleton, *Montesquieu: A Critical Biography* (Oxford, 1961), p. 209.

13. Gibbon's references to Voltaire are scattered through the footnotes of the *Decline and Fall*. [Identifying them has now been made easy by the excellent 'Bibliographical Index' included by David Womersley in his edition of *The Decline and Fall of the Roman Empire* (see above, n. 1). The comment that Voltaire 'was ambitious of universal monarchy' is in ch. lxviii, n. 25.] The judgment on *Le Siècle de Louis XIV* and the *Essai sur les moeurs* is in Gibbon's diary for 28 Aug. 1762: *Gibbon's Journal to January 28th 1763*, ed. D.M. Low (London, 1929), p. 129.

14. [Edward Gibbon, *Essai sur l'étude de la littérature* (1761), §. 53, in *The Miscellaneous Works of Edward Gibbon*, ed. John, Lord Sheffield, 5 vols (London, 1814), IV, pp. 67–68; *Decline and Fall*, ch. lvii, n. 13.]

15. Montesquieu to Mme du Deffand in her *Correspondance*. [*Correspondance complète de la Marquise du Deffand*, ed. M. de Lescure, 2 vols (Paris, 1865), I, p. 145: Montesquieu to Mme du Deffand, 13 Sept. 1753.]

16. 'Dans chaque lambris doré je crois voir un village de Savoyards prêts à mourir de faim, de froid et de misère'; *Gibbon's Journey from Geneva to Rome. His Journal from 20 April to 2 October 1764*, ed. Georges A. Bonnard (London, 1961), p. 18.

17. Hume's invitation to Lambeth was revealed by him to Boswell when the two were splitting a bottle of port in Edinburgh on 17 December 1775. 'David', says Boswell, 'was diverted with the thought of his being there among the chaplains': *Boswell: The Ominous Years 1774–1776*, ed. C. Ryskamp and F.A. Pottle (London, 1963), p. 201.

18. *The Heavenly City of the Eighteenth-Century Philosophers* (New Haven: Yale paperbound edition, 1959), p. 105.

19. See C.P. Courtney, *Montesquieu and Burke* (Oxford, 1963).

20. Gibbon to Lord Sheffield, 5 Feb. 1791, *The Letters of Edward Gibbon*, ed. J.E. Norton, 3 vols (London, 1956), III, p. 216.

Chapter 2: The Scottish Enlightenment

Delivered as a lecture to the Second International Congress on the Enlightenment, held at St Andrews in August 1967, but meeting for the occasion of the lecture in Edinburgh; published in *Studies on Voltaire and the Eighteenth Century* 58 (1967), pp. 1,635–58.

1. David Hume to John Clephane, 8 Dec. 1753, to David Mallet, 8 Nov. 1762, *Letters of David Hume*, I, pp. 182, 369.

2. Edward Gibbon to Adam Ferguson, *Letters of Edward Gibbon*, II, p. 100; Edward Gibbon, *The Decline and Fall of the Roman Empire*, ed J.B. Bury (5th edn, 1909), VI, p. 445, VII, p. 296 [in the edition by D. Womersley, III, pp. 728 (ch. lxi, n. 69), p. 1,057 (ch. lxx, n. 89)].

3. Lord Brougham, Lord John Russell, Lord Palmerston and the third marquis of Lansdowne were all educated at Edinburgh University, Lord Melbourne at Glasgow under Millar.

4. T.B. Macaulay, *The History of England* (1848), ch. 1. [Many editions, including the Albany edition (London, 1898); the edition by C.H. Firth (London, 1913–15); World's Classics edition, ed. T.F. Henderson (London, 1931).]

5. Henry Grey Graham, *Social Life of Scotland in the Eighteenth Century* (London, 1901), p. 160.

6. Henry Grey Graham, *Scottish Men of Letters in the Eighteenth Century* (London, 1908), p. 109.

7. On the philosophy of the Scottish school see Gladys Bryson, *Man and Society: The Scottish Inquiry of the Eighteenth Century* (Princeton, 1945).

8. Utrecht was long dominated by the great obscurantist Gisbert Voëtius; Leiden was reckoned to be a little more liberal, but not much: see the letter of Lachlan Campbell quoted in *Early Letters of Robert Wodrow 1698–1709*, ed. L.W. Sharp (Scottish History Society, Third Series, xxiv, 1937), pp. xli–xlii.

9. E.g. Sir Andrew Balfour, Sir Robert Sibbald, Sir Thomas Burnett, David Gregory, Archibald Pitcairne, etc.

10. Thus Andrew Fletcher of Saltoun, 'the patriot' who opposed with such eloquence both the royal 'tyranny' of the Stuarts and the national surrender of the union with England, solemnly recommended the introduction of domestic slavery into Scotland. He would also have presented some obstinate nonconformists among his countrymen to the republic of Venice, as galley-slaves. See his 'Second Discourse on the Affairs of Scotland' in *The Political Works of Andrew Fletcher Esqre* (Glasgow, 1749), pp. 84–106 [modern edition: *Andrew Fletcher: Political Works*, ed. John Robertson (Cambridge, 1997), pp. 56–70, with commentary on pp. xviii–xxii].

11. Gilbert Burnet, *History of his Own Time* (Oxford, 1833), I, pp. 108, 452, II, pp. 20, 88; A. Robertson, *Life of Sir Robert Moray* (London, 1920 [1922]).

12. G.D. Henderson, *Mystics of the North East* (Aberdeen: 3rd Spalding Club, 1934). James Garden's correspondence with Aubrey is in the Bodleian Library, MS Aubrey 12, ff. 122ff.

13. Sir Alexander Grant, *The Story of the University of Edinburgh* (London, 1884), II, pp. 217–22.

14. G.D. Henderson, *Chevalier Ramsay* (London, 1952); Franco Venturi, *Le origini dell'Enciclopedia* (Milan, 1962), pp. 16–26.

15. Graham, *Scottish Men of Letters in the Eighteenth Century*, p. 10.

16. *Boswell on the Grand Tour: Germany and Switzerland 1764*, ed. Frederick A. Pottle (London, 1953), p. 231.

17. James Gordon, *History of Scots Affairs from 1637 to 1641*, ed. J. Robertson and G. Grub (Aberdeen: Spalding Club, 1841), III, p. 242. On the Aberdeen doctors see R.S. Rait, *The University of Aberdeen* (Aberdeen, 1895), pp. 144–50. Their great monument is the edition of the works of one of them, John Forbes of Corse, published in Latin at Amsterdam, in 1702–3, by the deposed Episcopalian professor of Aberdeen George Garden.

18. See 'Scotland and the Puritan Revolution' in my *Religion, the Reformation and Social Change* (London, 1967). For the prosperity of Scottish Roman Catholics under Cromwellian rule see M.V. Hay, ed. *The Blairs Papers 1603–1660* (Edinburgh, 1929).

19. *The Letters of Samuel Rutherford*, ed. A.A. Bonar (Edinburgh, 1863), II, p. 398 [letter of 8 Aug. 1658].

20. This attempt was first made during the triumph of the Covenants in the 1640s, and revived after the abolition of Episcopacy in the 1690s. See Grant, *University of Edinburgh*, II, p. 210; Rait, *University of Aberdeen*, pp. 175–76; James Coutts, *A History of the University of Glasgow* (Glasgow, 1909), pp. 108–11. Also John Veitch, 'Philosophy in the Scottish Universities', *Mind* 2 (1877), pp. 74–91, 207–34. Even in physics, Aristotle was to be paramount.

21. 'Regenting' was abolished at Edinburgh in 1707, at Glasgow in 1727, at St Andrews in 1747, and at Marischal College, Aberdeen, in 1754. King's College, Aberdeen, clung to it till the end of the eighteenth century.

22. Dugald Stewart, *Collected Works*, ed. Sir W. Hamilton (Edinburgh, 1854–60), I, p. 550.

23. [The plea was answered shortly afterwards, by T.C. Smout, *A History of the Scottish People 1560–1830* (London, 1969), a work which Trevor-Roper described in a *Sunday Times* review as 'by far the most stimulating, the most instructive, and the most readable account of Scotch history that I have read (and I have read dozens)'. A subsequent collection of specialist scholarship is

R.A. Houston and I.D. Whyte (eds), *Scottish Society 1500–1800* (Cambridge, 1989); and a still more recent survey is Christopher A. Whatley, *Scottish Society 1707–1830: Beyond Jacobitism, towards Industrialisation* (Manchester, 2000).]

24. T.C. Smout, *Scottish Trade on the Eve of the Union, 1660–1707* (Edinburgh and London, 1963), pp. 27, 144–5.

25. *Ibid.*, pp. 74, 143–44.

26. For instance, Robert Morison (1620–83), the botanist, who took the degree of MD at Angers and became keeper of the duke of Orleans's garden at Blois; and William Davidson (1593–1669), who was the first professor of chemistry at the Jardin du Roi at Paris, 1647–51 – on whom see John Read, *William Davidson of Aberdeen, the First British Professor of Chemistry* (Aberdeen, 1951).

27. See A. and H. Taylor, *Jacobites of Aberdeenshire and Banffshire in the Rising of 1715* (Edinburgh, 1934), p. viii.

28. *Registrum de Panmure*, ed. J. Stuart (Edinburgh, 1874). The library list is in the National Library of Scotland, MS. 6305. [Fr Innes' *Critical Essay* is: Thomas Innes, *A Critical Essay on the Ancient Inhabitants of the Northern Parts of Britain, or Scotland*, 2 vols (London, 1729).]

29. *The Civil History of the Kingdom of Naples . . . by Pietro Giannone . . . Translated into English by Captain James Ogilvie* [2 vols (London, 1729, 1731)]. Ogilvie was a client of Lord Falkland and Lord Grandison, both Jacobites, and a friend of the Jacobite English scholar Thomas Rawlinson. He also translated from the French works by the Scottish Catholic Robert Menteith, secretary to Cardinal de Retz, and by an *émigré* Irish royalist, Riordan O'Muskerry, who, presumably, was a Catholic too (*The History of the Troubles of Great Britain . . . 1633–1650*, 1735). Giannone's contemporary biographer, the *abbé* Panzini, says that Ogilvie was a sea captain who translated the work while sailing on a voyage to Spitzbergen. The story is hearsay and *prima facie* unlikely; but since Josiah Burchett, secretary to the Admiralty, was a subscriber, the translator may well have been a captain in the navy. Another James Ogilvie, presumably a relation, was a captain in the army, serving in the 7th Dragoons and then in the 7th Hussars. He, and numerous officers of his regiment, were subscribers.

30. P. Giannone, *Vita scritta da lui medesimo*, ed. S. Bertelli (Milan, 1960), pp. 165–66 [and in *Opere di Pietro Giannone*, ed. S. Bertelli and G. Ricuperati (Milan and Naples, 1973), pp. 184–85].

31. For the intellectual effects of the discovery of America see G. Atkinson, *Les Nouveaux Horizons de la renaissance française* (Paris, 1935); R. Romeo, *Le Scoperte americane nella coscienza italiana del Cinquecento* (Naples, 1954).

32. Montesquieu's *De l'Esprit des lois* was published in full in English at Aberdeen in 1756 and at Edinburgh in 1762, 1768, 1773, etc.; Hume's edition of book XI, ch. vi, and book XIX, ch. xxviii, in French, was published at Edinburgh in 1750. Montesquieu's *Lettres persanes* and *Considérations sur les Romains* had already been published in both Edinburgh and Glasgow. See Alison K. Bee, 'Montesquieu, Voltaire and Rousseau in Eighteenth-Century Scotland: A Check List of Editions and Translations of their Works Published in Scotland before 1801' (1955). Typescript in National Library of Scotland, Edinburgh [published, under the name of Alison K. Howard, in *The Bibliothek* 2 (1959), pp. 40–63. But on 'Hume's edition' of chapters from *De l'Esprit des lois*, see above, note 2 to Chapter 1, 'The Historical Philosophy of the Enlightenment'].

33. John Millar, *An Historical Account of the English Government* (1803), II, pp. 429–30 [and in Lehman, *John Millar of Glasgow*, p. 363].

34. Smout, *Scottish Trade*, pp. 27–28, 47–49, 134.

35. See Gibbon's review of Lord Lyttleton's *History of Henry II* in his *Mémoires littéraires de la Grande Bretagne* (1767–68).

36. For Lord Lovat's household see Edward King, *Munimenta antiqua* (London, 1799–1805), III, pp. 174–76. J. Hill Burton, *Lives of Simon Lord Lovat, and Duncan Forbes, of Culloden* (London, 1847), p. 172.

37. It is interesting to observe the relative indifference of England to the work of Montesquieu. Gibbon, indeed, was bowled over by Montesquieu; but he discovered him in Lausanne, not in England, and the whole formation of Gibbon's mind was foreign, not English.

The historical revolution of the eighteenth century reached England indirectly, through Scotland.

38. [Henry Cockburn, *Memorials of his Time* (Edinburgh, 1856; repr. 1971), p. 28.]

Chapter 3: Pietro Giannone and Great Britain
This essay was first written as a contribution to the International Conference on Anglo-Italian Studies, Msida, Malta, held in September 1993. It was published in *The Historical Journal* 39,3 (1996), pp. 657–75.

1. E. Gibbon, *History of the Decline and Fall of the Roman Empire*, ed. J.B. Bury (5th edn, 1909), VII, p. 296 [ed. Womersley, III, p. 1,057: ch. lxx, n. 89].

2. Arthur Duck, *De usu et authoritate Juris Civilis Romanorum* (1653). Duck was an ecclesiastical lawyer who held office under Archbishop Laud. During the Civil War he took refuge in Oxford and wrote his work in the Bodleian Library. Giannone refers to it often, and always with veneration, e.g. *Istoria civile*, introduction; *Via scritta da lui medesimo*, ed. Sergio Bertelli (Milan, 1960), p. 40 [*Opere di Pietro Giannone*, ed. Bertelli and Ricuperati, pp. 53–54].

3. Although part of the *Triregno* was known to Panzini and published in his edition of Giannone's *Opere postume* (Naples, 1766), and a manuscript copy of the whole circulated secretly soon afterwards, the first proper edition of it, edited by Alfredo Parente, was published at Bari in 1940; on which see A. Omodeo, 'Il Triregno di Pietro Giannone', in his *Il senso della storia* (Turin, 1948) [and G. Ricuperati, 'Nota introduttiva' to 'Il Triregno', *Opere di Pietro Giannone*, ed. Bertelli and Ricuperati, pp. 581–92].

4. On the Neapolitan background see Salvo Mastellone, *Pensiero politico e vita culturale a Napoli nella seconda metà del seicento* (Messina-Firenze, 1965).

5. The best account of Rawlinson is the MS thesis of D.J. Enright (Oxford, 1956) in the Bodleian Library, which contains Rawlinson's MSS. His travels are recorded in his journal (MS Rawlinson D. 1,180–7) of which, however, two volumes covering the period June to Oct. 1723 are missing.

6. The episode has been described by Franco Venturi, 'Giannoniana Britannica', *Bollettino dell'archivio storico del Banco di Napoli*, fasc. 8 (1954).

7. Rawlinson's diary shows that he acquired Sebastiano Coleti's Italian translation of Lenglet de Fresnoy's book in Venice in 1722 and translated it during that summer, i.e. before it could contain a reference to Giannone's work, which was not published till 1723. Evidently his translation, as published in 1728, had taken account of the later edition – the same which would so infuriate Giannone when he read it in Vienna in 1730 (see above, p. 47).

8. Bodleian Library, MS Rawlinson D. 551. [The *Professione di fede* was printed in the *Opere postume di Pietro Giannone*, 2 vols (Venice, 1768), I, pp. 197–251.]

9. Panzini's biography of Giannone was published in his edition of Giannone's *Opere postume* (Naples, 1766) [in the Venetian edition, II, pp. 1–106].

10. George Villiers, duke of Buckingham, the founder of the family fortune, was the brother of Grandison's great-grandfather Sir Edward Villiers, president of Munster. Barbara Villiers, the mistress of Charles II, was his cousin.

11. Presumably the 'large estate' of his maternal grandfather, Sir John Fitzgerald of Dromana, County Wexford, which had caused his father to change the family surname from Villiers to Fitzgerald.

12. The two families remained linked in the next generation, when Falkland's son, Lucius Charles, 7th viscount, married in 1734 the widow of Grandison's son, Lord Villiers.

13. Falkland's secret visit to England (using the names Skinner and Stanley) and his consultations there with Bishop Atterbury, the chief Jacobite conspirator, are revealed in the report of the parliamentary committee which examined the evidence (*Reports from Committees of the House of Commons*, I, [1803], pp. 125–27, and Appendix D, pp. 27, 40, 41, 42). See also G.V. Bennett, *The Tory Crisis in Church and State 1688–1730* (Oxford, 1975), p. 255.

14. *Histoires des troubles de la Grande Bretagne . . .* (Paris, 1649).
15. *Remonstrance très humble faite au sérénissime Prince Charles II, roy de la Grande Bretagne . . . sur la conjoncture présente des affaires de Sa Majesté* (Paris, 1652).
16. Giannone, *Vita*, pp. 165–67 [*Opere di Pietro Giannone*, pp. 184–87].
17. The regiments are sometimes identified in the list of subscribers; I have identified others from Charles Dalton, *George I's Army 1714–27* (1910–12).
18. J.S. Burn, *History of the Fleet Marriages* (2nd edn, 1834), p. 116.
19. 'The Scottish Enlightenment', in *Studies in Voltaire and the Eighteenth Century* 58 (1967), pp. 1635–58; [above, pp. 17–33].
20. Mark Goldie, 'The Scottish Catholic Enlightenment', *Journal of British Studies* 30 (1991), p. 24.
21. Tallemant des Réaux, *Historiettes*, under 'Ménage'. [*Historiettes*, ed. A. Adam, 2 vols, Bibliothèque de la Pléiade (Paris, 1960–61), II, pp. 325, 329–30, on Menteith de Salmonet's connection with Cardinal de Retz, but with no mention of Mazarin's condemnation.]
22. This point has been made by John Robertson in an essay to be published in *The Historical Journal*. ['The Enlightenment above National Context: Political Economy in Eighteenth-Century Scotland and Naples', *The Historical Journal* 40 (1997), pp. 667–97; later, more fully, in *The Case for the Enlightenment: Scotland and Naples 1680–1760* (Cambridge, 2005).]
23. Giannone's letter to Lenglet is printed in Sergio Bertelli, *Giannoniana* (Milan and Naples, 1968), pp. 71–72, from the MS in the Biblioteca Nazionale in Naples.
24. For the jubilation, see the documents published in Bertelli, *Giannoniana*, pp. 172–79.
25. In *Bibliothèque italique ou histoire littéraire d'Italie*, vols IV and X (Geneva, 1730–31).
26. Cf. the letter from Marc-Michel Bousquet, at Geneva, to Giannone in Venice, 29 Jan. 1735, printed in Bertelli, *Giannoniana*, pp. 524–25.
27. Robert Shackleton, *Montesquieu* (Oxford, 1961), pp. 102–3, 113.
28. For details see Georges Bonnant, 'Pietro Giannone à Genève et la publication des ses oeuvres en Suisse au XVIIIe et XIXe siècles', *Annali della Scuola Speciale per Archivisti e Bibliotecari dell'Università di Roma*, Anno III (1963), pp. 119–38, with illustrations.
29. Vernet's account of the affair is printed in full, from the Archives d'Etat de Genève, in Bertelli, *Giannoniana*, pp. 573–92.
30. *The Autobiographies of Edward Gibbon*, ed. Sir John Murray (London, 1896), p. 143.
31. *Ibid.*, p. 235.
32. Gibbon made more than forty notes on Giannone in his commonplace book in 1755. See Patricia B. Craddock, *Young Edward Gibbon* (Baltimore and London, 1982), pp. 68–71. He also wrote 'Critical Researches Concerning the Title of Charles VIII to the Crown of Naples', which was printed by Lord Sheffield in *The Miscellaneous Works of Edward Gibbon* (London, 1814), III, pp. 206–22. Gibbon's debt to Giannone is emphasised by G. Giarrizzo, *Edward Gibbon e la cultura europea del settecento* (Naples, 1954). [Now also John Robertson, 'Gibbon and Giannone', in D. Womersley (ed.) with the assistance of J. Burrow and J. Pocock, *Edward Gibbon Bicentenary Essays* (Voltaire Foundation, Oxford, 1997), pp. 3–19.]
33. D.M. Low (ed.), *Gibbon's Journal to 28 January 1763* (London, 1929), p. 30.
34. Leopold von Ranke's earliest work, *Geschichten der romanischen und germanischen Völker von 1495 bis 1514* (1824), is in fact a history of the invasion of Italy by Charles VIII and its immediate consequences for Europe.
35. G. Bonnard, *Le Journal de Gibbon à Lausanne* (Lausanne, 1945), p. 143.
36. Gibbon's views on Naples are expressed in a letter, written after his return to England, to his uncle Sir Stanier Porten, who had previously been British Resident there. See J.E. Norton (ed.), *The Letters of Edward Gibbon* (1956), I, pp. 197–98: letter of 21 July 1765.
37. *Decline and Fall*, II, p. 322 [ed. Womersley, I, p. 759: ch. xx, n. 111].
38. *Ibid.*, VI, p. 167 [ed. Womersley, III, p. 471: ch. lvi, n. 1].
39. Giannone, *Vita*, p. 15 [*Opere di Pietro Giannone*, p. 26].
40. *Decline and Fall*, V, p. 171 [ed. Womersley, III, p. 25].

41. On the 'Gallicanism' of Muratori and Giannone, *ibid.*, II, p. 322, V, p. 257 [ed. Womersley, I, p. 759: ch. xx, n. 111; III, p. 98: ch. xlix, n. 30].

42. The subscriber is named as 'Edward Gibbon esq.'. In 1729–30 Gibbon's father was an affluent young man who was then still lingering at Cambridge and was about to go abroad before entering Parliament. The pupil of the non-juror William Law, he was a tory and, Gibbon insinuates (*Autobiographies*, p. 294), a Jacobite. Middleton, who subscribed for the book as university librarian at Cambridge, was also, at that time, a tory, and reputed a Jacobite. Incidentally, there were several subscribers from Cambridge – the work must have been well promoted there – but none from Oxford. The only other university from which subscribers came was Marischal College, Aberdeen, in Ogilvie country. But I cannot find a James Ogilvie matriculated there who could be identified with the translator. However, if he was a Roman Catholic, it is possible that he studied there without matriculation.

Editor's additional note on the identities of the printer of the *Civil History* and of Captain James Ogilvie

Further light has been shed on the printing of Ogilvie's translation of the *Civil History* by William M. Sale, Jr., in *Samuel Richardson: Master Printer* (Ithaca, 1950, repr. Connecticut, 1977) and by Keith Maslen, in *Samuel Richardson of London, Printer* (University of Otago, 2001). These identify the printer of the two volumes as Samuel Richardson, a printer before he became a novelist (Sale, pp. 109–10, 171; Maslen, p. 87). Richardson is not named as such on the title-pages. The work was 'Printed for W. Innys, in St. Paul's Church-Yard; G. Strahan, at the Golden-Ball, and R. Willock, at Sir Isaac Newton's Head, in Cornhill; A. Millar, at Buchanan's Head, in the Strand; T. Green, and J. Pote, near Charing-Cross; J. Penn, in Westiminster-Hall; A. Johnston, Engraver, in St. Martin's Lane; and sold by the Booksellers of London and Westminster: And at Edinburgh, by A. Symmer, in the Parliament Close' (Vol. I, 1729); and 'Printed for the Author; and sold by G. Strahan, in Cornhill; W. Innys, in St Paul's Church-Yard; C. Davies, in Pater-Noster-Row; and T. Green, at Charing-Cross' (Vol. II, 1731). A second printer, perhaps James Bettenham, was also involved in Vol. II. Trevor-Roper's contention that the publisher was Andrew Millar (above, p. 39) is therefore an over-simplification; the publication of so large a work clearly required a 'conger' of publishers, as well as the author and subscribers. These 'publishers' will have chosen Richardson as the printer. Maslen (p. 87) identifies fifty-seven of Richardson's printer's ornaments in Vol. I, and a further sixty-one in Vol. II, although other printers' ornaments were used too. Richardson also printed Ogilvie's translations of Menteith de Salmonet's *History of the Troubles of Great Britain*, and Riordan de Muscry's *True Causes . . . Which Contributed to the Restoration of Charles II*, published together in 1735 (Sale, p. 109; Maslen, pp. 106–7). The identification of Richardson as the printer of Ogilvie's translation of the *Civil History* strengthens the case for a Jacobite connection, since Richardson had previously printed works for Bishop Atterbury, his amanuensis George Kelly and the duke of Wharton.

Sale (pp. 109 and 372, n. 3) also suggests a positive identification of James Ogilvie, as Captain James Ogilvie in the earl of Orrery's Regiment of Scotch Fuziliers, noting that Orrery had been arrested for conspiracy in connection with the Atterbury Plot. This Ogilvie is listed in Charles Dalton, *George the First's Army 1714–1727*, I (London, 1910), p. 345, as having his commission renewed by George I on 1 March 1715. His earlier career can be traced in Charles Dalton, *English Army Lists and Commission Registers 1661–1714*, 6 vols (London, 1892–1904): commissioned as an ensign in Colonel Robert Mackay's Regiment of Fusiliers, 13 Feb. 1697 (IV, p. 182), he was a 2nd lieutenant by 1702, fought and was wounded at Blenheim, and was promoted 1st lieutenant in Aug. 1704 (V, pp. 80, 82, and Part II, p. 57). But, alas, this trail runs cold before publication of the *Civil History*; Sale did not notice the entry for the Royal North British Fusiliers (successor to the Scotch Fuziliers commanded by Orrery) in Dalton, *George the First's Army*, II (London, 1912), pp. 311–12, where it is recorded that Mungo Mathie was promoted captain on 5 May 1727 'in room of James Ogilvie decd.'. The puzzle of the translator's identity remains unsolved.

I am much indebted to Professor Angus Ross, of Sussex, for referring me to the works of Sale and Maslen, identifying Samuel Richardson as the printer of the translation.

Chapter 4: Dimitrie Cantemir's Ottoman History and its Reception in England

Originally published in the *Revue roumaine d'histoire* 24 (1985), pp. 51–66. The journal was a publication of the Académie des Sciences Sociales et Politiques de la République Socialiste de Roumanie.

1. Gibbon, *Decline and Fall of the Roman Empire*, ed. Bury, VII p. 199 [ed. Womersley, III, p. 968: ch. lxviii, n. 77].

2. [Dimitrie Cantemir, *The History of the Growth and Decay of the Othman Empire. Part 1. Containing the Growth of the Othman Empire, from the reign of Othman the Founder, to the reign of Mahomet IV. That is, from the year 1300, to the Siege of Vienna, in 1683. Part 2. The history of the decay of the Othman empire, from the reign of Mahomet IV, to the reign of Ahmed III. Written originally in Latin, by Demetrius Cantemir, late Prince of Moldavia. Translated into English, from the author's own manuscript by N. Tindal, . . . Adorn'd with the heads of the Turkish emperors* (London: printed for James, John, and Paul Knapton, at the Crown in Ludgate Street, 1734–35).] The title-page gives the date 1734. In fact the work was published in twenty-one serial parts beginning on 15 March 1735, as shown by the advertisement in the contemporary press (*Weekly Register or Universal Journal* 261 22 Feb. 1735; *London Evening Post*, 15 March 1735). Hereafter *Ottoman History*.

3. See especially the letters printed in L.N. Maikov, *Materialij dlja biografii kn. A.D. Kantemira* (St Petersburg, 1903), and Helmut Grasshoff, *A.D. Kantemir und Westeuropa* (Berlin, 1966); also the 'Vorbericht' and 'Vorrede' in *Demetrii Kantemirs . . . historische-geographisch-und-politische Beschreibung der Moldau* (Frankfurt and Leipzig, 1771).

4. For Guasco's relations with Antioh Cantemir see his introduction to his French translation of Cantemir's *Satyres* (London, 1759); also Marcelle Ehrhard, *Le Prince Cantemir à Paris 1738-1744* (*Annales de l'Université de Lyon, IIIe série, Lettres*, fasc. 6, Paris, 1938); Robert Shackleton, *Montesquieu* (Oxford, 1961), pp. 190–93.

5. This statement rests primarily on G.F. Müller's *Vorrede* to the German edition of the *Description of Moldavia*. Müller there states that he had heard some forty years ago (i.e. about 1724) that 'die Originalschrift sey von dem Fürsten in der moldauischen Sprache verfasset worden, und Ilinksy habe solche ins lateinische gebracht'. Since Müller was secretary of the St Petersburg Academy, and his account, in other respects, is confirmed by the original letters published by Maikov and Grasshoff, he is likely to be correct in this. The evidence concerning the original language of the *Ottoman History* is less explicit. It comes from a letter which Antioh Cantemir, in London, wrote to Gross telling him that 'les originaux de l'histoire turque de mon père', together with 'beaucoup d'autres cahiers de l'écriture de mon père', had been left in Ilinksy's hands and should still be among his effects. But almost at the same time Antioh Cantemir, in sending the English translation of the *Ottoman History* to Mme. de Monconseil in Paris, explained that he could not send 'l'original latin, puisque je l'ai cédé à M. Tindal, qui a fait la traduction anglaise' (Maikov, *Materialij*, pp. 88, 89). This suggests that 'les originaux . . . de mon père', which Antioh Cantemir had left in Russia, were distinct from 'l'original latin' which he had brought to England: and the natural inference is that the Latin text was a translation and that the original was in another language. From a statement in Dimitrie Cantemir's *System of the Mohammedan Religion* (*Sistemul sau intocmirea religiei muhammedane*, ed. Virgil Cândea, Bucharest, 1977, p. 467) it seems that this original language was Greek.

6. For this projected publication see the correspondence printed, or cited, in Grasshoff, *A.D. Kantemir* pp. 31ff., 260–74.

7. For the history of this map see Vintilă Mihăilescu, 'Harta Moldovei de Dimitrie Cantemir', in Dimitrie Cantemir, *Descriptio Moldaviae* (Bucharest, 1973), pp. 377–85.

8. For Antioh Cantemir's diplomatic activity, see D.K. Reading, *The Anglo-Russian Commercial Treaty of 1734* (New Haven, CT and London, 1938).

9. The doctor whom he visited was Claude Deshais Gendron, physician to the regent, the duke of Orléans. The *abbé* Guasco also came to Paris to consult Gendron.

10. *Satyres du Prince Cantemir . . .* ('Londres' [in fact, Holland and Paris], 1750).

11. 'Novye dannye k biografii kn. Antiokha Dmitrievicha Kantemira i ego blizhaishykh rodstvennikov' in *Zhurnal Ministersva Narodnogo Prosvescheniya* 274 (April 1891), i. pp. 352–425 and 275 (June 1891), i. pp. 252–333.

12. Nicholas Tindal's career can be traced through the dedication of his successive publications. See also Edward A. Fitch, 'Historians of Essex, I. Nicholas Tindal; II, Philip Morant', *Essex Review* 2 (1893) and 3 (1894).

13. This is apparent from a note by Morant cited by Fitch, 'Historians of Essex'.

14. Stefan Pascu, 'Dimitrie Cantemir' in *AJESEE* 11 (1973) p. 159; Alexandru Dutu, 'Dimitrie Cantemir, Historian of South East European Civilisation', *Revue roumaine d'histoire* (1974) p. 34; Virgil Cândea, *Dimitrie Cantemir 1673–1723* (Editura Enciclopedica Româna).

15. Shackleton, *Montesquieu*, p. 176.

16. Dutu, 'Dimitrie Cantemir'.

17. *Lettres d'un François* (The Hague, 1745), Letter LXIII. For other references to Cantemir, see Letters LXXVI, LXXXV. On le Blanc see H. Monod Cassidy, *Un voyageur-philosophe au XVIIIe siècle* (Cambridge, Mass., 1941).

18. Sir Robert Sutton was ambassador at Constantinople 1701–16. His despatches for the period 1710–14 have been published (Camden Society, 3rd series, vol. 78, 1953). See for Cantemir, pp. 53–54, 65.

19. *The Negotiations of Sir Thomas Roe in his Embassy to the Ottoman Porte 1621–1628* (London, 1740).

20. *Grub-street Journal,* 276 (10 April 1735).

21. See, for instance, the frequent references to the affair of Matthew Tindal's will (nos 212, 217, 220, 223, 231), the stories of his greed at All Souls College (265), and numerous editorials against Tindal and free-thinking.

22. Quoted in Grasshoff, *A.D. Kantemir und Westeuropa*, p. 282. The Russian ambassador in Constantinople was Antioh Cantemir's friend Aleksei Andreevich Veshnyakov, on whom see Grasshoff, pp. 68–69, etc.

23. In the last category, I am thinking particularly of Giovanni Giacomo Zamboni, the diplomatic agent of the duke of Modena, the Landgraf of Hesse-Darmstadt, and the king of Poland, whose papers, after his death, were sold in order to pay some of his debts and are now in the Bodleian Library (MSS Rawlinson Letters 116–38). They include one volume entitled *Miscellanea pornologica*, being the letters received by Zamboni from a series of obliging procurers and prostitutes. To pay for these activities, Zamboni acted as agent for the sale of Greek and other MSS from Italy and Holland, many of which were bought from 'that greedy segnior', at 'a most horrible price', by Humfrey Wanley for the Harleian Library. See *Diary of Humfrey Wanley*, ed. C.E. and R.C. Wright (1966), *passim*.

24. *Histoire de Charles XII* (1731), livre V. [Modern critical edition by G. von. Proschwitz, in Vol. 4 of the *Complete Works of Voltaire* (Oxford, 1996), p. 404.]

25. Maikov, *Materialij*, no. 73, cf. no. 82.

26. *Ottoman History*, p. 333 shows the Cantemir descent.

27. Voltaire, *Correspondance*, ed. T. Besterman, II (Paris, 1965), pp. 107 (à M. Thieriot, 28 Feb. 1739), 116–18 (à M. Cantemir, 13 March 39), 144 (à M. La Noue, 3 April 39), 161 (à M. Cantemir, 19 April 39); Maikov, *Materialij*, nos 144–45.

28. Voltaire, *Histoire de Russie*, Part II, ch. I (1763). [*Histoire de l'empire de Russie sous Pierre le Grand*, critical edition by M. Mervaud, Vols 46–47 of the *Complete Works of Voltaire* (Oxford, 1999), XLVII, pp. 713–14.]

29. Mr Besterman, for whom Voltaire cannot err, admires his independence in refusing the correction of a prince (*Correspondance*, II, p. 1,148). He overlooks the fact that a prince, on his home ground, may sometimes be right.

30. *Ottoman History*, p. 3.
31. Voltaire, *Essai sur les moeurs* [ed. R. Pomeau (Paris, 1963), I, pp. 820–25, in ch. xci]; cf. *Histoire de Charles XII* (1748), Preface. [The Preface to the 1748 edition was subsequently entitled 'Pyrrhonisme de l'histoire', and is included under this title in the critical edition by von Proschwitz, *Complete Works of Voltaire*, IV, pp. 567–78.]
32. Gibbon, *Decline and Fall of the Roman Empire*, ed. Bury, VII, pp. 202–3 [ed. Womersley, III, p. 971: ch. lxviii, with n. 84].
33. Maikov, *Materialij*, nos 89, 95.
34. The French translation, according to the title-page, is by 'M. de Joncquières, commandeur, chanoine régulier de l'Ordre Hospitalier du Saint Esprit de Montpellier'. That Guasco organised this is shown by his statement, in his life of Antioh Cantemir prefixed to the French translation of his *Satyres*, 'J'en fis faire en même temps la traduction française qui a été imprimée à Paris en 1743'. For the connexion of Cantemir with the Noailles family, see Ehrhard, *Le Prince Cantemir à Paris*.
35. See Mihăilescu, 'Harta Moldovei de Dimitrie Cantemir'.
36. The French edition was published simultaneously by two publishers. I have only been able to see one of these editions, that published by Despilly, Paris; I have therefore been unable to compare the texts. The portraits are not printed in this edition.
37. Montesquieu, *Oeuvres complètes*, ed. Nagel (1955), III, p. 1,048 [Montesquieu to Guasco, 1 août 1744].
38. It had been given to Tindal in 1734 and had not been returned in 1737, two years after the translation of the English version (Maikov, *Materialij*, no. 97).
39. For the history of this MS, see *Demetrij Kantemirs ... Beschreibung der Moldau* (1771), 'Vorrede'.
40. I refer particularly to the article of Franz Babinger, 'Die türkischen Quellen Dimitrie Kantemirs', in *Omagiu Profesorului Loan Lupas* (Bucharest, 1941), printed also in Franz Babinger, *Aufsätze und Abhandlungen zur Geschichte Südosteuropas und der Levant*, II (Munich, 1966), p. 142.
41. Hume, *History of England*, James I, *sub fine*. [Liberty Fund edition, based on the 1778 edition (Indianapolis, 1983), V, p. 154.]
42. [*The Rambler*, 122, Saturday 18 May 1751, in the Yale edition of the Works of Samuel Johnson, IV *The Rambler* (New Haven, CT and London, 1969), p. 290.]
43. *The Autobiographies of Edward Gibbon*, ed. J. Murray (1897), pp. 58, 121.
44. Gibbon, *Decline and Fall of the Roman Empire*, ed. Bury, VII, pp. 24, 34 [ed. Womersley, III, pp. 810, 818: ch. lxiv, nn. 40, 57].
45. It was first printed in *Magazin für die neue Historie u. Geographie* III–IV (1769–76).
46. Jones' 'prefatory discourse' was published by Lord Teignmouth in his *Memoirs of the Life of Sir William Jones* (1804), p. 513. It was evidently written before 16 January 1772, the date on which Jones informed a friend that his Turkish history – i.e. presumably the whole *Essay on the History of the Turks* – was ready for the press, and would be dedicated to Lord Radnor (*ibid.*, p. 103). The *Essay*, if it was completed, as the letter implies, has not survived, although Lord Teignmouth had seen part of the MS (*ibid.*, p. 106).
47. In preparing this paper I am indebted, particularly for the Russian and Romanian sources, to my friends Constantine Brancovan and Andrei Pippidi.

Chapter 5: From Deism to History: Conyers Middleton

Originally given as the Leslie Stephen Lecture at Cambridge in 1982, the essay has not previously been published. It is printed from the fullest of the typescripts now in the Dacre Papers, Christ Church, Middleton File.

1. Leslie Stephen, *History of English Thought in the Eighteenth Century*, 3rd edn, 2 vols (London, 1902), I, p. 270.
2. Norman L. Torrey, *Voltaire and the English Deists* (New Haven, CT, 1930; repr. Oxford, 1963), pp. 173–74.

3. James Monk, *Life of Richard Bentley* (London, 1830), p. 388.
4. The account of Walpole and selections from the account of Cole are printed in *The Correspondence of Horace Walpole*, ed. W. Lewis, Yale edition, XV, (London, 1951), Appendices I and II. The original text of Cole's account is in BL. Add. MS 5833 ff. 228–34. Another early account of Middleton's life is printed in *Biographia Britannica* (1766).
5. Giuseppe Giarrizzo, 'Fra Protestantesimo e deismo: le origini della moderna storiografia inglese sul cristianesimo primitivo . . . C. Middleton (1683–1750)' in *Ricerche di storia religiosa*, I, i (Roma, 1954), pp. 151–99.
6. The main manuscript sources for Middleton's life are: (1) the Heberden Papers, i.e. BL. Add. MSS 32457–59, being Middleton's own papers, obtained from the descendant of his executor, William Heberden, to whom they had been bequeathed by Middleton's widow; and (2) the Hervey Papers, i.e. the MSS of John Lord Hervey, now owned by his descendant the marquess of Bristol and deposited in the Suffolk Record Office. Two volumes of these (AC 941/47/8–9) contain the correspondence of Middleton with Lord Hervey from 1733 to 1737. The second of these volumes is from Middleton's own papers: apparently it became separated from them and was bought by the Hervey family. Leslie Stephen glanced at the Heberden Papers, but did not know of the Hervey Papers. Dorothy Margaret Stuart, for her article 'Some Unpublished Letters of John Lord Hervey and Dr Conyers Middleton', in *English* 2:7 (1938), used the Hervey Papers but did not know of the Heberden Papers: hence her erroneous statement that the correspondence 'seems to have flickered out' in 1737. In fact, the Hervey–Middleton correspondence is continued from 1737 to Hervey's death in 1743 in BL Add. MS 32458. Since the Hervey–Middleton correspondence is thus divided, I have cited the letters by date. [MS numbers have now been added, but note that the volumes in the Suffolk Record Office are not foliated. Thus, for example, AC 941/47/8 is the volume number: individual letters within the volume have to be identified by date.]
7. Letters to Middleton from Anglesey and Oxford are in BL Add. MS 32457. A letter from Middleton to Oxford, reporting university affairs, is in Historical Manuscripts Commission, Duke of Portland's MSS, VI, 30–31. Both peers had been tory MPs for the university before succeeding to their earldoms.
8. I infer this from a remark by Middleton in a letter to Lord Hervey of 8 Nov. 1733 (Suffolk R.O. AC 941/47/8): the high-church nonsense which he is reading is, he says, 'a penance which I impose in [on?] myself for my former sins of credulity'.
9. The proctor's report is in BL Add. MS 32459 f. 12. See also Monk. *Life of Bentley*, p. 224.
10. Middleton, at the end of his life, urged Horace Walpole to marry 'on the sense of his own happiness': Walpole to Montagu, 23 June 1750, *Correspondence of Horace Walpole*, ed. Lewis, IX, (London, 1941), pp. 110–11. He had made a similar remark to Warburton earlier: BL Add. MS 32457 f. 137.
11. They are *A Full and Impartial Account of all the Late Proceedings in the University against Dr Bentley* (1719); *A Second Part of the Full and Impartial Account* (1719); and *Some Remarks upon a Pamphlet* . . . (1719).
12. *Remarks . . . upon the Proposals Lately Published by Richard Bentley* . . . (1721); *Some Further Remarks* . . . (1722), both in Conyers Middleton, *The Miscellaneous Works*, 2nd edn, 5 vols (London, 1755), III, pp. 279–322, 323–459. [The works indicated in the preceding note are not in this collection. Hereafter *MW*, with volume and page numbers.]
13. Monk, *Life of Bentley*, pp. 449–50. In fact, Bentley continued to contemplate his edition until 1732, when he finally abandoned it. See R.C. Jebb, *Bentley* (London, 1882), pp. 162–71.
14. Monk, *Life of Bentley*, p. 198.
15. *Ibid.*, p. 456. A letter of congratulation from the earl of Anglesey to Middleton, of 3 Jan. 1721–22, BL Add. MS 32457 f. 5, makes it clear that the appointment was a reward for a loyal tory. [On Middleton's appointment, and the uneven course of his tenure of the office, see also David McKitterick, *Cambridge University Library. A History: The Eighteenth and Nineteenth Centuries* (Cambridge, 1986), pp. 166–86, 246–48.]
16. *Bibliothecae Cantabrigiensis ordinandae methodus*, 17°, in *MW*, III, pp. 45–82.

17. Middleton's claims to have been familiar with the learned *abbé* Giusto Fontanini, afterwards archbishop of Ancyra, and to have corresponded with him from England, are borne out by his letters in BL Add. MS 32457/14, 26, 51, 91. Cf. also Middleton's *Dissertations . . . Appendix* (1761), p. 13.
18. BL Add. MS 32457 f. 4.
19. *A Letter from Rome, MW,* V, p. 89: cf. C. Middleton, *Germana quaedam . . . Monumenta* (1745), p. vii [not in *MW*].
20. See the sale catalogue of his library. [*A Catalogue of the Entire Library of the Reverend Conyers Middleton DD, . . . Lately Deceased,* sold by Samuel Baker, Bookseller (London, March 1751). There are copies of this catalogue in the Bodleian and the British Library.]
21. Signor Giarrizzo refers ('Fra Protestantesimo e deismo', pp. 167, 181) to Middleton's 'conversion' to Newtonianism after his Roman visit; but I know of no evidence to justify such a 'conversion' or such a precise date.
22. His successor, Francis Parris, combined the office with the Mastership of Sidney Sussex. Parris' successor, Edmund Law, went further. He combined it with the Mastership of Peterhouse and the Knightbridge professorship of moral theology – and intended to keep all these offices when appointed bishop of Carlisle in 1769. D.A. Winstanley, *Unreformed Cambridge* (Cambridge, 1935), p. 140.
23. Middleton's comments on his duties, which perhaps he over-emphasised in self-defence (he admitted, 'and yet I am thought to give less of my time than I ought to this province'), are in his letters to Hervey, Suffolk R.O. AC 941/47/8–9: 18 Aug. 1734, 22 Sept. 1734, 24 Nov. 1734, 16 Dec. 1736. Cf. BL Add. MS 32457 ff. 60, 108.
24. *De medicorum apud veteres Romanos degentium conditione Dissertatio* (1726), in *MW,* IV, pp. 83–119.
25. *Dissertationis de medicorum Romae degentium conditione ignobili & servili* (1727), *MW,* IV, pp. 121–75.
26. The history of Middleton's 'Appendix' is given by his executor, William Heberden, in his introduction to the published text: *Dissertationis de Servili Medicorum Conditione Appendix seu Defensionis pars secunda . . .* (1761). Thomas Birch, writing to Lord Hardwicke in 1750, just after Middleton's death, says that the manuscript was given by Middleton, at Oxford's request, to Mead himself; but the survival of the MS among the Harleian MSS (BL Harl. MS 7515) shows that Heberden's version is correct.
27. *A Letter from Rome, shewing, an exact conformity between Popery and Paganism* (1729), *MW,* V, pp. 1–183.
28. Middleton regarded the *Letter from Rome* as 'the first of my writings that created me any enemies, whose resentment I have ever since been sensible of': Middleton to Hervey, 17 Sept. 1733, Suffolk R.O. AC 941/47/8.
29. *Reliquiae Hearnianae,* ed. P. Bliss (London, 1869), III, pp. 57–58.
30. See the account by Zacharias Conrad von Huffenbach printed in *Cambridge under Queen Anne,* ed. J.E.B. Mayor (Cambridge, 1911), pp. 397–405. [On Woodward and his geological ideas see Joseph M. Levine, *Dr Woodward's Shield: History, Science, and Satire in Augustan England* (Berkeley and London, 1977), chs ii–v.]
31. Winstanley, *Unreformed Cambridge,* p. 168, says that, 'except for giving an inaugural lecture', Middleton 'sedulously neglected his duties, which indeed he was incompetent to perform'. But this seems unfair. In his letter to Lord Hervey of 31 July 1733, Middleton writes that he has already given three out of the four lectures for that year, and must provide four more for next year. One of these lectures – different from the inaugural lecture published in the *MW,* IV, pp. 1–20: *Oratio de novo Physiologiae explicanae* – and entitled 'Oratio Woodwardiana', is in BL Add. MS 32459 f. 15. It is clearly one of his regular lectures ('In praelectionibus hisce quarum quattuor omnino singulis annis habendae sunt . . .'). The author of the account of Middleton in *Biographia Britannica* (who is not uncritical) states that Middleton 'held the office, and faithfully discharged the [duties?] of it', p. 3,097.
32. Middleton to Hervey, 31, July 1733, 25 Aug. 1733: Suffolk R.O. AC 941/47/8.

33. Stephen, *English Thought in the Eighteenth Century*, I, p. 257.
34. Macaulay's annotated set of Middleton's *Miscellaneous Works* (1755) is now in the library of Trinity College, Cambridge.
35. Daniel Waterland, *Scripture Vindicated, in answer to a book intituled, Christianity as old as the Creation*, Part I (1730), Part II (1731), Part III (1732).
36. Stephen, *English Thought in the Eighteenth Century*, I, p. 259.
37. *A Letter to Dr Waterland; containing some Remarks on his Vindication of Scripture; in answer to a book, intitled, Christianity as old as the Creation. Together with the sketch or plan of another Answer to the said book* (1730), in *MW*, III, pp. 1–66.
38. Zachary Pearce, *A Reply to the Letter to Dr. Waterland: setting forth the many falsehoods both in the quotations and the historical facts, by which the author endeavours to weaken the authority of Moses . . .* (London, 1731).
39. *A Defence of the Letter to Dr Waterland* (1731), in *MW*, III, pp. 67–163 esp. pp. 71–73.
40. *Some Remarks on a Reply to the Defence of a Letter to Dr Waterland* (1732), in *MW*, III, pp. 165–247; *Remarks on Some Observations, addressed to the Author of the Letter to Dr Waterland* (1733), in *MW*, III, pp. 249–78.
41. 'Phileleutherus Londiniensis' (John Burton), *An Attempt towards the Eulogium of Conyers Middleton* (London, n.d. [1750]).
42. The high stewardship was regarded as a stepping-stone to the chancellorship. See D.A. Winstanley, *Cambridge in the Eighteenth Century* (Cambridge, 1922). In fact, Oxford died in 1741 before the reigning chancellor, the duke of Somerset.
43. Middleton's breach with the tories and the earl of Oxford is documented by his own correspondence with Oxford (BL Add. Ms 32457) and with Hervey, and by 'Phileleutherus Londiniensis', *An Attempt*.
44. BL Add. MS 32457 ff. 84, 94.
45. Dr Johnson called 'the satire upon Sporus' 'the meanest passage' of Pope's *Epistle to Dr Arbuthnot*.
46. Walpole to Sir Horace Mann, 25 July 1750, *Correspondence of Horace Walpole*, XX (London, 1960), pp. 164–65.
47. Middleton's correspondence with Yorke is in the Hardwicke MSS: BL Add. MS 35605.
48. *Correspondence of Thomas Gray*, ed. P. Toynbee and L. Whibley, 3 vols (Oxford, 1935), I, p. 328.
49. BL Add. MS. 5809 f. 76 (Cole MSS).
50. BL Add. MS. 35605 ff. 54, 261.
51. Middleton to Hervey, 13 Sept. 1736, Suffolk R.O. AC 941/47/9.
52. *The Weekly Miscellany, giving an Account of the Religion, Morality and Learning of the Present Times* was published under the editorship of 'Richard Hooker of the Temple, Esq' (a pseudonym) from December 1732 until 1741. Selections from it were published in two volumes in 1736–38, dedicated to the earl of Anglesey, Oxford's successor as high steward of the University of Cambridge, and, after his death, to the Earl of Abingdon. Its avowed purpose was 'to defend *Revelation* against the objections of the *Deists*, the *Church of England* from the dangerous attempts of a powerful confederacy'.
53. Middleton to Hervey, 31 July 1733, Suffolk R.O. AC 941/47/8.
54. Middleton to Hervey, 27 Dec. 1733, Suffolk R.O. AC 941/47/8.
55. Middleton to Hervey, 31 July 1733, Suffolk R.O. AC 941/47/8.
56. Place published a work entitled *Reason an Insufficient Guide to conduct mankind in religion* (London, 1735).
57. Middleton to Hervey, 25 Aug. 1733, Suffolk R.O. AC 941/47/8.
58. Middleton to Hervey, 17 Sept. 1733, Suffolk R.O. AC 941/47/8.
59. Middleton to Hervey, 26, 27 Dec. 1733; Hervey to Middleton, 28 Dec. 1733, 1 Jan. 1734; Middleton to Hervey, 3 Jan. 1734, Suffolk R.O. AC 941/47/8.
60. Chubb had written a treatise on this subject [*Four tracts . . . III. The case of Abraham with respect to his being commanded by God to offer his son Isaac in sacrifice, . . .* (London, 1734)].

61. Middleton to Hervey, 12 March 1733–34, Suffolk R.O. AC 941/47/8.
62. Middleton to Hervey, 9 May 1734; Hervey to Middleton, 20 May 1734; Middleton to Hervey, 23 May 1734; Hervey to Middleton, 1 June 1734; Middleton to Hervey, 11 June, 1734, Suffolk R.O. AC 941/47/8. Middleton's unpublished document is in BL Add. MS 32457 f. 97.
63. Daniel Waterland, *The importance of the doctrine of the Holy Trinity asserted* (London, 1734).
64. Middleton's unpublished reply to Waterland's book on the Trinity is in BL Add. MS 32459 f. 53.
65. BL Add. MS 32457 f. 108.
66. Middleton to Hervey, 22 Sept. 1734; Hervey to Middleton, 19 Nov. 1734; Middleton to Hervey, 28 Nov. 1734; Hervey to Middleton, 3 Dec. 1734; Middleton to Hervey, 5 Dec. 1734, Suffolk R.O. AC 941/47/8.
67. Middleton to Hervey, 8 Feb. 1735–36, Suffolk R.O. AC 941/47/9.
68. A MS note by Middleton on the essay reads 'This wholly laid aside'. Cf. *Correspondence of Thomas Gray*, I, p. 349; but see above, p. 101.
69. R. Atkyns, *The Original and Growth of Printing* (London, 1664).
70. S. Palmer, *A General History of Printing* (London, 1732).
71. See Arundell Esdaile, *Manual of Bibliography* (newly revised edition, 1974), pp. 25–26.
72. *A Dissertation concerning the Origin of Printing in England: shewing, that it was first introduced and practised by our Countryman, William Caxton, at Westminster, and not, as is commonly believed, by a foreign printer at Oxford* (Cambridge, 1734–35), *MW*, V, pp. 321–72.
73. Middleton to Hervey, 24 Oct. 1734; 18 Aug. 1734, Suffolk R.O. AC 941/47/8.
74. *Reliquiae Hernianae*, ed. Bliss, III, pp. 171–72.
75. Middleton to Hervey, 31 July 1733; 30 June 1736, Suffolk R.O. AC 941/47/8–9; Middleton to Warburton, *MW*, I, pp. 374–76.
76. Middleton to Hervey, 18 Aug. 1734, Suffolk R.O. AC 941/47/8.
77. Middleton to Hervey, 30 Dec. 1735, 8 Feb. 1735–36, Suffolk R.O. 941/47/9. The Caput was a 'small and autocratic council' annually elected by the heads of houses and doctors from a limited list of academics. No grace could be voted on by the Senate unless it had been approved by the Caput. (See Winstanley, *Unreformed Cambridge*, p. 24.)
78. Middleton to Hervey, 13 Sept. 1736, Suffolk R.O. AC 941/47/9.
79. Middleton to Hervey, 24 Oct. 1736, Suffolk R.O. AC 941/47/9.
80. Middleton to Hervey, 4 Jan. 1736–37, Suffolk R.O. AC 941/47/9.
81. Middleton to Hervey, 8 Aug. 1737, Suffolk R.O. 941/47/9.
82. Middleton to Hervey, 15 March 1736–37, Suffolk R.O. 941/47/9.
83. *The Works of the Rev. Daniel Waterland, DD*, ed. W. van Mildert, 11 vols (Oxford, 1823), VI, p. 429.
84. Middleton to Hervey, 8 Aug. 1737, Suffolk R.O. AC 941/47/9; Townshend to Middleton, 21 Aug. 1737, BL Add. MS 32457 f. 122; Middleton to Warburton, 22 Sept. 1737 in *MW*, I, p. 390; Cole's account in *Letters of Horace Walpole*, ed. W. Lewis, XV, App. II.
85. Middleton to Hervey, 2 May 1738, BL Add. MS 32458 f. 40.
86. Middleton to Hervey, 4 May 1738, BL Add. MS 32458 f. 42.
87. BL Add. MS 32961 f. 133 (Newcastle MSS).
88. Middleton to Hervey, 30 May 1738, BL Add. MS 32458 f. 45.
89. Middleton reported the fact of his 'disagreeable conference' with the archbishop in a letter to Warburton of 28 June 1739, BL Add. MS 32457 f. 138. Compare Warburton's reply of 16 July 1739 (MS Egerton 1953), and Middleton's letter of 4 Sept. 1739, *MW*, I, p. 399). The substance of the conference is given in Middleton's later letter to the archbishop, BL Add. MS 32457 f. 149.
90. Hervey to Middleton, 17 Nov. 1739, BL Add. MS 32458 f. 130.
91. Middleton to Hervey, 4 Sept. 1740, BL Add. MS 32458 f. 164.
92. Hervey to Middleton, 20 Sept. 1740, BL Add. MS 32458 f. 168.
93. Hervey to Middleton, 13 Nov. 1740, BL Add. MS 32458 f. 171.
94. BL Add. MS 32457 f. 149.

95. Middleton to Warburton, 8 Jan. 1741, *MW*, I, p. 404–7 [with an anecdote at the expense of the late Dr Waterland].
96. Hervey to Middleton, 12 Jan. 1742, BL Add. MS 32458 f. 177.
97. Hervey to Middleton, 9 Dec. 1738, BL Add. MS 32458 ff. 68–69.
98. Hervey to Middleton, 12 Sept. 1741, BL Add. MS 32458 ff. 175–76.
99. *MW*, I, p. 399. BL Add. MS 32459 f. 1. The curious idea that Blackwell's *Enquiry into the Life and Writings of Homer* (1735) was an infidel book had been suggested in an article against Chubb in the *Miscellany* (Vol. II, no. 96). The writer of the article would have known that Blackwell was a friend of the two *bêtes noires* of the paper, Middleton and Warburton.
100. *The History of the Life of M. Tullius Cicero*, 2 vols, 4° (London, 1741).
101. Giarrizzo, 'Fra Protestantesimo e deismo', p. 180.
102. 'Dr Middleton's history, which I then appreciated above its true value, naturally directed me to the writings of Cicero': Gibbon, *Memoirs of my Life*, ed. G. Bonnard (London, 1966), p. 75; [*The Autobiographies of Edward Gibbon*, ed. John Murray (London, 1896), p. 138]. Macaulay's criticism is at the beginning of his essay on Francis Bacon.
103. Middleton to Hervey, 30 June 1736, Suffolk R.O. AC 941/47/9; *Life of Cicero*, I, p. xxi [in the three-volume 8° edn of 1755].
104. John Nicholls, *Literary Anecdotes of the Eighteenth Century*, 9 vols (London, 1812–15), V, pp. 412–16, note on pp. 414–15 says 'Dr Warton', citing his 'Essay on Pope', II, p. 324; i.e. Joseph Warton, *The Genius & Writings of Pope* (1756; 2nd edn, London, 1762).
105. S. Parr (ed.), *Gul. Bellendeni . . . de Statu Libri Tres.* (London, 1787), pp. iii–vii [quoted by Nicholls, *Literary Anecdotes*, pp. 416–17n]. Parr was known as 'Bellenden Parr' from his rediscovery and edition of Bellenden.
106. It is item 197 of the folio volumes. [*A Catalogue of the Entire Library of the Reverend Conyers Middleton DD*, p. 28.]
107. [But see M.L. Clarke, 'Conyers Middleton's Alleged Plagiarism', *Notes and Queries*, n.s. 30 (1983), pp. 44–46, for a contrary view, which takes account of Middleton's ownership of Bellenden's book.]
108. The house was Mount Morris, near Hythe, the property of his first wife. Some of Middleton's early letters are from it. He usually spent most of the summer there: MS Sloane 4049 f. 225: Middleton to Sir Hans Sloane, 1728.
109. Middleton to Hervey, 13 Sept. 1736, Suffolk R.O. AC 941/47/9.
110. Middleton to Warburton, 27 Oct. 1739, BL Add. MS 32457 f. 143; Middleton to Hervey, 21 Oct. 1739, BL Add. MS 32458 f. 129.
111. BL Add. MS 5486 f. 12 (Cole MSS). Cf. *Correspondence of Thomas Gray*, I, p. 276.
112. Middleton to Philip Yorke, 19 Aug. 1744, BL Add. MS 35397 f. 217.
113. Middleton published an edition of Cicero's letters to Brutus in 1743 and an account of the Roman Senate in 1747. [*The Epistles of M.T. Cicero to M. Brutus, and of Brutus to Cicero* (London, 1742): Preface in *MW*, IV pp. 305–408; *A Treatise on the Roman Senate, in two parts* (1747), in *MW*, IV, pp. 177–303.] The former was provoked by the attempt of James Tunstall of St John's College to prove these letters (which Middleton had used extensively in his *Cicero*) to be spurious. Tunstall was afterwards (1745) joined by Jeremiah Markland of Peterhouse, who agreed that not only the letters to Brutus but also Cicero's four speeches after his return from exile (also used by Middleton) were forgeries. The views of Tunstall and Markland were accepted by many scholars, including F.A. Wolf, but are now generally discounted. Middleton's edition is, however, a hasty work, and the translations were severely criticised. Macaulay declared them 'execrable', 'as incorrect as inelegant', with 'mistakes on every page', *Letters of T.B. Macaulay*, ed. T. Pinney (Cambridge, 1981), V, p. 460: to T.F. Ellis, 3 July 1855. But it seems that they were not by Middleton himself, but by an under-graduate of King's College whom he had hired 'at a cheap price' (Nicholls, *Literary Anecdotes*, V, p. 415n). Middleton's account of the Roman Senate was drawn from his corre-spondence with Hervey. Middleton also published, in 1745, an elaborate descriptive account of his collection of antiquities which he was selling to Horace Walpole: *Germana*

quaedam Antiquitatis eruditae monumenta (1745) [not in *MW*]. [On the debate over Cicero's letters to Brutus, see now Joseph M. Levine, '*Et tu Brute?* History and Forgery in 18th-Century England' in R. Myers and M. Harris (eds), *Fakes and Frauds* (Winchester, 1989), pp. 71–97, repr. in Levine, *Re-enacting the Past: Essays on the Evolution of Modern English Historiography* (Ashgate Variorum Series, Aldershot, 2004).]

114. *Biographia Britannica; Works*, I, advertisement.

115. 'Preface to A Free Inquiry', *MW*, I, p. xxx; 'Reflections on the Variations, or Inconsistencies, which are found among the Four Evangelists', *MW*, II, p. 375.

116. *A Free Inquiry into the miraculous Powers, which are supposed to have subsisted in the Christian Church from the earliest Ages, through several successive centuries* (London, 1748), in *MW*, I pp. i–cxix (Preface, Introductory Discourse, Postscript), 121–367 (*A Free Inquiry*).

117. Introductory Discourse, *MW*, I pp. xc–xcvii.

118. BL Add. MS 32459 f. 53.

119. *Free Inquiry*, *MW*, I, pp. 354–57.

120. John Wesley, *Journal*, 2 Jan. 1749.

121. *The Life of David Hume written by himself* (London, 1777), pp. 12–13, [repr. in David Hume, *Essays, Moral, Political, and Literary*, ed. E.F. Miller (Indianapolis, 1985), p. xxxv.]

122. 'A Preface to an intended answer to all the objections made against the Free Inquiry', *MW*, II, p. 242.

123. BL Add. MS 32457 f. 189.

124. Cited in G.O. Trevelyan, *Life and Letters of Lord Macaulay*, 2 vols (World's Classics edn, London, 1932; reissue, Oxford, 1961), II, pp. 385–86n.

125. A. Collins, *Discourse on the Grounds and Reasons of the Christian Religion* (1724).

126. *An Examination of the Lord Bishop of London's Discourses concerning the Use and Intent of Prophecy* (London, 1750), *MW*, V, pp. 185–319; *Correspondence of Horace Walpole*, ed. Lewis, XV, pp. 298–99.

127. [See the tracts listed as 'Posthumous' in 'A Catalogue of Dr Middleton's Works' in *MW*, I, and included in Vol. II.]

128. *Correspondence of Thomas Gray*, I, pp. 349–50. The Treatise on Miracles is in BL Add. MS 32459/21. The part played by Bolingbroke is described by Horace Walpole. A variant of the story is recounted by William Seward, *Anecdotes of Some Distinguished Persons* (1795–97), Supplement, p. 148.

129. 'Phileleutherus Londiniensis', *An Attempt*, p. 14.

130. *A Free Inquiry*, *MW*, I, p. 292.

131. Middleton always explicitly reserved the miracles of Christ and the Apostles from his criticism. He allowed that God could work miracles 'whenever He thinks fit', 'but whether He had wrought any or not since the days of the Apostles, is an enquiry which I do not meddle with: the single point which I maintain is that the Primitive Church had no standing power of working any': 'A Preface to an intended answer', *MW*, II, p. 251.

132. 'Reflections on the variations found in the Four Evangelists', *MW*, II, pp. 374–75.

133. 'A Vindication of the Free Inquiry', *MW*, II, pp. 138–42, III, p. 257.

134. Middleton to Hervey, 23 Nov. 1736, Suffolk R.O. AC 941/47/9; Middleton to Warburton, 30 Nov. 1736, in *MW*, I, p. 386.

135. Middleton to Warburton, 18 Nov. 1738, in *MW*, I, p. 398.

136. Middleton to Warburton, 11 Sept. 1736, 8 Feb. 1737–38, in *MW*, I, pp. 371–81, 383, 393; Middleton to Hervey, 14 Sept. 1735, Suffolk R.O. AC 941/47/9.

137. BL Add. MS 32459 f. 8. Cf. *MW*, II, pp. 259–60.

138. 'Prefatory Discourse' to the *Letter from Rome*, *MW*, V, p 79. Gibbon, in a note written, probably, in 1765–68 (Patricia Craddock, *The English Essays of Edward Gibbon* [Oxford, 1972], p. 91), says, 'Middleton, elegant and just in facts, carries his parallel too far. The Sacerdotal order on quite different principles from that of old Rome'. But this comment by Middleton shows that Gibbon's criticism is wrong: Middleton was well aware of the profound change of principle which was masked by the superficial continuity of rites and observances.

139. J.L. Mosheim accused Middleton of hypocrisy, since it must be clear to the careful reader that, through the later miracles, on which the truth of Christianity does not depend, he was secretly aiming to destroy those of Christ: *De rebus Christianis ante Constantinum* (Helmstedt, 1753), pp. 221–23. 'Cet homme avoit bien de netteté et de la pénétration', wrote Gibbon, on rereading the *Free Enquiry* in 1764. 'Il voyait jusqu'où l'on pouvoit pousser les consequences de ses principes, mais il ne lui convenoit pas de les tirer': *Le Journal de Gibbon à Lausanne*, ed. G. Bonnard (Lausanne, 1945), p. 224. 'You are a rogue and a sophist', wrote Macaulay (in Greek) in the margin of his copy of Middleton's works, 'but perhaps you are to be forgiven for it was not easy, or indeed safe, for you to speak freely.' Leslie Stephen, in his article in the *DNB*, roundly accuses Middleton of insincerity. See above, p. 117, nn. 174, 175.
140. In this 'Apology', Middleton describes his Letter to Waterland, of 1731, as 'thrown out . . . about 19 years ago' – which dates the writing of the 'Apology' in 1750, the year of his death.
141. Middleton to Hervey, 27 July 1735, Suffolk R.O. AC 941/47/9.
142. *Some Remarks on a Reply to the Defence of a Letter to Dr Waterland, MW,* III, p. 247. Macaulay, who wrote contemptuously of Middleton's character, nevertheless expressed enthusiastic approval of this passage.
143. Middleton to Hervey, 30 June 1736, Suffolk R.O. AC 941/47/9.
144. Middleton to Onslow, BL Add. MS. 32457 f. 118.
145. Middleton to Hervey, 12 March 1733–4, Suffolk R.O. AC 941/47/8.
146. Middleton to Hervey, 4 Dec. 1735, Suffolk R.O. AC 941/47/9.
147. Middleton to Hervey, 30 March 1735–36, Suffolk R.O. AC 941/47/9. See BL Add. MS 33491 f. 13 for Middleton on university professors.
148. Middleton to Hervey, 13 Sept. 1736, Suffolk R.O. AC 941/47/9.
149. William Warburton, *The Alliance between Church and State, or, the necessity and equity of an established religion and a test-law demonstrated* (London, 1736).
150. William Warburton, *The Divine Legation of Moses Demonstrated, on the principles of a religious deist, from the omission of the doctrine of a future state of reward and punishment in the Jewish dispensation* (London, 1738, 1741).
151. Twelve of Middleton's letters to Warburton were given by Warburton to Heberden and published in *MW*, I, pp. 371–413. The remainder were given by Warburton to Heberden in 1760 and are in MS. Add. 32457 ff. 114–48. Warburton's letters to Middleton are in MS Egerton 1953. Some of them are printed in R. Hurd, *Life of Warburton* [*A discourse, by way of general preface to the quarto edition of Bishop Warburton's works, containing some account of the life . . . of the author* (London, 1794), pp. 36–39, 67–69]. Middleton's private judgment of Warburton is given in a letter to Hervey of 9 March 1738, BL Add. MS 32458 f. 37: 'he has lived wholly in the country, and writes with the spirit of one who has been used to dictate to the provincial clergy around him'; and he adds that since Warburton is a *dévot* for Revelation, it is strange to see him attacked as 'a disguised infidel and real enemy of Christianity'.
152. On the breach between Middleton and Warburton see J.S. Watson, *The Life of William Warburton* (London, 1862–63), pp. 257–63.
153. William Warburton, *Julian. Or a discourse concerning the earthquake and fiery eruption, which defeated that Emperor's attempt to rebuild the temple at Jerusalem. In which the reality of a divine interposition is shewn; the objections to it are answered; and the nature of that evidence which demands the assent of every reasonable man to a miraculous fact, is considered and explained* (London, 1750).
154. [For this and the preceding paragraph: Gibbon, *Memoirs of my Life*, ed. Bonnard, p. 58; *Autobiographies*, ed. J.M. Murray (London, 1896), p. 84.]
155. *Essai,* § LVII [in *The Miscellaneous Works of Edward Gibbon*, ed. John Lord Sheffield, 5 vols (London, 1814), I, p. 70].
156. *Le Journal de Gibbon à Lausanne*, ed. Bonnard, pp. 114, 167, 214, 224.
157. Torrey, *Voltaire and the English Deists*, pp. 173–74. Torrey shows that Middleton was 'the most important English source of Voltaire's documentation against the historical argument of the truth of Christianity'.

158. *MW*, V, p. 89; cf. Gibbon, *Memoirs of my Life*, p. 134 [*Autobiographies*, p. 267].
159. Craddock (ed.), *English Essays of Edward Gibbon*, p. 91.
160. Gibbon, *Memoirs of my Life*, pp. 210–11 [*Autobiographies*, p. 249].
161. Craddock (ed.), *English Essays of Edward Gibbon* p. 115.
162. [S. Parr (ed).]*Tracts by Warburton and a Warburtonian*, (1789) pp. 219–20.
163. A comparison of the arguments used by Collins (*A Scheme of Literal Prophecy considered*, 1725) and by Gibbon ('To Richard Hurd', [c. Aug. 1772], *The Letters of Edward Gibbon*, ed. J.E. Norton (London, 1956), I, pp. 327–39) suggests that Gibbon had not seen Collins' work. Gibbon possessed a copy of Collins' *Discourse of Free Thinking* and all the works of Middleton, but apparently no other deist work; nor does he cite any other such work in his own writings. Collins' scholarship had been (unfairly, as Mr Torrey shows) denigrated by Bentley in 1733. Sir Isaac Newton's *Observations upon Daniel and the Apocalypse* had reasserted the traditional position.
164. Hurd first discovered that the letter was from Gibbon in 1796 when he saw it printed in Gibbon's *Miscellaneous Works*. He then wrote an Appendix to his lecture in which he confidently prophesied that Gibbon would soon be left without a single admirer. In his correspondence with Warburton Hurd invariably treats Gibbon with contempt.
165. Gibbon's biographer, D.M. Low, totally ignores the letter to Hurd and adopts (from Cotter Morrison) the psychological interpretation of the essay against Warburton: *Edward Gibbon* (London, 1937), p. 205. Even Mr Giarrizzo, whose work on Gibbon, *Edward Gibbon e la cultura europea del Settecento* (Naples, 1954), shows most awareness of intellectual history, leaves this point untouched. [But not Gibbon's most recent and authoritative biographer, Patricia B. Craddock, *Young Edward Gibbon, Gentleman of Letters* (Baltimore and London, 1982), pp. 276–80, on the *Critical Observations*; she too, however, ignores the letter to Hurd, mentioning it only in passing in her second volume, *Edward Gibbon, Luminous Historian 1772–1794* (Baltimore and London, 1989), p. 13.]
166. For the general convention of anonymity see Mossner, *The Life of David Hume* (Oxford, 1954; 2nd edn, 1980), p. 113. Anonymity was not merely, or necessarily, for protection – often it was very quickly pierced: it also conventionally allowed greater freedom of expression, as explicitly stated by Middleton, *MW*, III, p. 195. He makes the same defence in his letter to Archbishop Potter.
167. Gibbon, *The Decline and Fall of the Roman Empire*, Everyman edition (London, 1910), I, pp. 29, 31 [edition by David Womersley, Allen Lane (London, 1994), I, pp. 56–59, ch. 2, nn. 6, 8].
168. *Ibid.*, I, pp. 430, 442, 486 [ed. Womersley I, pp. 446, 457, 499].
169. *Ibid.*, I, pp. 460, 499 [ed. Womersley, I, pp. 473, 512].
170. Gibbon, *Memoirs of my Life*, p. 61 [*Autobiographies*, p. 88].
171. See Knowles' preface to *Letters between John Lord Hervey and Dr Middleton concerning the Roman Senate* (London, 1778).
172. Note by Heberden in BL Add. MS 32458 ff. 185–86. There are several other copies of these extracts in various collections: e.g. Cole MSS, BL Add. MS 5846, Ellenborough MSS (Edmund Law's copy), Stowe MS 305 f. 306 ('communicated to the Rev. W. Talbot of Kineton in Warwickshire'), etc.
173. BL Add. MS 5846 f. 12.
174. Thus Leslie Stephen based his censure on Middleton's statement that he would like some preferment as a return for his assent to the Thirty-Nine Articles, to which 'no man of sense can agree' (Middleton to Hervey, 13 Sept. 1736). But Middleton had written openly that 'Popery, Methodism and Infidelity' had been encouraged by 'certain articles professed and imposed by our Church' (*MW*, II, p. 258). To have subscribed to the Articles as a formality in order to obtain a benefice in the Church does not seem an unusual act, although Middleton was perhaps unusual in feeling scruples about it. Indeed, many of the university clergy, in the generation after Middleton, shared his dislike of the Articles and sought to replace them by assent to a more general formula. See Winstanley, *Unreformed Cambridge*, pp. 303ff.

175. [L. Stephen, 'Conyers Middleton', *DNB*.]
176. Gibbon, *Vindication, Miscellaneous Works*, IV, p. 606 [Craddock edn, *English Essays*, p. 288].
177. Gibbon, *Miscellaneous Works*, IV, pp. 588–89 [Craddock edn, *English Essays*, p. 277].
178. *Letters of Edward Gibbon*, III, p. 216 [to Lord Sheffield, 5 Feb. 1791].
179. *Letters of Edward Gibbon*, II, p. 321 [to Joseph Priestley, 28 Jan. 1783].
180. *Decline and Fall*, V, p. 237 [ed. Womersley, III, p. 178].
181. [On Gibbon's debt to Middleton, see now also: Joseph M. Levine, 'Edward Gibbon and the Johannine Comma' in his *The Autonomy of History: Truth and Method from Erasmus to Gibbon* (Chicago, 1999), pp. 157–240; and David Womersley, *Gibbon and the 'Watchmen of the Holy City': The Historian and his Reputation* (Oxford, 2002).]
182. Trevelyan, *Life and Letters of Macaulay*, II, pp. 385–86n.
183. [Macaulay to Macvey Napier, 27 Feb. 1843, *Letters of T.B. Macaulay*, ed. T. Pinney, IV (Cambridge, 1977), p. 107.]

Chapter 6: David Hume, Historian
This essay was written as a review of Giuseppe Giarrizzo, *David Hume politico e storico* (Turin, 1962), and was first published in *History and Theory* 3,3 (1964), pp. 381–89.

1. Giuseppe Giarrizzo, *David Hume politico e storico* (Turin, 1962) – the book under review in this essay; preceded by *Edward Gibbon e la cultura europea del Settecento* (Naples, 1954), and 'Fra Protestantesimo e deismo: le origini della moderna storiografia inglese sul cristianesimo primitivo . . . C. Middleton (1683–1750)', in *Ricerche di storia religiosa*, I, 1 (Rome, 1954), pp. 151–99.
2. I have dealt with this subject in my essay 'Scotland and the Puritan Revolution' in *Historical Essays Presented to David Ogg*, ed. H.E. Bell and R.L. Ollard (London, 1963) [reprinted in H.R. Trevor-Roper, *Religion, the Reformation and Social Change* (London, 1967)].
3. Sir Alexander Murray of Stanhope, *The True Interest of Great Britain . . .* (London, 1740).
4. When did Hume decide, or was any 'decision' necessary? Giarrizzo regards such a question as 'futile' and dismisses the reasonings of Mr Mossner on this, as on other points, with contemptuous asperity. Most students of Hume will feel too grateful to Mossner to relish Giarrizzo's adjectives, which he does not stay to support by reasoning.
5. Not that Hume had any illusions about the real character of Mary Queen of Scots. See his agreeable letter to Robertson on that subject, and his editor's equally agreeable note, in *Letters of David Hume*, ed. J.Y.T. Greig (Oxford, 1932), I, pp. 299–300.

Chapter 7: The Idea of The Decline and Fall of the Roman Empire
Originally published in *The Age of Enlightenment*, Studies Presented to Theodore Besterman, edited by W.H. Barber, J.H. Brumfitt, R.A. Leigh, R. Shackleton and S.S.B. Taylor, published for the University Court of the University of St Andrews (Edinburgh, 1967), pp. 413–30.

1. [*Autobiography of Edward Gibbon*, as originally edited by Lord Sheffield, World's Classics edition (Oxford, 1907), p. 160; *The Autobiographies of Edward Gibbon*, ed. John Murray (London, 1896), Memoir E, p. 302.]
2. [An allusion to Trevor-Roper's earlier assault on Toynbee's historical method and philosophy: 'Arnold Toynbee's Millennium', *Encounter* 7 (1957), pp. 14–28.]
3. S.T. Coleridge, *Table Talk*, ed. H.N. Coleridge (New York, 1835), II, p. 118.
4. [*Autobiography*, pp. 156–59; *Autobiographies*, Memoir C, p. 267.]
5. Having edited and published the autobiography and the other miscellaneous works of Gibbon, Lord Sheffield placed the Gibbon MSS among his private papers and, by his will, instructed his heirs to keep them private. They became public in 1896 when the third (and last) Lord Sheffield sold them to the British Museum.

6. *Gibbon's Journey from Geneva to Rome: His Journal from 20 April to 2 October 1764*, ed. Georges A. Bonnard (London and Edinburgh, 1961), pp. 6, 18.

7. G. Giarrizzo, *Edward Gibbon e la cultura europea del settecento* (Naples, 1954), p. 194; cf. G. Falco, *La Polemica sul medio evo* (Turin, 1933 [repr. Naples, 1974]).

8. See *The Letters of David Hume*, ed. J.Y.T. Greig (Oxford, 1932), II, pp. 104, 208, 269, 310, etc.

9. The last detail comes from Boswell's diary. See Boswell, *The Ominous Years 1774–6* (London, 1963), pp. 264, 337.

10. [*Autobiography*, p. 85; *Autobiographies*, Memoir B, p. 152, Memoir C, pp. 239–40.]

11. [*Autobiography*, p. 75; *Autobiographies*, Memoir C, p. 142.]

12. Edward Gibbon, *The Decline and Fall of the Roman Empire*, Everyman edition, with additional notes by O.S. Smeaton, 6 vols (London, 1910), VI, p. 91n. [Subsequent reprints of the Everyman edition followed this pagination, until the 1993–94 edition, to which Trevor-Roper contributed a new introduction. For scholarly and reading purposes the best edition is now that by David Womersley (London, 1994). This abandoned the earlier editorial practice of adding to or correcting Gibbon's notes, but added an invaluable Bibliographical Index. Hereafter cited as: ed. Womersley, III, p. 612: ch. lviii, n. 139.]

13. *Decline and Fall*, VI, p. 207, n. 3 [ed. Womersley, III, p. 728, ch. lxi, n. 69]; *The Letters of Edward Gibbon*, ed. J.E. Norton (London, 1956), II, p. 100: Gibbon to Adam Ferguson, 1 April 1776.

14. Boswell, *Life of Johnson* (1826 edn), I, p. 373, II, pp. 177, 217–18. Gibbon, *Decline and Fall*, VI, p. 293n [ed. Womersley, III, p. 810: ch. lxiv, n. 40.]

15. Pietro Giannone, *Vita scritta da lui medesimo*, ed. Sergio Bertelli (Milan, 1960), pp. 10–15.

16. *Letters on the Use and Study of History* (Basle, 1791), pp. 103–4, quoted by Harold L. Bond in *The Literary Art of Edward Gibbon* (Oxford, 1960), p. 13. The preface to Bolingbroke's work is dated in France in 1735. Montesquieu's *Considérations* was published in 1735.

17. Dugald Stewart, 'Account of the Life and Writings of William Robertson' in *The Works of William Robertson D.D.* (1821), pp. 61–62.

18. Giannone's direct influence has been shown by Signor Giarrizzo, *Edward Gibbon e la cultura europea del settecento*, pp. 136, 209. For Gibbon's admiration for Giannone, see his *Autobiography* [p. 76; *Autobiographies*, Memoir B, p. 143, Memoir C, p. 235].

19. *Decline and Fall*, VI, p. 543n; [ed. Womersley, III, p. 1,057: ch. lxx, n. 89].

20. [*Letters of David Hume*, II, pp. 170–71: Hume to Gibbon, 24 Oct. 1767; Gibbon, *Autobiography*, pp. 164–66; *Autobiographies*, Memoir C, p. 277. Between February 1767 and January 1768 Hume was under-secretary in the Northern Department, whose responsibilities included Canada.]

21. Bond, *Literary Art*, pp. 19–20.

22. [*Letters of Gibbon*, I, pp. 222–23: Gibbon to Hume, 25 Oct. 1767.]

23. This un-Englishness of Gibbon is brought out in many ways: his discomfort in the contemporary English literary world (as shown in Boswell's *Life of Johnson*); his complete independence of any English historical tradition; his apparently genuine failure to foresee the reaction in England to the *Decline and Fall*; his ultimate return – to the astonishment even of close friends like Lord Sheffield – to Lausanne. If he still thought in French in 1767, he was again thinking in French after 1783, and regrets, in his *Autobiography* [p. 204; *Autobiographies*, p. 333], that the language of his last two volumes may have been invaded by 'Gallic idioms'. It is some reflection both on the fundamental cosmopolitanism of Gibbon and on the fundamental insularity of his fellow-Englishmen that some of his best interpreters have been foreigners (I think of Georges A. Bonnard, G. Falco, A. Momigliano, G. Giarrizzo), while, as Signor Giarrizzo writes, 'nel mondo anglosassone e fuori, Gibbon è pretesto per le più banali esemplificazioni metodologiche e le chiaccherate più insulse' [*Edward Gibbon e la cultura europea del settecento*, p. 10].

24. [*Decline and Fall*, VI, p. 570; ed. Womersley, III, p. 1,085.]

25. [*Autobiography*, p. 205; *Autobiographies*, Memoir E, pp. 333–34.]

Chapter 8: Gibbon and the Publication of The Decline and Fall of the Roman Empire, 1776–1976

Originally delivered as a lecture at the University of Chicago Law School, and published in *The Journal of Law and Economics* 19,3 (1976), pp. 489–505. The notes have occasionally been amended to reflect the author's original intentions.

1. Richard Porson, *Letters to Mr Archdeacon Travis, in Answer to his Defence of the Three Heavenly Witnesses, I John v. 7* (1790), pp. xxviii–xxxi; and Table Talk, 15 Aug. 1833, in *The Complete Works of Samuel Taylor Coleridge*, ed. W.G.T. Shedd (London, 1856), VI, p. 475.

2. Horace Walpole to William Mason, 27 Jan. 1781, in *Horace Walpole's Correspondence*, ed. W.S. Lewis, Yale edition (London, 1955), Vol. 29, pp. 95–99.

3. Lytton Strachey, *Portraits in Miniature and Other Essays* (1931), p. 163.

4. Giuseppe Giarrizzo, *Edward Gibbon e la cultura europea del Settecento* (Naples, 1954).

5. Edward Gibbon to J.B. Holroyd, 6 June 1776, in *The Letters of Edward Gibbon*, ed. J.E. Norton (London, 1956), II, p. 111.

6. Edward Gibbon to Dorothea Gibbon, 15 March 1776, in *Letters of Edward Gibbon* II, pp. 99–100.

7. Gibbon to Georges Deyverdun, 7 May 1776, in *Letters of Edward Gibbon*, II, pp. 107–8 (translation by the author).

8. James Boswell, *The Life of Samuel Johnson LL.D* (1791), II, p. 27.

9. Edward Gibbon, *A Vindication of Some Passages in the Fifteenth and Sixteenth Chapters of the History of the Decline and Fall of the Roman Empire* (1779), p. 2 [reprinted in Patricia B. Craddock (ed.), *The English Essays of Edward Gibbon* (Oxford, 1972), pp. 229–313, quotation at p. 231]. See also Henry Davis, *An Examination of the Fifteenth and Sixteenth Chapters of Mr. Gibbon's History of the Decline and Fall of the Roman Empire* (1778), p. ii.

10. *Supra* note 9.

11. *Vindication*, p. 10 [ed. Craddock, p. 236]; *Autobiography of Edward Gibbon*, ed. Lord Sheffield, World's Classics edition (Oxford, 1907), p 186 [*The Autobiographies of Edward Gibbon*, ed. John Murray (London, 1896), pp. 316–17n.]

12. Edward Gibbon, *The History of the Decline and Fall of the Roman Empire*, ed. J.B. Bury (London, 1905), ch. lxvii, VII, p. 139, n. 15 [in the edition by David Womersley (London, 1994), III, p. 916, note 13.]

13. Gibbon to Adam Ferguson, 1 April 1776, in *Letters of Edward Gibbon*, II, p. 100.

14. *Autobiography* p. 95 [*Autobiographies*, p. 166]; and David Hume, *The History of Great Britain. Volume I. The Reigns of James I and Charles I* (Edinburgh, 1754), 'Appendix to the Reign of James I'; subsequently *The History of England from the Invasion of Julius Caesar to the Revolution in 1688* (London, 1778) in the Liberty Fund edition by W.B. Todd (Indianapolis, 1983), V, p. 154.

15. See *The Rambler* 122 (18 May 1751), Yale edition of the works of Samuel Johnson, IV *The Rambler* (New Haven CT and London 1969), pp. 286–91.

16. *Decline and Fall*, ch. lxiv, VII, p. 24, n. 66 [ed. Womersley, III, pp. 810–11, n. 41].

17. Boswell, *Life of Samuel Johnson* (1791), I, p. 231.

18. *Decline and Fall*, ch. lxx, VII, p. 296, n. 101 [ed. Womersley, III, p. 1,057, n. 89].

19. *Autobiography*, p. 32 [*Autobiographies*, pp. 57–58, 121].

20. *Autobiography*, p. 33 [*Autobiographies*, pp. 59, 122].

21. *Autobiography*, pp. 84–85 [*Autobiographies*, pp. 239–40].

22. [Not in Sheffield's edition, but in *Autobiographies*, p. 152.]

23. *Autobiography*, p. 75 [*Autobiographies*, p. 234].

24. Edward Gibbon, *Essai sur l'étude de la littérature* (1761) [repr. in *The Miscellaneous Works of Edward Gibbon*, ed. John, Lord Sheffield, 5 vols (London, 1814), IV, pp. 1–93].

25. See, for example, *Decline and Fall*, ch. x, I, p. 247, n. 41; and ch. xliv, IV, p. 469 and n. 96 [ed. Womersley, I, p. 262, n. 37; II, p. 805, and n. 95].

26. *Decline and Fall*, ch. lviii, VI, p. 319, n. 147 [ed. Womersley, III, p. 612, n. 139].

27. *Decline and Fall*, ch. iii, I, p. 78 [ed. Womersley, I, p. 103].
28. '. . . which age [after Domitian] for temporal respects was the most happy and flourishing that ever the Roman Empire, which then was a model of the world, enjoyed.' Francis Bacon, *The Works of Francis Bacon*, ed. James Spedding (London, 1859), I, p. 303.
29. *Decline and Fall*, ch. i, I, p. 10 (emphasis added) [ed. Womersley, I, p. 39].
30. *Decline and Fall*, ch. iii, I, p. 82 [ed. Womersley, I, p. 107].
31. *Essai sur l'étude de la littérature*, p. 1 [*Miscellaneous Works*, IV, p. 1].
32. *Decline and Fall*, ch. xxxv, III, p. 480, and ch. xxxviii, IV, pp. 161 [ed. Womersley, II, pp. 356, 509].
33. *Decline and Fall*, ch. lxi, VI, p. 446 [ed. Womersley, III, p. 728].
34. *Decline and Fall*, ch. xxxviii, IV, pp. 164, 166, n. 8 [ed. Womersley, pp. 512, 514, n. 8].
35. David Hume to Gibbon, 24 Oct. 1767, in *The Letters of David Hume*, ed. J.Y.T. Greig (Oxford, 1932), II, pp. 170–71.
36. *Decline and Fall*, ch. xxxviii, IV, p. 169 [ed. Womersley, II, p. 516].
37. *Decline and Fall*, ch. ii, I, p. 31, n. 8 [ed. Womersley, I, p. 59, n. 8].
38. *Autobiography*, p. 2 [*Autobiographies*, p. 418].
39. *Decline and Fall*, ch. xv, II, pp. 37–38; [ed. Womersley, I, p. 481].
40. Gibbon to Lord Sheffield, 30 May 1792, in *Letters of Edward Gibbon*, III, p. 263.
41. *Autobiography*, p. 78 [*Autobiographies*, p. 145].
42. Georges A. Bonnard, *Gibbon's Journey from Geneva to Rome. His Journal from 20 April to 2 October 1764* (London and Edinburgh, 1961), p. 31.
43. *Decline and Fall*, ch. lxviii, VII, p. 197 [ed. Womersley, III, pp. 966–67].
44. *Decline and Fall*, ch. xxxvii, IV, pp. 57, 62, 66–67, 74; ch. xxxviii, IV, pp. 162–63 [ed. Womersley, II, pp. 411, 416, 420, 428, 510].
45. *Autobiography*, p. 172 [*Autobiographies*, p. 285].
46. *Decline and Fall*, ch. xlv, V, p. 32 [ed. Womersley, II, p. 874].
47. *Decline and Fall*, ch. xlix, V, p. 264 [ed. Womersley, III, p. 105].
48. *Autobiography*, pp. 39–40, 138–39 [*Autobiographies*, pp. 74, 209]; *Decline and Fall*, ch. xxxii, III, p. 358, n. 1; [ed. Womersley, II, p. 237, n. 1].
49. *Decline and Fall*, ch. xxxviii, IV, p. 104, n. 25 [ed. Womersley, II, p. 456, n. 23].
50. *Decline and Fall*, ch. xv, II, p. 2 [ed. Womersley, I, pp. 446–47].
51. *Autobiography*, p. 180 [*Autobiographies*, p. 311].
52. David Hume to Gibbon, 18 March 1776, in *Letters of David Hume*, II, pp. 309–10.
53. *Autobiography*, p. 185 [*Autobiographies*, p. 316].
54. Gibbon to Joseph Priestley, 28 Jan. 1783, in *Letters of Edward Gibbon*, II, pp. 320–21.
55. *The Collected Letters of Thomas and Jane Welsh Carlyle*, ed. Charles Richard Sanders and others (Durham, N.C., 1970), I, pp. 115, 120–21; II, pp. 467, 314: quoted passages in letters from Thomas Carlyle to James Johnston, 20 Nov. 1817; to Robert Mitchell, 16 Feb. 1818; to John A. Carlyle, 11 Nov. 1823; to Jane Welsh, 26 March 1823.

Chapter 9: Gibbon's Last Project

Originally published in *Edward Gibbon. Bicentenary Essays*, edited by David Womersley, with the assistance of John Burrow and John Pocock, as a volume of *Studies on Voltaire and the Eighteenth Century* 355 (1997), pp. 405–19.

The principal sources for this article are *The Letters of Edward Gibbon*, ed. J.E. Norton (London, 1956), III, and letters to Gibbon from Lord Sheffield and Pinkerton, in *The Private Letters of Edward Gibbon*, ed. R.E. Prothero (London, 1896); *The Miscellaneous Works of Edward Gibbon*, ed. John, Lord Sheffield (London, 1814), especially II, pp. 490–94 and IV, pp. 559–90; John Nichols, *Illustrations of Literary History in the Eighteenth Century*, V (London, 1828); and *The Literary Correspondence of John Pinkerton*, ed. Dawson Turner (London, 1830).

1. Pinkerton expressed his belief in the authenticity of Ossian's *Fingal* in his *Select Scotish Ballads* (London, 1781) and recanted it in his *Ancient Scotish Poems* (London, 1786).

2. For Pinkerton's relations with Walpole see their correspondence in *The Correspondence of Horace Walpole*, ed. W.S. Lewis et al. (New Haven, CT, 1937–83), XVI, pp. 251–327, 357–58; also XXXIII, pp. 190–92, XLII, pp. 279–80; and John Pinkerton, *Walpoliana* (London, 1797), preface.

3. Quoted from memory; reference lost.

4. *The History of the Decline and Fall of the Roman Empire*, ed. David Womersley (London, 1994), I, p. 197, n. 110.

5. J. Pinkerton, *An Enquiry into the History of Scotland* (London, 1789), pp. xxxvi, 60, 122–24, 200. Gibbon's reference to the *Lives of the Saints* as historical sources is in *Decline and Fall*, II, p. 335, n. 34. As always, his words are carefully chosen: 'the *ancient* [his italics] legendaries deserve some regard, as they are obliged to connect their fables with the real history of their times'; cf. his remarks on the Bollandist collections (*Decline and Fall*, II, p. 292, n. 46).

6. Nicholas, *Illustrations*, V, pp. 676–77; *Literary Correspondence*, I, p. 328; *Miscellaneous Works*, II, p. 494 and III, p. 573.

7. *Decline and Fall*, II, p. 451, n. 1.

8. Nichols, *Illustrations*, V, p. 665.

9. Jane Norton, from whom I tremble to dissent, assumes that the initiative came from Pinkerton, that Pinkerton approached Gibbon, and that Pinkerton's emphatic statements that Gibbon sought him out – that he 'was pleased to *call me in*' as 'coadjutor in a scheme he meditated' (Nichols, *Illustrations*, V, p. 674), that he '*sought* my acquaintance', that the project was '*solely his*' (*Literature Correspondence*, I, pp. 347 and 343), etc. – were purely tactical, being written after Gibbon's death, when Pinkerton feared that he would be landed with the project without Gibbon as its sponsor (Norton, p.179). But Pinkerton had made similar statements before Gibbon's death: e.g. to Gibbon himself on 23 July 1793 (*Miscellaneous Works*, II, p. 491), and to Thomas Astle on 6 December 1793 (see below, n. 12); nor does it seem likely that Pinkerton, after his earlier impertinence, would have ventured to approach Gibbon, whom he did not know and who, at that time, had given no public indication of personal interest in such a plan.

　　Miss Norton bases her view on the date, 1792, given to Pinkerton's proposed prospectus, as printed by Lord Sheffield in 1814 (*Miscellaneous Works*, III, p. 582). This, she suggests, proves that Pinkerton had worked out the whole plan and prepared the document before he saw any prospect of co-operation with Gibbon, who was then still in Lausanne. But she admits that if this date is erroneous, her case fails. Surely it is erroneous. Pinkerton himself, writing to Gibbon on 23 July 1793, says that if Gibbon consents to his suggestions of detail, '*I shall begin to prepare* materials for the Prospectus'. His prospectus therefore had not been begun by that date. (My italics throughout.)

　　Nothing of this, of course, alters the fact that Pinkerton had been thinking along these lines since (at least) 1788.

10. Nichols, *Illustrations*, V, p. 676; *Literary Correspondence*, I, pp. 343, 347; *Letters of Gibbon*, III, pp. 340–42; *Miscellaneous Works*, II, pp. 490–92. Pinkerton's comment, 'Too true. Peccavi', is in a letter to Lord Buchan (*Literary Correspondence*, I, p. 351).

11. *Miscellaneous Works*, III, p. 579; Nichols, *Illustrations*, V, p. 676.

12. Pinkerton's letter to Astle, of 6 Dec. 1793, is in the Beinecke Library at Yale University (Osborne files, Pinkerton 31.109). I am indebted to Dr David Womersley for my knowledge of it. Astle's reply is printed in *Literary Correspondence*, I, p. 337.

13. This point was made to Pinkerton by the Roman Catholic antiquary Charles Butler (*Literary Correspondence*, I, p. 341).

14. *Literary Correspondence*, I, pp. 436, 449, 454; *Miscellaneous Works*, III, pp. 578–81.

15. *Literary Correspondence*, II, pp. 455–56.

16. *Literary Correspondence*, II, p. 459; Nichols, *Illustrations*, V, p. 673; [Sir Walter Scott,] 'The Ancient Caledonians' (review of Joseph Ritson, *Annals of the Caledonians, Picts and Scots*), *Quarterly Review* 41 (1829), p. 138.

17. See Pinkerton's letter to Lord Buchan, *Literary Correspondence*, I, p. 351.

18. *The Letters of Sir William Jones*, ed. Garland Cannon (Oxford, 1970), I, pp. 278–81.

19. Nichols, *Illustrations*, V, p. 676n.; *Literary Correspondence*, II, p. 449 (note by the editor, Dawson Turner). This account of the revival of the project is based on the introduction by Thomas Duffus Hardy to Petrie's volume *Monumenta historica Britannica* (London, 1848).

20. George Dempster to Lord Melville, 8 June 1813, in *Literary Correspondence*, I, p. 408.

Chapter 10: The Romantic Movement and the Study of History

Given as the John Coffin Memorial Lecture to the University of London on 17 February 1969, and published as a separate pamphlet by the Athlone Press, the University of London (London, 1969).

1. *The Letters of Edward Gibbon*, ed. J.E. Norton (Oxford, 1956), III, p. 216: Gibbon to Lord Sheffield, 5 Feb. 1791.

2. Leopold von Ranke, *Zur Eigenen Lebensgeschichte*, ed. Alfred Dove (Leipzig, 1890), p. 47.

3. Gibbon, *The History of the Decline and Fall of the Roman Empire*, ch. VI, ed. J.B. Bury, (London, 1905), I, p. 129 [ed. Womersley, I, p. 152].

4. *The Letters of David Hume*, ed. J.Y.T. Greig (Oxford, 1932), II, p. 310: Hume to Gibbon, 18 March 1776.

5. J.G. Herder's essay 'Über Ossian und die Lieder alter Völker', was published in *Deutsche Arte und Kunst* (1773).

6. See Paul Lieder, 'Scott and Scandinavian Literature', *Smith College Studies in Modern Languages* (Northampton, Mass.), 2 (Oct. 1920), pp. 8–57.

7. I have dealt with this subject more fully in my essay 'The Scottish Enlightenment', *Studies on Voltaire and the Eighteenth Century* 58 (Institut et Musée Voltaire, Geneva, 1967). [See above, pp. 17–33.]

8. See the enjoyable account by Scott's old tutor, James Mitchell, in J.G. Lockhart, *Memoirs of Sir Walter Scott* (Library of English Classics, London, 1900), I, pp. 87–94. Mitchell wasted his time, on the occasion of this meeting, trying to enlist Scott's patronage for 'the strict and evangelical party in the Church of Scotland'.

9. Edward Gibbon, *Miscellaneous Works* (1837 edn), pp. 836–42 [1814 edn, III, pp. 559–77]. George IV, who had a delicate taste in such matters, chose, as his gift to Scott, the fifteen folio volumes of Montfaucon's *Antiquities* (Lockhart, *Memoirs*, IV, p. 152).

10. J.A. Froude, *Thomas Carlyle; A History of the First Forty Years of his Life* (new edn, London 1890), II, pp. 321–22.

11. Lockhart, *Memoirs*, III, p. 84.

12. McCrie's (anonymous) review of *Old Mortality*, 75,000 words long, was published in three successive numbers of the *Edinburgh Christian Instructor* (Jan.–March 1817), and was afterwards reprinted, both as a separate book and in *The Miscellaneous Writings of Thomas McCrie* (1841). The editor of the *Christian Instructor* was the Rev. Andrew Thomson: his letter to McCrie is quoted in *Life of Thomas McCrie DD, by his Son, the Revd. Thomas McCrie* (Edinburgh, 1840), p. 221. Scott replied (anonymously) in the *Quarterly Review*, April 1817. See also his (anonymous) review of Charles Kirkpatrick Sharpe's edition of James Kirkton's *Secret History of the Church of Scotland* in the *Quarterly Review* in 1818. Anyone who examines the matter will see that, although he made errors of detail, Scott used more and better sources than McCrie, and used them more critically and historically. McCrie (like Macaulay after him) ignored the best available source and relied exclusively on what Paget very properly described as 'the trash of Wodrow'. See John Paget, *The New Examen* (1861 [repr. The Haworth Press, 1934]): 'Viscount Dundee'.

13. In the library of his house in Edinburgh Scott had only one picture: a portrait of Claverhouse, 'that beautiful and melancholy visage, worthy of the most pathetic dreams of romance'. Lockhart, *Memoirs*, III, p. 86.

14. The Greek ballads were collected and published by Claude Charles Fauriel (*Chants populaires de la Grèce moderne*, Paris, 1824, 1825). A German translation by Wilhelm Müller appeared at Leipzig in 1825. For the Serbian ballads see below, p. 185.

15. The MS of the *Nibelungenlied* had been discovered in 1755, in the library of Hohenems, in the Upper Rhineland, by J.H. Obereit. It was published in 1756–57 by J.J. Bodmer.
16. 'Das Wichtigste ist das Ergebnis plötzlicher Lichtblike und Divinationen', Niebuhr wrote in a letter of 20 Dec. 1829 (*Lebensnachrichten über B. G. Niebuhr . . .*, Hamburg, 1838–39), III, pp. 248ff.
17. Jacobus Perizonius, *Animadversiones Historicae* (Amsterdam, 1685), caput VI.
18. Niebuhr, *The History of Rome*, trans. J.C. Hare and Connop Thirlwall (Cambridge, 1828), I, pp. 212–18.
19. Charles Beard, *The Reformation of the 16th Century* (1883, repr. Ann Arbor, 1962), p. 346.
20. Fritz Renker, *Niebuhr und die Romantik* (Leipzig, 1935) seeks to dissociate Niebuhr from the romantic movement by emphasising his classical interests and his sound Protestant views, as opposed to what Niebuhr himself called 'das Katholicisieren und die Überschwenglichkeit der romantischen Schule'. By that definition Scott was not a romantic either.
21. Ranke, *Zur Eigenen Lebensgeschichte*, p. 31; *Das Briefwerk*, ed. W.P. Fuchs (Hamburg, 1949), pp. 69–70; *Neue Briefe*, ed. B. Hoeft and H. Herzfeld (Hamburg, 1949), pp. 264, 484, 737.
22. E.g. Augustin Thierry, whose *Histoire de la conquête de l'Angleterre par les Normands* (1825), as Eduard Fueter says (*Geschichte der neureren Historiographie* [Berlin, 1925], p. 445), could hardly have been written without Scott's *Ivanhoe* (1820).
23. Ranke, *Zur Eigenen Lebensgeschichte*, p. 61.
24. Ranke, *Geschichten der romanischen und germanischen Völker von 1494 bis 1514* (1824, 3 vols Leipzig, 1885), Preface.
25. Ranke, *Zur Eigenen Lebensgeschichte*, p. 64; *Briefwerk*, pp. 166, 174, 204, 269; *Neue Briefe*, p. 153. For Kopitar and Vuk see D. Subotić, *Yugoslav Popular Ballads* (Cambridge, 1932), p. 9.
26. Ranke, *Zur Eigenen Lebensgeschichte*, p. 621.
27. For Macaulay's strong disapproval of Scott's way of life see Sir G.O. Trevelyan, *Life and Letters of Lord Macaulay* (World's Classics edn, London, 1932 [repr. Oxford, 1961]), I, p. 438. The complacent panegyrist of the bourgeois virtues and suburban villas of provincial England naturally deplored the genial feudal extravagance of the new laird of Abbotsfield. Scott (in Macaulay's eyes) should have settled down in Edinburgh and been a good, steady, solvent whig.
28. It is published in the Albany edition of *The Works of Lord Macaulay* (1900), VII [or in the Edinburgh edition (London, 1897), V].
29. Trevelyan, *Life and Letters*, I, pp. 170–71.
30. *Ibid.*, I, p. 343.
31. *Ibid.*, I, p. 181.
32. *Ibid.*, I, pp. 404–5.
33. Niebuhr, *Roman History*, I, p. 220.
34. Quoted in Trevelyan, *Life and Letters*, II, p. 172.
35. J.W. Croker in the *Quarterly Review* 84 (March 1849), p. 551. The historiographer royal was G.P.R. James, an imitator of Scott. He was the author of *Richelieu*, *Darnley* and over sixty other historical novels.
36. Trevelyan, *Life and Letters*, II, pp. 55–56.
37. On the obliging Rev. R.S. Hawker of Morwenstow, see the article in the *DNB*.
38. Thomas Carlyle, *Critical and Miscellaneous Essays*, 'Sir Walter Scott' [5 vols, (London, 1899), IV, p. 77].

Chapter 11: Lord Macaulay: The History of England

Originally published as an Introduction to: Lord Macaulay, *The History of England*, edited and abridged with an Introduction by Hugh Trevor-Roper (Washington Square Press, 1968, repr. Penguin: Harmondsworth, 1979), pp. 7–42.

1. [George Otto Trevelyan, *The Life and Letters of Lord Macaulay* (1876, repr. Oxford, 1961), II, p. 317n.: letter to Edward Everett [7 May 1849]; also in *The Letters of Thomas Babington Macaulay*, ed. T. Pinney, V (Cambridge, 1981), p. 52.]

2. G.S.H. Fox-Strangways, 6th Earl of Ilchester (ed.), *Elizabeth Lady Holland to her Son 1821–1845* (London, 1946), p. 108n.

3. This essay was published in the *Times Literary Supplement* on 1 May 1969.

4. Earl of Ilchester, *Elizabeth Lady Holland*, p. 184.

5. [Trevelyan, *Life and Letters*, I, pp. 398, 409: letters to Thomas Flower Ellis, 8 Feb., 30 Dec. 1835. And now in *The Letters of T.B. Macaulay*, III (Cambridge, 1976), pp. 129, 158.]

6. [Macaulay to Macvey Napier, 5 Nov. 1841, 18 Jan. 1843, also 22 Feb., 11 Aug. 1845, *Letters of T.B. Macaulay*, IV (Cambridge, 1977), pp. 15, 96, 242, 264.]

7. 'History', *Edinburgh Review*, 1828 [*The Works of Lord Macaulay* (Edinburgh edn, London, 1897), V, pp. 157–58].

8. Maria Edgeworth lamented that in Macaulay's first volume 'there is no mention of Sir Walter Scott throughout the work, even in places where it seems impossible that the historian could resist paying the becoming tribute which genius owes, and loves to pay, to genius' (letter to Dr Holland quoted in Trevelyan, *Life and Letters*, ch. XI, II, p. 172). Croker singled out 'the example and success of the author of *Waverley*' as the 'true source' of Macaulay's design (*Quarterly Review* 84 (March 1849), p. 551).

9. [Trevelyan, *Life and Letters*, I, pp. 442, 463, letter to Napier, 20 July 1838 (*Letters of T.B. Macaulay*, III, p. 252); Journal for 18 Dec. 1838.]

10. [Trevelyan, *Life and Letters*, II, pp. 204, 207, Journal, 7 Dec. 1849, 12 Jan. 1850.]

11. [Trevelyan, *Life and Letters*, II, p. 52, letter to Napier, 5 Nov. 1841; *Letters of T.B. Macaulay*, IV, p. 15.]

12. [Trevelyan, *Life and Letters*, II, p. 185, Journal, 27 Jan. 1849.]

13. [Trevelyan, *Life and Letters*, II, pp. 157–58, Journal, 8 Feb. 1849.]

14. [Trevelyan, *Life and Letters*, II, pp. 196, 213; Journal, 29 June 1849, 28 July 1850.]

15. Macaulay to H.S. Randall, 18 Jan. 1857; printed in H.M. Lydenberg, 'What Did Macaulay Say about America? Text of Four Letters to Henry S. Randall' (New York Publishing Library, 1925), p. 23. [Now in *The Letters of T.B. Macaulay*, VI (Cambridge, 1981), pp. 74–75.]

16. [G.O. Trevelyan, *The American Revolution* (London, 1899–1907); G.M. Trevelyan, *England under Queen Anne* (London, 1930–34), *History of England* (London, 1926), Book V: 'From Utrecht to Waterloo'.]

17. David Knowles, *Lord Macaulay 1800–1859*, a lecture (Cambridge, 1960).

18. [Trevelyan, *Life and Letters*, II, pp. 223–24 and note.]

19. On 26 June 1838 Macaulay wrote to Macvey Napier, the editor of the *Edinburgh Review*, that he was willing to be judged by his historical and political essays, 'but I have never written a page of criticism on poetry or the fine arts which I would not burn if I had the power' (*Letters of T.B. Macaulay*, III, p. 245).

20. See his essay 'Mill's Essay on Government', *Edinburgh Review*, 1829; also his letters to H.S. Randall cited above, note 15 [and in *Letters of T.B. Macaulay*, VI, pp. 94–96, 171–72, 186–87].

21. For Macaulay and Ranke see Sir Charles Firth, *A Commentary on Macaulay's History of England* (London, 1938), pp. 249–56.

22. *Quarterly Review* 84 (March 1849), p. 613.

23. [*Ibid.*, p. 608.]

24. [John Paget, *The New Examen* (1861, new edition, The Haworth Press, 1934), 'William Penn', p. 147.]

25. [Trevelyan, *Life and Letters*, II, pp. 185–86, 188–89; Journal for 2, 5 Feb. 1849. Firth, *A Commentary*, pp. 272–73].

26. *Edinburgh Review*, Oct. 1861.

27. [W.E. Gladstone, 'Lord Macaulay', *Quarterly Review* 142 (1876), pp. 17–18.]

28. [*Ibid.*, p. 12.]

29. [Trevelyan, *Life and Letters*, I, pp. 170–71.]
30. Essay, 'Mill's Essay on Government' [*Works of Lord Macaulay*, V, p. 270].
31. Essay, 'Sir James Mackintosh' [*Works of Lord Macaulay*, VI, p. 77].
32. S.R. Gardiner, *Cromwell's Place in History* (London, 1902), p. 17.
33. Lord Acton, *Letters to Mary Gladstone*, ed. H. Paul (London, 1904), pp. 173, 210.

Chapter 12: Thomas Carlyle's Historical Philosophy

Published in the *Times Literary Supplement*, 26 June 1981, pp. 731–34. It was published without references. An earlier, heavily corrected but still not final, typescript of the essay, retained in a file marked 'Carlyle', has some annotation, but it is by no means comprehensive. Rather than provide references which the author evidently did not think essential, I list the editions of Carlyle's works and other secondary works from which Trevor-Roper copied quotations and took his own notes, likewise kept in the preparatory file.

Thomas Carlyle, *The Early Letters of Thomas Carlyle*, ed. Charles Eliot Norton, 2 vols (London, 1886); *Critical and Miscellaneous Essays*, probably vols XV, XVI and XVII of the Ashburton edition of Carlyle's *Works* (London, 1887–94); *Sartor Resartus* (1831; in the Everyman Library edition with an introduction by W.H. Hudson, London, 1908); *The French Revolution* (London, 1837; apparently in the two-volume edition, London, 1869); *On Heroes, Hero-Worship and the Heroic in History* (London, 1840, in the Everyman edition, London, 1900); *Chartism* (London, 1840; edition used not identified); *Past and Present* (London, 1843, in the World's Classics edition by G.K. Chesterton, London and New York [1909]); *Oliver Cromwell's Letters and Speeches, with Elucidations by Thomas Carlyle* (London, 1845; edition used not identified); *The Life of John Sterling* (London, 1851); *History of Friedrich II of Prussia, Called Frederick the Great* (London, 1858–65), edited with an introduction by John Clive (Chicago, 1969); *Reminiscences*, ed. J.A Froude, 2 vols (London, 1881).

J.A. Froude, *Thomas Carlyle: A History of the First Forty Years of his Life 1795–1835*, 2 vols (London, 1882); and *Thomas Carlyle: A History of his Life in London 1834–1881*, 2 vols (London, 1885); Norwood Young, *Carlyle: His Rise and Fall* (London, 1927); H.J. Grierson, *Carlyle and Hitler* (Cambridge, 1933); Jacques Cabau, *Thomas Carlyle ou le Prométhée enchaîné. Essai sur la genèse de l'oeuvre de 1795 à 1834* (Paris, 1968).

Other works consulted include: W.C. Abbott (ed.), *The Writings and Speeches of Oliver Cromwell*, 4 vols (Cambridge, Mass., 1937–47); Lord Acton, *Letters to Mary Gladstone* (London, 1904), and *Essays on Church and State*, ed. D. Woodruff (London, 1952); Waldo Hilary Dunn, *James Anthony Froude: A Biography*, 2 vols (Oxford, 1961–63); *Hitler's Table Talk*, with an introductory essay by H.R. Trevor-Roper (London, 1953); G.M. Trevelyan, *Clio, a Muse; and Other Essays* (London, 1913).

Chapter 13: Jacob Burckhardt

Delivered as a 'Lecture on a Master Mind' at the British Academy on 11 December 1984, and published in *The Proceedings of the British Academy* 70 (1984), pp. 359–78. It was published without annotation. The following notes, which provide references for the quotations from Burckhardt's works and correspondence, are derived from annotation to the lectures on Burckhardt which Trevor-Roper gave at Oxford in the 1970s. They have all been inserted by the editor.

1. *The Letters of Jacob Burckhardt*, trans. and ed. Alexander Dru (London, 1955), pp. 49, 61: to Heinrich Schreiber, 15 Jan. 1840, Louise Burckhardt, 5 April 1841. Hereafter: *Letters*. They were the subject of a review essay by Trevor-Roper in the *New Statesman* (6 Aug. 1955), reprinted as 'The Faustian Historian: Jacob Burckhardt' in the author's *Historical Essays* (London, 1957), pp. 273–78.

2. *Letters*, p. 71: to Gottfried Kinkel, 13 June 1842.
3. *Letters*, p. 97: to H. Shauenburg, 28 Feb. 1846.
4. *Letters*, p. 158: to Friedrich Nietzsche, 25 Feb. 1874.
5. *Letters*, p. 152: to Von Preen, 28 June 1872.
6. Jacob Burckhardt, *Die Zeit Constantins des Grossen* (1853); J.G. Droysen, *Geschichte Alexanders des Grossen* (1833).
7. *The Age of Constantine the Great*, trans. Moses Hadas (London, 1949), pp. 225, 242–43.
8. *Der Cicerone* (Leipzig, 1854); translated as *The Cicerone: An Art Guide to Painting in Italy, for the Use of Travellers and Students*, trans. A.H. Clough (London, 1879). *Die Kultur der Renaissance in Italien* (Basel, 1860).
9. *The Civilisation of the Renaissance in Italy*, trans. S.G.C. Middlemore (1878), in the edition published by Phaidon (London, 1944), p. 2.
10. *Ibid.*, p. 261.
11. *Ibid.*, pp. 172–73, 181–83, 212, 326.
12. Jacob Burckhardt, *Baukunst der Renaissance in Italien* (1867).
13. Jacob Burckhardt, *Weltgeschichtliche Betrachtungen*, ed. Jacob Oeri (1905), in the edition by Werner Kaegi (Bern, 1941). New edition by Peter Ganz, as *Über das Studium der Geschichte. Der Text der 'Weltgeschichtliche Betrachtungen'* (Munich, 1982) (on which, Hugh Trevor-Roper, 'The Historical Spirit', *Times Literary Supplement*, 8 Oct. 1982, pp. 1,087–88).
14. *Letters*, p. 151: to Von Preen, 26 April 1872.
15. *Letters*, p. 129: to Friedrich Salomon, 15 Feb. 1863.
16. *Letters*, pp. 151–52, 207, 220: to Von Preen, 26 April 1872, 13 April 1882, 24 July 1889.
17. Werner Kaegi, *Jacob Burckhardt, eine Biographie*, 7 vols (Basel, 1947–82), VI, p. 125.
18. The quotation is translated from the Ganz edition of the *Weltgeschichtliche Betrachtungen: Über das Studium der Geschichte*, p. 182. See also *Weltgeschichtliche Betrachtungen*, ed. Kaegi, pp. 50–51, 67–68.
19. *The Age of Constantine*, pp. 323–25.
20. *Letters*, p. 157: to Von Preen, New Year's Eve 1872.
21. Friedrich Nietzsche, *Die Geburt der Tragödie aus dem Geist der Musik* (1872); Jacob Burckhardt, *Griechische Kulturgeschichte*, ed. J. Oeri, 4 vols (Berlin [1898–1902]). A substantial selection from the latter has been published as *The Greeks and Greek Civilisation*, trans. Sheila Stern, ed. Oswyn Murray (New York, 1988).
22. Kaegi, *Jacob Burckhardt*, VII, pp. 42–43, 98. Wilamowitz's judgment is also quoted by Oswyn Murray, 'Editor's Introduction' to *The Greeks and Greek Civilisation*, p. xxxiv.
23. Kaegi, *Jacob Burckhardt*, VII, pp. 15–16; Murray, 'Introduction', *The Greeks and Greek Civilisation*, p. xxxiv.
24. *Griechische Kulturgeschichte*, quoted in Kaegi, *Jacob Burckhardt*, VII, p. 91.
25. Kaegi, *Jacob Burckhardt*, VI, p. 125.
26. *Ibid.*, VI, pp. 135, 138; Georg G. Iggers, *The German Conception of History: The National Tradition of Historical Thought from Herder to the Present* (Wesleyan University Press, 1968, rev. edn 1983), pp. 226, 252. There is an English translation of Meinecke's lecture on 'Ranke and Burckhardt' in Hans Kohn (ed.), *German History: Some New German Views* (London, 1954), pp. 142–56.

Index

Hardy, Thomas Duffus, editor of the Rolls
  Series 174
Harris, Samuel, first Regius Professor of
  History at Cambridge 89
Hastings, Warren 202
Hearne, Thomas, 'the great Hearne of
  Oxford' 92–3
Heberden, Dr William 105, 106, 287n6,
  288n26
Hegel, G.W.F. xxi, xxii, 251, 260, 264
Heidelberg 22
Helmont, Jean-Baptiste van 68
Helvétius, Claude Adrien 130
Henderson, Alexander 32
Henderson, G.D. 24 & n
Henry IV, of France xvi
Henry VIII, of England 193, 245
Hepworth Dixon, W., biographer of William
  Penn 214
Herder, J.G. xxii, 149, 178, 182, 183, 186, 224,
  233, 247, 248, 250, 252, 255, 257
Heron, Robert, pseudonym of John Pinkerton
  (qv), 163, 165, 166
Hervey, Augustus, 3rd earl of Bristol, son of
  John Hervey, 117
Hervey, John, Lord xvii, 86, 88–9, 91–4, 96–8,
  101, 105, 111, 112, 117, 287n6
Highlands, and Highlanders, of Scotland
  124–5, 165, 178–9, 180, 189, 198,
  214, 217
Hildersham, nr Cambridge, 100
Hitler, Adolf, his enthusiasm for Carlyle's
  Frederick 242–4, 265
Hoadly, Benjamin, bishop 87, 92, 100, 132
Hobbes, Thomas 29, 126, 220
Holbach, Baron d' 130
Holland 22, 25, 26–7, 140
Holland, Lady, her prejudices 198–9
Holland, Lord 196–7, 204
Holland House 196–7, 198, 199, 206
Homer, 178, 182, 183
Hooker, Richard 29
Horace xii
Horner, Francis 200
Hotman, François 193
Humboldt, Alexander von 237
Humboldt, Wilhelm von 249
Hume, David viii, xi, xiv, xix, xx, xxi, 1, 2 & n, 3, 5,
  6, 8, 11, 12, 13, 14, 17, 19–20, 21, 25, 29,
  30, 31, 32, 34, 65, 67, 68, 104, 116, 120–8,
  129, 133–7, 139, 141, 142, 147, 154,
  158–9, 160, 176, 178, 179, 187, 195–7,
  199, 205, 208, 210, 215, 219, 269–70

History of England (1754–62) 11, 12, 14,
  31, 120–8, 136, dismissed by Pinkerton
  163, but not by Gibbon 164, 195–6
Hurd, Richard 67, 113, 114, 115–16 & n
Hutcheson, Francis 20–1, 27, 32

Ilinsky, I.V. 56
India, Mackintosh in 197, Macaulay in 200–1,
  207, 219, 221
Innes, Lewis 25, 45, 46
Innes, Fr Thomas 24, 29, 45, 46, 164

Jacobins, French 8, 199, 204
Jacobites, Jacobitism xii, xv, 18, 23–5, 27, 28,
  29, 30, 36–7, 41–7, 53, 73, 76, 77, 89,
  121, 122, 124, 125, 180, 186, 219
James VI (of Scotland) and I (of England) xvi,
  41, 68, 121, 126
James, duke of York, subsequently VII of
  Scotland and II of England 24, 45, 126,
  194, 197, 205, 213, 217
James, the Old Pretender see Stewart, James
Jefferson, Thomas 17
Jeffrey, Francis 200
Jeffreys, Judge 219
Jerome, St 103
Jesuits (Society of Jesus) 11, 38, 46, 80
Jesus College, Cambridge 96
Jews 3, 9, 84, 107, 112, 134, 233, 243
Jocelyn of Brakelond, chronicle of 233
Johnson, Samuel 32–3, 67–9, 78, 98, 133–4,
  136–7, 142, 145–7, 151, 178, 230,
  289n45
Jones, Sir William 66, 70 & n, 172–3
Joseph I, Emperor 35
Justinian 5, 138

Kaegi, Werner 261
Kames, Henry Home, Lord 25, 32, 136
Keble, John, 232
Keith, George, Earl Marischal 25
Kidd, Colin xix, 266–8, 270, 272–3, 276n12
Killiecrankie, battle of 23
Kingsley, Charles 223, 244
Kirk (or Church) of Scotland 12, 14, 18–19,
  23, 25–7, 45, 181
Kirkcaldy 225–6
Klopp, Onno, historian of diplomatic
  affairs, 222
Knapton, James and sons, publishers 59, 62
Knollys, Richard, Dr Johnson's model
  historian 68–70, 137, 147–8
Knowles, David 209